Supreme Being Trilogy
How To Step To The Path*
Angels Ecstasy
The Rejoicing

Channelled by Kitty Lloyd through the Entity Michael,
High Beings and Angels

Copyright @ 2016 by Kitty Lloyd

Published by:
Mountaintop Healing Publishing Inc
P.O. Box 193
Lantzville, B. C.
Canada   V0R 2H0

email inquiries: mountaintophealingpublishing@shaw.ca

First Edition print version
ISBN: 978-0-9948745-6-6

Imprints: Mountaintop Healing Publishing Inc

Cover designs by Tara Cook
Chart graphics by Tara Cook
Painting, Marianna Vanderklift

All rights reserved. This book may not be reproduced in whole or in part, stored in a retrieval system, or transmitted in any form or by any means; electronic, mechanical or other, without written permission from the publishers, except by a reviewer, who may quote brief passages in a review.

*The first Book in this Trilogy ***How To Step To The Path*** by Kitty Lloyd is available on Amazon in print and ebook format.

Dedication

Supreme Being Trilogy, a gift of Purity to humanity.

We teach all Souls to the millions
in many lands, of many earth stations.
We are the teaching force of all spiritual avenues to the tao.
We answer to sincere Souls on a quest for Truth:
the stones, the hands, the cups, the cards, the mediums,
the friends of the desire to look outward to the tao.

Michael

Supreme Being Trilogy
Table of Contents

Angels Ecstasy

Dedication		page 12
Foreword		page 14
Introduction to the six		page 16
Preface		page 18
Introduction		page 19
Chapter One	Spirit	page 37
	Visions	page 114
Chapter Two	Co existence	page 183
Chapter Three	Idyllic	page 212
Chapter Four	Returned	page 243
Chapter Five	Rapture	page 275
Appendix A	Daily East Ritual	page 288
Appendix B	equation of T	page 289
Appendix C	Book List	page 290

The Rejoicing

Dedication	page 294
Foreword	page 296
Introduction to the six	page 298
Preface	page 300
Introduction	page 301

Chapter One	Confirmation	page 321
	Visions	page 332
Chapter Two	Timeless Travel	page 396
	Farside and Other Worlds	page 417
Chapter Three	Triads	page 454
Chart, *Parallel Worlds*		page 492
Chapter Four	The Web	page 493
Painting, *Creations of Light*		page 584
Chapter Five	The Beginning	page 585
Epilogue		page 648
Glossary		page 667
Appendix A	Daily East Ritual	page 669
Appendix B	equation of T	page 670
Appendix C	Book List	page 671

Foreword

The twenty first century has propelled our world into a new paradigm of a dizzying variety of scientific discoveries which offer an unheard range of new opportunities and pitfalls in all aspects of life. Science is in the process of conquering space, flight has enabled us to conquer the limitations of time and distance, we are finding new cures for ailments assuring us of an ever extending life expectancy, assuring some of us of an ever higher standard of living.

The fly in the ointment of these undeniable achievements is that we have concomitantly acquired bigger and better methods of eliminating our enemies in times of war, both local and regional. We are engaged in the headlong exploitation of nature to the point where we now have to face the result of climate change and the imminent extermination of many species of flora and fauna to name but a few obvious perils facing contemporary societies in all parts of the world.

But again, these are only the obvious dangers facing contemporary humanity. The greatest danger lurking behind is the need to develop a new paradigm of values to assure the very survival of life on earth in some semblance of civilized society. In recorded history such norms developed to accommodate changing environments and/or changing social requirements either in terms of legal strictures or by moral dictums based on religious teachings. In some rare instances such constraints were based on philosophical considerations, but if pragmatically expedient they were soon absorbed by secular or spiritual organizations for their own pragmatic ends. In all instances these teachings and demands were and continue to revolve about the egocentric concerns of a tribe, a social group, a linguistic group or a national or racial affiliation, and in some rare cases for the benefit of humans in general. At no time have we given credence to the equality of all existence, be it on earth or beyond it, be it the sparrow or the willow or the mountain or the star.

The patient reader who persists in studying the multifaceted text of <u>Supreme Being Trilogy</u> will find an exposition of a new paradigm which reaches beyond the immediate concerns of an individual human or of humanity as a group of beings, both on earth and beyond. Not only does it encompass all existence on earth; animate and inanimate, human, animal and plant, living or deceased, but also the spiritual energies inhabiting worlds upon worlds beyond our ken, including their Creators of other Creators.

The reader may well become disheartened by the relative insignificance of the individual human being in this overwhelming plethora of existences and feel relegated to some irrelevant particle in the soup of the cosmos, but nothing could be further from the truth. We would encourage those who can access an old fashioned watch or clock to spend a few moments admiring the intricate interaction of numerous wheels and cogs which allow the mechanism to function optimally. Consider the consequences if any one minuscule cog were to bend or break! Is the cog on a small wheel consequently the most important part of the clock? Patently not, but it does remain indispensably important to the intended purpose of the whole. Just so does each human assume the function of an individual cog on a wheel which represents humanity among many other large and small wheels of creation.

The text of <u>Supreme Being Trilogy</u> offers the latest and most comprehensive revealed communication on what the Spirit world consists of, its hierarchical structure, its interactions, its purpose, limitations and aims. Such revelations have been communicated to humanity on an ongoing basis as far back as history allows us to trace them. They were received by the founders of the world's great religions and formed the basis for the teachings of the great mystics and clairvoyants throughout recorded history. We are told that at times such messages were misunderstood or contaminated by subsequent oral transmission, later transcription and at times by ulterior motives to advance a particular point of view or interpretation.

The medium and compilers of the present volume were under strict instruction to record all transmissions by mechanical means and not to change any detail in the transcription without verification from the source of the message. This we have to the best of our ability and understanding.

Introduction to the six

My name is Kitty Lloyd. I am a medium. For much of my life until 1994, I read tea leaves, palms and tarot cards. If there was a beginning to a new phase of my life, it was in 1994. A friend and colleague, Joanne, brought me a copy of <u>Messages From Michael</u> by Chelsea Quinn Yarbro[1]. I read with great interest about our spiritual selves and the how and why of our existence on earth. Not long after we had finished reading the book, Joanne bought a Ouija board and suggested we try it to see if we, too, could reach this Michael Entity. I was extremely sceptical, but reluctantly agreed to try. Almost immediately we found that the board worked and we began to record the teachings.

Soon words were directly channelled and the board was discarded. I was filled with concern and doubt, often feeling responsibility for the words. Yet in spite of skepticism and reservations, we continued, because the teachings brought truths we had not considered and this changed our outlook on life. I have always been a great believer in God. This information did not interfere with my belief system. If anything it enhanced it. I know that what we receive is not from my inner self. I can not verify this except through the many instances that occur throughout our sessions which provide information that I could not possibly know.

In 1995, the information we were recording seemed so important that the idea of a book took root. When we asked the Michael Entity, they verified that the channelling would be published. One evening in 1995, Joanne invited Tara to come to a channelling. At first skeptical, she, too, became enthusiastic and helped with recording the sessions. Until the spring of 1997 the recording was all done in longhand. After that we recorded the sessions on a computer. Since September 12, 2000 we started taping the sessions. The sessions consisted of answers to personal and spiritual questions, as well as teachings.

In 1996 Lucy, an old friend of Joanne's, came for a visit to see and hear the channelling. She was also a skeptic until she began studying the spiritual teachings and received information that was valuable and expanded her understanding. She volunteered to help us sort the material we had collected and place it into categories. By late 1997 we had a great deal of material accumulated and sorted. Lucy sent some of this to her friends, Grace and Roman, for their input. After reading the text and

---

[1] Berkley Publishing Group, 1995.

attending some channelling sessions, they also became committed to bringing this message to you.

The teachings of the Farside explicitly state that there are no coincidences. The Spirit world tells us that these events originated with a solemn agreement on the Farside before we chose to become reincarnated in our current lives in order to bring these messages to humanity. It therefore comes as no surprise that the earth life experiences of the six diverse people matched the skills required for the task, and that one link led to another. We were gently guided to find within ourselves the separate gifts we were able to contribute beginning with the Creator Trilogy (available on Amazon). It has been a long process of reflection and growth for each of us during the gathering and sorting of thousands of pages of channelled text.

Given the significance of the message being communicated to humanity, we have retained the original text without any changes to syntax or vocabulary.

Tara Cook
Joanne Drummond
Lucille Dumouchelle
Kitty Lloyd
Grace Piontkovsky
Roman Piontkovsky

Preface

Dear readers,

Within a sentence there often will be a word capitalized, yet that same word in another sentence will not be capitalized. The capitalized word is specific to the Farside; the uncapitalized word is specific to earth.

For example, humanity comes to earth armed with Truth. Capitalized Truth is an attribute of Creator that allows humanity upon earth to recognize and overcome negativity created by man. Uncapitalized truth is a reference to earth conceptuality of the word, truth, a truism. An earth plane truth changes as wisdom, knowledge accumulates. What was truth for you as a child, more than likely changed as you matured. Capitalized Truth does not change, remains always true.

Angels Ecstasy

SUPREME BEING
ITH /15th Creator
Yawn of Consciousness

Breath　　　　　　　　　　Matter
Matter　　　　　　　　　　Ion
　Ion　　　　　　　　　　Echo
Volume　　　　　　　　　Intent
Echo　　　　　　　Awareness
Existence　　　　Breath of Void
Vacuum
Vacuum　　　Flame
Flame　　　　Breath　　14 Creators' Yawn
Awareness
Intent　　　　V A N G U A R D

　　　　　　　　　　EYE

　　　　　　　　　　SEE
　　　　　　　　　　　　　　　　　　Breath of Void

　　　　　　　　　Flame
　　　　　　　　　Breath

　　　　Death　　　　Existence
　　　　Ion　　Rend　Energy Matter
　　　Awareness　　　　　Presence
　　Intent　　Chaos　　　　Life
　　　　　　　Fire
　　　　　　Sireen Sound
　　　　　　PULSE -
　　　　　　14th Creator

7 Dark Energies　　　　　　7 Light Energies

　　　　　　13th Creator
　　　　　　12 Lights
　　　　　　12 Creators

　　　　　　7 Dark Levels

　　　　　　3rd Creator's Yawn

Supreme Being Trilogy
How To Step To The Path *
Angels Ecstasy
The Rejoicing

Channelled by Kitty Lloyd through the Entity Michael,
High Beings and Angels

Copyright @ 2016 by Kitty Lloyd

Published by: Mountaintop Healing Publishing Inc
P.O. Box 193
Lantzville, B. C.
Canada V0R 2H0

email inquiries: mountaintophealingpublishing@shaw.ca

First Edition print version
ISBN: 978-0-9948745-4-2

Imprints: Mountaintop Healing Publishing Inc

Cover design by Tara Cook

All rights reserved. This book may not be reproduced in whole or in part, stored in a retrieval system, or transmitted in any form or by any means; electronic, mechanical or other, without written permission from the publishers, except by a reviewer, who may quote brief passages in a review.

* The first Book in this Trilogy ***How To Step To The Path*** by Kitty Lloyd is available on Amazon in print and ebook format.

Dedication

Angels Ecstasy, a gift of Purity to humanity.

We teach all Souls to the millions
in many lands, of many earth stations.
We are the teaching force of all spiritual avenues to the tao.
We answer to sincere Souls on a quest for Truth:
the stones, the hands, the cups, the cards, the mediums,
the friends of the desire to look outward to the tao.

Michael

Angels Ecstasy
Table of Contents

Angels Ecstasy

Dedication		page 12
Foreword		page 14
Introduction to the six		page 16
Preface		page 18
Introduction		page 19
Chapter One	Spirit	page 37
	Visions	page 114
Chapter Two	Co existence	page 183
Chapter Three	Idyllic	page 212
Chapter Four	Returned	page 243
Chapter Five	Rapture	page 275
Appendix A	Daily East Ritual	page 288
Appendix B	equation of T	page 289
Appendix C	Book List	page 290

Foreword

The twenty first century has propelled our world into a new paradigm of a dizzying variety of scientific discoveries which offer an unheard range of new opportunities and pitfalls in all aspects of life. Science is in the process of conquering space, flight has enabled us to conquer the limitations of time and distance, we are finding new cures for ailments assuring us of an ever extending life expectancy, assuring some of us of an ever higher standard of living.

The fly in the ointment of these undeniable achievements is that we have concomitantly acquired bigger and better methods of eliminating our enemies in times of war, both local and regional. We are engaged in the headlong exploitation of nature to the point where we now have to face the result of climate change and the imminent extermination of many species of flora and fauna to name but a few obvious perils facing contemporary societies in all parts of the world.

But again, these are only the obvious dangers facing contemporary humanity. The greatest danger lurking behind is the need to develop a new paradigm of values to assure the very survival of life on earth in some semblance of civilized society. In recorded history such norms developed to accommodate changing environments and/or changing social requirements either in terms of legal strictures or by moral dictums based on religious teachings. In some rare instances such constraints were based on philosophical considerations, but if pragmatically expedient they were soon absorbed by secular or spiritual organizations for their own pragmatic ends. In all instances these teachings and demands were and continue to revolve about the egocentric concerns of a tribe, a social group, a linguistic group or a national or racial affiliation, and in some rare cases for the benefit of humans in general. At no time have we given credence to the equality of all existence, be it on earth or beyond it, be it the sparrow or the willow or the mountain or the star.

The patient reader who persists in studying the multifaceted text of <u>Supreme Being Trilogy</u> will find an exposition of a new paradigm which reaches beyond the immediate concerns of an individual human or of humanity as a group of beings, both on earth and beyond. Not only does it encompass all existence on earth; animate and inanimate, human, animal and plant, living or deceased, but also the spiritual energies inhabiting worlds upon worlds beyond our ken, including their Creators of other Creators.

The reader may well become disheartened by the relative insignificance of the individual human being in this overwhelming plethora of existences and feel relegated to some irrelevant particle in the soup of the cosmos, but nothing could be further from the truth. We would encourage those who can access an old fashioned watch or clock to spend a few moments admiring the intricate interaction of numerous wheels and cogs which allow the mechanism to function optimally. Consider the consequences if any one minuscule cog were to bend or break! Is the cog on a small wheel consequently the most important part of the clock? Patently not, but it does remain indispensably important to the intended purpose of the whole. Just so does each human assume the function of an individual cog on a wheel which represents humanity among many other large and small wheels of creation.

The text of <u>Supreme Being Trilogy</u> offers the latest and most comprehensive revealed communication on what the Spirit world consists of, its hierarchical structure, its interactions, its purpose, limitations and aims. Such revelations have been communicated to humanity on an ongoing basis as far back as history allows us to trace them. They were received by the founders of the world's great religions and formed the basis for the teachings of the great mystics and clairvoyants throughout recorded history. We are told that at times such messages were misunderstood or contaminated by subsequent oral transmission, later transcription and at times by ulterior motives to advance a particular point of view or interpretation.

The medium and compilers of the present volume were under strict instruction to record all transmissions by mechanical means and not to change any detail in the transcription without verification from the source of the message. This we have done to the best of our ability and understanding.

Introduction to the six

My name is Kitty Lloyd. I am a medium. For much of my life until 1994, I read tea leaves, palms and tarot cards. If there was a beginning to a new phase of my life, it was in 1994. A friend and colleague, Joanne, brought me a copy of <u>Messages From Michael</u> by Chelsea Quinn Yarbro[2]. I read with great interest about our spiritual selves and the how and why of our existence on earth. Not long after we had finished reading the book, Joanne bought a Ouija board and suggested we try it to see if we, too, could reach this Michael Entity. I was extremely sceptical, but reluctantly agreed to try. Almost immediately we found that the board worked and we began to record the teachings.

Soon words were directly channelled and the board was discarded. I was filled with concern and doubt, often feeling responsibility for the words. Yet in spite of skepticism and reservations, we continued, because the teachings brought truths we had not considered and this changed our outlook on life. I have always been a great believer in God. This information did not interfere with my belief system. If anything it enhanced it. I know that what we receive is not from my inner self. I can not verify this except through the many instances that occur throughout our sessions which provide information that I could not possibly know.

In 1995, the information we were recording seemed so important that the idea of a book took root. When we asked the Michael Entity, they verified that the channelling would be published. One evening in 1995, Joanne invited Tara to come to a channelling. At first skeptical, she, too, became enthusiastic and helped with recording the sessions. Until the spring of 1997 the recording was all done in longhand. After that we recorded the sessions on a computer. Since September 12, 2000 we started taping the sessions. The sessions consisted of answers to personal and spiritual questions, as well as teachings.

In 1996 Lucy, an old friend of Joanne's, came for a visit to see and hear the channelling. She was also a skeptic until she began studying the spiritual teachings and received information that was valuable and expanded her understanding. She volunteered to help us sort the material we had collected and place it into categories. By late 1997 we had a great deal of material accumulated and sorted. Lucy sent some of this to her friends, Grace and Roman, for their input. After reading the text and

---

[2] Berkley Publishing Group, 1995.

attending some channelling sessions, they also became committed to bringing this message to you.

The teachings of the Farside explicitly state that there are no coincidences. The Spirit world tells us that these events originated with a solemn agreement on the Farside before we chose to become reincarnated in our current lives in order to bring these messages to humanity. It therefore comes as no surprise that the earth life experiences of the six diverse people matched the skills required for the task, and that one link led to another. We were gently guided to find within ourselves the separate gifts we were able to contribute beginning with the Creator Trilogy (available on Amazon). It has been a long process of reflection and growth for each of us during the gathering and sorting of thousands of pages of channelled text.

Given the significance of the message being communicated to humanity, we have retained the original text without any changes to syntax or vocabulary.

Tara Cook
Joanne Drummond
Lucille Dumouchelle
Kitty Lloyd
Grace Piontkovsky
Roman Piontkovsky

Preface

Dear readers,

Within a sentence there often will be a word capitalized, yet that same word in another sentence will not be capitalized. The capitalized word is specific to the Farside; the uncapitalized word is specific to earth.

For example, humanity comes to earth armed with Truth. Capitalized Truth is an attribute of Creator that allows humanity upon earth to recognize and overcome negativity created by man. Uncapitalized truth is a reference to earth conceptuality of the word, truth, a truism. An earth plane truth changes as wisdom, knowledge accumulates. What was truth for you as a child, more than likely changed as you matured. Capitalized Truth does not change, remains always true.

INTRODUCTION

870   It is reflection and retraction.
You are humanity.
Human are flesh and blood.
You are also Energy.
The Energy that you are is called Soul.
The Soul is mere fragment of the Essence of your being
        that has as its triad coordinate, Spirit.
The Essence of your being is mere fragment to Creator.
You who are a part of your own Creator,
        Soul of Creator as mankind.
You who entered in, not first as Angel,
        but Archangel of the Legion of Creator.
You who have found a path to be mirrored over and over
        that you might bring those lost unto the Deity.
Deity indeed for humanity to behold Creator
        would be a containment you could not survive.
For the Energy Field that you are as Archangel,
        you could be in the presence.
You have been in the presence as Archangel!
Indeed, you know this, for you are connected
        as all earth is connected to the origins of your being.
Energies that flow in the endless night of being,
        from a presence of such magnitude extending forth
        into that place of Void,
        crystalline particles so minute,
        and the shards impale themselves
        into the darkness of the Void.
And the Void opened its way.
And worlds began, galaxies expanded
        with the minute particles of Breath
        released into the endless night.
Some took one form and
        others another and another and another.
And some held within their being
        growths of infinite numbers of beings
        and so your world was set with trees and animals
        and fish of the sea
        and sands to settle upon the sea,
        as stars within the skies, as orbs of planets

and you see a portion so small in your galaxy.
Zillions could not contain
> the numbers from one Breath alone.

871   Holy, men of earth, Holy art thou.
Unto you is the care of humanity given.
We ask, Souls, that you cry outrage in your being.
Defend those of earth defenseless.
Souls of earth, register that you are human,
> that you have an affinity to all Energy,
> that you are of Creator's attributes
> in the belief of Truth, of Purity, of Love.

Souls of earth, the bowels of earth
> are giving forth putrid energy,
> for man has placed within the very sanctity of earth,
> the evil of their doings.

You who speak in the name of sacred,
> you who lift your arms in blessing unto all beings,
> show unto earth's people
> the strength of your Energy,
> for you , you are the shepherd left to tend the flock.

You are giving to those benefactors of your truth.
What truth is this, they will say,
> that you have not spoken forth?

We do not judge,
> Soul, we do not.

What we do is speak the Truth
> of humanity, the Holy ones, the blessed ones.

Your world, to the east, to the west,
> to the north and to the south
> have escarpments of evil upon them.

You have, Souls, the power to dislodge
> in the Energy that you have.

Do not depend on the armories of earth
> to cleanse that which is evil.

That which is evil is cleansed through Energy!
Call the people of earth.
Call those who understand the power of Energy.
To place calmness, serenity upon the troubled waters,
> upon the bleeding lands,
> upon the surging emotions of negativity.

You who see yourselves as blessed,
> speak of the blessed that you are.

Register in the name of Holy
> that you have power
> that is yours and all humanity's
> to alter the negativity of humanity's energy.

Souls of earth, your world is fractious.
Who would seek and lift their Energy
> to draw down unto all those who are troubled.

Souls, you have the power to withhold the knife,
> the bullet, the carnage, the fire.

You, that which you have,
> create miracles upon your earth.

Speak of the miracles that you have.
Cry outrage with your Energy.
Souls, you are the fountain of Energy.
You who are the devout draw yourselves into conclaves
> that you might be understood from the energy
> that arises round about you.

Holy beings we draw you unto the Circle of Saints
> that you might be strengthened in your courage,
> that you might be known throughout earth
> as the giver of Truth, of Love, of compassion,
> that you recognize within yourself
> the Purity of whom you are;
> Energy of Humanity from the realm beyond earth.

872 Soul, behold thou art Holy.
Behold, Soul, humanity is Holy.
Humanity often in the many lives they have lived
> have cleaved unto negativity.

Negativity bribes the mind
> coerces the energy to sway to its favour.

Soul, negativity of earth
> is not connected to the Negativity of Farside.

It is the illusion that man creates.
It is the pain that man discovers is possible.
It is the great precipice upon which man stands.
You have a choice, Soul.
It is always choice,
> the choice to reach in to negativity.

You, you who are caught in the pain of your day,
>	you who find yourselves with men and women
>	who have chosen to diminish
>	that which is humanity,
>	see the humanity you are.
See the glory of that which you are.
See the Light
>	that was in your being as you entered in to earth.
Indeed many humans find themselves
>	in a path of destruction that is not their own.
They have not created
>	the denseness of negativity round about them,
>	they have been brought into the pain.
But you have a choice even in the densest pain to know
>	that humanity reaches for a greater Truth,
>	a Truth that rises unto Purity,
>	a Truth that knows Love,
>	a Truth that has compassion.
We ask you to understand
>	there is a great battle being fought.
It is being fought with great Love.
It is being fought with Truth.
You, Soul, are one of the contenders within this battle.
You and we,
>	even upon Farside
>	we share your portion of the battle
>	for we too enter in unto where you are.
Souls of earth, gather the might of your being.
Gather the might of Mohammed who struggled
>	and brought great truths into being:
>	feed the poor,
>	hold women high, give them equality,
>	for you are one equal unto.
You, who are humanity, you who speak of Jesu,
>	the Jesu who taught you to Love all beings,
>	lay down that which would harm another,
>	see your brother as your equal.
You have before you upon your earth
>	examples of Truth, high Truth, Soul.
e ask you that you acknowledge the high Truth.
This is the Truth of the high mind.

This offers to you
> the greatest key to share one with the other.

No single man may hold the key.
It is not for one,
> it is for all!

For only with the Energy of all
> may the key fit the lock to open
> a door wherein all will enter.

The lock is Truth,
> simply Truth, Soul, the highest Truth.

You are the children of your Creator.
You are precious beyond your knowing.
You are numbered and in the numbering accountable
> for that which you do.

873 Souls of earth, speak not unto the deities.
They do not exist.
Speak not unto the cathedrals, the domes.
They exist but they do not speak true.
Speak, Soul, unto those who sit and beg,
> for indeed they mean more of earth,
> of Energy, than all palaces.

Before you place a mat to sit upon
> that you might contemplate
> > your nights and your days, the stars of the night,
> > the blue of the sky, the clouds
> > that gather before your being,
> > feel, as the wind and the rain,
> > the cold and the heat of the sun,
> > place themselves about your body.

Be familiar with that which is of earth
> for it is of you to learn while you are upon it.

You may learn to gather unto you wealth as the kings.
You may learn to gather wisdoms from others,
> but we would have you gather Truth.

For in gathering Truth you will come to a wisdom
> and in coming, Soul, it will be a new truth for you.

Do not be desperate in your being for any one thing.
Allow the wash of the ages to enter upon you.
For you have been upon your earth
> and you know in your being

   that which is new
    and that which you have learned before.
Understand you are on a great journey.
Your journey leads you into a place of occupation.
By many Souls it is a purposeful occupation.
It is to bring a beloved unto your very Creator.
It is to draw unto you that which has given outwardly
   Energy to find that which is perfection.
Gather all that you are.
Gather all that you have been
   and know the way will be laid for you
   and you will rejoice
   for you will behold within your being
   an Energy that ignites even unto a great Light
   and you will feel
   the shiver of the ages through your being.
You are not, Soul, without purpose.
For you are the dart,
   you are the missile.
You are the Light that moves forward that others might see.
You are the gallant warrior
   with a mission deep within your being
   to conquer evil
   with great compassion, with great Love.
Enwrap your being with this purpose.
Gather all that you are.
Reach deep within your Soul
   to see that which is available unto you
   for you have given yourself the map.
You have the way.
Endeavour to know that you travel not alone.
When you separate yourself you lose yourself.
In any issue of earth
   we would have you know
   when you separate yourself
   you lose yourself.
You are one with your God
   for your Energy is of your Creator.
You are strong in your purpose
   for you have dared to enter in
   to a negative ion, a negative state of being.

Dance with the Angels, sing with the Angels.
Draw your Energy into the very realm of the Angels
    for you are at one with them.
You are glory and you perceive it not,
    yet we say this unto you,
      "Do not dalliance upon the way
        but know the time to enter in is the now!"
Of the twelve tribes from the twelve spheres of perfection
    for even as they have been touched,
    they have become as Idyllic,
    many have even entered unto your earth
    that you might know them in their perfection.
Souls of earth, you see only before you the obelisk.
See that unto which the obelisk is centred.
See it is outward from your being.
See it is grounded unto earth but it reaches far.
Allow your Energy to be as the obelisk
    outward from where you are.
Enter in and know you have a purpose to blend,
    to blend with the Angels,
    to speak unto them, for you are Holy.
You will hear that which is said
    and they will speak of the purpose of your being.
They will speak even unto you of that which was lost.
They will give you, Soul, a map of purpose,
    a chart that holds a record of all that is and will be.
Lift your voice in song
    and know that the song carries the colour and song
    of that perfection when it is cast forth in Purity.
Souls of earth, you are the salt of the earth.
Recognize that you have all entered in to earth.
Some have entered in with an agenda other than your own.
Even though they are of you and you of them,
    humanity has entered in with the purpose
    of bringing forth the Blessed Angel,
    of bringing Negativity,
    the Wilful Child, unto Creator.
Yet others carry an added burden.
It is that of seeking that which is Idyllic.
It has always been so.
Would you speak of the infidel?

Would you speak of the gentile?
These are not negatives, Soul.
They are beings
      who have the purpose you have entered in for.
But unto the tribes of Abraham is a greater purpose.
It is to seek the sound, the echo that is Idyllic.
Do not separate yourselves in this purpose.
Do not alienate yourselves one from the other.
For earth has a mighty inveigler,
      it is negativity
      and it will draw you apart one from the other.
But you are brothers!
You are the sons of Abraham!
Lift your hearts and know this will overcome chaos
      to know that you are indeed chosen,
      not the Jews alone,
      but all the sons of Abraham
      and the tribes there gathered.
Within the tribes are the sacred ones ensconced.
They are, Soul, deep in their purpose and radiate Energy
      from their being,
      do not speak in platitudes and fork tongues,
      they speak with the clarity of Truth, of purpose,
      of a river that runs through the land
      and cleanses the people in the wash.
Touch your Soul with your heart.
Touch your mind with your heart and know that
      from the heart is the longevity of nations
      for it is not with knowledge
      that nations are held together,
      it is with the vision of the heart.
Gather in your beings by the tens and the thousands,
      by the ten thousands
      and speak unto the Energy of Abraham
      to open the way that you might see clear
      the blend of nations.
You are soldiers in a battle.
The battle has a Truth.
There are battalions.
The battalions have a single purpose.
Draw that purpose to your Soul.

Draw that purpose unto all obelisks
> that all nations might know the purpose
> of the melding of the Jewish and Arabic states.

Rejoice that chaos will be lessened upon your earth
> and the purpose in your being
> will become strong to seek for that perfect world
> wherein you learned
> and lived and spoke as one.

You are the vision that has always been
> but the clouds have distorted the visions
> so that through the clouds you see different nations,
> when indeed you are one nation
> under your Creator.

Speak indeed of Krishna, of Mohammed,
> of Buddha, of Jesu
> and know that you are a voice of perfection.

You are voice of strength.

Do not give static unto that which is clear.

Do not muddy the waters of the pristine river
> with that which was given unto you was golden
> a son as no other son, a glory as no other glory.

Waste not your lives upon earth
> to dabble in bitter wars of contention
> when you have a single battle before you.

It is the battle to overcome negativity
> which is done with compassion unto all.

Bring forth the children.

Speak into their ears.

In the cradles give them words of union,
> of brothers and sisters,
> of fathers and mothers with a single purpose.

Allow the fissures to heal.

Allow the blood to congeal and the wound to heal.

Rejoice as brothers rejoice who have long been apart
> and have found the heritage of their being
> and let go of the manmade idyllics
> that have placed distortion

> into the meld of your being
> for there is a Humanity apart from earth.

It is with your Creator.

It is, Soul, of your Creator
> wherein you are one with a single purpose.

You who are of the Arabs and the Jewish,
> understand that as the Light shines upon you
> you radiate that others might see.

Understand you cannot place
> the Light of your being within a barrel.

It will not be sealed.
You cannot place it under the straw
> for it will ignite and ravish the nations.

It must be a clear Light,
> a Light of the mind and the heart and the Soul.

It must be a Light that is unto the Path of your Creator
> for all nations have the same Creator.

You must not hide your being with robes of contention
> that blazoned colour of, I am this or I am that,
> for you are one and upon your earth being
> you have not recognized this
> but upon the Farside
> you fall upon each other in Love, in sob
> upon the shoulder of Abraham
> for the battle is not yet won
> and the chaos reigns upon your earth.

You are diligent to see the differences
> but you blind your eye to see the similarities.

Brother unto brother, sister unto sister,
> hold the siblings that are young in years
> and whisper unto them,
>> *"We sing the same song.*
>> *Our voice goes forth in the same chord.*
>> *Might we be brothers one unto the other!*
>> *Might our purpose be of one!*
>> *Might we all become*
>>> *one again with Abraham!"*

874 Soul, earth humanity, you who have been lost,
> who have not yet found
> within the dispensation of time
> that you are a part of your particular attachment
> to all other humanity, we say to you, it is time.

The way is clear.

The Path predestined.
You are one of humanity.
You are indeed one of a battle
      but your battle is not against your fellow being.
It is to recover that which is negativity;
      to bring forth the Blessed;
      to open doors in a manner
      that only the knell of humanity can do.
Soul, you can be in oneness.
In great peril,
      you can come together in a state of oneness.
There is an alternative.
It is to come together in a bonding of humanity
      to behold that you are one and the same
      brought forth unto the Path of Creator
      with the very Breath of Creator.
Souls of earth, you have strong within you
      a determination to Truth.
Your will is ever antagonistic toward contrary beings.
Yet, are you not one?
Do you define the state of being one of tranquillity!
There are few upon earth, Soul, who have such a state.
We ask that you erase from your mind
      your determination to thwart that which is different.
We ask that you behold that
      in humanity that is so very much equal,
      charged with Truth.
Feel.
Value.
Behold.
Within each of humanity is the Angelic being of Purity.
We say this to you not that you have arrived upon earth
      to that Angelic state.
Indeed not, but it is the destination of your being!
You are gathered that you might overcome.
You are gathered that you might draw unto compassion.
You are gathered that you might send forth
      the clear pure voice of humanity,
      the very sound that draws the Angels to hear.
Behold humanity how tethered you are one to the other.
Behold humanity how in your weakened state,

       can even give forth that which you have
       or another will come and draw
       nigh unto you with offerings.
Souls of earth, you are upon your earth
       for the briefest of moments.
It is as a lightening flash in the sky.
It gives great Light for each humanity gives Light.
For all are arriving at perfection.
Some Souls take longer to arrive but all are arriving.
All have a moment in time
       but in the Timeless state you are one.
In the Timeless state you have but to gather yourselves
       unto the completeness of one.
Souls of earth, see that which you are.
Behold who you are.
One Soul greater than another,
       a king and a pauper, a priest and a peon?
Soul, you are equal!
You are one in the brotherhood of man!
Souls of earth, forward unto us the glory of your being.
Forward unto us that which only you can arrive unto,
       the perfect note,
       the clarity of joy.
For it is joy within the being to give unto another.
It is joy to behold that which is a gift being sent forward.
Soul, place unto your being Truth.
Clasp, Soul, that which you have and offer unto all a song,
       a word, a step, a deed, an action.
Equate as you will,
       but earth beings behold the humanity that you are,
       that you are Soul, equal one unto the other.
You are charged with a great purpose.
The purpose is a gift unto Creator.
Humanity is destined to ride into the path of Love;
       to arrive and enter through
       a gateway of such profound Purity
       that it opens the dimensions of all that you are
       and you behold once again who you have been.
For that which you enter in to is from another illusion
       and you understand how profound is perfection.
How profound is the manifold attributes of Creators

>   who have sent forth unto you
>   from a single state of perfection
>   an opportunity to behold that you, you have a key.
> The key is the utmost of Truth for it unlocks all gateways.
> It is given unto you from Light, Supreme Being,
>   all that is IS.
> Souls of earth, you have carried in your being a Truth.
> It is imbedded within each one of you
>   that you have been charged,
>   as the Archangels charged with a Truth,
>   to blend that which is chaos unto all things,
>   to see that which is individual, united;
>   the oneness of humanity, individual in oneness,
>   but coming together as one.
> And so it is in the place of perfection that even chaos
>   will come together united as one perfection.
> So shall it be.

875   We speak to you that you might know
>   the intent of that which you are,
>   that you might feel
>   a oneness in the gathering of those about you,
>   that you might behold a Truth
>   that is high above the truth of earth.
> For humanity is above the truth of earth.
> You are reflected forward unto your earth
>   but you are Humanity.
> You have a dwelling place where we are.
> You are of the Armada.
> You are, Soul, a warrior against negativity.
> Do not gather negativity about you.
> Do not warm yourselves in the heat of negativity.
> See, Soul, the positive steps.
> See that negativity sends a great swarm upon thy being,
>   it marks and lays trenches.
> And you, you do not become less,
>   but you do not accomplish.
> So we ask that you work in oneness ,
>   that you hold that which you do as sacred,
>   that each step is guided from Farside.
> You have Holy energies.

You do not work, Soul, as singularly alone.
You have the Spirit of your being.
You have the Purity of your Essence.
Do not see the dark corners
        for there are many upon your earth.
Do not see the hidden places,
        they will always reign upon your earth,
        see the sunlight shine upon thy being.
See the glory of that which you are and know
        that you have entered in to earth to accomplish
        and you are not accomplishing alone
        but you are accomplishing one with the other
        those who have left and those who remain.
Some will leave and some will stay.
And yet that which is will be done.
Do not fear.
There is not a step that will be allowed to falter.
This, Soul, is not a threat!
It is a statement for you have entered in with this knowing!
Each has entered in with a purpose to accomplish.
Be humble in thy being.
Reach out, do not reach in.
Seek to magnify not to belittle.
Seek to strengthen not to weaken.

876   To earth religion.
You have had many messengers, Souls of earth.
You have encountered many teachers.
Each from the Farside have a program one to the other,
        supporting the teachings of all.
Mankind holds the teachings true.
Man distorts.
In the Path of Energy,
        teachings are given to earth for their understanding;
        that you might become illuminated in your being,
        that you might understand
        the vibrational volume of creation.
Your earth tampers with that which the teachers have given.
Seek to know in that which you call sacred:
        Love, Purity and Truth.
Hold those truths as powerful unto you.

The verbalization of man counters the Truth.
For as the garland of flowers that are pure,
    they may become less in attraction by the negatives,
    the negative blight upon their being.
So it is with religion, that which has been given
    has a Truth, and a Love, and a Purity.
Yet, mankind distorts and places a blight upon Truth.
We ask, Souls of earth, that you endeavour in your being
    to hold open to the mind
    the lesson of consciousness,
    for it is available to evaluate all that you hear.
You may place it, Soul, to the vibration of consciousness
    and in your being you will know of its Truth.
Man does not receive value for truth in Truth.
Man only receives value in distortion of Truth.
That which is pure is pure.
The Blessed are pure.
The child entering in is pure.
The distortion comes from holding on to the pain within earth.
It places a blight upon the form,
    upon the mind of humanity.
Love in Creator is Agape, Holy Love.
It is available unto all mankind.
Yet, man distorts Love and places negative, want, upon Love.
We would have you see open unto you all the comparisons
    of Truth, Purity and Love from the Farside.
The Angels will beacon at your call.
The guides will nurture your being.
The Energy of your Creator will send glory outward unto thee.
You have but to ask.
You have but to know in your being,
    there is no countenance unworthy of Love.
There is no pain so great, Love will not enter forth to it.
Unto all humanity is Love offered.
In Love there is no caste.
There are no lesser or greater.
There are, Soul, only the warriors
    having entered in to battle
    to bring forth the Blessed unto Creator.
So be it.

877   Come to order!
Is that not what your teachers have said!
When a portion of knowledge is going to be given,
        students have always resisted the lesson
        and teachers always re teach.
For we would have you understand growth,
        for growth is a lesson.
Growth is not an easy lesson.
It is not for your earth an easy lesson.
For humanity dwells in the state of negativity.
Not only within the state of negativity
        but carries the seed of negativity within
        so that the opportunity is there
        to cleave unto negativity.
But the opportunity, Soul, is also there to cleave unto
        the portion of Truth that is given unto thee!
The seed is placed and the expectation is
        that with nurturing the seed will come to full growth
        and bloom, and form seed and re grow.
And often within the seed pod itself there is a lesion
        and a substance alters that which the seed is.
And the seed grows
        and instead of the creation that was to be glorious,
        it sends forth a rapetious, inveigling self.
It has carried an alteration.
Your world has seed pod in varied forms.
Creator has designed it so.
Within these pods come forth life forms.
Each one altered or altered by.
And the seed has awareness within its being.
It understands the negativity within itself,
        but that negativity
        has become a part of the wholeness.
And how does one eradicate a part of self?
It does not make self less loved than perfection.
Does the planter of the seed
        wish to drag it from and destroy the creation?
Or does the planter of the seed want to contain the vine
        so that the vine may grow within the fullness of itself!
Does the Creator of the seed nurture the difference
        and see the seed that will be thrown

    from the fullness of the fruit?
You understand we do not speak in riddles.
We speak clearly of Creator and the garden of seeds
    that has been willingly entered in
    and fed upon the lesion of negativity itself,
    and it has been altered each and all by the negativity.
And yet some
    have allowed the negativity
    to enlarge their understanding.
It is made the Truth of the seed fuller,
    it has expanded the goodness within the seed.
Each humanity is that seed.
Some have followed the path and become the clinging vine,
    searching endlessly for that which it knows not.
But others have gathered the negativity within
    and altered, and re sprouted from that negativity.
And Truth combined a glorious bloom of humanity
    that is giving and honouring and loving.
Growth is what humanity does best.
Growth is that which you are in.
The purpose of your being
    to grow in Truth that you might fulfill
    the bringing forth of the Blessed.

878 It is a need to register the times
    of three great Gateways opening.
One, the Gateway unto Farside
    when the beings will be lifted from transition
    and Angels will walk the Path
    between earth and Farside
    and energies of many nations
    will find the Path a welcome place.
And they will know the joy of Humanity,
    they will uphold the banner of Humanity.
For the Light in that day will shine so the sun
    will seem as a dim star and the energies of Humanity
    will resonate a note upon earth.
Within the thousand years,
    that note will have reached such a vibration
    that at the Second Gateway the doors will be opened
    and energies will behold that Energy that is Creator.

And you will be known
       by that mark of Purity upon your being,
       for you will have brought forth the Blessed Angel,
       as united in Oneness you enter in
        to the placement of Godhead.
You will understand the resonance in your being
       that will draw you unto the Third Gateway
       wherein you will behold a desolate sorrow.
And you will enter in to the darkness
       with the Sound of Humanity
       and you will reach unto the Blessed Archangel
       and you will have become
       in that existence of being, such Light,
       for you have been reflected forward
       and upon return you have gathered reflection again.
And the brilliance of your being will Light the darkness
       and all that was dark
       will see the Light of the Purity you are.
And the Archangels will feel within their being your power,
       for you will have the touch that Lights their Being.
You will restore unto them that which they have lost.
And in the darkened recesses of the Void,
       will be heard, Negativity.
And the voice you have gathered unto your being
       that carries a resonance of perfection
       will be carried forth and touch the Wilful Child.
And in that day, you will feel no grappling hold,
       but only the gentle thread of Energy
       touching thy being.

Chapter One
SPIRIT

879   We speak to you of the Soul of man,
        that which resides
           upon both Negative Void and Positive Void.
Upon Negative Void, the Soul enters in with a Path
        unto the Positive Void but not the recall.
As the human also has no recall,
        only in the gathering of knowing,
        as the human accepting the Soul's high being
        is the Soul able to access information
        pertinent to the level
        wherein the Soul is upon Farside.
There is within each Soul a consciousness.
It holds no judgment.
It is a template that may be read upon Farside.
It is a conscience and a conscious memory.
It is, Soul, holding all the pain,
        all the positive of the human upon earth.
As the issues of earth life are lived, as they are resolved,
        the Soul has the ability to release the karma.
If it is not resolved the Soul holds the karma unto it.
The Soul has the ability to expand, to swell and shrink.
To aspire is not within the Soul's realm.
That is for the human.
The human aspires
        and the Soul gathers that which the human aspires.
It is translatable unto the Spirit.
It is, Soul, an Energy of great calm.
It has a reserve of wisdom
        to encourage the human
        to defend against negativity.
It has a linear that is attached to the Spirit.
But the way is not viable until the human allows access.
There is within the Soul of man
        the great ability to lead the human into the Path,
        not with judgment but with gentleness,
        calming that the Soul might hear the Spirit speak.

The Angels sing unto the human.
They might hear the guides who see the Path
    the Soul is willing to enter
    and urge the being to retreat
    into the calmness the Soul offers.
You are human.
Every earth being of mankind is human.
You have the ability to enter in to the Path the Soul offers.
It is the path of gentle calm.
It is the Path wherein no harm may come unto you,
    understanding you are Energy,
    you are of the form of Energy.
You are abiding within the human flesh.
Your flesh is merely a reflection
    of a template you have chosen.
The mask is but a mask until the Soul is revealed.
Through the eyes of a human,
    you may see that Soul received.
Through the eyes of a human,
    you may behold that which is of great beauty.
You may discern wisdom through the eyes of a human
    that will lead you to the path of goodness and mercy.
You may cleanse your being of all words of misconception
    for the human does not always understand
    the purpose for which they have entered in.
The great telling is in the gentleness of the Soul.
For the man, the woman,
    who holds the Soul available unto them,
    they issue from them an Energy
    of calmness, of gentleness,
    of fervour, but in a gentle manner.
Behold that which is your Soul.
Lift unto the Soul's Path.
Guide your flesh by the Soul's wisdom.

880   You will understand upon your earth
    there has been enormous injustices done to humanity.
Your earth as at no other time is in karmic repayment.
There are groups of people who have created great injustices
    upon the flesh of mankind.
They have diligently, systematically

       worked at eliminating humanity.
All of these beings are not in the field of this endeavour,
       many sit in opulent places and send forth indictments
       that create great pain.
These Souls, many, are now caught
       in the repayment of karma.
They do not do it simply for the sake
       of being bludgeoned, tortured.
Karma has far greater interpretation.
For each being as your selves
       behold that which as has been done
       and you learn from this experience.
You adjust, Soul, the thought processes of your mind.
You are taught by the action of others.
Karma is not simply torture for torture, an eye for an eye,
       a tooth for a tooth, Soul.
It is, indeed, the opportunity for mankind
       to behold the evil of man
       that you might understand
       the great need for compassion.
Each being who has been in the place of sending forth pain
       has been the receiver of such pain.
Will you inflict such pain?
No.
For in your being you have seen the mirror and the mirrored.
Within your earth there is the contention always
       of negativity even as you meet.
Negativity would ask to misinform, to alter that which is Truth.
We speak to you of Truth.
Humanity dwells upon earth, upon Farside.
Unto all worlds Purity reigns.
There are levels of Purity, as there are levels of Holy.
Upon earth the holiness of the Soul is persuaded by negativity
       and even upon entering in,
       must leave at the station of karma unwanted negativity.
Upon Farside Purity reigns.
Upon Farside the Spirits hold Purity,
       Holy Spirits, Holy unto Holy Spirit,
       but beyond the Holy unto Holy Spirits
       are the Holy Spirits.
Even the teachers who have spoken unto you,

>   these beings who give unto you messages,
>   Truth that you may render unto mankind
>   that which is in their being.

Even as they enter in to earth, Purity, holiness,
>   so they will have within their being
>   the ability to gather Truth
>   needed to overcome negativity.

You have only, Soul, humanity
>   as your earth has a form upon the orb in which it dwells.

The glory placed upon the orb was placed for mankind.
It was brought unto earth.
Soul, you brought with you your holiness unto earth.
You are formidable in that holiness.
Humanity, minute in all manner,
>   unto other beings you are seen
>   as the holiest for you have entered in to battle.

Holy beings witness whom you are.
They have accepted the greatness of your being.
They have witnessed even as you have entered in
>   and overcome negativities through reincarnation.

You have chosen to re enter time and again
>   and as the Purity in you becomes greater
>   the magnitude of holiness grows.

Some humans of humanity have become Holy Holy Holy
>   as Angels themselves.

Some Souls have entered in
>   unto the Holy Holy Holy level of the Circle of Saints
>   and some have entered in with the High C,
>   even to lite the way for the lost.

Sacred beings you are,
>   Holy Spirits who have entered to earth,
>   many who have grown within their being
>   unto the state of Ecstasy.

Consider the smallest of seeds entering in
>   unto the aridness of the desert
>   and the seed lies dormant
>   until the desert chooses to feel the drops of rain.

So is the Spirit grown.
The desert wasteland is earth for humanity.
Upon Farside it is in Purity itself that grows, expands.
Upon Farside there is no reincarnation but growth.

There is growth that is ever billowing outwards
        to offer unto all Energy
        the holiness that is is, to become Holy unto Holy.
Holy Beings who teach and offer,
        as Buddha has chosen to hold himself to earth
        at level five,
        that mankind might see the Truth of holiness.
Hell is your very earth.
It is a battleground with negativity.
But even upon the battleground are all beings Holy,
        yet they choose to delve deeply
        into the mire of negativity
        before in a glory of reincarnation.
Often through many lives they understand
        they have entered in to overcome.
Negativity is a Brother.
We would not have you harm Negativity.
We would have you enfold Negativity in your compassion.
For even your Creator enfolds Negativity with Love.
You are a portion of the Triad of Creator.
You have within you
        all the attributes of your Creator;
        Truth, Purity and Love.
You have been brought forth unto earth
        that you might magnify the Truth that is within
        and in your holiness unite as one, to rise as one.
And all that have been caught in the mire of transition,
        in the levels of their own pain, you will bring them forth.
You will teach as High Beings unto them.
You will lift the Angels from the depths of transition
        unto their brothers.
Behold you are Holy.

881   Souls of earth, unto you we speak
        from where we are upon your starry nights,
        far into the way of the spheres.
Your beings could not travel
        with the flesh and the blood you hold
        for they would collapse.
But you, you have entered in many times unto our side.
For you have reincarnated lifetime after lifetime

in your effort to overcome negativity,
not to befriend, but to yearn in your being
for the stability of life's goodness.
For deep, deep within each human being
is the memory of that which is Purity.
When you are far from Purity your being echoes,
resounding echoes of that which is lost to you.
So you find yourself yearning for this Purity
and as you mature in Soul level,
so you understand what fully you have lost
as you enter in to the earth plane.
But you also have the recognition
that it is returned unto you
in an instant that you return.
Fair weather or foul, so it is as you enter in,
do you carry the great burden of karma
to release from you.
Or do you just flit through unto where we are?
Or have you, Soul, persecuted your being
that you must leave off the entering in
to remain in transition's grasp?
Negativity, Soul, holds prayer separate, but not unto you.
For the Blessed are always sending forth
Amens and Amens
unto all men of humanity.
Souls of earth, grasp unto you the Purity of whom you are.
Grasp unto you the dedication of your Soul
to enter in time and again
unto the throes of negativity.
Be aware not of whom you are.
Be aware of that clinging vine that holds and grasps
and contains in it all the possibilities of pain,
for upon your earth, negativity has dereliction
and contains great confinements for the Soul.
You are, Soul.
Just that, Soul.
As you enter in you cloak yourself
in the form of human but you are Soul.
You are the Purity from whence you came.
You hold in your being all possibilities
and so we give unto you the knowledge

that you may derive a quickening of Spirit unto you,
that you may not be satisfied just to be human
but to equate in your being
that you are so much more than human.
For humanity is your name upon earth
but it is an expansive name upon Farside.
And as you have entered in,
you have not understood
the fullness of this Humanity.
You have not understood its connection
to the Armada, the great Battle.
You are not derelict in your attentiveness to this,
for the very purpose of not being aware,
that you might grow in your being
by overcoming the pain of negativity.
And yet there are times
when humanity needs to understand
how great they are.
They also need to understand there is a purpose
in this dual personality of human.
Farside human and earth human,
one in Spirit, one in Soul,
one tied unto the Purity
and the Love of the Essence of being,
the other one tied to the flesh,
the blood and the bone of the earth being.
Yet, both are continually aware
of that which is the overcoming of negativity.
They drain negativity from their being
to become even skeletonized
in the weary path of overcoming pain.
They age in their being and they recognize
as the flesh becomes gaunt upon the bone,
the skin hangs low,
that there is so much more than the human form,
and wisdom has entered in.
The wisdom of all Farside is available unto you.
You are Truth.
You are held in the arms of Angels.
You are, Soul, grasped in the very connection
that echoes unto where we are.

You are mighty in your understanding of pain.
Upon Farside you are mightier
      in your understanding of Purity and Love.
We give unto you a vision of the chiasm that is yours
        that you might see the dual self
        and witness all growth as containing
        to the Essence of being.

882   We speak to you of beginnings and endings.
We speak of earth's awakening in your earth year 1994.
Within that year was a conscious awareness laid
      upon the men and women of earth.
Many beings heard the call of Energy
      and lifted the awareness of their being
      to behold that which was given unto them.
In all nations of earth in all languages in all terminology
      came the lifting of Energy unto mankind.
For earth spoke unto Creator
      of the great need for pain to be lifted.
Still is that need awakened unto mankind.
Still is the awareness of the Energy
      charging through humanity,
      becoming a talisman for earth
      to heed its own destruction and create a solution.
Negativity is not the solution.
Brother against brother is not the solution.
Using Energy to create havoc upon earth
      is not the solution.
We give you the solution:
        it is to see within the eye of all humanity
        your own eye,
        to see within the heart of humanity
        your own heart,
        to see within the mind of humanity
        your own mind,
        and lift the knowledge to its highest transport
        that it might be beheld
        as coming from other than earth.
For you are human,
      but human did not begin upon your earth.
Human resides upon Farside.

Human has a Holy estate with your Creator.
You are called Armada.
You have a goal.
You have a vast intelligence available unto you.
You have a Circle of Saints who present to you solutions,
    if you will but hear, if you will but ask,
    if you will but abide in the Energy of Farside
    rather than the chaos of your earth.
You are not randomly where you are.
You have entered in.
The entering in is purposeful.
It is Truth.
It is chorused with a song of Angels.
It is voiced by your Creator,
    "Human, go forth
        that you might become Humanity."
May the songs be sung.
May the bells ring out.
May the harp and the zither be heard.
May the dance begin, the dance of Energy,
    the dance that begins and ends with Love,
    the Love that carries compassion as its ultimate goal,
    the Love that beholds all fellows
    as compatriots one with the other
    to overcome negativity.
Not with evil, not with the sword,
    but with a flame of White Light
    so that your Light may be seen in all worlds,
    your goodness shine forth in all worlds.
Hold the precious life
    that you bring unto your earth as sacred.
Hold the young, the adult and the aged as learned beings
    who have offering unto you of goodness.
Behold in all those who have not the capacity of fullness
    within their physical, mental or emotional being,
    see them as teachers
    that you may learn from their being.
For they have come to teach you of compassion.
They offer to you a testimony of that which is mankind.
Be vibrant in your Energy.
Dance the dance.

Give an invitation to dance in the holiness of Energy
> for the vital Energy of your being is the sacred self.

All holy men and women
> have voiced the Energy they have felt within.

It is not offered only unto Saints.
It is offered unto all beings.
It is available, Soul, for it is who you are.
You have no great excursion.
You have but to accept that you are Energy
> and the form that will cast from you and die
> is merely that, a form.

Rejoice in the leaving, rejoice in the entering in.
For each gives the other an opportunity
> and you gather as the Joseph coat,
> the shades of many colours.

And you behold, as in all sacrifices, a Truth
> that life is Holy and death is a shared part of life.

883 And so we teach you how to be,
> how to strengthen your resolve
> while you endure the turbulence of your existence.

Firstly, Soul,
> you must see it as the mirror of whom you are.

For have you not always known
> you were other than just who you are!

Indeed, you are the Energy being and often you are Holy,
> the Energy being, so that you look at your humanity
> and you wonder at the poor Soul caught.

And how could this be?
For upon the Farside is no woe.
The triad of whom you are is the capsulation.
We would have you
> draw dignity from the mirror of your being.

They would have you
> seek the strength of the tree in your being.

We would have you see yourself in the forest,
> among many different, yet like who you are;
> some strong, some weak,
> some colourful, some desperate
> but that is only, Soul, the reflection.

When you look unto earth

>   you may see the mirror on both sides.
So understand, you may draw
>   from the Spirit the Energy of whom you are.
You may know the path on which you have set yourself.
You may gather strength from the Spirit.
And you may make appointments
>   with your guides and your Angels
>   for they are there to help you
>   on the path you have chosen.
Humanity, you are in all shades of green,
>   you are warmed by the green.
The green will blend to the yellows and the blues.
But the green, as it blends to the red,
>   brings you back to earth,
>   to the troubles of earth, to the pain of earth,
>   to the chaos within earth.
We say unto you:
>   "*Rise above!*
>   *Lift your being*
>   *to see the Essence of whom you are,*
>   *to see the golden Light*
>   *that is about your being,*
>   *to see the Spirit of your being.*
>   *Gather in all that you are*
>   *that Truth of your Creator.*
>   *You are of your Creator.*
>   *You are the Energy.*
>   *You entered in by choice to overcome negativity.*"

884   Humanity, Truth.
Humanity, be in Spirit and be in Truth.
To walk in Truth is to recognize the battle,
>   for you are Truth.
To be in Spirit
>   is to be aware of all possibilities of humanity,
>   of the human Soul.
To be in Spirit is to be in consciousness,
>   consciousness of High Being.
To be in Truth is to honour yourself
>   as participant in the great Armada.
You have entered in willingly.

You have battled through many lifetimes.
You have been brought
      to the great Negativity that will not see Truth.
And as you have gathered in your Soul self
      a recognition of whom you are,
      you behold the Truth in you
      that you are indeed a part of humanity,
      that you are indeed together,
      the Soul of your Creator.
The Spirit is there to feed the Truth knowledge.
It is there to recognize that you have an avenue, a passageway
      to the great teachers, to the Angels,
      to the Souls and guides
      who have participated with you in lifetimes,
      that you may use the wisdoms to understand
      the purpose of the Truth that you are,
      not that you will become, that you are!
We would have you look closely at the savant
      and recognize the gathering of knowledge
      that comes from the high consciousness of the mind.
The avenue that is taken is the third eye,
      the mind, the mind's eye,
      the mind's eye that has a clear vision
      if acceptance is a portion of the mind.
To have acceptance
      the being must enter in to the knowledge of Truth.
The Truth is!
The Truth will set you free.
The Truth will bring you to a plateau of knowing.
The Truth cannot be shared.
It cannot be, Soul.
It must be entered in to individually.
As a gathering of humanity,
      there is a knowing of the Truth in that humanity.
But the Truth we speak of cannot be shared.
It must be entered in to.
And in entering in to,
      you lose the individuality of who you are,
      for you see yourself in a common bond
      with all humanity.
Your earth has spent many futile civilizations

without the understanding of Truth.
Even within your own civilization,
> you have not fully comprehended
> that you are less attached to your earth
> and more attached to where we are.

For the thoughtful man sees himself vulnerable.
The wise man lets go of identity
> and becomes the Energy of consciousness,
> therein recognizing
> the Truth of the purpose of being on earth.

You are ever reaching outward from your being,
> you are ever concerned
> that it will lessen who you are.

Souls of earth, to reach outward from your being
> is to enhance the Energy field round about you.

It is to enervate unto all beings the Creator's Masterpiece.
You were formed with Truth as your ultimate possibility.
You are endowed in your being with Purity.
And many have lost the Purity in their earthly endeavour.
Yet the reflection always is there to behold
> if they will but look up
> at that which is there before them.

Love is endlessly available unto you.
The Creator holds all Energy as one.
There is no less Energy.
None!
So the negative Soul is not less than,
> merely has not attained the wisdom of knowing,
> of the Truth that they are.

You are of the pattern of your Creator.
You are the fragment sent forth willingly
> to become the ultimate Truth.

You do not stagger under the weight.
At times you are oblivious
> to the great weight of being that you have accepted.

And you play at childish things
> and you enter in to great battles of nonity
> instead of the purpose of the battle
> for which you entered;
> to overcome all negativity with Truth,
> to grow in understanding

of the great adventure you have entered in to.
You are not at the frontier of your universe, Soul.
You are the frontier!
You are the great passion brought forth in music
  to be understood by man.
You are the tongue of your Creator.
You are the chord that comes forth.
You are the touch that can remove pain.
You are the mind that can enter in to the high mind.
You are the consciousness of all that is upon your earth.
Be at one with all the energies of your cosmos,
  for you are that which is the most enlightened
  and you know it not.
As your Creator has brought forth
  great intricacies of creation,
  so are you bringing forth
  great intricacies of creation.
But the single web does not behold the design of the whole.
Only the spider beholds the design of the whole.
The web of humanity is beheld by Creator.
And you, you humanity, are each a single web,
  a thread that makes the intricacy
  wherein many domes of enlightenment are
  and rely on the Truth you will come to.
Humanity
  behold in you in the vulnerability of the flesh
  is an Energy.
It moves and it vibrates.
It has a mind and it has a heart.
It has a high mind and a high heart, and you are that Energy.
Each of you attached one to the other,
  as each thread of the spider web
  is attached one to the other.
In perfect formation you have entered in,
  each with a purpose, each with an intent.
Do not behold a fallen humanity as less than who you are
  but send forth your blessed Energy
  to lift and assist in overcoming pain.
For they have entered in to pain that they might overcome.
And as the Blessed Angels
  found the weight of Negativity upon their being,

        so do many humanity
        find the weight of pain upon their being
        more than they can bear.
Should we not be as blessed as the Angels!
This should be your mantra,
        that you, humanity, might speak
        unto the being that you are,
        not to your brother, indeed not, to who you are
        that you might recognize the power in you,
        that you might see in you the blessed Saints,
        that you might behold in you the power of Truth.
You have entered in with Truth
        that you might overcome negativity.
It was but a seed within you
        and for those who have gathered purpose
        to their humanity,
        it will grow and it will enhance humanity
        and humanity will heal
        because you have allowed the Truth to grow.
Truth is the saviour of Negativity.

885   Souls, we speak to you of Truth.
Magnify your being in Truth.
All that you are, all that you have ever been is rewarded
        in the growth of Truth.
You have entered in to earth.
You have felt the energy of negativity barb your beings.
You have many times challenged that negativity with Truth.
Truth alters, it changes, it grows, it diminishes.
Your world has a truth.
The actual Energy of earth was brought to be in Truth
        that it might be the foundation
        for which your truth will grow.
All that is of earth is maintained
        through the influence of truth,
        the truth that mankind places upon it.
Mankind seeks and Energy responds.
Until a Soul has entered in to earth many times,
        time and time again,
        the purpose of truth defeats them
        for they are swayed in the halls of negativity.

They echo and echo and beseech unto humanity
      offering the curiosity,
      offering ever the path of least challenging.
Yet, Souls, you are given a cover to your being.
It is the cover that is a shield.
It protects your being.
It is the aura wherein you have gained
      many truths through your lives.
The barbs of negativity build up against the aura
      and you recall in your being the challenges
      that are recorded in your mind, in your aura.
You become Truth.
For you climb a mountain burdened much in your being
      so that your very Soul is heavy with the negativity.
And then you surmount the negativities
      and you release from you
      the burden as you gather the Truth.
You hold the Truth as a shield,
      "*I know I have gained this.*", is your cry.
And yet the spirit often falters,
      but always the Truth gains the way
      for you have entered in to earth to overcome much.
You have before you the sparkling waters of your earth.
They flood throughout your world.
You have the energy
      within the waters cordoning all your earth
      to become one united earth.
Your very Energy does the same with humanity.
It draws in its Truth
      and it energizes throughout all of humanity
      until you find a one and a one and a one,
      until you become many,
      until you become known for Truth.
Not the truth, Soul, of complexity, the truth of simplicity,
      the Truth that has a record of knowing
      there is a high Energy,
      an Energy beyond where you are
      to which you are attached,
      an Energy wherein you thrive in your being.
For you know you can gather from that Energy
      all healing, all Purity, all Love.

It is not, Soul, to defeat negativity that you have entered in,
    it is to overcome negativity with the Truth.
You are grasping in your being as you enter in
    but each entering in gives you a foothold
        higher and higher to the mountaintop of knowing.
At times you are ought to look about you and see beings
    who have not gathered the truth
    and it is in you to feel compassion
    and to reach out your very being
    with the compassion of knowing.
For that which you have become
    belongs to a core of Energy.
That core of Energy resonates.
It resonates to a chord of High C.
It is sounded throughout your earth.
It is carried at such height that the air
    does not always comprehend the sound
    but the Energy of your being
    receives it and rejoices.
You open your being in so much that you are vulnerable.
You are vulnerable, Soul.
You feel the depths, you feel the angers,
    you feel the heights of ups and downs.
You feel the inners and the outers
    and you cry unto your Creator,
    "*Why me. Why?*"
For Soul, you have become totally human.
You have felt all there is in that humanness.
Rejoice!
Rejoice that you can be angry
    and release from you the anger.
Rejoice that you can be sad
    and release from you the sadness.
Rejoice that you can have doubt
    and be fulfilled with the strength of your Energy.
Souls of earth, you are simple.
You are minute and you are treasured.
You are not forgotten.
Do not be cast down.
Do not be formidable.
We would not have you stand forefront

and cry in your energy,
> *"Hear that which I have."*

We would have you rather exude from your being
> that which you are,
>> a sparkling diamond that ever Lights
>> as you walk among men,
>> that ever speaks of your goodness.

Lift your hearts,
> rejoice in the Purity you have entered in to.

Hold your being.
Allow the earth feelings.
Allow, Soul, that you are so very human.
For is that not that purpose that you have entered in unto!
Allow the tears to fall.
But know as you are angry, it is your anger.
Know as you tear, they are your tears.
As you cry and sob, as you laugh and sparkle in your being,
> you are human.

Excite yourself for you are human.
You are delightfully so
> and as human we see your pain and your struggle.

We see your laughter and your sadness.
We see you attempting to enter in
> and challenge in your being
> that you have naught.

And even as you challenge your being you have entered in,
> for you have become the very purpose
> for which you have entered in.

You have become the full human, vulnerable,
> holding all the humanity that is.

886 Souls of earth,
> come to understand the Registry of being.

Behold the commitment of humanity unto its form.
Within the Register of many lives
> is always the return of Souls.

There is within the Register the mark of humanity.
It flows singularly unto a togetherness.
It is as a river that comes
> from many areas in to a strong source.

It is as the roots of the tree that form the trunk,

        the branches, the leaves,
        that have the power of Energy.
Souls of earth, be committed unto the Register of being.
It is the Register that accounts
        that which you do as human,
        that which you do in the Spirit form.
All that you are is beheld within the Register.
Documentation, Soul, is a source of understanding.
It is the ability to see.
It is the ability to behold that which you do.
You may return upon Farside
        and see all that is within the mark you have laid.
Who are you, humanity,
        if not the single portent of all that will be!
You are the purpose.
You are the acknowledgment of that purpose.
You are the end of that purpose.
Within all that is you are Energy beheld magnificent,
        Energy beheld in form inconsequential
        in accomplishment greater than the Angels.
Who art thou humanity
        to be called greater than the Angels?
How is it that you have come
        unto the Place of Shining with your glory?
Beheld before you a Light
        that even though you have not entered in
        it shines within unto the Place of Godhead,
        unto the Place of Creator.
Upon the tapestry you have weaved
        is the purpose of your being.
Within the purpose of your being
        is that which reaches outward from you
        a Light, a Light of power unrequired by you,
        for it shines even beyond where you are.
The significance, Soul, is great for you have sent forth
        even in the place of darkness an orb of Energy
        so strong it resonates.
With the Void it is heard,
        even as your earth trembles,
        even as the very power you see of ego
        within self manifested itself.

You who are human can step a side from the ego
        and reach unto the greater form that you are,
        magnificence in self,
        manifested into the power of Farside!
You are beheld.
You are gathered.
The Spirit of whom you are accomplishes this
        for the Spirit knows
        that which the Soul has acquired.
The Spirit holds all that is of the Soul
        within the positive realm of the form.
You are positive in your being.
Do not gather yourself unto the negativity
        of each day you are in.
Do not wrestle with the ego.
Accomplish, Soul, for yourself the placement of Truth.
Give fortitude.
Give grace.
Give generosity.
Give all that is you are able to give.

887   Souls of earth,
        welcome your being unto where we are.
Welcome your Energy,
        recognizing Energy is of ion.
Understand, Energy is of ion.
Matter you leave.
The form of matter you may take with you,
        but matter you leave.
Ion, the Energy of whom you are, you gather unto you.
The consciousness of your high mind is unto you.
Your earth mind, your earth conscious, is of no matter,
        for all is indelible upon the Farside.
You have every whit of recognition upon Farside,
        as you do upon earth.
It is, Soul, all your being that you will gather unto,
        the form of your matter, the ion of your Energy,
        the consciousness of your high mind.
You are one, complete in being as you enter in to Farside.
We are gentled by the Spirit you enter in with.
All Souls who enter in unto Farside

        meet the Spirit of their being.
All Souls who enter in to Farside
        have the recognition
        of the many lives they have lived.
All Souls who enter in
        know mankind's connection to the Armada.
There are avenues of connection for you.
There are counter ways in which you may,
        replete each nuance you have lived then
        indeed, Soul, satisfy your being.
You are a being.
You have been formed being.
You have not always been so,
        for Energy has a connection unto consciousness.
Matter has a connection unto ion.
Breath is the connectiveness of all three.
You are a connected Energy.
Wither you are, what will you transverse?
You are connected to the original Energy of your being.
You would understand deity.
You would worship deity,
        it will give you upon your earth a security of being;
        but, Soul, you must reach past
        the form of earth's religions,
        you must reach past the form
        of earth's insecurities.
For much that is done in the name of God,
        be it one or the other,
        it is to replace the inadequacy of the humanity.
It is to give a fear in that Energy
        might receive an earthly token.
But the Energy does not originate upon Farside.
For upon Farside there is no token to be.
You are, Soul, a being.
You do belong.
You are a portion of your Creator.
You are a fullness of the Energy.
The ion of your being gives forth
        unto the high ion a state of being.
Holy Holy Holy magnified, your Soul a shard of Purity.
Magnified you are given forth of Love.

It matters not what hand you have had
> in your bringing forth unto earth.

The Creator of your being
> has given you forth in Love, in Purity,
> has gifted you with the discerning of Truth.

Pledge not your allegiance unto earth.
Pledge your allegiance unto whom you are.
For you are the chalice, you are the perfection,
> you are the capability of the fullness of Love.

You travel your world and you look one upon the other
> and you see variations that create,
> hierarchies when indeed you are one.

There is no Soul greater than another.
You all enter in in the same manner.
You all enter in and you all leave and return
> into the place of Purity.

Bring forth a just self.
Bring forth a true self.
Bring forth an honourable self
> and you will be recognized as a being of Light.

For lightness can bear to be looked at
> and darkness will show forth Light.

Behold that which you have within your being is Purity.
Purity is Light, Soul.
You are entered in of Light.
You will leave, Soul, as Light.
How much pain you offer unto your being
> before you enter in,
> is your growth to overcome.

888   The value of the Soul
> is in carrying information of humanity,
> the individual humanity.

The chord that humanity creates is the chord
> that unites with all other humanity.

But the individual record
> is carried by the Soul unto the Farside.

At the Gateway of One,
> as the Soul re enters back unto Farside,
> it is relieved;
> not of negativity but of the negative lessons.

How is this done?
Awareness, Soul.
You are being taught ever by guardians and Souls
    who have the awareness
    of that which your earth lesson
    and that which you accomplished
    in your earth lesson.
And you release from yourself,
    we will call them, conversations.
In these conversations with Aura,
    you release from you the burden of humanity.
For indeed it is a burden to be humanity.
You have carried a great load upon your being.
You have all that you have unloaded,
    carried for you by the guardians of the stations.
All the information is carried to the station.
It is left at the station
    until you who have entered in to the Spirit self
    decide to come back to earth.
Should you never decide, Soul, it sits and awaits.
But as you decide, 'I will re enter the battle.',
    then you are invited to go
    to the station of learning,
    that you might once again choose
    the complexities of your earth existence
    and that which would help you achieve,
    not your Spirit level, but your Humanity level.
Your Spirit level is done through Purity.
Your Humanity level is done through Truth
    and the Truth
    is the discussion of the learning station.
It is where Souls go.
It is as you would go to a great meeting place
    and you would find yourself
    placing within your computer
    that which you would choose to accomplish,
    to help the purpose of humanity.
And you choose Souls that are willing to help you,
    and you have been
    in their endeavour to help humanity.
There is no need to make you purer than you are.

You are pure.
You do not go to your earth
      to achieve a more pure being.
You attend earth that you might overcome negativity
      not for your individual life,
      but for the life of Humanity.
Each return is done at a personal level.
Each parent picked at a personal level,
      but the purpose for all beings
      before they enter to earth
      is to overcome negativity.
As you enter in to earth,
      indeed the majority of humans are inundated
      by the negative barbs.
And you come to a place of overcoming pain.
You come to a place of achieving humanity.
This is your goal.
This is your purpose.
This is why you have entered in.
You are indeed most glorious.
You are indeed pure.
It is Love, the fullness of Love which is compassion,
      that you are achieving.
Do not look at another humanity
      and see them stranger to who you are,
      for nobody could be in your close proximity
      and not have a inflection upon that which you are;
      not even a glance in a crowd that meet your eye,
      not even a thought that crosses your mind,
      each held and balanced
      and weighed and sent forth.
It is your humanity that is measured in each action.
It is your purpose to overcome.
For it is why you have entered in.

B293   Souls, respond to inquiry of Humanity.
Seek to know that which is Humanity.
Endeavour to behold that Humanity
      that is within where we are, the Farside.
For you are in the turbulence of negative ion.
But we, Soul, we are in the positive Energy of Ion.

We have reached into the vicissitudes of where you are
	and we understand
		the great leaps and bounds you take in faith.
But we seek to have you relinquish faith
	by a simple knowing,
	by the sight that is offered unto you
		from where we are.
You are Soul of Purity.
You are sanctified in your being,
	not by yourself, indeed not,
	but by the Creator who has agreed
	that you go forth to overcome that which is
	to return the Brethren unto Creator.
Souls of earth, hold in your being
	the countenance of peace.
Hold in your being the register of calm.
We ask you, Soul, to find discussion
	and know it is an offering to resolve
	in your being issues of one Energy to the other.
To bring forth severity in discussions is to be at war.
To bring forth complacency is to withdraw
	from being an active part of humanity.
It is inevitable, Soul, that unity will be
	for it is the purpose of your entering in.
You have no intent, Soul, of withdrawing from the battle.
Upon Farside it is known that humanity
	is involved completely
	in their being of overcoming negativity.
You are grand in whom you are but grand, Soul,
	in whom you are upon Farside.
Upon earth you have many fallibilities
	for you are human
	and negativity entices
	all energy unto you, even itself.
You may be in a quagmire of negativity, Soul,
	but you may always reach forth
	unto the Energy of your high being to withdraw,
	to emerge from the negativity unto the Truth
	that you have entered in to find.
Only those beings who untangle the waiting hands
	and shift momentum

    into the forward movement of go
    will reach the clarity
      to understand the purpose of their being.
Soul, that which is written is written.
You have, each one, sat within the station of learning,
    a being surrounded by teachers of great Purity,
    resolving
      "How shall I live that I may offer unto Creator
        the greater Purity of my being?"
And many resolves are taken,
    and all the energies of your being
    have formed the projected place, the destiny.
And the child is born,
    and awakens to that which has been planned.
And all the tools are in the little being, child,
    and the Purity of that child.
Even the negative tool is received.
A negative tool,
    it is that which is passed from a being to a being.
Often, Soul, your very being
    carried through into another form.
There is karma involved in a Soul who produces a child.
The depths of pain of the child must be resolved karmically.
And this has been arranged.
This is pre ordained.
This is at station.
All Souls enter earth for growth.
All!
The tools are many to perform that growth,
    to overcome the negative step,
    to abound in the positive Energy.
Do not fear!
All life has purpose.
All Energy has purpose to one end,
    to overcome negative energy.
It is the purpose of your birth,
    it will be the purpose of your vibrational leaving.
We speak unto you of the Energy of being.
Motion, Soul, is in the Energy of being.
It is the messenger.
It is the mission.

It is the result,
> for all humanity must energize their being.

They must understand that lack of Energy
> within their being
>> creates a body that is dormant.

It creates an energy of consciousness that is dormant.
To vitalize the Energy gives forth movement.
It gives a path.
It gives a mission.
It gives a result.
You have entered in with a mission.
It is to overcome negativity.
It is, Soul, not casually to entertain negativity.
It is, Soul, to overcome the energy of wilfulness.
It is to behold that the unification of mankind's intent
> must be in oneness.

It is the universal Energy of oneness
> that is the collected Energy that will give forth
> the result of the mission of mankind.

You may hold your energy.
You may walk in your energy.
You may seek knowledge of the mind,
> but the mind will give you earth solutions.

You may seek knowledge of the high mind,
> this will give you Farside solutions.

But without the intent of use the avenue is stilled.
Even this becomes dormant.
It necessitates, Soul, that you become actively involved
> in the Energy of being,
>> that you behold you are a portion
>> of the Energy of Farside.

It is connected to you.
It is the Spirit of your being.
You hold Truth within you.
It is the ultimate Truth of your being.
It is the pulse that heals and resolves issues.
It is the pulse that sends forth.
It is the pulse that gives result,
> for in the active use of the mind,
> in the active use of the high mind,
> in the resulting transfer of Energy,

   there are solutions.
There are, Soul, projections.
They do not wither at the wayside.
They are brought into being.
They come to fruition.
Behold the path, the path of your energy,
   of each individual humanity.
Where is your Energy upon the Path,
   not of creation, but of existence,
    of the very existence you are upon earth,
    upon Farside, as the Angel that you are,
    as the Archangel you have reflected from?
Where are you on the Path?
Have you lost your being within the form of negativity
   or have you gathered the Truth
    and lifted your being offering unto negativity?
The scope of choices have been yours.
Throughout your many reincarnations
   you have been choosing
   that which is to draw you closer
   unto the return of being
   so that you might re gather unto who you are,
   the Holy Holy Holy transfigured as an Angel,
   as an Archangel.
Behold the Light.
Behold the scope of possibilities within
   to travel beyond where you are
   into the realm of distant views.
It is your Energy that takes you there.
It is not your human form.
It is not your human mind.
It is but the avenue.
It is but the first Path,
   but there are Paths beyond
    of which you may choose to enlighten your being.
There is the Path unto Love, unto Ecstasy.
There is the Path unto value and echo.
There is the Path and as the keeper of Light
   you have available unto you
   that which is the Path,
   for each of humanity

   is the keeper of the Light within.
You have the venue in your being.
You are, Soul, Energy of Energy of Energy.
You are a portion of Holy.
Cleave unto all that is Holy.
Cleave all that is sacred in your being.

889 Souls of earth, render yourselves defenseless.
For in that defenseless self is great power.
Arm yourself only with Energy.
For when you understand Energy
   is of the greatest power,
   be it water, wind or human,
   the Energy will alter all things.
It will alter the flesh, the blood, and bone.
It will alter the way of the mind.
It will alter the Energy of all worlds.
It will alter all needs.
Energy is positive or negative.
How you alter
   is dependent on the form of the Energy you take.
The wind also will alter.
The balance of the wind is chi.
And in the balance of the wind can be great calming.
In holding the wind of rage,
   it can blight a child for its existence in that lifetime.
The water is silent in its running,
   yet the sound is great within,
   not of the animal lapping at its shore,
   not at the life form within,
   but the water itself
   carries sound for the Energy ebbs over and over;
   the Energy from the old
   at some distance from you
   alters that which is.
And sound echoes forth if it will be heard.
Energy is powerful
   and we ask you to relinquish from your being
   the need to hold negative energy.
Relinquish from your being the need to judge.
You are, Soul, of great fortitude.

You will maintain a direction of Energy
>   for long periods of time as humanity.
You will do this in a unified effort
>   or you will do this in a singular form.
We ask you to look at that which you hold.
If it carries judgment
>   you know you are holding a negative.
We would have you dance the dance of Energy.
We would have you understand the liquidity of Energy.
Indeed, liquidity!
For it gives a drink to the Soul.
It gives vibrational food and drink.
You have the power to alter with the Energy that you are.
You have the power
>   to receive and embellish in a positive,
>   that which is land and seeking Light.
You can offer the Light within your Energy.
You can offer laughter,
>   it instills Energy.
You can offer compassion,
>   it heals Energy.
There is upon your earth a great momentum at battle,
>   negativity against positive.
It is continuous as the waves of your ocean,
>   and you must decide which side of the battle to be in.
As individual Human, as Humanity,
>   you are in the battle of Truth that is human.
You are also in a battle,
>   and this battle rides many waves.
It is, Soul, powerful in its Energy to overcome.
We ask that you battle with no judgment.

890   Soul, behold the Light.
Behold that which is Light.
Know that within the Light
>   there is structure, tensure, value unseen,
>   yet consciousness sounds forth,
>   gives forth energies
>   held of their own accord in darkness
>   that they might know that which is darkness,
>   for darkness is death.

Darkness is done.
Darkness withholds from Light.
Light must enter in to darkness.
Darkness does not enter in to Light.
It is victory when Light enters in to darkness.
It is defeat without Light, for Light is life.
Light focuses.
Darkness despairs.
Universes collide, expand, collapse.
They enter out of darkness.
They enter in to darkness.
They flow.
They pierce in howling screams of sound.
Had your earth not been cordoned off in its galaxy,
      had the Yawn not been held in the perfect Breath,
      your ears could not bear sound
         that would enter in unto where you are.
You are cordoned off.
You are in the Light yet you are in darkness
      for the Soul must evolve to become.
The truth must enter forth to become enlightened.
Ecstasy is Light.
You have the power of Light.
Earth, hold your head.
Hold the crown of your pate.
Know that the knowledge deep within is feeble knowledge
      unless you reach unto enlightenment.
This is the entering in.
This holds only that which is given to human.
Upon earth side
      you must enter in to the Energy of your Farside self
      to know that which is the knowledge
       you hold in your being,
      your song of entering in, your voice of giving forth.
The echo will resound and you will know
      that which you hear is of your being yet not of earth
      and you will be enraptured in that which you hear.
You will be found in great Light.
Light, Light entering forth from your being
      and you will see the chord
      that is the sound of your being.

You will know that which you are.
You will understand that you hold negativity still, is B flat.
You will understand that you have reached beyond
      unto that which is you.
You will reach High C.
You will see the glory of Angels.
You will behold the Sound
      which is that which they sent forth
      and you will recognize
      it has touched your being before;
      when you have drought upon your earth,
      you have known the touch of Angels
      but not recognized the Energy as such.
You are the simple;
      you are defective in so many ways,
      for you carry in your being taunts and jeers.
You mouth from the perfection of sound
      that which is negative,
      yet you are Holy beings.
You send forth words unto your humanity other than Love.
You have the power to speak in the gentlest of tones
      to give forth sounds of healing, echoes of knowing,
      responses of Purity.
And you tether your tongue unto negativity and we ask
      that you release the tether,
      that you offer from your being
      the words, the sound of Purity.
Be generous with the Purity that you are.
Give forth of the Truth that you carry.
Share all that is of earth
      for earth is only a dwelling place of illusion.
Supreme Being.
Can you fathom the power of creativity
      to separate the very Self into Energies to send forth!
As your Supreme Being has this power so, human, do you
      to send forth from your being,
      to separate that which is negative and positive,
      to voice forward that which is positive.
It alters not that which you are, Soul,
      but all those who will hear that which you are.

891   You are formed as the tree is formed,
        as the leaf is formed.
Indeed you are radiant and you have change.
As you enter in, you can enter in
        adorned in glorious colour
        or you may enter in muted in your being.
Yet each Soul entered in in the perfection
        they have intended.
And as you live throughout your earth existence,
        you are born and reborn
        many times in a single existence,
        you are one creature then another
        and another and another.
And at the time of your refining
        as the hairs upon your head
        become whitened and thinned,
        do you then to gather the wisdom
        that time presents to you.
And as you gather the wisdom, Soul,
        you think of what use is this life
        when wisdom only comes at the end?
Of what purpose?
You do not see the many lives you have lived.
You do not see
        there is no connection through the many lives;
        it is simply a pathway that you are walking.
You are on a path within the earth's sphere
        and you take yourself from that path
        to rest, to gather strength upon the Farside.
And you re enter over and over again for battle,
        as a soldier who takes himself
        from the battlefront to rest,
        that others might go in and battle as he rests;
        so you have done many times.
And you are often content to watch the battle.
And then, the urge to re address negativity
        overwhelms your being.
And the Spirit rises within you
        and you look at that which you have accomplished.
And you enter in to the foray again.
And so it is as you enter in each time,

it is simply a single battle.
It is not battle after battle,
    you have merely taken a rest
    from that which you do.
Some Souls, they are caught in the battle.
They have been overcome in their being by negativity.
And they lay upon the battlefield
    and their energy is caught
    and they are gathered into transition.
Do not think you enter in to battle alone.
Do not think the Souls in transition suffer alone.
There is no Satan.
There are Angels who hold great comfort,
    who have the glory of gathering.
There are humans of Farside Energy of manifestation,
    who have given of their being
    to enter in to the deluge of pain.
And they enwrap their Energy over the levels of pain.
There is no pleading,
    for the Soul must be accepting
    of the life they have lived.
But there is comfort
    and there is gathering of the innocents
    who merely wait and are caught,
    who are taken home to the Light.
Hold in your being a tear.
Allow the tear to fall.
Allow, Soul, the hands to meet in acceptance.
Allow the Energy to open
    and be sent forth unto all beings upon earth;
    the C that you have, the Energy,
    not to mete out, Soul,
    but to glory out Energy from your being.
For you are a field of Energy.
You are enwrapped with Energy.
Allow the Energy to flow and magnify from your being
    unto all Souls of earth.
It will bring peace to unknown beings, to children,
    to soldiers in battle,
    to Souls who have found their being isolated
    without home, without food.

You cannot change their step, Soul,
    but your Energy can alter the moment they are in.

892   To the Souls of earth,
    we would have you see
    the greatest of trees upon your planet.
We would have you see the length and breadth of these trees.
We would have you see the many connections to the trunk,
    the leaves upon the tree.
We would have you see the bracts.
And we would have you see how the leaves are maintained
    by the very root.
And the flow of Energy rises within the tree
    and the tree is nourished
    and fed by the Energy flow.
You who are humanity, you are in such a path.
You are in the space of such growth.
For the tree is of a single component that is attached
    to all other energies of earth.
You who are human,
    you have absorbed from your being Energy
    from a great Energy Flow.
This Energy Flow
    has the strength and endurance of the tree.
It has the graciousness of the tree.
It has the Energy that allows the Light to shine through,
    so do you have such Energy as the tree.
For as you absorb Energy unto you,
    it shines through you and becomes.
You are tinged in your being as growth is often tinged.
And in the tingeing, negativity may enter.
Negativity may appear as blight, as a very hole,
    as a gnarl within the tree.
As human, you too can become gnarled and blighted
    in your perceptions of humanity.
You are as all others, you are as all humanity,
    even the blighted Soul is yet humanity.
The blighted leaf is yet a part of the tree.
If it falls from the tree,
    it yet maintains the Energy of the tree.
This is for humanity.

All Energy is related and part of a single Energy:
Energy called Supreme;
    Energy with a Voice that projects outward
    in a Flow of Energy.
It is heard in the deepest recesses of the dark.
It is heard within the ambiance of the Light.
It is heard by the smallest of fragments and by the greatest.
The Energy calls forth unto all Energy to return, to return
    and so does all Energy return.
The flesh becomes dust.
The Energy of your being flows
    unto the Creator who cast you forth,
    all Souls of earth.
Would that it were a direct flight.
Yet it is not.
For it holds to it the choices
    you have made upon your earth.
It holds to it the choice upon the Farside
    to achieve greater Purity.
It holds to it the recovery of the beautiful,
    of the Idyllic, wholeness, completeness.
How can you say, "*We are not whole.*", you cry.
Wholeness of Energy is of that which we speak.
The flesh and blood is but illusion
    it is only for your growth's sake.
It is the Soul's venture in to earth
    that allows the fullness of perfection.
Each and every Soul upon the earth
    is blanketed in Energy.
Some shift from this Energy,
    others will allow the Energy
    for portions of their earth time,
    then shift from it.
Yet, it is always available unto them.
You are endowed with the possibility of perfection.
This is attainable for you
    because you have entered in from perfection.
Souls of earth frequent our station.
It is a station of learning.
It is not to return unto earth,
    it is for manifested Souls wherein they select

        that for which they would achieve,
           be it the Crystal Cave or the Circle of Saints,
           or high guide or research.
In each segment there is an opportunity to enter in.
You may enter in unto the Circle of Saints
        and behold that which is.
You may enter in to the Crystal Cave
        and speak with the energies who you have chosen.
You may see yourself as the Angel you are
        and the ability of high guide to earth beings.
All things taught are taught within the aura.
All things taught are irretractible.
It is an onward step of choice.
There is within the research the ability to travel
        as your space programs attempt to travel
        within the sphere of planets.
So does Farside seek to travel into, unto the great Void.
Souls of earth, upon your planet
        you have acquired great knowledge.
You have acquired so much more,
        greater than knowledge is compassion.
Upon the earth, earthlings create compassion
        within their being.
It is not a form.
It is created by the overcoming of chaos,
        by the acceptance that greater than negativity
        is Love and Purity and Truth.
You have saints, saints who are bound in compassion.
But we would speak to you of the Saints of the Farside.
All of the Saints upon the Farside are of Humanity
        but not all Saints have entered in to earth.
Few who enter to earth and have become Saints
        find themselves in the Circle of Saints.
Souls who have acquired great compassion,
        Souls who have given of their very being
        for a step unto humanity,
        these are the Saints of earth who have
        a portion of the Circle of Saints.
Upon the Farside there are many Humanity
        who never enter in to earth.
There are many of Humanity who have begun as human

                and acquired greatness in the stature of Purity
                through their ongoing receptiveness
                within the Field of Purity.
To be within the Field of Purity
                at the level of the Circle of Saints,
                one must understand Love.
One must behold Love
                and one must enter in to total Love.
Now therein for earth beings is a question.
Do not all Souls of the Farside have Love?
And we say to you, many being of the Farside
                understand love as you understand love.
They have a Purity that is not tethered
                in any way to negativity.
And they live throughout their Energy
                in the total acceptance of whom they are.
Yet there are purities
                that have brought their being
                to a higher understanding
                for they have heard the Angels, the Archangels.
They are tethered to the Love that is of Creator.
They are of great Purity, of great Love
                 and hold compassion prominent
                 unto whom they are.
You forward compassion
                unto the Archangels within the Cauldron.
They hear your echo.
The sound is threaded, it is nurtured
                and it is caught
                at the sounding board of the Circle of Saints.
For all that is humanity is heard at the Circle of Saints,
                all the nuances of growth,
                the manner in which compassion has been gleaned.
For all Souls are not compassionate
                in the same pattern as another.
Some give of their hearts in great compassion.
                others give of their action in great compassion.
Upon the Farside within the Circle of Saints
                compassion is.
It abides.
The Circle of Saints hears all sound,

    all colour, all vibrations.
It is brought unto their being
    through the Energy Field that is theirs.
Within the echo of their known
    is the beatification of the Angel
    who will return unto them.
They will be emancipated from the field they are walked in.
And we say unto you, walked, Soul,
    for they are inert in their being
    both within transition
    and within the Cleansing River.
Only is negativity virulent within the Farside.
Highly active within transition, it is a state of mind;
    within transition, within the human negativity,
    is a reality, but it is a reality of the mind.
For the Souls who are Brethren of the Angel,
    these are inert in their being.
That is negativity.
The Blessed Angels, indeed, guard,
    have locked the negativity still from you.
But in that day when humanity enters in,
    the gateway will be unlocked
    and negativity will be gathered
    unto the Cleansing River
    as it rises from the chasm.
Souls of earth, be aware that the Circle of Saints
    is ever watching over you
    as the Energy of Creator watches over you.
Indeed, that which is the helm is always touchable
    for is not the Energy the helm!
Blessed art thou humanity
    for you have much to understand,
    you have much to behold.
When you have entered in unto the Path of your being,
    sound will resound within you.
Colour will flow unto your being
    and you will see the Angels as they draw you
    unto the Circle of Saints if it be your will.
For all are escorted by the very Angels.
All are delivered in the Energy of their entering in
    in this the Essence of their being.

893   Soul, call forth unto your Energy.
Call forth unto your Soul to hear,
        to reach out unto the High Being,
        to collect for you
           that which you have left to be collected.
For as you are within the learning station,
        you give unto your Soul, directives.
You even leave opportunities
        for Angels to enter in and nudge your being.
And you call forth,
        "Holy one, come speak to me,
            for I have strayed from the Path of Purity.
        Show to me which is the path in which I erred,
            that I may find my way again.
        Was it ego that took me from the Path, or selfishness
            or pain or jealousy or greed?
        Give unto me, please,
            that I might know wherein my feet should be.
        That Path that is ever sacred,
            where my Soul knows my Spirit
            and my Spirit may speak to my Soul
            and I no longer is,
            but the Holy one is powerful, instead."
Holy, remember the possibility of your being,
Holy unto Holy, the reach is not so far.
The generosity of greatness from Farside
        is ever available unto you.
You have before you a great Path.
It is possible to reach the end with many levels achieved,
        wherein you would not have to re enter again and again.
You would be as the blind man who cannot see.
You would be in the depths of darkness
        and yet you would behold a Light and not fear.
And you would know where you are on the Path.
For the human may see with the eyes of sight,
        yet be blind to the Path.
It is when you lose your earth eyes
        and recognize the Eye of Beholding ,
        that you allow the Path unto the Purity,
        that you are Spirit of self.

894   We speak of the Soul
        and the need for the Soul to be fed.
Indeed.
For the Soul constantly is bombarded
        with the extremities of negativity.
That which is heard can bring the grief to the Soul.
For the Soul has an awareness
        of that which is the Writing on the Wall.
The Soul has the understanding
        of why you have entered in.
The Soul has a response to all that you do.
For it is upon the Soul that that which you do is written.
It is within the aura of the outer form
        that the Soul absorbs
        and translates unto the Spirit
        that which is about the human entered in.
There is a great need to understand
        the great tenderness of the human's Soul.
The great avenue of Light that can be given
        through the Soul's aperture
        and the language of the Soul is receptive
        and it interprets on hearing, on seeing.
For the Soul has both sound and colour attached.
The Soul has within the expansiveness
        to absorb anything that the human might give.
It can define that which is for earth
        and that which is for Farside.
It does not send forth
        that which would be detrimental unto Farside.
But it does alert the Spirit
        to the need for guides and Angels to attend.
Within the Soul itself
        is an awareness without judgment unto itself
        or those who might inflict or offer,
        propose or depose, destroy or build up.
All that occurs to the human
        is absorbed unto the Soul, not into, unto.
That which is negative, that which is deeply scarring,
        is felt
        and response can only be given unto the Spirit.

The nudges will then come from the Spirit of the Soul,
    or the Angels, or the guides.
But they cannot come from the Soul itself.
For the Soul has not entered in with the ability
    to alter the life of the human.
The life of the human is a gift unto Creator.
The gift must be received by the Soul
    in whatever form that gift will take.
It is measured in the negative form
    by that which is overcome
    or that which is entered in to.
It is defined by karma.
It is, Soul, not laboured in understanding of the Soul.
Indeed not.
For it is the human who has
    the exact deliberation
    within the heart and the mind.
It is the human who must overcome the negativity
    and receive the scars.
The Soul may not even rejoice at the overcoming.
This, the Spirit may do.
The Soul is a balance and registers all things human.
Each and every occurrence of the human
    is indelible unto the Soul,
    that which is negative,
    that which is balanced equal one to the other.
But that which has karma attached,
    the Soul will release before entering in to Farside
    upon passing through the curtain of care.
All that is of the Soul of Farside
    is separate on entering in unto the negative ion.
All that is within the substance of the human life
    is then for the Soul to receive.
Think you, then, that the Soul is as your great sponge
    and in truth not unlike!
But the Soul has the consciousness of the Spirit
    but has relinquished the ability
    to act upon that consciousness.
It relinquishes the consciousness unto the human
    until the human is willing
    to awaken the consciousness of the Soul.

It is not in servitude to the human.
Indeed, not.
It is the great wonder of Farside that such greatness,
    the Soul of man, can render itself without will
    and relinquish that will
    unto the human born unto earth.

895   Freedom, Soul, is greatly exaggerated
    for Souls of earth are seldom free.
Each being has a connection to many lives.
Each being having made commitments
    for the ongoing connection to many Souls
    to help them in that which is their life walk.
When you step, Soul, into the path of another,
    you affect the other
    even outward for infants unto thirty five feet.
As the aura is allowed to protect itself
    that distance becomes less
    for the Soul gathers fear and doubt.
And yet the aura knows the connection to other Souls,
    each Soul being taught or a student of another;
    this is common knowledge upon your earth.
But you also teach the blessed Angels as they teach you.
For they may teach you of Purity.
They may teach you of Love.
But you teach them of Truth.
You have a grasp of understanding
    beyond even that of Angels in your high being.
You have the thread always with you of that connection.
Your weave in that which you do to gather truths is pattern,
    not by the Angels but by your Creator.
Even the Angels
    do not have the attribute of Truth in them.
It is not they are not truthful in their being
    but they do not strive
    to gather the fullness of all truths.
They are accepting, always accepting of the goodness,
    of the Purity of a human being.
Whereas you have the attribute of Truth within you.
It comes from your Creator.
You are driven in the choices you make

    to gather higher truths
    in our articulates unto the Angels,
    the wisdom of truths.
And it takes them into a sounding board that gathers
    and channels itself into the darkened way
    wherein the Wisdom gathers Light
    and the Light illuminates the Dark.
Wisdom illuminates the mind of your being.
You may gather knowledge throughout your life
    but without the wisdom
    to use that knowledge correctly,
    you stand still.
For the Angels they gather that wisdom from you.
How can you, who are so spontaneous
    in your need to leap in to negativity
    able to teach unto the Angels?
And yet you do for truths do not accept.
Purity accepts, Love accepts, truths do not.
They continue from one truth to another.
They are always in search of.
You, humanity, you are always in search of.
You inspire the sound that echos forth from where you are.
It is not the sound of your ears.
It is not, Soul, the sight of your eyes.
It is not Soul the touch of your being.
It is, Soul, the continuous thread that ever grows in truth
    that glows as it gathers wisdom.
Your Soul ignites the thread to carry it unto the Spirit
    and the Spirit is astounded
    at that which you have overcome.
We would not have you
    lessen the use of your mind for knowledge
    even though it is ever unto you.
For earth beings it is a forage
    into the denseness of the forest
    gathering fruits of knowledge
    that assist in the walk of mankind.
But we, we would have you seek always the higher truths
    and that you would share
    in your being with the Angels,
    acknowledging the purities.

We do not ask that you bow unto them,
> they do not request it of you,
> but that you give unto them
> the emotional truths
> that you gather within your self
> offering unto them
> that which you have overcome.

896   Soul, we would have you look
> at a word within your earth vocabulary,
> whatever the language, the word, investment.

Soul, you are humanity first and foremost.
We ask you to make an investment in humanity.
We ask you to partition the word; in.
Enter in.
Enter in to the reality of whom you are.
You are subject only to your own growth.
In your earth's moment you reside.
Then, Soul, we ask you to look at vestment.
What vestment will you honour yourself with?
What is the glory of whom you are?
What raiment do you have round about you?
Do you have, Soul, a single colour?
Or do you have the prism of your earth's humanity?
We ask you to see aura,
> to see the colour that is around you.

See the flame of glory that you are.
Enter in to the high flame of violet.
Know that in the violet is the in to the Spirit.
Know the full form of investment.
Wherein will you invest?
Of your earth?
What have you in your earth
> that is worthy of your investment?

What material form
> will you seek to surround yourself with
> that is so mighty that it will override
> the investment that you have
> where we are upon the Farside?

Where we are, you have all that is.
You have the fullness of the Spirit that you are.

You have the Essence of your being,
> a part of your Creator.

Negativity does not reign.
Would you have the Soul invest in the materials of earth?
They are short lived.
They are there but for a moment.
Invest upon your earth in the well being of mankind.
Invest upon your earth in the breathing of whom you are;
> for the breath that flows from you,
> that gives you the possibility
> to do saintly things upon your earth,
> Angelic behaviours upon your earth,
> Love unto compassion upon your earth.

You are in a domain that is fragile.
It is ever been fragile.
It was formed that it might be fragile.
Why?
So that you could invest your worthy being unto earth,
> stabilize all Energy, even unto Negativity.

Souls of earth, children are born.
People live and grow old upon your earth.
They pass in form from your earth
> and the form becomes that of earth itself.

Your Energy, your Energy soars as the eagle soars.
It triumphs above where you are.
It meets the moon and the sun and the stars.
It transfixes a site upon the Farside
> and we await your Energy.

And we glorify your being in your triumphant entry,
> for once again you have entered in
> and gathered the vestment of your Purity.

Souls of earth, be present in your earth.
We do not advocate that you remove yourself from earth.
We do advocate
> that you make an investment in whom you are,
> whom you truly are, that which is your glory,
> that which is your rising star.

Soul, invest in
> the purpose of your being, humanity, the oneness!

You are the flame.
You have been the fire.

You have been and are the flame.
And in the Energy of the fire are all colours,
> is strength that is energized by the breath of all.
For a single breath brings a glow to the flame,
> but many breaths, Soul,
> > the flame once again becomes fire,
> > the fire of Purity, the fire of goodness,
> > the fire of Truth.
Upon your earth
> you have misconstrued the flame that you are.
You use the flame to incite, to provoke,
> to be crass and inane.
When in truth you are making an investment in negativity!
It is a choice.
It is the choice of humanity.
You slaughter, you violate.
The Angels, the Archangels,
> the legions of beings beyond where you are,
> would have you see the investment of earth.
They glory in your being, Humanity upon Farside.
But tears are brought to behold
> that which mankind would do
> and does to mankind, to creatures upon your earth.
Value, Soul, who you are!
Value the fire in your heart
> but have the flame rise for mankind's goodness,
> for mankind is the purpose of your being,
> to glory in its oneness.
A flame dances.
A flame vibrates.
Vibrate your Energy.
Send it outward from your being so the violet flame,
> the glory of whom you are will reach unto all beings.
You are of earth and we treasure you as such.
But it saddens our Spirit when earth's bowels cry
> at the internment of humanity by humanity.
See yourself as the star that glistens upon your sky.
See yourself as the angel of earth.
See yourself as the flame
> that has the breath of goodness attached,
> that all things might be unto the good of all,

and chaos will cease to reign.
Chaos will become a word rather than a state of being.
Souls of earth, transfix your mind unto the Mountaintop
    where you may see
        the glory of all things round about you
        and alit your eye upon that
        which you can aspire to heal in your goodness.
Peace unto you.
May the flame within your Spirit soar,
    that your earth flame might match its being.

897 Souls of earth, be entered in
    to the name of Humanity.
Be entered in to the call of humanity.
You are humanity.
You are Farside Humanity.
Be caught in the whirl of goodness.
Be caught in the whirl of Truth.
Understand your entering in
    and entering out of that which is illusion.
Recall unto you all that is of whom you are,
    the Essence, the Spirit, Soul of your being.
Do not confound your being.
Do not seek in dark places that which is.
Do be in the place of Light,
    Light within your being,
        then you will illuminate all dark palaces.
You are forever a part of Purity.
You are forever a part of that which is your Creator.
You are of Farside.
Enter in to the knowledge of whom you are.
Your world is triumphant in its ability to entertain negativity.
It is triumphant in its ability to exercise untruths.
It is triumphant even in the wanton activities of humanity.
Now we say unto you,
    garb your being with the Purity that is you.
Garb your being with the abundant truth
    you entered in to grow round about you.
Acknowledge your Energy to overcome
    that which is negative within your being.
Hold from you that which is untruth.

Gather the ultimate of Truth.
Gather the glory of Purity.
Acknowledge that you are each, humanity.
You are not the foil of negativity, Souls of earth,
      nor are you tribes and clans.
Indeed, that is only your illusion.
You are one in a battle to overcome all negativity,
      to gather in your humanness
          the confounding truth of compassion.
Holy beings, you have entered in unto a sphere
      that holds great beauty that holds great comfort.
Yet, it has within the swirl of motion
      a motion that can bring about
      a constant energy of negativity.
Do not be confounded.
Do not see the swirl as an invitation to dance
      but dance the Holy dance.
Dance the dance of Truth.
Dance with the Angels.
Dance with one another in your Energy
      that your Energy becomes one
      that you hold close unto you
          all that is the ultimate Truth that you are Spirit,
      that you are of your Creator gathered as one.
You have entered in to earth to recall unto Creator
      that which is the Brethren
          Loved and beloved of Creator.
You are Holy.
You are Holy unto Holy.
You are the very fragment of your Creator.
Allow the Light to so shine to acknowledge
      that you have a Holy Energy that disallows untruths
      that holds only the candle of Light.
As all energies gather into one
      the candelabra becomes a unified force of Truth.
Holy unto Holy art thou blessed humanity.

898   We speak of breath, of earth's need for breath.
Of earth's need for continuous breath,
      deep and abiding breath,
          not shallow but deep within the being.

When the breath is shallow
> the breath has difficulty seeing.

When the breath is deep
> the humanity that holds that breath
> is willing to look at all things.

We would have you carry deep and abiding breath
> and the avenue to that breath is acceptance.

Acceptance of your earth plane,
> of the great difficulties you have intent to incur.

Indeed, you have entered in to earth
> with a purpose of incurring great difficulties.

Those difficulties bring growth.

When the human breath is shallow
> the Soul is rejecting growth.

That is not a negative, Soul.

Do not impugn thy being but recognize each step,
> for humanity carries a purpose,
> the purpose is often unknown to who you are.

Only in enlightened Souls do you truly understand
> where you have come.

When you encounter a difficulty upon your earth,
> the earth being may see an enormity of pain
> and create within their being a lessening of breath.

They retreat as it were.

And as the Soul sees that which the being of self has done,
> the Soul may recover, find courage
> and encourage the breath
> to breathe deeply into the body.

For the Soul may hold the breath willing life to stop.

Breath is indeed an avenue to life.

Your Creator breathed forth a great Breath
> and in that Breath you reside.

As Creator is able to draw unto self the Breath once again,
> you will return into the space of thy Creator.

Breath is Holy; breath of breath of breath.

You have the power to expand the breath of self
> by releasing from you fear.

Hold no fear.

Know the greatest power of the mind
> to hold no fear,
> to see within the humanity, no action, no deed,

no placement that does not have purpose.
Therefore no fear is needed.
No fear is required for growth.
Fear gathers unwellness to it.
Fear holds the breath stagnant.
As you have purpose, breathe.
As you have life, know that breath is contingent to life.
Know, Soul, that your purpose is life not death.
Death is not within the space of Creator
    only is there renewing of life, expanded Breath.
You, Soul, do not die.
You invigorate your being.
You gather unto you an expanded breath,
    an expanded vitality,
        that which you have known
        in many in between lives of earth.
It should be familiar to you,
    for Soul, it is deep and everlasting.
It holds clearness that channels do not clog.
They flow free.
Reach unto the breath that is everlasting
    and know you can gather
    that breath unto who you are.
You can breathe and let thy breath reach for it and heal.

899   In the openness of life is the fulfilment of life.
Your existence in illusion will be done best
    in contemplation of Spirit.
For the recognizing of Spirit is the expanding of wisdom,
    is the crown of consciousness
    that envelops beyond illusion.
Within the place of worlds beyond your own,
    there is carried no recognition,
    for recognition is absolute.
It is!
It does not require awareness.
You are!
Only within your fallible earth,
    do you have the need to register recognition.
In entering in to the high consciousness of being,
    a Soul has a revealment of whom they are.

So that, Souls of earth, the Energy of your being, hidden,
> is revealed,
>> for the need to be clandestine is no more.

The need to withhold is no more.

The need to be overt is no more.

For fear and doubt have left your being,
> for in entering in to high consciousness
>> there is a recognition of Truth.

There is a recognition of the ego
> held in the flesh and the heart.

Ego is a result of the heart's dismissal
> of the mind's wisdom.

It withdraws from the mind and enacts.

To await is a lesson of patience,
> to behold is to
>> recognize the mind's teaching of wisdom.

As a human, as an Energy, as a Holy being,
> you have the power to enter in to Holy unto Holy.

In entering in to Holy unto Holy,
> you behold in you that portion
>> that is of the human race.

You see yourself equal to.

You see yourself entering in
> and welcoming in all variances of Light,
> for only in the entering in of all variances of Light,
> may you enter in
> to the White Light of understanding.

This we say unto you,
> *'See yourself as a part*
>> *and recognize you are apart from,*
>> *but you are also a part of.'*

In recognizing the difference
> of whom you are you hold a value for self.

In recognizing the difference of another,
> you recognize an opportunity
> to gather wisdom and share.

You will be met by three
> and you will contemplate the teachings presented
> and evaluate
> where you are within those teachings,
> and from the level you are in

   reach out to be as one.
See yourself as the swallow
   that enters in from a distant place
   and seeks to find the place where it has been.
And know the swallow has a companion.
The companion has ever been and knows
   that when one flies forth, the other flies also.
And know the place that was is no more
   and the burden to find home
   is felt strong within the female.
And the male searches and seeks to find an abode
   and the abode is found
   within the home of another.
Indeed the other does not fly.
The other is human.
Yet the other has set up a domain.
The domain is structurally sound and welcoming
   and the swallow sees the opportunity of home.
And all that is nature, including the human,
   give forth that which the home may be built with.
And the family do not see the creature as invasion
   but as a welcoming.
The differences are unseen.
Only the generosity is seen.
Seed will grow well with the nurturing and the care,
   and the family will recognize
   the return of members.
For family holds the memory of kindness.
To fold your hands and await the opportunity
   of offering from your being, has no evil intent.
It does not alleviate pain.
It does not alter distress.
Available unto you is the opportunity to alleviate
   whatever portion of pain that enters in to your space.
If no pain enters in to your space,
   recognize how fortuous you are
   and reach out to return a token
   of that blessing unto you.
You are even in the poorest of your need
   able to reach out and give.
The three mights given may alter.

You who have the opportunity to give, give,
      when you cannot give, you may bless.
You may use the self
      and physically, emotionally assist another.
We ask for earth's needs to be fulfilled.
In the quiet despair of a child
      is the opportunity to offer forth.

900   Souls of earth, we delight in your presence.
You have become as the ray of sunshine unto your earth
      for you send forth Light that we may see.
From the depths of your negativity,
      from the great valleys wherein you dwell in pain,
      you look unto where we are in your being
      and you say,
          "Bring forth joy that negativity
               might be released from us."
And you have all the capabilities within your being
      to release negativity!
Souls of earth, you grow old and you hesitate in your being
      to take the leap unto where we are.
You hold yourselves upon your earth.
Souls, leap!
Find yourselves rejoicing
      in the crossing over unto where we are
      for, Souls, we have what you have.
We enjoy life.
You seek to enjoy life, we enjoy life.
It is inescapable, Soul, as your recognition to Farside
      for you know you have appointed yourself to earth.
You know there is a purpose for your entering in
      and you know in your being
      the greatness of that entering in.
Now we speak to you
      that you might hear with the earth ears
      the song of Energy that you may hear
      in each being that you meet;
      the song of their Energy.
For all beings hold a note.
All Sound and Colour respond in the human
      and is sent forth in vibratory notes

   unto other of mankind.
Your Energy travels great distances.
You are not limited to that which you can see.
You have the spiralling Energy that sends forth a vacuum
   that draws Energy to you
   and sends forth your Energy
   outward forth from you.
You have ability, Soul.
You have abilities not to ponder in,
   but to exact a science of,
   to reach into, to accept.
And in accepting magnify the abilities of search, of heal,
   of Truth, of desire.
You may feel in your Energy the goodness or the falseness.
You may feel in your energy the purpose or lack of.
Being contented is not why you have entered in to earth.
Being contented is a form which many of humanity take
   but we advise
   from the calendar of mankind is a purpose
   that purpose, Soul, to overcome negativity.
It is resonate in each entering in.
It has great purpose.
In your life we advise that you do not wallow within the mind
   for this is not the purpose of mankind.
The purpose of mankind
   is to reach beyond the mind into the high mind.
To dwell in the cavernous way of the mind
   ever seeking knowledge
   does not allow experience.
You must gather both.
Knowledge without experience
   is like charm without being applied.
We ask, Soul, be gracious in your being.
Share that which you have of the mind.
Be not content to hoard knowledge unto you but give forth.
When the mind is saturated it seeks elsewhere.
It may seek unto negativity or it may seek unto the high mind.
You have your earth.
You have the glory of your earth.
It is magnificent in its multitude divisory
   of all forms of existence.

Yet know it is a replication of that which is.
Your earth in its sister form is pristine as ere it ever was.
Your earth is continuing to repel negativity from it.
It is caught in the chaos of energy both from mankind
      and the force of chaos
      and as radar emits unto
      so does your earth send forth cries,
      gathers, reaps, bleeds.
Only mankind has the power to restrain the knell of pain.
In whatever form the energy is
      mankind has the power to repel
      but also to impel and send forth altered with Light,
      changed unto a perfect note, a High C
      that resounds in the outer energies.
Innocence is yours to gather and hold and cherish.
Innocence is yours but as humanity you witness innocence
      and you say naught as it is scourged.
Speak for innocence.
Speak in a voice for those who have no voice.
Who are you but humanity who has gathered
      for the purpose of overcoming pain,
      overcoming negativity.
It is why you entered in to earth,
      it affects he very being of whom you are.
You can cordon yourself off.
You can gather piousness unto whom you are.
You may speak unto others that they might do your dwelling.
But, Soul, the Truth dwells within you.
You have the purpose.
You have the power.
As you are young, as you grow unto your age
      speak for the rights
      of human for you are human.
And those who are caught in pain, pain has always been.
It is only replicated even now upon your world
      as in replication after replication.
No word is spoken of the similarity.
Souls, love is for your earth, Love is for humanity.
Love is for humanity even, Soul,
      for the expression of your life is unto your purpose
      and the purpose of your entering in is to overcome negativity.

Passion, Soul, Love is passion.
Be passionate in that which you do.
Do not casually walk through a life.
Do not fear.
Do not wait.
Stand at the highway and know there is a way for you.
It is the way with purpose.
It is the way that has positive outcome.
Soul, you are treasured
    and you are held in the palm of your own hand.
You are valued as humanity.
Lift the power that you have that all beings might see.
Speak with words of Truth and in the words of Truth
    come unto the ultimate Truth
    that of the high mind.

901   Souls of earth, understand Truth.
Understand the Truth of where you are,
    of that which you have entered in for.
Souls of earth, you are counted within
    the Truth of your being.
Understand you have entered in for the purpose
    to grow in Truth, overcoming negativity.
Do not be contentious with Truth.
Allow your being to confront each truth
    and grow in each manner unto you.
You are Holy.
You have entered in unto the very being of earth.
You have entered in that
    you might immerse yourself in negativity.
Indeed, understanding negativity, understanding
    the how, the where, the why, the within of negativity.
You are offered a generous helping to confound your being
    in that you might know that fully
    that which is your confrontation,
    that which is not your enemy,
    but the source of your overwhelming desire,
    for negativity is mesmerizing unto humanity.
It draws you into the thick talons of inextricable pain.
It draws you that you might know
    and unhinge the hold

       that negativity has on your being.
You are the balance of Truth.
Can you search in your being for an understanding of Truth
       that will give you reign over negativity
       that will give you the power
       you seek to confound negativity!
Be strong in your will.
Wilfulness is not power.
It is to overcome will that gives you power.
Intrigue your being with the purpose of your entering in.
Know round about you
       your world has immersed itself
       in the negative throng of evil.
You, Soul, you have the power to alter energy.
You have the power to change the will of men.
You have the power to alter the will of your being.
Contain your energy in silence.
Ponder well on that which you see as truth.
Know that Truth that grows within you.
Know the Truth grows within the mind of whom you are.
Truth grows within the understanding of the heart.
Soul, you have the power
       to refrain from entering in unto negativity.
You have the power to seek to prevent a resurgence
       of negative within your being.
Alter the path you are on.
Each road you walk, each path you take
       give understanding in the way of Truth.
You may cry.
You may refuse to understand.
You may designate your pain unto another.
You may saturate your energy in selflessness
       but to seek to the Truth
       you must circumnavigate negativity,
       you must, Soul, not enter in.
Balance the weight that negativity has upon you.
You will never be free from negativity upon your earth.
While you abide upon your earth sphere
       negativity will always be
       brought unto you at some form.
That which is your survival

>   is the ability to balance negativity
>   with the positive Energy of self.
> We are held from the great triumph of our earth life
>   yet we have been given as teacher unto you.
> You may reach into the depth of your being
>   and you will see that which we are,
>   not unlike who you are, a human of Farside,
>   once of earth pattern to overwhelm negativity.
> We have not returned
>   for the battle is upon both spheres.
> It is within the depths of Farside and within earth.
> We assist you in your battle of negativity
>   as others assisted us as we dwelt upon your earth.
> Souls, do not despair.
> Know that your earth is altering
>   but even as you feel there is none beside you,
>   know there are many.
> Know that even as the alien beings
>   once inhabited many spheres round about you
>   so will they inhabit again.
> Souls, you are treasured.
> You are brother of brother, sister of sister,
>   you are human upon your earth.
> Upon Farside you are Energy of Energy.

902 Soul, we delight in the words of humanity.
We learn from the words of humanity.
We will express to earth how Farside expresses self.
You see, there is no negativity, Soul.
So our conversation that addresses any form of negativity
>   has to be from an experience that a human,
>   attached to Humanity on Farside has experienced.
Upon Farside each human is only Humanity.
They are not individual being.
They are classified as Humanity,
>   so that the entering in
>   separates themselves from that Humanity,
>   to enter in to an earth learning station,
>   to be that portion, that fragment that is human.
As you enter in to a learning station,
>   you do not separate alone.

Even in that choice that you have at Farside,
> to enter in again is traumatic, Soul.

And within that station of learning,
> there are Souls who coach you
> > on the pitfalls of earth,
> > for baby Souls who enter in, this is.

We cannot measure for you in your earth years.
Our Time is different, Soul.
It is a vibratory acceleration
> that allows the Energy of Humanity
> to absorb and release from their being
> the purpose for which
> they have entered in as humanity
> and become simply human.

So that to separate, there is a vibratory increase.
To enter in to the station of learning,
> there is a slowing of that vibration
> to nearly the point of stillness.

And as the Soul is received upon earth side,
> that vibratory motion begins to accelerate,
> but only as fast as the human on earth allows
> in the growth of their being.

It is not simply to separate as human from Humanity.
It is a great step.
To be in the place of Love, of Purity, of vibrancy,
> the vibration is overwhelming.

And to be without that vibrational self,
> in the cohesive oneness of Humanity,
> is to feel an aloneness.

It is why the arms of mother enwraps the child,
> to hold them
> until they can adjust to the negativity of earth.

903   Souls who are upon the planet earth,
> know that you are watched.

Know that you are watched with the eye of care.
Know that you are watched
> with the intellectual advantage of our station.

For we have the fence to view.
All that is within your world's turmoils is seen and beheld.
It is not for us to question the rights or wrongs.

It is not for us
>	to send forth even energies
>	to alter that which you do
>	for you are on a mission and the mission is yours.

Only the Blessed Angels could change your step.
And they know that which you do and would not alter
>	for the sake of their beloved Brethren.

All negativity upon your earth is frozen in time
>	for it will be as though it were not,
>	for what you do is illusion.

The pain is not illusion and we know this.
But you have willingly entered in to the pain.
You willingly have knowledge of the turmoil
>	and the great misery wherein
>	>	there is no consolation, no sack clothing
>	>	that could cover the agonies of the multitudes.

We speak unto you that you might know
>	you are a Light in our sky.

As the sun shines and is a light unto you,
>	so are you beheld as a Light unto us.

For all that you do, your beam of Truth shines forth.
For all that you do your being ignites the darkened way.
How deep is your valley and the pain therein?
And we cannot lift it from you.
But we are aware of the great pain inflicted
>	upon the Souls who deserve it not,
>	>	dastardly deeds that are amuck upon your earth.

You are wizened and old,
>	you are careworn and in need of sustenance
>	and we cannot sustain you in a manner that we would.

For as humanity, you have asked us
>	to separate ourselves from your battle,
>	that it be the battle of humanity
>	and we have agreed for we know in Truth
>	that your step of wisdom is greater than ours.

You have taken a lift beyond that of Farside
>	for you are called born of Creator,
>	Humanity born of Creator.

Indeed, the term is born.
Terminology, Soul, is in the hearing.
It is needful for earth know,

    to understand the great mission
    you have entered in to,
    that it is not of your earth alone.
It is carried beyond the realms of your dimension.
It is carried beyond the realms of Farside.
You have delivered unto all existence a map,
    a Path that is beyond Truth,
      that is beyond Purity, that is even beyond Love.
It enters in to the breath of all that is
    and it stills as the voice of Humanity is heard.
It stills the chaos, it calms the wayward motion.
This we have seen, this we have beheld,
    not throughout the Fields and levels,
    but within Fields and levels have we witnessed
    the serenity of chaos.
And we understand that to alter chaos
    one must first bring motion to still
      before it can continue in the force of earth.
Earth humanity, our being is not as your being.
Our features are not true to yours, but we are kin.
We are of brotherhood, the sisterhood,
    the family of existence.
We meet at the drawbridge
    and we consult the flowing path of Light,
    and we see therein the creation's plan.
And we behold the stars that lighten the Path
    and we know you have travelled
    beyond where we cannot go.
Why could we not go, Souls?
Because of negativity,
    because of the great distortion
    that would befall our beings.
But you, you have entered in to the distortion
    and indeed it distorts in great ways
    that which you are
    and we see your being torn and twisted.
We see your Energy lifted and lowered.
We see the will of man bent.
And then, we see the crown lifted to ego.
And we say to you,
    "*You travel alone but our care we send with you.*

Our Love we send with you
   and the battle is yours and we know it."

904   What is the mark of a man?
We ask humanity, what is the mark of a human?
What at the end of your tethered time to illusion,
   do you say, "*This is who I am.*"?
It is simple.
It is the measure of Truth gained.
It is not the measure of that which you have accumulated
   as treasures upon your earth.
It is not the idiosyncrasies
   that make you particularly who you are.
It is simply the measure of Truth you have gained.
To gather the ultimate Truth,
   you must leave aside earthly treasures.
To gather the ultimate Truth,
   you must overcome pain,
   overcome fear, overcome doubt.
You must recognize in the being
   you are a Soul that is simply tethered to earth,
   but has a homeland that is palatial in its richness,
   that is garland and carries with it all knowledge.
And you who are tethered to earth,
   you have availability to that knowledge.
It is not classified from you.
It never has been.
It is available unto all mankind.
You do not even have to diligently search out.
You have but to become aware of the Path to it.
It is a transforming pathway,
   for it beholds who you are.
It beholds not the inadequacies within the human,
   it recognizes, Soul, the smallest step,
   the most minute action of goodness,
   of mercy, of compassion.
Truth; simple you say, to gather truth.
And yet, it is not, Soul.
For it requires of you all things.
It requires of you the extension of self
   to reach outward from your being.

It requires that there are no noble men,
> only noble deeds.

There is no challenge for it is a voluntary path, Soul.
There is no accountability,
> for there is no measure except your own.

There is no time involved.
For you have eons of time, many lives,
> to gather unto you the ultimate Truth.

You may feel the heart of your being
> pulsing within the container
> but the aura is much more silent.

The aura does not inflame or incite.
It merely gathers knowledge
> and takes strides outward from you
> that it might give your intent.

To be in the place of Truth is to relinquish
> the mind of humanity
> and gather to the high mind of your reality.

It is to persevere in light of great want and need.
It is to humble self without humbling.
It is to enter in to the greatest of visions.
It is to see integrity of humanity in the smallest act
> and in the greatest deed.

It is to want for nothing in the greatest deprivation.
For your meal is the meal of manna,
> and your healing is the Balm of Gilead,
> and your home is the home of Angels.

And you are but traveling the Path that will take you there.

905   Brilliantly, brilliantly shines the Light
> in the heart of a child.

Brilliantly seen the Light
> as the Soul receives itself back unto the Farside.

Only in the holding of pain does Light be dim.
The darkness gathers round
> as the Soul invites the negativity
> to take part in the dance of life.

Behold unto you who have known the value of pain.
See that which is pain.
Endeavour to know its capability of lingering within
> the humanness of man.

And know that you may alter that which is negativity
      by holding it from thy being, allowing the Light
      to be the distance
      between negativity and whom you are.
What is this Light you speak of, say you?
We say unto you, it is the Light of your inner being.
It is the Purity that you have entered in with.
It is the avenue to all other shards of Light.
It is not your sun or your moon or your stars,
      they are there to comfort you,
      to remind you of the Light you have left.
It is the Essence of your being,
      it is the starlit way,
      it is the glory of Entering In.
Look upon negativity, Souls of earth.
See clear in thy being.
Do not shun thyself from it.
Indeed, not.
Gather unto you and offer it out.
Do not embed it in thy being.
Offer it unto only that Energy that is pure enough
      to gather unconditionally all negativity.
Would that earth beings could gather round about
      all the negativity and offer it forth.
For then humanity would see themselves
      as the crystalline self,
      as the shard of Purity.
You who are human are very human in your being.
You allow pain to enter in.
It is only in the understanding
      that humanity is that which you are about,
      not the human, but humanity,
      the entirety of that which is human
      becomes the foremost, the essential in your being.
Gather you not material worth unto you
      as a form of who you are.
It is not who you are, Soul.
You are the portion of Light that is contained within you.
That is who you are!
Be at peace.
Be thyself in the Purity in the Energy of Farside.

Do not hope for clarity.
Accept clarity unto thy being.
Do not reach for the impossible.
Reach for that which is possible in you,
     which is the Light of thy being.

906   Souls of earth, be in peace.
Bring harmony unto all that you do.
Bring accord unto the platform of earth.
There is within each humanity a variance of chord.
It is necessary to bring a oneness unto the sound.
Beloved of earth,
     you want nothing that is not available unto you.
Your earth has been given all power
     to access into the realms of all possibility.
You have within you a tapestry barely filled.
You have a possibility of cantation of good.
You have before you a great realm to bring forth.
It will be as a garland of colour.
It will have the chimes of chord unto you who are, Souls,
     visitors upon your earth.
Do not become bogged down in that which is
     not the fullness of truth.
Truth carries contention if you will.
Truth carries a whisper, a mere whisper of oneness
     but to hear you must allow the din to cease.
You must allow the wing of a moth to be heard,
     to hear the sound of the wind,
     to hear the buoyancy of air.
Blessed humanity do not pattern your being in all things.
Hold yourself apart so that you have become an example
     of that which is serene.
Enter not into the fray with loud boisterous sounds
     but hear the echoes
     that come unto you from the Farside
     for you have the capability of sound.
You have the capability of colour.
You have before you all the possibility to create
     a masterpiece within the emptiness of your being.
Fill, so that your cup runneth over with the calm
     and the gentle mind, heart,

>   so it enters in to the Soul
>   and carries you unto where we are
>   for we await the resonance.
> We gather at the fence
>   to hear the optimum sound of oneness.
> We relegate those who would hear
>   so it may enter forth on the Energy of Farside.
> Gather the sound.
> Send it forward, the sound of peace, the sound of oneness,
>   the sound that makes all healing possible.
> This we say unto you for your world is in need of healing.

907   We speak to you, Soul,
>   the flame that you are, the Energy of fire.
> Fire that ignites flames other than within itself.
> This is why you are fire
>   to ignite the Energy within others of mankind,
>   to recognize that your flame
>   is not singularly your own
>   but a part of fire.
> To understand that as the fire enlarges,
>   the Light is seen at a greater distance.
> The Energy is felt within the flame.
> Behold the power that you are, human in yourself.
> Behold the Energy that you are.
> As you reach into the fullness of your Energy,
>   as you behold
>   the Spirit and Essence of whom you are,
>   as you behold the entirety of mankind,
>   not just of earth, but of Farside,
>   that your intent is the same,
>   your echo is the same,
>   your value is the same.
> Would you understand the great pain
>   you have entered in unto,
>   the horrendous pain you have inflicted
>   upon others of creature, even of flora and fauna,
>   even of earth itself,
>   so that the Angels have cried in their being,
>   the Tears of Creator
>   have reached to the very Hem of Being!

But when you seem
>   at the farthest distance one from the other,
>   we find that you reach outward in your being
>   to embrace
>   even those of the most depraved of being.

And the negativity, Soul, that overwhelms their being,
>   you wash away with the very tears of your Purity,
>   with the very tears of your Love that is compassion.

All that ever was was minuscule.
Think on this!
All that ever was was minuscule!
A thought enlarges itself.
Even, Soul, a negative thought
>   can expand itself unto greatness
>   and wisdom is brought forth.

But a thought spoken is contagious,
>   it gathers yet another thought
>   and another and another thought.

It is explosive in an outward thrust and it cries for solution.
It delves into possibilities.
It becomes as the stars of the heaven
>   and travels through energies, through verticals,
>   through linears and becomes.

It becomes.
It becomes a tangible,
>   but not always a tangible form of earth.

But often it becomes a star set in the sky
>   that others might behold the Energy.

Often it travels into the darkness
>   that others might see
>   the completeness of the thought
>   that has been formed and brought forth a solution.

Your ego will place forth a bold or tenuous issue
>   and your being of earth,
>   the aura connected to earth,
>   will send it forward.

There are thoughts that have such Purity,
>   that have such completions within that are beheld
>   and sent farther and received.

For they are pure thoughts.
They can travel through the curtains of care

        into the realm of Purity.
They can travel even beyond unto Ecstasy.
They can travel unto the Creator
        that they might behold the Light of solution.
And this is a circle completed
        this is a reflection returned.
This is a Path you have found.
Mankind began the return
        upon first entering in unto the world of your being.
Then the Path, Soul, was lost
        for it was necessary to enter in to
        the conflict with negativity
        that the ultimate solutions might occur.
Some have entered in to earth for so many lives
        that they have not forgotten
        the purpose of their entering in.
But on entering in their Energy
        is absorbed by the negativity
        to which they have become accustomed
        and they carry in the pain.
Yet, many overcome
        and find in their intent the greatest desire
        to reach from within their being unto all humanity.
There have been Humanity of Farside
        that have entered in
        for the single purpose of showing,
        the violet and the indigo, the many lives of Souls,
        who have entered in just to teach
        how humanity can overcome pain.
You, Soul, would be devout.
You, Soul, would be pious.
You, Soul, would be clothed in recognition of purpose
        and yet you offer less
        than those who would give forth
        a crust of bread to the starving.
Seek not to anoint your head with oil.
Seek not to cloak your being in robes of adornment.
Seek not to entrap your mind with replicas of devotion,
        but in your being,
        in the strength of whom you are,
        find the commitment of your humanity

    unto all earth beings,
     unto all creatures, unto all flora and fauna,
     unto all that is earth.
You have entered in.
You are Holy beings.
You are pronounced in your Purity as of your Creator.
You are Souls of earth but you are citizens of Farside.
Your home is where we are.
The time, the length of your stay is for a solution.
Only a solution, the purpose to overcome negativity
   within yourself
     and then outwardly in compassion unto others.
Hold your hands cupped that you might receive.
Hold your Energy full that you might send it forth.
This we say unto you, for you are of Purity.

908 Beloved, enter in to the circle of well being.
Draw nigh unto
   the time of releasing all pain from thy being.
Souls of earth, respond to perfection.
Respond to introspection.
Drawing from thy being the Holy Light of Purity,
   see with the eye of thy being.
As Egyptians circle the eye, so circle thy eye with Purity.
Know in thy being, the eye responds to introspection,
   it is, Soul, the receiving of goodness,
   it is the cloaking of all negativity.
And with the magician's furl,
   know it will disappear from thy being.
Behold the seed of Purity.
Behold the Light covers the seed
   and the Light causes the growth of the seed.
Soul, know the same seed
   and know the cloak of negativity
   will draw the seed into itself to turn and die
   as the gnat at the seed's core
   causes the daffodil leaf to turn.
Blessed, blessed Purity.
Respond to thy being!
Do not look outward.
Do not look to the far field

    but seek within thy own field
    that which is there for thee!
For within the mind of man is incredible power.
To be enlightened to the fullest possibility of enlightenment
    would be to be a Farside Soul upon earth.
It is where the Purity of thy being
    will bring humanity at the Gathering Time.
It will be that pure thought,
    that pure healing that will alter the sum of man.
And man's heart would open as a flower opens
    to nourish all those within the region of their being
    and gather unto themselves
    so that they may share in the well of Purity.
For only in giving may a Soul absorb total Purity.
Beloved, mankind is fraught with ineptness.
Mankind may not countenance his brother's inferiority,
oh Souls of earth, why, why
    does earth have the distorted vision?
Of course,
    they have not overcome negativity!
Oh behold, behold, children of earth,
    behold the Light that may enter in if thou wilt.
Behold the Light that will draw itself unto thee.
And yet mankind will flounder in minuscule problems
    that will hold no matter
    in the true existence of his being.
Reserve thy Energy,
    reserve thy Energy to move outward
    from thy being.
Do not hold thyself to a framework of position.
Do not hold thyself to a framework of employment
    if it does not allow thy being
    to reach unto all mankind.
For only in the reaching out may the ladder be climbed,
    the ladder that takes thy being
    into the true step of humility.
Who can open the flower of the heart not to say,
    "*What will you do for my heart?*"
    but "*What may my heart do for you?*"
Earth Souls, blessed be thou man.
More blessed is it to give than to receive.

909 Beloved, we speak to you of Purity
   and we speak of earth Purity.
Earth has pristine Purity.
Earth is committed to Purity.
Within the earth there are beings
  who have entered in with such Purity,
  who have not lost that Purity.
They have not forgone by choice that Purity.
Humanity has Purity.
We would have you know they have chosen
  to allow the throes of negativity to be upon them
  and in that negativity is often lost
  to bring tears to humanity.
Upon the earth there is such Purity
  as is held and treasured and beloved of all Farside.
Again even within humanity there are beings who
  have gathered unto themself while upon the earth
  the understanding of Purity
  and in as much as their humanity allows them
  they are of the pure state of being.
You are not pure.
You are not contained in Purity
  for you hold within the power
  to be swayed by the negative seed you carry.
You are bombarded
  from the outward extensions of your being
  by negativity of earth people
  who convey evil unto you.
Many earth citizens grasp at this evil as in hunger,
  holding on to it in a mighty avaricious state.
They become a part
  of the very evil they have been bombarded by.
And within the earth there is text that would say
  you have lost your Soul unto evil.
You have not lost your Soul!
You have merely stagnated your growth.
You have given unto yourself a great darkness
  when Light shines before you.
You have assailed yourself
  with darkness covering the Light of your being

   from that which would be your glory,
    your place of being.
Purity is not just a word.
It is a commitment of being.
For the mind in the thought process for the physical self,
   in extending outward from the aura
   in a negative form,
    it is seen lashing as a whip would inflict itself
    outward unto another in the voice
    that can carry unto another Soul
    great depressions of being.
Upon the aura,
   it can cause the aura of another to move inward
   decimating the Light of the being
   for they have been struck with fear
   until they regain their stature,
   their presence of mind that extends to them
   that the Soul is not required to hold fear.
It is held in abeyance for the karmic station,
   a reality is the mind, is focussed
    to the connection to Purity
    that withers evil, even is astounded by goodness!
It is threatened by the very pure sense of thought.
The aura will convey unto evil
   the power of the Truth of Purity.
Action of humanity may indeed kill,
   destroy a defenceless Soul
   the karma is huge and must be repaid.
There is the Purity of the wandering Soul
   wherein thought is placed upon beings
   in a great extension of Purity.
It allows goodness to reign.
It allows tenderness to speak.
In the greatest turmoil of your earth,
   the voice of thought projected outward by the aura
   can succour many beings in to Purity.
You cannot change all there is to change
   as a single Purity.
We say you cannot.
But you can alter in your being
   the fragmented energies of many.

We ask you to send outward from your being Purity,
      the pureness of thought that lites itself
      upon the human flesh and creates an awareness.
A Soul in the state of Purity will gather the extension.
A Soul in the state of evil
      will become aware there is a choice.
You cannot alter the choice,
      but you can send awareness to that choice.
Indeed, we ask you to arm yourself with Purity.
We ask you to behold in your being
      the greatest armour is Love unto ecstasy.
Covet no thing,
      see in your being no earth value.
Strengthen the armour of your Truth
      with the understanding that earth is a term,
      a qualified time
      connected to the Writing on the Wall
      upon which you have committed yourself to live.
The choices are for the growth of the Spirit
      as well as the Soul.
For as you gather understanding,
      you will understand it is the Spirit
      that enters in to the Crystal Cave.
You will understand
      Light will connect to Light and you will be one
      where your Light travels.
You will be, Soul, apportioned those to Enter In
      who have reached
      the greatest level of Truth, Love and Purity.
For only they will reach the door.
Only they will understand the total connectedness
      of you unto your Creator.
You will be, Soul, wiser in Spirit.
You will be of the Wisdom
      that holds an understanding to Negativity of Farside.
You will understand
      that which is Love unto the Blessed Brethren.
For you will have understood Love for all humanity.
You will have become a part in body, mind and Spirit.
The wholeness of who you are is joined together
      to become one in Energy,

    that your Light may so shine in its Purity,
    that outward from your being
    you will ignite thought in a manner
    in which thought has not been conditioned.
You will understand consciousness of thought
    in the purest achievement of mankind.
For all equations will be made known unto you.
And you will have the awareness of the chords
    that strike a mathematical genius, a musical genius,
    a scientific genius to dedicate all Energy
    to bringing forth that which is the purest,
    that which is the Idyllic, that which is Light,
    that which hides within the Energy of galaxies
    wherein all Energy
    thrusts itself outward from matter.
And such Light will be seen and echoed.
And all that is good and Holy are Truth,
    will gather the chords that are heard
    and the hearing
    will bring forth a manifestation of that which is lost.
And the Brother of Creator,
    lost in a search of Purity will be caught in the Light.
And the Light will measure the time of existence
    that was thrust forth into the darkness.
And the sound will be heard and draw in
    the united goodness of all Light Beings,
    the purest of the pure
    into the Path unto which it was lost.
You are the glory that awaits all Energy.
From you is the Light of Purity to be
    that will beam itself, Soul,
    as no other beam has ever been felt.
For you in your minuscule self
    widen the doorway of our vision.
You broaden the window of our awareness.
We perceive through you that which is possible in us.
We who are of Farside,
    who have entered in as you upon earth
    know the entering in was noble,
    was the greatest gift unto Creator
    for indeed you became vulnerable

        apart from Creator's plane.
You have not been protected in the manner that we are,
        for you are thrust as we were into negativity
        wherein choice gave way to will.
For it is the Will of Creator that no harm enters in.
It is, Soul, the choice of mankind to choose evil over good,
        the choice of mankind
        to conquer then evil with good,
        the choice of mankind to raise themself
        unto the Purity of being,
        wherein Purity is radiant in humanity.
Souls of earth, draw thy being unto the ever changing skies
        and know in your being
        that you are as the ever changing skies.
And as beneath the storms that weather your skies
        you know the sun shines,
        so in the conflict of your human self,
        know behind the conflict is the Purity of your being.
For you are of Farside.
You are treasured and Loved.
Souls, unto you be peace and goodness given.

910   Souls of earth, you are brought
        unto a place of learning.
You have before you a vision of all that you are,
        all that is, of positives.
Only that which is karma is brought unto the Farside,
        that which is negative is seen as overcoming negativity.
As it is overcome
        there is no need to bring it forth unto learning stations.
Only that which is karma is entered in to.
That life that you plan to enter in to,
        this will be established through
        many interactive lives with others
        but only for growth, Soul.
The teaching that is yours is for growth.
All that you are propels you, Soul, to the positives of growth.
To grow you must enter in to negativity.
To grow you must respond unto negativity.
It is not a growth life to only acknowledge negativity.
That is a teacher life.

Fragment your being,
> offer your Energy.

Acknowledge that you are not perfect.
Give forth sound, sound, Soul, exquisite sound,
> that revives the Soul, that lifts the heart,
> that enhances humanity.

You have the power in your being
> to reach in to the heart of your brothers,
> of your sisters, of your mothers, of your fathers.

You have the power to alter the lives of humanity.
You are a pendulum that may respond
> to the energy around
> but the pendulum always seeks the centre of being;
> the centre of being the Energy of positive power.

And we say to you, Soul, "*It is power for it motivates*".
Grasp your Energy within your mind.
You are teacher.
You cannot say,
> "*This is negative. It is in my way*".

You can say,
> "*This is negative.*
> *How may I transform that which is negative?*
> *How may I lift that which is negative?*
> *How may I respond*
> > *with positive thinking to that which is negative!*"

The world is grounded in negativity.
It is, Soul, desperate to reach unto your being,
> for it searches outward from itself.

Send forth all the compassion that you have,
> for we would return that which is negative,
> even unto Creator.

For cannot Creator alter that which is negative
> to become Truth, Wisdom!

You have a det.
You have, Soul, held it, det, within.
It is not unto your Creator.
It is unto the very ideal that you are,
> the Human that you are.

Det, you can recover from.
You can come forth from.
Resolve all det.

Visions[3]

911   Humanity is a plane that is visual to us.
We see all.
We have no judgments.
We have no interest in the human element.
We reason the life perceptions.
We are guardians of the Soul.
We have a mission to keep.
Station planes guard you.
It is for us a dedicated walk to our own next space.
We chose to help you.
Knowledge is to be transmitted through us,
    only if it is received.
Cleanliness is a part of growth that bears burdens.
If people do not recycle, the world will contaminate itself.
But, the millions of tons of waste that is toxic
    is the greatest challenge.
It has its answer in mathematics.
The Soul is living who can research this.
Wisdom only grows.
[January 1995]

912   Soul, Michael will teach crop circles, alien life.
Endeavour to think not of alien life
    but of brother sister, mother uncles, wife and lover.
The gaze is fixed from all worlds, from all worlds,
    all worlds upon the globe that is earth.
Flight to simple earthlings, a jet,
    no form, we call the jet the microscopic nothing.
On worlds beyond your own are capabilities.
The great minds have a gathering on earth
    and complexities of mathematician.
Puzzles are brought to the eye.
And the Souls beyond gaze down and cast the answer.
Decipher, decipher the message within the crop.

---

    [3] Visions - the dates at the end of each passage indicate when the channelling was received.
It does not indicate the date of the vision.

Extend the mind, not to the mathematician,
> but to the view of the contemporary association.

These are messages, Soul.
They are brought as a vision to your space.
The waters have bowed
> and turned their head from the complexities
> and must stand as a chained man
> stands before his captor
> and cannot loose the cord
> upon which the sacrifice is being given.

The benevolent father gazes at a sacrifice
> and would alter the course but cannot,
> but can offer wisdom.

Remove from the sacrificial lamb, alter the place of the lamb.
Remove from the sacrificial altar the inner scent.
Soul, gather the toxic waste.
Gather the bend of humanity
> before the vision is taken to a vortex
> of great turmoil, of great agitation
> and babies are cast downward and lifted forth.

Then the Angels sob
> at the death of the vision that had beauty.

Soul, gather all Souls and say,
> *"Behold, the place of Purity has been defiled.*
> *Sweep with a cleansing.*
> *Sweep with a cleansing mother earth*
> > *before the wash erases the form of being."*

[July 30, 1998]

913   Blessed, Blessed, Souls of earth,
> people who look for signs,
> the signs have been placed in multitude before you.

The Souls gasp at your lack of recognition.
Souls, encourage not the mind.
Encourage the Farside thread.
There has been deception.
There will always be deception upon the face of earth.
Know the plan.
Aliens, Soul, alien is not a name to give the many worlds
> who have carried pure thought to save earth Souls
> from a step of great deception.

Crafts of great complexity are brought into a space.
There is Energy in very concentrated forms;
      that as your camera takes a picture,
      the form of camera gives a picture.
It is an Energy float.
It is sent as a beam with great complexity.
It is carried in swoosh.
Swoosh and the fibres cannot withstand the Energy,
      and the form bends before the axiom of itself.
Soul, crop circles are gifts of enlightenment.
Who will hear?
The learned will not hear,
      the learned have fear.
Who will hear are the Souls who lift their eyes
      beyond the mind into the place of heart.
Be profoundly touched that earth carries the magnetic field
      that enables the flight in the space of great science.
Soul, for the space of one week no flights will be seen or heard
      because there is no silence in which to travel.
Polarity will cease.
Look to the crop circle and know no fear, but know,
      the reach for earth to hear the beat of the earth Soul.
Know the vibration, know the tears, and bow the head
      that earth would only be brought to a place of joy
      from what it perceives
      as only cosmetic entertainment and life.
Reach beneath the energy of the surface
      and feel the beat of agony
      at the distress put upon the land.
Why?
Why do you think that the crop circles
      have been placed on fields of food?
Contaminants, Soul.
The earth is being shaken and trembles in pain.
Create a huge arm, Souls of earth.
Reach arm to arm.
Enfold the earth and heal the pain.
[August 28, 1998]

914   Soul, you have not received all that you will receive.
If the flesh is willing

and the Souls hold the union of their being,
there is beyond where you have entered in
much to know.
There are worlds that will help your world.
There are sciences to be taught.
There are energies of life to be given.
There is Soul, cure to be placed.
To reach into the Keys requires the human,
 not to be persuaded to hear, Soul,
 but to be totally aware of their cosmic Energy
 that they might travel to where these worlds are
 that have purities.
These are gifts that will be offered, are readily accessible.
The Souls could not gather in space vehicles
 that which is to be given.
They will learn in the wellness of whom they are
 to travel to different worlds.
They will achieve great knowing
 and the knowing will be brought unto earth
 and recognized.
The mind will be read.
Young children of earth will offer their being
 to be clairvoyant in the receiving of knowledge.
These children will be recognized as the indigo children.
They will have within their being the ability to travel.
Upon earth all man has this ability
 with the solution of the equation.
[April 1 1999]

915 We will come often as a minute cylinder
 with swiftness beyond man's ken.
Our ship enters the water
 at 45 degrees angle with no motion.
It does not alter the wave.
We slice in.
There is grave concern for the seaman.
The air is fetid and many are fallen.
We have an impossible task to be with brave men
 and not be allowed to alter their fate.
But were earth to work together,
 the men would not have fallen.

Each is being solaced.
Each is being held from pain by the thread of Creator.
Many Souls linger, and many Souls writhe.
It is dark and darkness brings fear
      to the bravest of earth men.
Our beings have Light and it is luminescent in their space.
They will only remember the entrance of peace
      in their coming forth.
You will see deeply in to the seas.
You will behold the candles glow.
You will see Light when there should be no Light
      and you will know that we are tending
      the canopy of the sea that the Light may shine.
For the Light gives forth release unto the bottomless pit
      and the sea adjusts herself
      through the candles that glow.
You will hear.
The seas will clap and earth will spew forth funnels
      and the funnels will lift in great clouds
      but many are they that are in the deep.
The seas will rage above.
Yet, below will be thousands
      who will protect the tunnels
      that the Light might escape,
      for the sea cannot enter in with cold to the depths,
      for this will create a change
      in the candles that burn in the sea.
And you will know, as we lift our voices
      you will hear the sea candles belch forth outing.
For the coldness has touched and altered their Light.
Know as you hear the sound,
      hear also the sound of our voice
      for we will be heard and many will be seen,
      each rising to be replaced by another and another
      that we might lite ourselves to air
      and return to the depths.
Hear the belch and know
      we will be with the earth and all her people.
[August 16, 2000, December 29, 2010]

916   Souls, earth has a voracious appetite for goodness.

Earth will receive all of the goodness that mankind will offer.
It will invite the generosity of mankind.
It will offer unto mankind days and nights of growth
    and air as pure as the Soul can receive.
Earth will repel no gift.
It will gather unto her bosom all that is given,
    even in the space of negativity will earth receive,
    because earth is goodness.
Earth has no evil.
Earth has only the will of man invested in it.
All pain, all joy, all sadness is gathered.
All bones, all refuge, all blood poured in is gathered.
But earth has a framework and earth has a breaking point.
There is naught that earth can do to prevent it.
The Soul of earth is powerless to prevent
    the giving and the taking.
It is only the receptor of mankind.
The struggle of negativity
    is affording earth many great scars.
The struggle puts stress upon the framework of earth
    and the dalliance that earth
    has with the sun and the moon
    is also affected by the spoils of earth.
How precious is that orb
    to the humanity that gives the Farside.
What goodness is in the being of earth
    that offers unto man all creature comforts,
    all sources of life.
Mankind, see into the Soul of earth.
See that the earth trembles with great pain
    under the unholy structures you place upon her.
Her waterways are bombarded with vast negatives
    and earth has soil that rejects the seed
    because of man's endeavour
    to persecute his brethren.
Souls of earth, look you well, for darkness is about to fall
    and the pale moon
    will reflect the blood of mankind
    and the sun will turn from earth.
[March 28, 2001]

917   Souls of earth, be in the spiral of all creation.
You are downward from where we are, not lesser than.
Within the great spiral of existence are corridors
        that lead outward into realms you know not.
Upon your retirement from earth,
        you have the opportunities
        to look and see and dwell
        within the many outward worlds.
These worlds are inhabited with many energies.
The variations of these energies are manifold.
The surety that you will be at one with them all
        is in the Purity that you are.
For they too dwell in Purity.
You, you who carry tribulation within your being do so
        because of your existence influenced
        by the negatives about you.
You will understand
        as you embrace
        the great realm of positive Energy that is Purity.
Your world will expand in the Truth of that Purity.
You will know
        within your being that you are connected
        to the homeland,
        for you will feel the vibrancy within your being.
The Souls of earth who cling in their truth to negativity,
        understand too that negativity
        accelerates and grows outward
        to proportions
        that they will have to conquer and overcome.
Souls of earth, you are redeemed within your being
        by the Truth that you gather.
In the positive realm you are Humanity.
You are greatly in tune with Creator.
For you have within you all that is possible to become
        as the Son of Creator, the Light of Creator,
        the very Joy of Creator.
You are carrying within you the expansiveness possible
        to spiral upwards into the Energy of Ecstasy.
You have the great power within you
        to be brought to balance by registering your intent.
It is needful upon your earth to register intent.

For if you do not register intent, Soul,
>   you will always meet chaos,
>   for chaos abounds within the realm you are in!

When you choose a realm apart from chaos
>   it draws you into the positive.

You may even be inventive in that which you do.
For indeed has your Creator not been inventive!
Create within yourself all the possible ways
>   to gather Truth within the positive.

Gather all the positive ways to shun negativity
>   from within your being
>   that you might overcome
>   and know the depth of degradation
>   it may draw you into.

Holy Holy Holy
>   in the Circle of the Blessed Angels
>   are you brought Holy Holy Holy into the realm
>   of all that watch over you.

For you have the purpose of all that we are.
You carry the agenda for all of existence.
You are the gentle ones far from home
>   and you are Loved as the lost child
>   is loved and sought.

Soul, upon your being Light doth dwell.
You may hold the Light a lamp unto yourself.
The Light that is ever!
It has no dimness.
It dwells not within the righteous Soul
>   but within the pure of heart.

As you gather the Purity of heart,
>   your Light illuminates from you.

It shines forth.
As the flame that you are, you are illuminated
>   that all earth beings might see how great thou art.

You may behold those in greater pain,
>   you may see their despair.

You may witness their great fall,
>   yet you may not cast dispersion unto them.

For as you have become great,
>   the greater must Light the way,
>   the path for those who are lost.

Carry the food, carry the lodging.
Give unto them what is their need
      for you are the keeper of the Truth.
You have become as Creator;
      outward in your thrust of Purity.
Your world is precious unto all worlds.
It is so, so very minute.
It holds upon it only a portion of humanity.
These Souls are formidable in that over and over
      they fight the good fight.
They re enter to battle with negativity.
They hold within their being
      such possibility for all existence.
It would amaze you to hear
      the great sounds of joy that are created
      as any human surmounts
       the negativity within their being.
You are never lost in your darkest moments,
      you are always seen.
The Angels hold thee in their Light.
They bless thee
      and they carry within their being
      the weight of your pain.
From all that you are to the magnificence that you will be
      is such a great step and you know it not.
For you see only the reflection of whom you are
      and you are ever so much more.
You are gathered unto the spiral of existence
      and you see the many worlds
      that you meet in your time
      upon your homeland.
And you feel within you
      the great admiration of other worlds.
For you have stepped out of Purity itself.
You have stepped forward unto the Armada
      to participate in the drying of Creator's Tears.
For the Blessed are lost and are to be brought home.
And the beloved Brother you have called out to,
      you have been touched by the Energy.
And the Soul of beloved Brother has been wakened
      to the great possibilities you hold within your being.

Idyllic will resound and be heard
      and you will carry the clarion note
      within your being,
      clarion!
The High C will resonate throughout all that is.
The spiral, the endless spiral
      through which the note will heard,
      will be carried into the outer realms.
Do not, Souls, be pious in your being.
Do not strengthen your Energy with needless prayer.
Be about the business of humanity,
      which is the gift you give unto Creator,
      the very reason you have entered in!
Precious unto you is the flower that is white,
      for white resonates as the Light of your Creator.
You have the greatest purpose, both on earth and Farside,
      for you are humanity and you are coming home.
Blessed be humanity.
Souls, be in receiving of great news.
For earth can rise in a moment of Purity
      when mankind would be one!
In the time before Abraham and Isaac,
      in the time of Methuselah,
      were a people who stood in a unified effort
      to live in accordance with the laws of nature.
They took no thing to destroy
      and sacrificed only that for which there was need.
They honoured all life and came together
      to offer unto Creator a response
      for the recognition of life that was bestowed.
Their thought was pure and no selfish intonation entered.
They laid down all arms that would alter the life of another.
In the gift of new life, they burst forth in song.
Their motion was synchronized and unified in its intent.
There was no discordant note within their being.
Each of two Souls have the possibilities within them
      to create such accord.
Each of six have the possibility
      within them to create such accord.
We have in our space the Purity of this unified Soul effort.
They are teachers to your being of earth,

in what you call Mesopotamia.
They were not called anything but Zionist.
They knew.
They accepted all that was in their being.
They heard within their being all the nudges from Angels.
They allowed the still small voice to enter
      and they held out their hands to the other,
      and accepted the brother as self
      and the pain of one was the pain of all!
The joy of one was the joy of all,
      the despair of one was the despair of all!
The solution was unified.
Soul, you have but to hear.
Those who teach are ever present.
They came as you to earth.
They looked upon their neighbour
      and saw themselves and they bestowed Love.
In the presence of Love you are lifted, Soul,
      beyond where you are,
      unto the Realm of your Creator.
These Souls entered unto six.
[May 26, 2010, February 25, 2004]

918   All humanity, all humanity is in battle together.
There is no lesser or greater.
Each is striving to overcome Negativity.
None will be left without.
The confusion is in perception.
Indeed, ships will come.
Indeed, they are in preparation
      and have navigated many times into your atmosphere.
At the time of lift Souls will be brought upward unto them
      and many earth beings in their negativity
      will be lost upon the face of earth.
Not lost to the purpose of the Battle.
Indeed, we will receive them unto Farside.
But does not exist, Soul.
Those within the craft
      will be brought down when earth stills.
Those will be the beings who will enter in
      with those of five to receive the Blessed.

The Thousand Years
> will have all Humanity within the Path,
> receiving and teaching,
> clarifying and releasing negativity.

And the Path will seem as a golden stairway
> with Souls in continuous movement.

When the Thousand Years is in completion,
> the heavenly throng will stand at the Gateway
> and all humanity and all Purity will enter in.

And the Path will continue,
> and the Archangels will open the way unto seven.

And all earth, all Farside,
> all energies beyond third will enter through,
> save negativity that will remain.

All energies beyond three, at the Gateway of Two,
> will enter through unto the Gateway of Two,
> the Second Gateway.

And you will see a gathered Light
> such as no existence to your field has seen.

And you will see the Essence of your being
> from which you have mirrored forth.

And you, humanity, will behold how great thou art.

And you will see the fruits of your labour
> and behold the Blessed in their ethereal state.

And you will look unto a distant field
> and you will see the Energy Source,
> and you will see the Holy Beings that you are.

And Humanity will be renewed in the Spirit of Love,
> for Ecstasy will have been viewed.

[April 30, 2004]

919 Holy Holy Holy, blessed be the time you are in.
Blessings to shatter the pain.
Blessings to ignite the Energy of your being.
Children of the Creator,
> blessed art thou for you walk upon pain.

Blessed art thou for you teach the Angels compassion.
Blessed art thou
> for you carry the everlasting star within your being.

You see the great Light
> for you have it particled within your being.

You are Loved and beloved.
You are, Soul, the morning sun
      and the light of the moon at night.
You carry darkness in your being,
      yet the smallest portion of Light shines great in you.
You are the dancer without the mask,
      vulnerable in your being.
You are the cascading rivulet of water
      that does not count wherein it falls.
You endure and overcome where you are.
Unto you is the blessing of your Creator fallen upon you.
Is there no random moment?
Each moment precious in your time,
      for the greatest pain
      is carried by the Love of Angels unto you.
The greatest shadow is the shadow of the Angels
      that mark your space.
The greatest clarity
      is the discordant note that you have heard
      and reached out to.
Blessed humanity, you are all enduring.
Blessed humanity,
      you have shown yourselves
      to be capable of great endurance.
The time is gentle upon you,
      for the ray that marks the Gate has touched.
Holy being, Holy human, blessed are thou.
The mark on the Gate is naught for protection
      from your Creator,
      rather you have placed the mark
      to show the worlds wherein to gather.
Set the bow that will ride high in the sky.
Set the bow and your earth will know,
      not the prism of colour
      but the solid blue.
You will see, Souls, the transfiguration of the rainbow,
      for no fear will be felt by those who are gathered.
They will rise in the tumultuous roar of earth
      to behold the awakening of Spirit.
There will be no trampling rush,
      for each being has its space marked.

Each thread is woven with a design of acceptance.
And you will drink from a cup of Purity,
        for you will behold the Angel realm.
You will see the significant form blessed.
What vast beauty you will behold,
        for the way will not be unto your sky.
The way will open and your vision will behold!
The blind shall see, for the way has no woundedness within.
All who touch the Path are altered in their being.
And the great emancipation of the Soul in torment
        will bring forth a glorious throng
        to anthem forth as they come,
        the Sound as translucent as pearls.
The Sound of Creator will flow to the Path
        and all humanity will ride the first wave forth.
Who will be all?
None to be sacrificed!
Holy unto Holy, blessed ever blessed.
And the cascading Tears of joy
        will fall unto the Beloved Brethren
        and all will see clearly that vision.
Beloved brethren, humanity has resisted all pain
        and forth into the Light you may enter in.
And who could refuse such a Purity!
Who could hold themselves apart from such a gift!
Beloved brethren, the heavens call to you to return.
Beloved brethren, each is no longer separate.
That which must be done, can be done by all.
Redeem thy space.
The way is clear.
The path is open.
The door has the mark.
Holy Holy Holy, the Blessed Brethren
        have given of themselves for you.
See that which they have given unto you
        and walk in the Path they have walked.
For they show the way unto thy brethren.
There is no tablet of stone that marks a distant path.
That which is Purity will be recovered!
We speak unto you.
That which is Purity will enter home!

Souls of earth, send forth to the Brethren
        to hear and see the burden of scars
        you have endure,d
        and hold unto you the great way.
For we say this:
        "In your beloved state, you create chaos.
        In your beloved state
                you alter that which you would not.
        Come for that which is,
                is in preparation for thy return.
        Pain is unrelated to the vision of Purity.
        Discordant Note, hear the thread of thy aloneness
                and hear the call we send forth."
[November 5, 2008]

920   Upon your earth, humanity does not always
        radiate with the same Energy field.
Much of humanity has a diminished Energy field.
We would tell you, Soul,
        the Light of Purity shines in the particles of earth.
Where we are, from the orb of Source,
        can be seen the Energy Field
        of violet and indigo children.
Particularly, Soul, the violet.
For they bring themselves together
        that they might pass from earth together.
Their Purity excels.
Their Angel Being excels.
We say to earth, prepare yourself for the great waterway
        that will divide continents, not one, but two.
Indeed, the Mediterranean Sea will find itself greater
        as the oceanic surge reaches from Holland
        in a direct line through to the Mediterranean.
It will then apportion a path through Guiana.
This will come to be.
And where water is not, there will be more than is wanted
        from the toe of Italy to Guiana.
[March 25, 2009]

921   Earth is preparing for the great struggle
        when all men unite to be on a single path.

For the finality to occur, there will be great insurrections.
There will be great inhumanities.
There will be great successes.
For that which has been taught,
    by Jesu, Mohammed, Krishna, Buddha,
    will be held high.
And leaders of earth who do not envision
    the structure of the teachings,
    will lose to the onslaught of mankind.
Humanity is devious and willful.
And the path of Truth is not easily won.
And those who have not the power to stay the sword,
    will fall by the sword of brutality, of starvation.
And many will fall,
    but those who stay the course
    will succeed in the building of mankind.
The path is now being structured for world peace.
The path is built by individuals who rise
    from the depths of deprivation.
And all that is upon your earth
    will have a window that all might see.
And there will be no hidden places
    for all is visible in the eye of technology.
[June 17, 2009]

922   You cannot carry weight within the mind
    without it affecting that which is visible
    and affecting that which is within.
It is important for life to be buoyant,
    to allow all that you are to ride the wave of buoyancy
    that anxiety might not settle upon your being,
    that illness might not lock your form.
Souls of earth, you have such ability to ride the giant wave
    that is always in your consciousness.
It is the endless journey that has no end.
It has no coming and no going.
It has a ride in perfect stillness
    where the air holds no sound
    and the eye sees the sound.
And the eye beholds before it all that is visible
    and you see through layers and layers and layers.

And you part the curtain,
> the veil that presents itself,
> and you behold the magnificence of all that is.

It is as though your whole being
> is laid upon a jellyfish of your sea,
> a great jellyfish that allows its being
> to float upon this wave,
> and it moves in rhythmic motion,
> and it has before and after it energies.

And you feel the light, and you sense the darkness.
And you hold in your being a need to release from you
> and you know that this buoyancy is the place
> that you can release all anxiety,
> all that has stopped your being need no longer exist.

All that has formed fear and pain need no longer exist,
> for you have entered in
> to the consciousness realm of the Spirit
> and the Soul stands aside holding your negativity
> as you sort through.

You are no longer human, yet, you are not Farside.
You are the visitor and you see.
Yet, you only see what you are willing to see,
> not what we would show you.

We would show you all there is to see.
We would show you the gardens of Farside.
We would open to you the temples of art.
We would show you
> the kaleidoscope of the Akashic Record.

We would take you there,
> but your willingness may not be as ours.

But you will behold energies.
You will see children at play.
You will be brought to the land of creatures you know
> who await to blend once more
> with the energies of earthling,
> for you have built a bond
> through the many lives you have lived
> and you will know these creatures.

You will identify to them
> and they will run forth unto who you are.

Even though your humanity is not fully a part of your being,

        if you will, you will behold the Angels.
Many of earth have seen Angels.
They walk with you.
Your earth has many Angel beings
        who walk before you walk,
        who talk unto you, who give you solutions.
Upon Farside you will have the ability to hear.
You will hear with a discernment you have not had on earth.
You will hear with the Purity that you are.
And as many alien beings
        who enter from where we are unto you
        and cannot abide the field of negativity for long;
        you will not be able
        to hold your Energy to us for long.
It will be short intervals until you come unto us from earth.
But you will learn to cloak your being and ride the wave.
And you will know the doorway
        and you will gather many members with you, Soul,
        not alone;
        but come unto us and excitedly we will welcome you.
        You are who we are.
        You are Purity.
        Soul, a key is to be given.
[July 22, 2009]

923   We speak to you of the event
        that will bring earth its saviours.
Many of earth will feel lack of breath
        and it will be important to sustain the breath
        particularly in the small children.
There is a great need for earth to prepare
        for the coming onslaught of deprivation.
For the wind will not be harnessed.
The rain will be exceeded only by the cold.
And the Souls who hold dear to them the children
        will protect them in the night hour.
For hunger will search the land for victim.
Within the passageway of the Great Lakes,
        a sound like a lion's roar
        will awake Souls from the deep sleep.
At the same time the sound will come from China

and a portion of the Great Wall will find itself flat.
There is no preparation.
We ask, Soul, that you do not judge in any way.
For only in not judging will the knowing accelerate itself.
You will send, Soul, around earth
> a great awareness of the crafts that will save you
> from annihilation, Soul.

And many there will be who want to stay
> to assist those behind, and we say to you,
> *"Do not, Soul.*
> *Earth must go through the pain it has created.*
> *Humanity will overcome the pain of earth."*

[September 9, 2009]

924 Soul, the awareness
> of your world's people is altering.

You are ever to be brought to a higher ground.
For in the Mountaintop is the knowledge of wisdom.
In the mountaintop is the solution to pain.
In the mountaintop is the gathering of all healing.
You hold within your being the power
> to reunite Soul to Spirit while on earth.

This religions have not done.
They have been caught in the conflagration of dispute.
They have been caught in the great energy of no thing
> while humanity flounders and begs for guidance.

The great dragon awakes.
The sleeper has been touched
> and the vision of the dragon
> will be seen by the world.

The dragon who bring to all beings a great understanding
> of that which is written.

Within China will the young boy speak to the grandfathers,
> will the young boy discern
> that which all humanity has not discerned.

And the Mountaintops of the world
> will be enlightenment for the world.

For the consciousness
> will be touched within the being of man.

And that which is guarded will no longer be guarded.
The Spirit of man will be beheld by man

            in a transfigured child called Sun.
We speak to you of the growing state of Purity
            of your small boy who lives in China.
He is gathering his goodness.
He has reached unto the shaven head to sanctify his Energy.
And we say to you it, is pure indeed.
It requires no sanctification.
He is, Soul, closing unto his eighth year.
He is rich in the knowledge of the Spirit.
He is rich in the knowledge of coordinates of the sky.
He has knowledge of the passes of moons and suns.
He knows each individual star that rises and sets
            within his earth space.
He is within two facilities, one a Christian monastery,
            the other a lightened being who has entered in
            to teaching of the heavens
            wherein he must be to fulfil the prophecy.
The young boy is awakened unto his Purity.
He has been to the aperture many times now.
He has felt the eye.
He has felt transfixed upon the eye.
His is tablet will give knowledge of Lantosia.
It will give coordinates of the night sky.
Earth will see the Purity in the eyes of this human.
They will see the golden goodness in who he is.
They will find the text unreadable for two earth years,
            then cipher it in Israel.
[October 28, 2009, October 13, 2010, July 22, 2009]

925   This young man is close in the space of your earth
            to those Souls forming one of the Keys.
This person is to be questioned
            by a scientist who is in Switzerland.
The person will find himself creating a paper
            using the findings of this young man
This being is honourable
            and he has challenged this young man
            to bring his findings to a human body.
The young man is not of a maturity that is listening.
But the Soul is determined to use the findings
            and has asked permission

>   to use the concept he has been shown
>   to the human body.
> It would totally bring all elements
>   of the human Energy to a stop,
>   as though dead and then revitalize,
>   but in revitalizing,
>   will place inside the code of wellness.
> But the man is young and years have yet to pass
>   before he will come to the understanding.
> And the healing manual will have a great place.
> Souls of earth, upon the mountaintop
>   will be a large structure.
> The structure will be using Energy
>   from the sun and the wind.
> It will be giving people the opportunity to enter through.
> This healing will not be immediately accepted, Soul.
> Before one can live one must die.
> There will be fear in the stopping of the heart
>   and the restarting of the heart.
> This, we say to you.
> Upon earth, there will be many, seven in all.
> From one connection, it will take time, Soul,
>   before earth believes that wellness can be,
>   to create enough to heal all of earth.
> The procedure will take less than half an hour.
> So you do see how time consuming it will be
>   and how so few beings may be altered.
> As earth understands,
>   there will be octopi of such instruments
>   leading from a single one.
> But again, Soul, that will be time.
> [October 28, 2009]

926 We speak to you of timeless Energy.
We speak of the destination of all
          that is within the Negative Void,
          for you will be carried through in a wave of Energy
          unto the very door of your Creator.
You will rise in your being
          from that which you know as earth Energy
          to understand the fullness

of the Energy of Humanity.
For earth has been but a causal visit.
The tranquility of your being
>has always made its domicile upon Farside
>in the timeless orb of Creator's Breath
>within the Positive Void.
Now we bring you to the very understanding
>of the beings that inhabit your home.
These are first and foremost humanity
>and you wonder that you should be first.
You are first, Soul, because you have chosen to overcome.
There are inhabitants of many worlds.
These worlds are as complex and varied as your creatures,
>insects, fish upon your sea.
The flora and fauna of your Energy upon earth
>has been adapted from originals upon Farside.
Anticipate to see the glories of your world
>but in the vibrancy of perfection.
There are Souls extending out
>from the Dome of the vertical spiral
>in which you adhere to.
There are Domes horizontally from you
>wherein also complex inhabitants exist.
To these you have not been.
And yet you know of their Energy.
For the blessed Angels and Archangels
>have awareness of their being
>>but more so have the ability because of their Purity
>>to enter in to those Domes.
Souls of Farside, worlds of Farside,
>that are at level one and two and three
>do not have the Purity to exist other than
>they are outside of the Dome they are in.
There have been brought forth in much simplicity
>compared to the complexity of energies
>within the eleven other Fields.
The Archangels seldom reveal their Being
>unto the lower worlds,
>>Angels, yes.
Why is this so?
It is not because they lack the ability.

It is because the agenda no longer is of Farside.
Only within the spiral does the Archangel
      reach downward in great numbers.
You are, Soul, vital to all existence.
You are the wine
      that is brought to the mouth and savoured.
And the savouring is of more important than the tasting.
For Soul, your Energy exudes possibilities
      that have not been visible in existences before.
You have taken the perfect argument
      and placed it before the Wilful Child.
And the Wilful Child has turned an ear
      to hear what is humanity's echo.
For we have heard the sound
      of our Brother, Discordant Note.
Your world will cease to hold as its agenda
      a night and a day, a month and a year,
      for time will cease to be in the measure you hold it.
There will be a new formation of time for earth.
And you will find yourself accounting your span of years
      not as years but as yar.
The night time cometh
      and the bride awaits the bride groom.
There is no condemnation upon a Spirit
      who prefers to stay at a level of Purity.
Indeed they are pure.
The purpose of mankind was to redeem the Fallen Angels,
      thereby permitting the Second Gateway
      to open wide, to draw back in a reflection
      of all Farside, of all earth,
      of all that was created back unto their own.
It must be done in unison that none is left outward.
Soul, there is no fault in their being,
      there was never a persuasion to go forward.
They have within their being no need to progress in Purity.
It does not mean they are not pure.
They have entered in, they have chosen to withdraw.
It is a choice.
What is unknown is within the Second Gateway,
      and yet you have lit the way,
      for do we not know that all Humanity

        who have reached manifestation will enter in
           to Light the way through the Cauldron!
This you know.
Soul, within the Second Gateway is Creator.
You have then become the Archangel you are.
As humanity moves forward through the Second Gateway
       unto whom they are, will Love of Creator BE.
Through the extension of that Love behold and embrace
       unto self the wayward, the lost,
         and the Father will reach unto his son
         and welcome him home.
[March 3, 2010, October 7, 2003]

927   Soul, we speak of the Energy Source.
You have not entered in and we would have you enter in
        to portions that may be visible to you.
The most visible is not that of your Creator.
The most visible to you is that of the twelfth Light Being
       and all the energies available unto that hierarchy.
The reason, Soul, is that this is the accountability.
This is the Record.
This is the great darkness enlightened.
Within it is as a beehive,
       it has pockets of Energy, great Energy
       deriving from all known worlds,
       not within your Creator's realm alone,
       but far into the Void.
For the Energy Source is set within the Void
       and has the advantage
       of picking up Sound and Colour
       within the consciousness of the Void.
It has within it an echo that is not available
       in the stationary existences
       upon the Fields and planes of the Domes.
There is within the Energy Source
       a manipulation of targets to be directed
       for the acknowledgment of your perfection,
       when we receive.
We will simplify, Soul, a notation from your world.
It is said to a chamber that will quickly place it outward
       where it might be heard.

It is echoed forward, echoed,
      not echoed forward in a fashion you might know
      but in a density of colour
      wherein knowledge can travel with greater speed.
It is the blue black, Soul.
It is not the Light shard that makes it carry itself forward.
It is in dark matter that it is sent forward.
Dark matter also is a conduit
      to both Void, Ion and Matter.
Therefore anything lost within the Void at some point
      must meet the echo sent forward.
Your earth has done this in a very simplistic way.
It has sent forth echoes vibrationally outward.
Your technology is comparable in the minuscule fashion
      to that which we have.
It is not your technology that amazes us, Soul.
It is that which comes
      from the humanness of whom you are.
It is the compassion that astounds and amazes who we are.
So, as we receive tricklings
      of this compassion from your world,
      it is forwarded out into the dark matter
      that it might echo as in the chamber of a drum.
You will understand the vibrational path
      is in the vortex of your head.
It is caught and held,
      then relinquished at decibels from your being
      and you know it not.
As you do some small insignificant humanness,
      it is caught and carried unto us.
The mind chamber can be shattered
      but it also has within it an ability
      to send forward great communications
      unto whom we are.
You enter in as a sounding board
      upon which all humanness,
      all earth is resounded against.
And the echo and the decibel of that echo is counted
      and channelled to its origin, if possible,
      that all things might return.
You would say,

>"*Have you not made us a mechanical being then?*"

And we say to you, "*Indeed not!* "
For you have entered in of choice,
>you have given yourself
>>to be that upon which all else rests.

You are the pivotal point of the pyramid upward.
You are the eye of the chamber.
You are the beginning at the end.
Yet in your perception, you would see yourself as the end,
>that all things are reflected unto you.

Perceive this and you will perceive the Energy Source.
Within the power of beings within the Energy Source
>are, what you would call, great ships.

They can travel without travelling.
They can glide without gliding.
They can reach a periodic timetable
>of the Void of Consciousness.

It is, Soul, discernible in portions unto you
>and shall be forthcoming to you.

[March 10, 2010]

928   In the Yawn, Soul, there is only
>the forward unto perfect Energy, Idyllic.

You have the ability to hear the resonance of sound.
You have gathered about you
>the creations of sonar properties
>>that carry much of what is upon your earth
>>into the atmosphere outward from you.

You are unaware of the capsulating of that sound
>that travels at great velocity through a time vacuum,
>not timeless, Soul, time vacuum.

It is carried in a velocity where sound
>allows travel to be projected by breath.

The more sound is available
>by the amount of breath cast forth,
>>so your Purity is casting forth a sound.

It is sent forth as a tear is dropped
>from the eye in a capsule and let loose.

It creates many tear drops in minuscule fashion.
So it is with the sound of humanity
We have encapsulated only that amount of Energy

  that you have sent forth,
    for you have given it freely.
In the very near future you will hear
    there has been a return of sound.
When this occurs you will inform those that be
    of what we have said, that:
    "*Sound encapsulated creates a farther distance.*"
It will have been received in a distant world.
It will be significant in that earth
    will have created an Energy field of humanity
    and sent it forth into a dimension
    that is other than the third.
[June 16, 2010]

929 That which you do is sacred.
That which you do comes from a great Light.
A Light, Soul, that diminishes your sun,
    the Light that makes small
    your outer realms of your planets.
Much that is held
    within the centre of Lantosia is in preparation
    to receive you unto those who would give you shield.
There is, Soul, a great dimension brought into being
    to see forth far beyond where we are,
    even into the darkness which is many Fields away.
The corridor is extending,
    but only you on earth have extended it out for us.
Had you not extended your energies unto earth,
    we could not be where we are.
We would speak.
Within your world are many so gathered.
You are but a few of those
    who see the realm beyond where you are.
We carry a designation to you.
We have a direct way.
We know, foray your planet.
We have permission of the Circle of Saints.
Our hold is from Lantosia.
You are but shorely from us.
Upon a great ship will be an intervention.
You will see our coming forth.

You will hear a tattoo of sound to announce our coming.
Earth will make much of that which was seen.
But to those who have the higher contemplation of being,
> we speak to announce,
>> *"There is no untoward force that will be presented.*
>> *We come for a single purpose.*
>> *It is for the survival of the human race upon earth."*

The calibration that is set in the depths of earth is faulty.
It must be altered.
This will be done
> through impelling force
>> to prevent a flow of earthquake.

There is a power to be set in force.
It will have a resolution for earth's search into space,
> but it will have an adverse effect upon the planet.

As light years take time,
> so is the sound caught and held.

Before earth will feel the great power of sound,
> your research will be altered by us.

This has not been attempted or permitted before.
It is the change of a single note that will bring
> the sound more immediate
>> to the vibrational aura of the world.

The outer realms will not feel the resounding thrust
> for two years into the future.

Then earth will shake.
This is what we alter.
Souls, we do not share to give you consternation,
> we share to alert earth that earth is not falling.

Earth will survive.
Earth will endure.
You will hear, Soul, the low B flat
> and you will respond in B flat, not High C,
>> for you are allowing passage through.

You are only acknowledging those planets that fly by,
> not earth's ships, not ships, crafts of other nations.

Hopes, fears, Soul.
Whole spheres will send forth their Energy.
It will be, Soul,
> creating as little intrusion as possible to your earth.

Yet we know it will be there

and we see you in a state of panic.
For that which the sound is, is low and residual,
    in that it does not leave for four hours of your earth.
It is low, a hum as in the electric of your earth.
The hum is not always heard, yet to some hearing it is valid.
You have the knowledge to give forth.
[August 4, 2010, December 9, 2009, October 13, 2010]

930   We bring to you tidings of great joy.
These come, Soul, from Lantosia.
We are not of Lantosia but we have been asked
    to bring forth the message for delivery
    unto the people of earth.
There is a opportunity for earth to register Lantosia
    if you will change the decibel to four zero.
This upon the outward flow of Energy.
We will direct unto earth a coordinate
    by which you may fix your landing gear
    unto a moon drop.
Storage will be underground at all moon drops.
Secondary will be a positioning, not for Mars,
    indeed, not.
For Lantosia.
For you will see an Energy of vast intelligence.
They say it is theirs.
And we can but believe.
They ask the coordinate be met for 2017.
If unsuccessful, not again until 19, Soul.
Message complete.
Souls of earth, within the night sky
    you will see a dispersement of three stars.
They will be far from you
    but your earth will feel an echo
    of their bursting forth.
And as they implode they will feel unto earth as an echo.
All of humanity
    will have a depression of Energy at that time.
It will create great tribulation if earth humanity is not told.
We ask those of astronomy
    to declare the burst of three earth stars.
And from the timing of the burst will be nine months.

Then a wave of three months depression.
Although light years will be thought of as a calculation,
      we say unto you, you will see it after the fact.
We will ask, Soul, that you will carry a magnet with you
      to be held strong.
We ask that you do not depend
      upon the use of your pharmaceutical powers.
They will not help.
We do ask that you use foot massage
      upon the ball of the foot and sole,
      the cushions of the toe.
You have the great telescope
      that sees far into your galaxy and beyond.
Souls of earth, you have seen nothing.
For soon you will behold a portion of what we see.
Soon you will enter in to the green sphere
      and you will see before you
      a great swimming landscape
      encircling itself as your great hurricanes encircle.
So will you see the gaseous forms before you.
We will tell you, when you have come to this space
      you will behold where we are.
You will have entered in and through
      and behold a great form.
It will be seen as an enormous shadow.
And you will know it to be the Energy Source.
It will appear to you dark and we do assure you it is not.
We have merely placed encircling about a fume,
      to prevent any form of documenting.
But to those who will recognize, we ask you to understand
      if you will allow your Energy to travel through
      what will appear to be a great vacuum,
      you will be able to lite your being
      on the Energy Source
      at the platform of the Second Creator.
For those who are willing, we ask that you do not fear.
You will find yourself being condensed in such a manner
      as you have not been condensed before.
And we will ask that you know the breath to be real
      and not far from you.
We ask that you use the eye

> to clear the debris that we have placed
> and you will enter through.

All earth beings may visit the form of the Energy Source.
It is available unto all.
We ask that you
> allow your Energy to enfold itself like so.

If you do not, Soul, the breath will not be enough
> to sustain your body in the travel.

[May 12, 2010, February 24, 2010, September 9, 2009]]

931 We speak to you Souls,
> of Stephen Hawking.

We have to remind you with necessity
> of the great respect that the Soul is held in regard.

Yet we address to you, the mind wanders
> and there will be much that he will see
> that will be seen as faulty.

Yet time will allow the voice to be heard.
For he is catching without
> the voice the tremulations of attitude.

It is something that has not been available to this human,
> for the vibrational pull of Farside is upon him
> and he registers the B Flat
> when the churn, the chord, has changed.

He would not permit himself to be that human,
> therefore he disallows within his righteousness
> that which he knows to be true.

As the life span shortens, he will come to terms
> with the vibrational field he is entering in to.

And his words will recognize the alien nation.
You from what you hear will recognize it as Lantosia.
[June 2, 2010]

932 Souls of earth,
> what will thou do without all that is yours?

What will you do when the name of your being
> is no longer stamped
> upon items of value to earth inhabitants?

How will you glory in who you are
> when you hold no item greater than another's?

Souls of earth, we bring you glad tidings of great joy.

Upon the Farside ownership is non existent.
There is not even ownership to the Soul of your being.
Think you on this!
Your very Soul is so freely given
    that all other Souls might behold
    the Spirit of whom you are,
    the glory of whom you are.
The secret place is of no value.
The counter plot is non existent
    and that which would fill your being with joy
    is in the Purity and Love of others.
That which provide you from one galaxy to another,
    from world to world,, from existence to existence,
    is free, free to the extent of Purity you are.
The choice is ever yours.
Wherein is the sun and moon and stars, you will say?
But they are!
They have ever been, as all spheres within the Void,
    known unto Farside, unto to where you are.
And you are the voyager.
You are the Soul who enters in to the great causeway.
You have armed your being and you have set forth.
And we say to you,
    all that you have ever done
    is for the glory of your Creator.
And we say more unto you, Soul,
    you have succeeded in great glory.
Before you, another vista opens
    and earth humanity is preparing to enter in.
Within the great crack of earth will come a sound
    such as humanity has not before heard.
It will be within the waterway.
And earth will open and water will disappear
    and it will reach
    through the continent of North America.
The sound so great
    that within the Void the sound will be carried.
From the depths of the valley will come rushing forth
    waters and bubble as steam from the geyser.
And earth will tremble in her being.
From the north and from the south,

        the seas will join the heat of the water
        and become mighty in its flow.
We can tell you, Soul, the sea will rush
        first from south to north,
        then will it rush slowly from north to south.
There will be a constant change in the level of the water
        as it flows ultimately
        south to north and north to south.
The sound will be heard
        and will be channelled from Lantosia outward,
        that the great call of humanity will be heard.
At that time humanity will come together
        as at no other time on the face of the earth
        and send forth a great High C
        unto the outward places of Void.
Upon the place of Lantosia, within the register,
        there will be a redirecting
        of this sound outward unto fourteen Realms.
It will alter that which is in your Light and Dark.
For only by the magnification of sound
        can it be effectual in reaching into the Void.
All that is is in preparation.
Do not, Soul, tremble in your being.
All that is will be found in the time of change
        and earth will know the moment the valley becomes.
[June 23, 2010]

933   You speak of gold.
Gold has a value, even upon the Farside.
We speak of value.
Value, unlike the value of earth, is not monetary, Soul.
It is indeed connected to echo.
It is the sound of the colour that is the value.
It is the great connector that carries the echo
        into the hinterland beyond where you are.
It is, Soul, worldly that you value gold.
But it is your Farside mankind that understands
        the true value of the Path that provides in the echo.
You will be soon astounded at the availability of colours
        that enter in unto your world from outer space.
You will reap from the hinterlands

    the great bombardment that will excite mankind.
It will be such as will create a gold rush.
And yet, the beauty will not be in that which is entered in.
It will be in that which is in.
For you are receiving from outer space
    a bombardment of shards
    that come from the area of Lantosia.
And you will behold there will be
    what you will call gemstones within
    that will excite the psyche of mankind.
Souls will feel the eyes as they peer into the stone.
It will be seen as Energy and felt as Energy.
The placement of these shards upon the flesh
    will bring healing,
    not from the Energy, Soul,
    but from the attachment to the Energy.
It will bring a great atmosphere of search in your world.
There will be a recognition by governments
    to forbid the touching of these shards
    but mankind seldom obeys.
And healings will occur
    that will demonstrate the uniqueness
    of the outer realm of Energy.
A fallibility will arise and a great horizontal Energy
    will spear itself diagonally
    across the southern to northern hemispheres.
From this will be a raiment clothing the earth
    for approximately thirteen miles wide.
It will find its destination in the area of Japan.
It will find its beginning in the area of South Africa.
[July 21, 2010]

934 To visit unto earth is a voyage into time.
For that which your earth is,
    is so far from that which our earth was,
    that to vision is to behold yet a different world.
We have before us a great ship.
A ship that carries great Energy.
It holds within it all that is available
    not for transporting humanity,
    but for holding humanity.

It is one of very many, Soul.
We will not be a part of that armada.
But we have visited unto the Energy Field of its reality.
All Souls of earth will be held in their present form
    available to breathe and interact.
The beings who man the ship
    will only complete the function
    of holding the ship in the Void,
        they will not relate to earth beings,
        for their mission is not, Soul.
The mission is to prevent the deluge from decimating earth.
There is only Purity in the intent of these ships.
There is no evil intent, no controlling mechanism
    that would alter the minds of men.
You will behold that all function of the human will be static.
It will hold itself at bay.
You will be as in, Soul, your atmosphere
    will be controlled as earth's,
        there will be one alteration.
You will have released babble from your being.
Each will speak as the other.
Each will know the heart of the other.
For you will be in the state of Soul.
All that is Truth will be beheld,
    and you will be as a brother, one unto the other.
You will find yourself brought unto the powerful
    and they will not seem weak,
        they will merely have lost the will
        to hold themself above the other,
        for their hearts are at Purity.
There is within the field of space travel a lack of purpose
    which will be altered soon.
And the greatness of germane scientific exploration
    will bring to be an atmosphere
    that will form a single language for all mankind.
We have spoken of this before, Soul.
It will be as China's language.
And it will form the world language for humanity.
As you become connected in your oneness,
    you will find the greatest need
    to be that of language.

All advanced educators will speak the language of Queing.
[July 21, 2010]

935   Soul, behold that which is the spiral.
It is the spiral which contains a purpose,
        a purpose to overcome chaos.
We and you are within that spiral.
As, Soul, all of your knowledge and our knowledge,
        it is echoed through the spiral.
And we see and know much
        of the length and breadth of the spiral.
We see that which holds
        the sacred Energy called Cleansing River.
We see beyond that
        which is into the lower depths of negativity,
        for we see a challenge of great Purity separating
        those who dwell in Lantosia.
And we tell you of the Energy there,
        which impels negativity
        from entering in to the sphere
        where world's inhabitants have entered in
        to assist in a search for that which is Purity, Idyllic.
There is an atmosphere encircling the sphere of Lantosia.
It is profoundly dark, even unto a deep black red.
It will be visible, not too far into your earth history
        but you will not be able to see beyond the shield.
For it protects.
Not for the purpose of hiding
        but for the purpose of protecting,
        the beings in Lantosia are of Purity
        and to assist earth they must be
        in the lower echelon of the sphere.
They are not targeting any one area.
At no time do they target earth.
They have within them a weave of delicate energies
        that project a clarity into the Field of four.
It has been configured
        into a visible occurrence for earth to see.
They will understand the science of your globe,
        that which they are and must acknowledge,
        is for those profound,

        for the eye will be deep and dark.
It will, Soul, sap the Energy to visually approach.
There will be required an adjustment for the eye to focus.
It will be an Energy alteration that will be done.
It will be done through a beam
        and then the eye will adjust to that which it can see.
You will see not Lantosia,
        but you will see worlds of fragmented Energy
        that stores great leaps of useable material
        to draw into the lens and materialize.
It will capture fragmented energies from great distances
        into a material projection readable by man.
It will bring unto mankind the greatest search
        that will fit into the equation.
What you have brought forth is simple
        but it will be a key in the implosion of worlds.
[July 28, 2010]

936   We would have you know
        in Lantosia's central system
        there is a great eccentricity.
It is, Soul, a gathering of conglomeration of beings
        that hold variances of such misnomers,
        it would be difficult for earth to behold
        for they would find themselves acknowledging
        the missing of this or that
        or the extra this or that, or the added to.
They would make an immediate detriment
        that size does not always give intelligence,
        and mediocracy will not be beheld,
        for there is no middle point
        to any definition of being.
They cannot view with the eyes of earth.
Yet they do not feel with appendages.
Indeed, not.
Often they do not hold that which you refer to as head.
Yet, they hold intelligence beyond your own.
They have no need in many cases
        to lift a hand to touch or feel,
        for that which they are is Purity
        and knows and responds.

We would have you understand,
    that which is Purity is often not of your description,
    not the Angels with their vibrant wings.
Are there such beings?
Indeed there are, Holy unto Holy, Holy Holy,
    Holy Holy Holy precious to Creator.
But there are other beings as precious and Holy.
Greatly profound in their being,
    absorbing all Energy unto them,
    able to use not a mind such as yours,
    an intelligence beyond yours
    but used in the Aura of their being
    to manipulate all things.
Were you to use your mind in its nondescript self
    to move a this to a that,
    you would have a glimmer of understanding,
    where to be the gray matter that you used,
    not your hand or your foot
    or your tongue or your physical self.
Within Lantosia there is a gaiety, a great joy,
    a great happiness.
These are not Souls who are confounded always with
    that which is of earth,
    which that great road unto Idyllic.
They know the atmosphere wherein they are charged
    and they know the creativity
    of that which is possible within that atmosphere.
And they have available unto them all creativity
    and they use that creativity to bring into being
    creations that extend outward from their realm
    and beyond what you would call the safe zone.
So we ask you, Souls of earth, to be mindful as you peer in
    to the black red Energy, the charges of Energy
    that come up and out of it,
    for it is creation from Lantosia
    and you have found where we are.
Now, enter in and draw out that which we will give unto you.
Were we, Soul, to draw from you,
    you would find a drain in your field
    and the magnetic force would leak as all things leak.
[July 28, 2010]

937   Within the corridor of Lantosia is much to be given.
From the central cosmopolitan area
      are many influences to be given.
There is within Lantosia,
      the Jinn who hold fast to the arm of many
        to guide that which is written, that which is spoken,
      that it be held accountable unto the Volume.
There is, Soul, a blight visible in distortion.
There is a causal effect when it is so.
There is a numerical compound to all things.
Each word uttered,
      each move taken is equated to numerical.
This you will understand clearly
      as your science projects itself into
      the realm of the Void.
There is still within the Ion Void the negative influence.
When the Souls of earth
      project themselves past the Negative Void,
      the vision will clarify and that which was
      will soon be seen in great magnitudes.
There is a complexity within the equation of simplicity.
There will be a drawing brought forth unto man.
It will be given in the outward heavens.
The Soul Ivan will receive it.
[August 4, 2010]

938   The sweetest sound is that which we hear from you.
For we are reminded of the many lifetimes
      we have been upon earth.
We are reminded of the many beings
      who still remain to fight a fight.
We are reminded
      of the great catacombs within the Basilica.
And we are, Soul, taught that man is very human,
      that a man even within robes
      can hold disdain for another,
      can hold from another that which is truth,
      the very purpose of entering in.
And we were given
      a reason to resign our self to the catacombs.

For deep within the depths of church are signatures
> that cast a shadow upon the greatest of icons.
For they have been brought forth
> upon the bodies of men, of women and children.
We are carried into ligature of law
> that we may aid in the understanding of humanity.
We are programmed to adhere to Canon Law.
For the educated only can see within the curates' volumes.
These hold the atrocities.
This will be unto the Canon.
[October 6, 2010]

939 We have been in your world and loved your world.
We have treasured our moments
> and recall our gracious companions.
We have walked and we have taught
> and shared that which is religion.
We have been to the depths of despair
> and to the heights of joy.
We see no valid position for religion
> when we are upon earth.
But from where we are now,
> we see the poignant purities of humanities
>> who hold in their hearts the blessedness of religion.
They come from many of your cultures
> and many of your religions.
And they give to those humanities a strength of being,
> a tie that binds, a chord that holds
>> the heart form withering in the despair they are in.
Religion has a purpose upon your earth.
It is led by negative men
> negative, Soul, who lose the focus of religion.
Men as in mankind
> gather together often with negative vibrations.
They do not always hold the best interest of mankind as one.
But we say to you,
> "*There will be a change*".
Religions of the world will alter from earth's ground up.
For that which is religion
> will become the recognition of good against evil,
> of positive against negativity,

   of feeding the poor against starvation,
    of clothing the poor against gathering the extra cloak.
And the simple of the earth
   will become the heart of mankind.
And those who deem themselves
   learned in the name of religion
   will find themselves with only the gold
   to hold to their hearts.
Be pure of heart in the name of your religion.
[November 10, 2010]

940 Souls of earth, within your earth,
   within the construction of your earth,
   for your earth is constructing itself daily,
   is a change that will affect the moon,
   the polarity of moon to earth.
The moon is traced from a great shield.
It is connected by particles within the earth.
Those particles have great power
   to alter the tracking of the moon to earth.
It will be called trecheolite
It will be necessary to shield the earth
   from great generosity of fragments.
For each offering of fragments is accepted by the trecheolite,
   being an attraction unto space particles.
Each offering of the moon and the sun
   enhances the thrust forward.
It is done and cannot be undone.
Each forward thrust will create within the moon
   a great hovering of particles
   that will discharge themselves upon the surface.
This will directly affect the night sky of your earth.
It will prevent vision.
This will clear over a period of twenty years.
The moon will then shine brighter,
   only because within the moon
   are fragments of trecheolite itself.
[November 17, 2010]

941 Soul, indeed many earth beings call the Energy,
   mother ship.

For they have suppositions.
It is indeed the beginning of Purity of Truth.
It is the perfect founding for all chaos to reconstruct.
What you bring forth, Soul, is the Energy of perfection
        in that chaos may re coordinate.
Idyllic will be.
This we know.
Indeed, Soul, it will come forth.
You have but to draw the Energy as you are purified.
What you bring is further testimony to humanity's greatness.
It is, Soul, the ability to reconfigure that which is Idyllic.
This has never been challenged with success.
It would take many such stations to send forth
        even your weakest signal
            but you are building greatness
                that will have the ability to send forth.
Earth humanity you have the sounding board.
You have the resonance within the Rend.
It no longer resounds.
The Energy Source is within the Void.
The resonance must come from a coordinate of existence.
You are that existence.
We ask, as we have asked before,
        that you search out 45 megahertz.
We further give you coordinates.
Those coordinates are twenty nine by sixteen,
        inward of three.
They may not, Soul, have meaning to you
        but they will have meaning
        to those who study the stars.
Entering in to the equation is entering in to implosion,
        unto where we are, Soul.
The coordinates you have been given are the frequencies,
        are the vibrational tone for Idyllic.
Your Yawn, Soul,
        the fullness of the Yawn and all within,
        all the worlds, all the purpose, not of humanity;
        but to overcome and enter in to that which is chaos.
To know as a blend that which occurs!
All purities unite in an effort to know awareness,
        the fullness of awareness and all that is.

Presence, Soul, is not a register.
It is a hearing of all registers.
It monitors all that has been and sends it forth.
It gathers all incoming unto.
You have entered in for a purpose.
All illusion has entered in for a purpose.
Life and Death itself has entered in for a purpose.
The very Idyllic has become for a purpose.
[December 15, 2010]

942   We speak to you
        from the coordinates of that which is the Rend.
We bring to you that which is vibration.
This vibration, Soul, within the Presence.
We say to you,
       "*That which was lost, Idyllic;*
           that which was Light, Idyllic,
           that which was of the pure
           and blessed state,
           Idyllic has sent forth a single vibration."
We say to you, Souls of earth, to gather in great numbers
       and hold your Energy to a vibratory of twenty four.
We say to you to listen through the register of sixteen
       to assume the immediate location of Idyllic.
You may hold within your being a flame of humanity.
You may coach the flame to be united.
And in the sixteenth, a frontal,
       you will find a dark, slithering Light.
Catch to the Light.
Carve it , Soul.
Configuration of twenty nine by sixteen, inward of three.
It is a labyrinth that carries an echo
       that draws Energy from the Soul.
It is a corridor of travel that is unexplored.
It is within the Rend the Path of Idyllic.
[December 15, 2010]

943   Hear the voice that is to be heard in the wind,
       in the sea, for the land will groan
       and the mystics will come down
       from the mountains

and proclaim earth has completed its course.
We say to you,
>"*Earth's time is not done.*
>*Earth's glory is not complete.*"

The sun will shine and the moon will glow
>and the stars will come forth
>>and ignite before man that which the heavens are.

And man has yet many explorations to encounter.
For earth has a destiny to fulfil the Timetable of Man.
Earth is a joyous place to be
>but man has instilled upon earth a fear,
>a dread, interlocking with negatives
>>shaping the drone of that which earth could be.

The sound of despair, of want, of greed,
>ripples forth from the energies of men.

And yet, we say unto you,
>"*You are our horizon, you are our glory.*
>*You are the table that is prepared for our being,*
>>*you are the constant.*"

And all that is chaos will feel that constant.
And that which is revealed of man will come forth
>and a Light, a sound will vibrate throughout earth.

When earth trembles in its fro,
>man will reach in a single voice unto Creator.

And the sound of High C will radiate,
>and the score of perfection will be sung.

And all that is is the tuning fork.
The vibration will strengthen a search forth to heal.
You are fearsome and feared.
You are troubled and trouble.
You are good and goodness itself.
You are Truth, yet holding tight to negativity.
And we sing with you, albeit in discord to your perfect C.
And you will say to us,
>"*You are the Angelic.*
>*How can you be in discord to who we are?*"

 But we say to you,
>"*All that is of Purity is strengthened by you*
>>*for you have the Truth of Love,*
>>*the Truth of Purity,*
>>*the fullness of Truth itself.* "

You lift the ring that is ever the Pillar of Light
      and you strengthen all that are within,
          all that have ascended, all that have descended.
And you gather them within the heart of your being.
Humanity, soon is not to be contemplated.
When is not to be contemplated.
It is, Soul, that you are who you are,
      that you are glory, that you are Light.
It is to recognize within yourself.
Then the time shall be.
So be it.
[December 29, 2010]

944   Soul, come with us into the depths of the sea.
Enter down in to the cavernous way of earth.
There is a rift of great dimension.
It is filling with toxicity.
We ask you to do what we cannot do.
We are containing the toxicity
      but we cannot send it within the rift
      and we ask you to do this.
We ask those of earth to know
      that the instability of your earth
      has created much damage.
But it is the same Energy of earthquake
      that can gulp and swallow the pain of nuclear leak.
We would have you see the energy in the depths.
We ask of you to call upon the rift to open
      and gulp forth and close.
For therein will a lethal, vile energy be contained.
And we who travel the seas will rejoice.
Spare the young, the infinitesimal, from the toxic waste.
We ask this of humanity.
The inner rift will open.
It is at that moment you will send forth the toxicity.
Weigh it down with weight of Energy.
Keep it down until the rift closes.
Our children will live.
You will be aware, for the whales will call unto earth.
Soul, there is within Lantosia
      a centre for research

    of all active violations of Negativity.
We will explain this, Soul.
Negativity, chaos as we understand Negativity outside
    of your third Negative Ion Void,
      there is a recognizable trait to all Negativity.
It repels.
It searches.
It is continuous in its movement.
Upon your earth, Negativity differs.
Negativity attracts.
It is violent only when mankind creates the violence.
It is, Soul, struggled to be separate for it must attract
    and its nature is to be separate.
Therefore for those in chaos upon earth,
    there is a natural struggle to be apart,
    even as atom attract and reject.
There is a compound prepared to be given
    that will in all manner attract.
But we, we in our research
    are guiding you to a component of repelling
    that will guide science to
    hold a loosed atom confined.
For it will be always attracted and repelled
    to the same place without collision.
Soul, Lantosia is spurred
    to a to a high degree of celebration,
    for many Souls have entered in.
They are holding a deep intellect.
They have, given themselves to assist earth.
They come from many worlds upon the Farside.
They come to assist mankind
    in the research of scientific expertise
    upon the catastrophe of nuclear equation.
It is, Soul, more than earth is able to complete.
It is not as the disasters of the moment
    but it is within the deep crevasse
    of the waste that seeps and drains.
It is, Soul, to encapsulate in a manner that will not drain.
It cannot be accomplished
    with the minds upon your earth today.
There is not a single mind

    that can stand to accomplish this feat.
Therefore you will hear three sciences bonding together
        to coordinate a perfunctionary drill
        that will deep compounds within
        the site of leaking fumes, acids.
There is a contention that this will be successful
        and we say to you, it will not.
It will require a greater stirring. Soul.
It requires a fifth longer
        to exhibit the strength and endurance required
        to seal the compound.
It will also be necessary to undermine the container.
This will then receive a compound
        stirred to the fifth longer than the designed.
This then will be successful.
[April 13, 2011, March 23, 2011]

945   Souls of earth, hear from Lantosia.
Hear, Souls, the words.
We see, we know.
We entrust to you this knowing
        that earth is gathering momentum
        to estrange itself from the sun.
It is Soul, a minute portion that will cause a reach
        to rise deep within the Himalaya.
It will be seen to rise at a degree that will shake earth.
It will create a chasm deep unto Indonesia.
The corridor of Australia
        will be seen to lower itself in the mid section.
The frequent swelling of pockets of mud
        will burst to vent a gaseous explosive.
The vents will reach high in to the atmosphere.
There is a rendering of useless land
        that will become forced to the sea
        and will rise to give a mountain range.
This will be given in to the darkness of the cavity.
The whorl lungs are heard to gasp from the noxious vents,
        the throats are burned
Souls of earth, prepare to defend
        long stretches of earth's land from inland seas.
Reaches of catastrophic proportions

       will be found to demolish standing waters.
Your earth is formulating a bitter four years.
Prepare to assist mankind.
Soul, we are Jinn.
[May 11, 2011]

946   You have been reminded of your earth's great pain.
You have been given diagrams of earth
       on coming calamities.
And you, countries who collaborate to control,
       we say to you,
       "Prepare for the rising of humanity."
Humanity is becoming clear in its vision.
The minions understand that earth desires peace.
So the flesh of their being is driving them to look inward
       even unto their mind to know
       that which is in humanity's interest.
The collective Soul of humanity is taking on an awareness
       such as never occurred upon your earth before.
Each of humanity is providing a path for another to walk.
As you find in your being freedom,
       so does your vibration move outward
       and offer it to another.
The hierarchy of earth's economy holds great anger.
For upon your earth the metals
       that can be formed into tanks and guns
       provide greater personal wealth
       that spews forth great pain.
They do not care!
They do not care and spew outward.
And still they do not care.
They do not understand the need for earth
       are the plow shares to feed.
But the people, the people understand.
Their awareness is global.
See the horizons of your earth spewing forth pain
       in the sky, in the land.
No longer will it tolerate the battles of the flesh
       when the flesh cannot be well, cannot be fed.
And the lamb, it is time to lie with the lion
       in the place of serenity where battles are not.

You may not place food in a trough for humanity.
They are not animals.
They will not be placed to be fed as animals.
When we enter in, the last wave of the indigo and violet,
      we will speak of freedom for all.
We will live a virtuous life unto all neighbours.
You will see us as thus.
Truth will be in our works.
[June 15, 2011]

947   The earth is finding its divisions.
It is thrusting itself deep.
The Souls of beings
      who have entered in to earth to assist mankind,
      are preparing a readiness,
      for many who will be lost in the seas.
We say to you, do not extract from this
      that your earth is complete
      in its life cycle for humanity.
It is not.
Do understand that the chaos will be enormous.
And from the chaos will come circles of energies
      that will be seen as great orbs.
You will understand these as the alien creatures.
They are not distortions of film,
      for they will be seen with the naked eye.
They wil lift and energize and draw Souls so that you will see,
      these orbs gathering together in great streams to rise.
It will give you comfort to know
      that they carry with them the energies,
      the Souls of human.
They will not be left alone.
[July 3, 2011]

948   Souls of earth, upon the Farside is little of disarray.
That which is of disarray is within the field of flowers,
      it is within Creator's Masterpiece,
      it is within the design
      of all mineral rock formations.
Now does that astound you, Soul?
For indeed upon Farside there is rock.

There are minerals.
There is deep ponds of living water.
There is great fronds of ivy, flowing, not clinging,
    expressing, free.
There is worlds of such sharp edges
    as needles that would bite at the human flesh.
Yet upon Farside they do not,
    they do not bind and bleed
    as the wounds are ought to do.
They gentle their thorns.
Upon Farside there is a vision of all things.
There is much that is available
    so that the bearded one is seen
    and the hair flows from the form
    and delights the Spirit.
For these are worlds that are tender.
These are worlds that are prepared for joy.
These are worlds, where all that is,
    is brought within the mind
    and the delights of the mind are formed into realities.
Upon the Farside it is not magic it is merely desire for joy.
Joy and Purity is the remembering.
Earth would see the heavenly fount
    as lascivious squanderings
    of imbibing of love that is craven unto need.
But, Soul, this is not so.
Farside's value is measured by Purity, by goodness.
Joy is Truth.
Joy has form, the form that each alien world might choose.
But these beings have not known the wantonness of earth.
They are pure in their being.
They know that which
    mankind enters in to earth to give unto Creator.
They know the negativity
    that is strong in the negative ion human.
They even witness the depravation of Souls reality
    as they live in the illusion of materialism,
    of negative cravings, of wanton deeds.
For these Souls have worlds of Purity.
They have not reached to the strength of Angel.
They have not reached to the strength even of mature Souls.

But they have goodness
>> and they can bring into their world
>> that which they see,
>> but cannot pass the barrier of the curtain of care,
>> is negativity.
Nor would any being of Purity have such thought to enter in.
For indeed Negativity has brought them low.
They have in their being been challenged in their Purity
>> and the Angels have gifted them with life once again,
>> the fullness of thought once again.
Do not feel to be within the Farside is to be deprived.
Souls who are young carry
>> great commerce within their being,
>> one world to the other.
They create challenges for each other.
Indeed, there is a mastering of trade between them
>> but not in the form of goods,
>> in the form of that which the mind will exchange.
This is the trade of the Farside.
This is that which brings joy
>> for deep within the bowels of earth
>> are visions of beings you cannot see.
Within, Soul, the great convex of the Yawn
>> is a Truth that is other than
>> that which is outer from it,
>> for chaos reigns outward from it yet again.
It is not within the form of negativity that earth endures.
Soul, earth will wrapt her being,
>> so that one portion will blend and meld to the other,
>> and earth will dizzy itself.
And the fragile places will be brought low
>> and the strengths will be brought high.
And all that is upon the earth will appear to shadow,
>> for earth will see a vision of that which is to come.
[September 28, 2011]

949 Souls, the maggots upon the flesh
>> are creatures of great value.
They scourge the land of pain.
They create within themselves
>> an existence from that which is past.

You, you have a maggot self.
Indeed, for you have a self that is past!
You have reincarnated into a new beginning
    from a life that you will forge ahead from.
As the maggot creates a new life from the old
    so have you created a new life from the old.
You have done it, Soul, with much forethought.
You have been upon the stations of learning
    to receive instruction and intent from past lives,
    from guides and Angels.
You have received fortitudes and strengths
    to give to your weaknesses upon your earth life.
You have a mirror
    instilled within your being of whom you were.
Within the very aura of your being
    you have the recall of your many lives.
They are imprinted with that which you have gained
    in the knowledge of life as human.
You are generous unto your own self
    in that you have given yourselves beliefs
    within the very fibres of the threads you weave.
You come across them as you thread the cloth of your life
    and you are nudged to know this is a knowing;
    "Why have I known this?
    What is the purpose?"
And the purpose reveals itself,
    for you have absorbed the memory unto who you are.
Calibrate with care the strengths of the weave.
Refurbish the strength of the weave by the tightness,
    yet not overly as to take away the strength
    for the cloth that is bulged is not strength.
The bulging gives way to weakness.
Always is their strength in the continuity of the fibre,
    in the consistency of the weave.
Upon your earth
    you have many Souls who give you great strength.
They are Souls set before men
    that all men might see whom they are.
They are iconic in their being.
There are men to widen the eyes
    and the hearts of their fellows.

They hold truths within them that enlighten the Soul.
They are not always great men.
They are not always men but women also
      who have lifted the hearts to recognize
          that each man in them may see a nobler being,
      a more fully human being,
      a being with the strength
      and attributes of their Creator.
Men who have entered in to earth,
      Four of which will Light your world,
      Four who have created vast Lights of purpose,
      each one different from the other,
      each one in his own life a beacon to tether to.
Humanity, you are brought to see.
You are brought to see that which all humanity has,
      a cornerstone, a north, a south, an east, a west,
      the quadrant,
      a purposeful vibrant rainbow of such voracity
      that the world will be stilled by their coming.
Krishna, Buddha, Mohammed, Jesu,
      beatific in their Being of Light, of Love,
      offering unto earth a purpose fulfilled.
Soon will the Light be lifted.
Soon will the darkness be seen.
Soon will the shades of colour vibrate
      upon the earth's bosom.
And all will see the wonders of the glory of Four.
There will be no man separated from man,
      for all will know the Four
      are of one high mind, of one purpose;
      to bring forth the lost,
      to dispel the negativity from earth.
Each being will find themself on one side or the other.
There is no fence in that day.
There is only the purpose of Entering In.
There is only the fulness of that
      which you have entered in for.
You who have seen and understood
      will find a lift for your being.
Those who see and will not see will vibrate in a turmoil
      until the barrier is lifted

and the Angels enter forth unto humanity.
[October 26, 2011]

950   Souls of earth, you are in never ending circles.
Each Soul spiral one to the other.
You are the movement within the circles.
You are the Energy that flows upward unto your Creator.
You unfurl before your wisdom,
> you have gained upon earth,
> you give unto who we are
> the learnings within negativity.

Are you amazed that you learn in the field of negativity?
Indeed we are, for you grasp great truths.
You behold great honours unto you,
> for you receive with graciousness
> that which the alien nations give unto you
> and you know it not that you receive.

They are ever in your space.
They are ever giving of themselves unto humanity.
You are the purpose of their entering in
> that you may maintain
> the highest truth possible for you.

They are not in collaboration with you, Soul.
They are an entity unto themselves.
But they assist wherein they can.
They have the greatness of Spirit
> that human does not always account to.

They grasp the full meaning of the word give
> for they give with no recompense offered to them.

Who could deny such generosity?
Indeed!
There are many alien nations gifting unto humanity.
There are worlds awaiting
> that which will come when the earth spirals.

For earth shall spiral.
Indeed!
Many will call forth unto their Creator
> but those who would call with Truth
> will have been lifted.

There is a noxious odour
> that will be the forecoming of the catastrophes.

It will be sent throughout the earth.
It will be visible as a yellow spume throughout the airways.
Laughter will not be taken from earth.
Laughter will cease to be,
> for the Souls left will have great lamentations
> and the dearth of sound will be deeply upon them.

You are humanity.
You have beckoned unto who we are.
You have even asked as the Armada
> that we support you in all human efforts.

And these in Truth we do for you.
You are called to us the Pathfinders
> for you give unto us a Path we will follow.

You will take us into the glare
> that is known as the Place of Shining,
> alight, illuminescent,
> wherein the Idyllic echo resounds.

Calm your being.
Rise to the greater humanity that you are
> for each individual has a choice
> unto the purpose of their humanity.

Your footfall will be heard in each humanity
> as you rekindle the lives of earth lived.

We have come to know each and every being.
Many have entered in time and time and time again.
Many have entered in never growing past the energy.
For negativity is dastardly in its effort
> to collapse the human Soul unto it.

But you, you have fortitude,.you have become of high man.
You have lifted yourselves above the negativity of low man.
With negativity of low man you use the low mind.
With the strength of high man, you use the high mind.
You bring yourself into a conscious awareness of th Spirit.
You see the Light as formed
> not only as the sun and the moon and the stars
> but the Light of your Creator, of our Creator.

You grasp the sensitivity of that which is Holy.
Yet there are men upon earth
> who use the word holy lightly.

They place golden threads about their being.
They cry in great cathedrals and mosques,

        even in barns
        do they call forth the presence of Creator.
Who are you human
        that you can call forth the presence of your Creator,
        you may enter in to the Hem of your Creator!
But even we who are Holy
        have not entered in to the presence of our Creator.
The lowliest, the most humble beings of earth,
        are often those who are worthy to enter in.
You are fragile in your being, you are easily broken in spirit.
You are easily set asunder by the playful words of negativity.
You are coerced into believing
        that evil has an invitation for you,
        when indeed it drives you in to the hallowed pit.
All things are hallowed,
        even the deepest, darkest cave
        wherein lies the tormented of earth.
Man's mind is always open for us to see.
We can see the truths within the words you speak.
It is not an intrusion, Soul.
It is a Truth you have offered unto us.
All earth cries "*Woe is me*!" and the mask falls away
        and the crown of iniquity is open unto us.
The hallowed aura of Light is seen
        and all who witness earth's mankind
        understands the confliction between the two.
The growth of humanity as man is difficult.
The mind is swayed by the negativity it is brought to it.
It inveigles the choices of wisdom that could be made
        and sways the simple minded.
You have a simple mind for it is little used.
Even the most intellectual of earth
        seldom express the extremities
        of the mind available to them.
They give only a copious amount of nonentities
        outward from their being,
        when indeed they have intellect
        resounding within them.
The aura translates from the mind and sends forth linears.
The great expanse of the Soul is brought to weigh
        and accountabilities of humanity

    are laid upon the Soul
    and the Soul equates
    that which will be left as karma
    and that which will be carried with it
     unto the Farside.
You are Holy and we as alien beings, we know this.
You are treasured.
We know this too for we know that you are of our Creator.
We know that the wisdom which you have gathered
    comes from a portion within you
    that allows wisdom to become a part of your being.
Fractious though you are, you are beloved.
Humanity, know that we are with you.
We give this to you.
We will not leave you alone.
Where you are, we will be also.
In your turmoil, we will lift those that we can.
In your pain,
    we will release from you the hold you have on earth
    that you might be transported unto Farside.
[November 4, 2011]

951 You are soldiers caught in a battle
    and you have not esteemed yourselves
    to see it as such.
Woe, commanders seek colours for themselves
    and the echoes of the battleground
    is the roaring of machines
    and the detonations to eradicate the spirit of man.
As one, perch your way into the chart rooms,
    the command centres
    and ordinations will come forth
    to sound a new echo unto outward energies,
    not aliens, but beings you have known.
Allow the resounder to echo.
You are of the army of Melchezidec.
You are of the force of Truth.
You are of the Light of your Creator.
Beckon all that you know to give forth the echo.
For the echo will sound greater than the burst of a star
    and the sun will rise on the following day

        and the night will see the dark
        but earth will have a new calendar.
It will, Soul, be the day that united Souls awakened
        to send Energy forth unto Purity
        and the stars will shine
        and the sun will glow
        and the heart of man will lift as one
        and send forth such a charge of Energy
        that will enter in unto the darkened way.
And those that are lost will be found.
The song will be sung as the songs of David sang,
        for peace will enter in to the hearts of man
        and Idyllic will be seen in the shadow
        of man's beginning
        for man will see a reflection
        of that which is truly human
        and bestow Light unto darkness.
Be it as it may.
[September 26, 2012]

952   Behold humanity.
Behold who you are.
Behold your entering in unto that which is negative
        and know that your battle is nearly done.
You have been upon your earth in many forms.
You have transfigured that which humanity is.
You have been in a new land,
        given hope unto spheres far from you.
You have held in your heart and your mind
        that you are not alone.
For you have always known this.
The Angels walk upon your earth.
They speak unto your ear.
They guide your footsteps.
Upon your earth are beings
        and you see them in glimpses
        and you feel their Energy.
They also nurture your being.
All other creatures have entered in to fulfil your need
        in the battle you have begun.
You are well into the battle.

Your Soul has been carried forth many times unto Farside.
You know the intricacies of your humanity.
You know the fallibilities of that which is human
      and yet, you refuse to stay home.
You continue to re enter in to the battle of Truth.
Souls of earth, you are participants with all other energies.
Far beyond where you are are existences of such greatness,
      of such Purity, of such Love.
Souls of earth, there are Creators
      and you have not visioned them.
There are legions of Angels that you eyes cannot behold
      and yet have beheld.
Holy beings that you are
      you have destined yourself to enter
      in reflection after reflection unto your earth.
You hold yourself ready to overcome negativity
      and we follow the plight that you are in
      and the gathering of Truth that you have come unto.
In the place known as Energy Source
      is a fathomable depth of Truth.
There is an echo within the chamber
      that gives forth and resounds outward
      from where you are unto the Source.
This re echoes even into the darkened way.
Souls of earth, as you become the Crystal Cave
      in the condensed form of being,
      as you allow your Energy to minute itself
      so that all Energy is one Energy,
      do you become the Light,
      do you become the star
      in the Crown of your Creator.
For you send forth a Purity beyond the Light of Angels.
You send forth a goodness beyond the realm of Archangels.
You become even as the Creators,
      a Truth, a Purity, a Love unto itself
      an orb of such crystalline goodness.
Souls of earth, you are pure
      in the potential of whom you are.
You are pure from that which you have come.
You are pure
      as you enter in unto the homeland of your being.

We would lift you farther in your knowing.
We would lift you into the frame we can see.
For beyond far beyond where we are
      and we do see much, we see worlds.
We see all that you see within your telescopes,
      your microscopes, your audioscopes.
Soul within the theatres of your understanding
      we see all and more
      and beyond that which we see
      is the Light of Humanity
      and we glory in the knowledge
      and we behold that
      which came from fractious energy,
      could so illuminate itself to be seen in the darkness
      unto the Light into the realms beyond where we are.
In the Void of Consciousness is the echo of thought.
In the Void of consciousness is the ultimate of knowledge.
In the Void of Consciousness is the breath of existence.
In the Void of Consciousness ion and matter are.
Souls of earth, you have been heard.
You have been heard
      as no other Energy before you has been heard.
You have resounded
      in your minute call forth for compassion.
When many of humanity
      would see their brethren lost unto them
      there are those
      who have gathered strength and goodness
      who have taken Love of fellow man
      unto the realm of compassion
      and have brought about their being
      a luminous presence that ignites the aura
      so as to present the halo of goodness.
They are, Soul, always gathered together.
Aloneness is not possible for them
      for they uplift each other in their oneness.
Souls of earth, be you one of them.
Be you as they are.
Be you in the heart of your being,
      in the Soul of whom you are,
      in the mind you present a Truth of honour.

For it is the luminous fragment
> that is humanity that echoes forth.

It is the Truth of all truths.
It is, Soul, the Light of all Lights,
> you, greater than Light Being,
> greater than Angel and Archangel,
> for that which you have echos.

It is not, Soul, only about the being,
> it echoes within the Purity, the Ecstasy of the Angel,
> of the Archangel is such Light
> as your eyes could not rest
> upon the very Energy of the Being.

But it does not echo as the Light of Humanity echoes.
Even in the fragmental particle that you are
> is the echo for you have entered in,
> you have entered out.

You have loved and you have hated.
You have overcome the hate with goodness.
Oh, Souls of earth,
> send forth from you all that spews from your being
> but ultimately, ultimately, through your many lives
> you become compassionate,
> you wrap your Energy about
> that which is evil and you Love.

You beseech even when death is upon you, you beseech.
Souls of earth, blessed of all heavens,
> accept that you are Holy.

Accept that you have entered in unto battle to overcome
> that which is negative, to gather Truth of truth.

Souls of earth, you are blessed.
You are the star in the Crown of your Creator.
[November 14, 2012]

953   Souls, Souls, bring your attention.
Hear the sound of Energy.
Hear all that Energy is.
Hear the nuances within the travel of Energy.
You, Souls, you are Energy;
> as your Energy of earth, as your Energy fields.

As all that travels in Energy has sound so do you have sound,
> so does the Energy of your being carry itself

    in and unto the thresholds of many fields.
You are not forgotten.
You have not been gone long.
You carry a sound.
There is no other.
There has never been
    an Energy Field united such as those of High C.
You carry the intricacies that Energy invites.
You are drawn into an outward realm,
    for that which you are
    travels farther in unto the dark.
It travels in unto the Fields of existence.
It travels even in unto the Path of perfection.
You are the startling sound that reverberates.
You are held in moments of timelessness
    as you are lifted in a chord.
Only in accord, Soul, one or two, three, five,
    a hundred, a thousand,
    the sound is lifted and carried.
The sound triumphs over all other pathways
    that reaches deep into the darkness.
It reaches and overwhelms the energies of all that hear.
Within the galaxies of existence,
    within the barriers that create contention,
    within those in the space of time,
    the Energy of High C travels through.
You cannot travel through as you are B flat
    without the coordinate of another that creates,
    united High C.
There is a form where earth
    will meet with many beings from outer realms.
You will know that you are of the same species.
You will understand you have travelled
    in the same configuration
    and you will be delighted
    that you have a variance of the same language.
You will require no Rosetta Stone.
The call will enter in and the fleet will gather round you.
You will see the brethren of whom you know.
You will meet these beings.
We want you to know this.

We want you to understand this,
>   that your earth is on a coordinate
>   to meet an entire species of humanity.
We do not in any way create misnomers.
What we bring to you is exactness.
What we bring to you is a reality.
Your earth species will confront another species
>   as alike unto you as brothers.
You will see the fullness of whom they are
>   and you will enter in with joy unto them.
This, Soul, is that which is called the Gathering Time
>   when the gates will open unto you
>   and you will become aware
>   that you have leeched negativity from your being.
You have allowed no residues within so that you have
>   the Energy of highest Truth that you have, Soul,
>   the goodness of Purity to return unto humanity.
You are, Souls, caught in a space,
>   you are formed in the will of your own.
You have been sent forth as human unto human
>   but that which you enter in
>   as is a choice of your own.
That which was cast out from humanity
>   was the pure Energy of Humanity.
Souls of earth, know the way is quickening.
Know the Path is not yet but the numbers have grown.
Know there are spurting humanities upon the earth
>   that ignite the very fibre of that which humanity is.
They seek to draw humanity into a musical note,
>   a sound, a cadence of joy.
They know the sound.
They know that which is to be,
>   but humanity is slow to respond.
They are not quick to enter in to perfection.
We say to you,
>   see the numbers round about you.
See the incredible speed upon which your life develops.
Time has accelerated and you have accelerated with time.
Time upon earth is speeding
>   even as the oceans and rivers and lakes
>   are confounded by the energy

        and swell when the heat of earth is responding.
The vitality of earth is quickening.
Even as the Energy of humanity excels in its Timetable
        and speeds forth so does earth speed forth.
You cannot delay.
You cannot reserve for another time that which is to be.
The Truth is yours.
The vanity is of nothing.
Expediate that which you do.
Send forth a continuum to refrain from delinquency.
Your world will be tantalized by that which you give forth.
Your world will receive
        and explore that which you give forth.
For even as you configure,
        your earth people are setting an agenda
        that will meet all that is within.
Your earth is vast in its potential to err.
It is vast in its delight with negativity
        but the Souls who have heard the note of High C,
        those who have been touched
        in the pain of negativity,
        those who have entered in unto earth as teachers
        as speakers of the Light, they have come to know
        there is a Truth waiting to be heard.
There is a Truth that will bring forth an understanding.
Seven Tomes of Truth, seven pathways of understanding.
You are an avenue.
You are a vehicle to carry forth
        that which you have written upon earth many times
        but never given to understand why.
You are, Soul, the deliverer of Truth.
[November 21, 2012]

954   Humanity, you who are in the dispersal of goodness,
        give forth of that which is you,
        give forth of that which is worthy.
See within yourself that which is goodness.
Enter in to the way travelled by the Angels.
You are far from where you are,
        not ignoble, but advancing back unto,
        releasing the negatives from your being,

    echoing a volume of perfection.
You are the receiver of goodness
    but you are also the giver of goodness.
Far beyond where you are in the landscape
    you have come to know in your recent days
    are worlds such as have been
    inhabited by many beings,
    are inhabited by truths,
    conscious energies, viable thoughts.
You will understand the concepts learned,
    you will understand to behold the echo
    that strains down unto you.
You will see a manifold likeness of your own.
You will behold the struggling of an earth.
It will become visible unto your astronomers.
They will see through the small eye
    and behold a target on which to dwell
    and we speak to you as you see this earth
    as you behold the beings upon it,
    that as much as they are like you,
    they hold none of that which is evil.
They could not be approached
    in any manner by mankind
    for mankind would dissolve their being
    without the transformation
    that the new day presents.
To enter in unto their verbalization,
    you would behold a manner of being
    who holds gently the form they are in.
They manipulate their Energy to be that which they will.
They travel within the galaxies
    fearing no heat or light rays upon them.
They are conglomerate unto a vast number of sources
    that provide them with visuals.
They see you before you see them.
They behold your energy as sickly for it is
    not held in the state of flesh
    to a high degree of Purity.
Do not, Souls of earth, approach them.
You have not their Purity.
[December 12, 2012]

955   Souls of earth, we speak to you
        from the great oceans of timeless space.
We speak to you from Lantosia.
Soul, there are more energies of earth
        entering in to our reality.
We are delighted for they have understood
        there is a dimension
        that can be reached by the Soul unto us.
It does not require
        that the Energy enter in unto Farside first.
It does require the leaving of the earth existence
        that you might allow your being
        to have a dimensional alteration.
There is within the scope of mankind an ability
        to lessen the vibration of their being
        to such an extent
        that the very breathing has come as an oddity
        not decipherable from earth physicians.
You will understand this ability is not presentable
        unto all bodies in form of human.
First, they must learn themselves, Soul, to no fear.
Then, they must allow the body to shrink,
        encapsulate itself into a small chamber.
Then the movement
        will be caught in the Energy of a thread
        that will be brought unto us.
Many are learning the scientific ability
        to use the thread as a possibility
        for transferring material goods.
They have not connected the ability to send forth
        humanity by this same connection.
Therefore we alert you that this is feasible
        and the platform exists on
        which you may transport your being.
Souls, you do not have a fear
        that you will pass where we are,
        for we have out an extension of Dome
        to capture all errant forms.
You would be caught as a web offers a spider to be grasped.
Thus you are in a web of your own for you are as we are.

We are one.
Those of Lantosia have a single purpose,
      to bring forth Idyllic.
You are, Soul, under constant surveillance.
It is in a benign way.
For all that is shrouded by form are researched
      that we might know how they travel.
Souls of earth,
      we continue to send forth unto you soundings.
The soundings could be caught with more intent
      if you would place a 45 megahertz label
      to the random sway.
You are visiting often but you cannot realize
      the full impact of where you are.
For you are in a diagonal line of reversal.
Cohinge the variables.
Enter in to the sound of megahertz.
Hear within the continual sway, Soul.
There is a variable that has been caught.
Leverage the variable
      that you might see clearly that which we are.
You are random, Soul.
There is a variable.
Overreach the variable.
Do not tamper with the cohinge.
[February 12, 2014]

956   Soul, you may not enter without time lapse.
It is not possible, Soul.
There is from us, where we are, a great flare sent upward
      that will not permit entry without co sway.
Hinge into, Soul, hinge.
All collaboration will be done through hinge.
There is, Soul, a great moment.
There is a great entry in to your world.
It is vibrant in its vision.
If the Soul come into the southern sky,
      it is redemption itself
      for it will be seen as the northern lights
      in the southern heavens
      wherein all reflections will be seen.

Lights of earth will be dimmed.
Sixteen days in length for sun.
No scheduled lifts from earth will be able
    to withstand the vibration.
The energy will be begun by a great volcano
    that erupts in three magnitudes.
Each of six will light forth in varying degrees.
There will be a huge fire seen and heard,
    heard echoing throughout the earth's ligatures.
Sixteen days of semidarkness.
This will come before the great light is exposed dancing,
    within the skies.
The heavens will seem to open unto space itself
    and earth will feel a vibrant shake.
Waters of the northern inlets will reach.
Many will cease to be.
There is a resounding clap in the sky.
Man will put their rifles upward but see only a great blue.
The blue will appear in the shape of a woman devout.
Souls of earth, hear that which can be altered.
[February 12, 2014]

957   Soul, the mountaintops echo,
    send forth vibrations one to the other.
You will see triad within triad in the linear.
You will see the Energy flow.
Sound accelerates with the flow of Energy.
You will find that earth is aware of all that you do.
Earth has a continuum of existence.
It will not decimate from any act of mankind,
    from any flow of nature.
It will rock and roll.
It will be brought to great Energy flow.
Earth will respond to the movement of truth.
For earth is as aware of mankind's energy as is mankind.
Do you understand?
All that is upon your earth is formed of Farside.
All that is upon your earth
    has a purpose in being upon your earth.
As earth struggles in her being,
    as mankind overcomes

       the desperation of negativity,
       so earth is uplifted
       and earth resounds in great sound.
The negativity of earth is continuous.
It is writhing.
It is, Soul, uplifted by the knowing
       that soon the travail will be ended.
[February 12, 2014]

Chapter Two
CO EXISTENCE

958   Humanity, be eloquent as the giver of Truth.
Speak unto earth of graciousness in giving.
Speak in compassion to the young.
Speak in compassion to the wounded.
For they know not that woundedness is illusion.
We ask you who are olded in the age of Soul,
       to reach into the wisdom you have gathered
       and find no judgment,
          that you table your agenda for material goods,
          for all that you have will be as nothing in turmoil.
That which you will reach unto, Souls of earth,
       are each other.
That which you will reach unto
       will be the wisdom you have gathered.
You will seek to know who is the carrier of wisdom.
For knowledge will seem as naught.
Only the Truth that has risen beyond earth truth
       will have meaning.
Chaos abounds in your earth,
       in the universe beyond,
          that which you call universal.
Indeed chaos is rampant.
For chaos deflects against chaos.
Chaos knows no right, knows no wrong,
       knows no up or down, only outward thrust.
It does not consider from whence it came.
It does not look back at that which has been altered.
Chaos is alterable.
Chaos is riding the wave of humanity's Truth.
It is tethered to the tone of humanity.
For it is in the coattails of humanity
       that the best results have been.
For humanity is ever embellishing negativity.
It has restructured negativity, even to become evil,
       that there might be a greater overcoming.
All is of purpose, even negativity.
All is to return unto its origin, even negativity.

For the energies that you know as power,
    that you see, indeed, as deity,
        these know your beginning and your end.
They have the Timetable of Man well written
    and you are participating willingly
        in the thrust of negativity from you.
You enter in to overcome, not to place pain
    but to overcome pain.
Your earth also is riding a wave.
Your earth is caught in the upward thrust of earth pain.
And in the upward thrust, the waters must cleanse
    and earth will feel the cleansing
        throughout the lands.
Do not fear to be a part of earth.
Do not fear to value that which you are.
Do not seek to look for paths apart from your earth.
You have but to be in the Path of your intent
    and you will know all worlds.
They are abundantly available to you
    as are the Angels who ever beckon unto your Truth.
The negativity will not hear but the Truth will hear.
Bring joy into each moment.
We ask you to see each animal in your life,
    each drop of rain, each ray of sun,
    each web spun by the creature,
    each growth
        that raises itself above the soil of your earth
        and within the soil of your earth to remind you,
        indeed, that there is goodness within and without.
Within the very core of your earth there are caverns
    that have the Timetable of Man accountable.
There are Souls who have entered in to your earth
    to maintain that Timetable.
You are never alone upon your earth, Souls.
The Spirits are ever around you.
They ever ask for you to participate
    in your Purity, in your Truth.
When you have entered in to that knowing,
    the understanding of Energy consciousness,
    you then have the ability
        to know the energies within your space.

Indeed, you may feel their closeness.
You may hear the words they pass unto you.
There is no blend as dear to the Angel
    as the blend of humanity and themselves.
They enter in to earth to watch over who you are.
They tread the very ground for you.
Discipline your Energy to hear the song of Angels.
Rise above the mind.
Rise into the consciousness of being
    and know the Light that is Holy
    will attend thy being.
Know that you are truly a child of the universe.
Know that you are truly a part of all Energy.
The tone of whom you are sings to all that is.
The fragment that is called by your name
    lifts and lifts unto the very blend of one
    that is Love, that is Truth, that is Purity.
Indeed, you are no less than Angels, humanity.

959   We teach unto thee the value
    of all creatures inhabiting your earth.
Each creature enters in with a vibratory chord.
It is within the mechanism
    of the strands of DNA Energy of all beings.
It is connected to other beings whether wild or tame.
The animal has a connection to a human.
There is no coincidence
    in the liting of an animal unto thy Energy.
You are brought together of accord.
You are brought together
    because you have agreed upon Farside
    to be brought together.
These beings who choose
    to have a language unto themselves,
    have given their Energy a psychic ability
    to read within your mind.
They may connect unto you from many miles,
    even unto the hundreds of miles.
When an animal is lost, were you to call it unto you,
    it would feel the vibration of your mind's will
    and follow throughout your earth

unto where you are.
You will not search needlessly
        to recall where the animal might be.
We will have you also understand the wild animals.
Even in the giving of a life as in a trophy animal,
        Energy does not leave.
Remember this!
It teaches as it is,
        were it even to be mounted
        and placed upon a wall,
        the animal would continue to teach unto energies
        were it at some distance.
Even through the threads of them,
        a being would be drawn to that animal.
The Energy of your being
        may not be lost through the incarnations.
Indeed you carry upon your being five close animals.
There is rarely beings who hold greater numbers.
That comes only when they cannot accept humanity,
        in other words,
        they have discarded the chord of Energy
        and replaced it with the wild.
It is seldom done with the tamed,
        as you refer to animals.
But more often
        with herds of horses or cows or goats
        or sheep or lamb,
        wherein the caregiver empties their Soul
        into the caring of these creatures,
        rather than attending humanity.
It is a life of teaching of the animals to the human,
        for the animals often respond
        in a favourable or negative way.
It is a lesson, Soul, in that incarnation.
Much of the creatures of earth
        are connected to the Faeries,
        particularly the larger.
These Souls respond and are in tune with negativity
        in a manner that they can alert all creatures
        who are tended by man in groups,
        as in herds, gaggles.

It is a great curing of negativity within that life,
       to be drawn into the classroom of the animal.
They are profound teachers,
       often violent teachers,
            even more often incredibly gentle teachers.
Do not lightly see an animal
       of any description within thy space.
A camel, a yak upon the plains, the buffalo, the cattle,
       all have purpose for humanity.
See that which is the lesson for you.

960   We tell you, Soul,
       earth inhabitants were not the original inhabitants.
The original inhabitants were not upon your earth.
They are in a Path of Creator upon Farside.
You have humankind upon Farside,
       not only upon your earth.
The entering in to earth is your growth.
Your reality is upon Farside!
It is these beings that were gifted from Second Creator
       to enter in unto the Path of Creator
       from other worlds.
These beings called Humanity by your Creator.
Indeed many beings offered.
Many have entered in unto your earth.
Still yet are many beings who hold themself in readiness.
There are others who do research.
There are many who have never yet entered in,
       yet act as guides.
Many of these come from the original.
Souls of other worlds many who have been upon earth,
       who have lived in the Light and the Dark,
       even are the beings of the four alien nations;
       the Jinn, the Gray Beings, Pleiadians,
       Souls from Lantana
       who have entered in to earth,
       not all of whom are original earth beings
       but many from the sister earth of yours.
Your earth is but a shadow of that which it was.
It is merely a reflectory of that which it was.

961   Within your world you have great books of learning.
You have great connection to word.
It is for most people upon your earth, communication.
And to have it written gives it validity
        in the mind of many of humankind.
Yet much of that word that is written is false.
It has no basis.
Within Farside there is a great storing of record.
It is visible for all to see.
It is called Akashic.
It is attended to and grows
        as all worlds within and without the Yawn fulfill.
The little that we know outside of the Yawn
        is placed in the Akashic.
As human you rely much upon the written word,
        yet your written word is becoming less written.
It is becoming visible through energy.
You will find yourself relying upon that energy.
But you must not be bound by all the energy word.
We ask that you learn to detect fallacy.
It is simple, Soul,
        rebound it against your aura.
For your aura has all knowledge,
        finite and finite to the level you are.
You can access that which is true against that which is negative
        by allowing it to enter the aura.
It is simply done.
If it is written material,
        simply hold it within the Energy field.
The Energy field scans quickly.
It need not have the book opened.
Your being can read page after page
        quickly with the book shut
        and the Farside Energy you are
        would discern a truth or an untruth.
Within the form of Energy word,
        we ask only if you have a question of authenticity,
        you simply place your hand
        upon the tome that it might receive.
There is no time or space within the aura.
It will quickly transport itself to the beginning and feel

        whether negative or positive.
You will then understand
        the need to respond to that which you will feel.
Listen to the inner voice that you have
        for it will receive the message
        through the consciousness of being
        and relay it to the mind.
It will be the consciousness of being that will nudge the mind.
The mind then has the choice to receive or be deceived.
The ability of human is far greater than has been discovered.
You have the ability to transfigure form.
Upon your earth you use skill to carve the flesh.
Yet the flesh can be altered by the mind
        and all pain removed by the mind.
There is within your earth powerful energies.
These beings are alien to you.
They often alter flesh and blood.
They have the power
        to turn the time back to a brief time only.
In doing so they lose great power within their own being.
For five of your earth minutes,
        they can respond to what has been flow of blood.
It can only be done at the will of the Soul injured
        and only for the purpose of Purity to humanity.
The Souls who can do this are called Jinn.
They are of the most maligned of alien Souls.
Yet, they have given Energy
        that has not allowed them the quickening to return
        and are caught upon earth until the closing of time.
Indeed not all Jinn
        but those Jinn who have made the choice
        to give their Energy to alter humanity's pain.
Their Energy is such that they do not behold
        the gift they give as gift.
It is that for which they have entered in.
How can you communicate?
Speak to them.
They will move.
They move things, Soul.
This is how you will know you have reached them.
They are playful, the Jinn.

They move your realities.
They do, Soul.
They have great Energy, the Jinn.
They are tireless, they are.
Words do not come from the throat of their being.
Their words are sent forth by the extremities
     so that you feel a dart
        and you will know a Jinn is about.
You will feel a trickster is touching your being.
Then you will listen to what your being has heard.
And you will repeat it aloud
     until you have become accustom to accept this.

962   We would speak to you, Soul, of those beings
     who are diligent upon your earth, the alien.
We would speak in a timely report of that which they do.
Our agenda is the accountability
     of alien Souls upon your earth.
We are collective in this purpose.
Our world has a single agenda.
It is to account the pain, not of earth Souls,
     of alien Souls upon your world.
You must know there is a cost to these Souls entering in.
There is a diminishing of protectiveness.
In order to enter in to earth to achieve
     that which they must achieve,
        there is a need to be contaminated by the pain
        they lift from earth.
Only in the acceptance of the lifting of that pain,
     are they able to do so.
We will give you an accounting of such a lift.
Within each detonation, the Soul of alien enters in.
The Jinn enter in to speak to the Souls
     who are caught in the carnage
     and to place those scattered
     into the hands of the other,
     for their humanity has not lost
     the acknowledgement of the body.
They still acknowledge the body self.
The Jinn bring the Souls together and place their beings
     hand to hand and help them lift from earth.

Upon their own being they collect pain.
Upon their own being they hold the tears of your earth's
      whys and wheres and how.
They see before that which is negative is spewed forth,
      the devoutness of this being,
      indeed, we do say devoutness.
For in the Energy they have this acceptance.
They may not deny of a purpose,
      and they see it in the best Light unto their being.
They do not see until they leave earth
      that which they have done.
And the Love of the Angels reaches out to them
      and a portion of their being
      would stay upon earth and linger,
      for they are caught in the dreadfulness
      of the act of carnage.
It is the Jinn who speak to them,
      who give unto them the need to move forward.
Who hold in their Energy and offer the Soul unto Creator,
      and the tears of the being is mingled
      with the Tears of Creator and the tears of the Angels.
And the Soul is caught in the looking back of the carnage
      and the Jinn remind them of the life to come
      that they may alter.
We would explain, Soul, to you another happenstance.
It is of the innocence of children.
The Jinn work with the children
      left alone upon earth to fend for their being.
They bring unto them an awareness to gather together
      to find security in the Spirit, not the flesh,
      they can do naught for the flesh,
      but in the Spirit they do.
So that the infants are gathered by the old
      and together they walk in the pain
      and know the presence of the Jinn.
And the Jinn is the mother and the father
      until they reach the arms of the Angel.
For they know the purpose is they must leave earth,
      but they will not be allowed to leave uncomforted.
It is the Jinn who respond to the comfort of their being.
It is the Jinn that gathers the flesh and the blood.

They cannot alter but they can hold.
You do not work alone in your mission to alleviate pain
      upon this earth that you are in.
Your orb is in genuine stress.
Even the little children are privileged
      to acknowledge the place of the Jinn.
Know that the stress they can alleviate, they do.
Know that they work with you.
They are active in their working.
Be as the Jinn, active in your working.

963   Hold silent that which is sacred.
Hold calm
      for all that is cannot be held within the space of two.
It must be three.
It must be altered that all might be triad,
      where there is two
           it must be changed and altered to become three.
For three is sacred.
Three carries the spiral from one Energy field to the other.
Three brings joy, two brings pain.
Three lifts to Love,
      two endures.
Three becomes whole,
      two is always wanting.
In all existence this is so.
Throughout all worlds this is so.
In the great valleys, in the mountaintops,
      in the deepest forests,
          in the most barren desert, this is so.
Unto all that is is the knowledge of the triad,
      for who, what, where and how
          are always seeking three, the complete.
There is upon your earth a tremor of knowledge
      that is formulating the perfect three.
It is drawing a formation upon the land
      that will be seen from distant places.
And we can tell them,
      "Souls, you have no need for we see you clearly."
Indeed, we are alien life form.
Indeed, we visit earth frequently

and we know your calibration, the two.
You are visible unto us
>   as we are not always visible unto you.
You are brought into the great realm of physiology
>   in order that you might examine who we are.
But you will find us deceptive,
>   for we can be illusive in our matter.
Our matter can be lost and then visioned.
We are seen greatly, not for the whim of the alien,
>   but that you might become accustomed
>   to who we are, what is,
>   we who will greatly man those ships,
>   even though not those who have entered in to earth.
To re enter unto our world we are scourged,
>   not painfully but cleansingly
>   that all that is of negativity
>   might be erased from our being.
Our tenure upon your earth
>   is always one hundred earth years.
It is the same for the Michael who teach to you.
It has been flittingly timed
>   and yet our endurance
>   is required to exist upon earth.
Although we enter in to your earth,
>   we are not timed by your earth time.
We merely use the hundred years that you might estimate.
To enter in to earth we must endure what is earth,
>   for earth is Holy unto us.
We do not detest earth.
We merely have difficulty with the endurance of negativity.
It is a clinging draining energy.
This many Souls of earth find it to be.
We chose to come to earth,
>   at the time humanity chose to come to earth.
We chose as nations to uphold humanity.
For humanity's endurance is long
>   and all creatures of your earth chose at the one time.
And we tell you many have formed
>   and been altered in their form
>   by the stresses of earth.
And this is as it should be, for it shows unto humanity

　　　　the great negativity that can be caused.
Upon returning to Farside, each being returns as whole.
We came to earth, and we speak only of our,
　　　　we use the term nation,
　　　　unto you that we might uphold
　　　　　　those who have fallen and have lost their way.
We search forth Souls who are human, who are lost.
And we do say to you,
　　　　it is not unto transition that these Souls are lost.
They are lost in the passing of their being,
　　　　for thy are neither in transition
　　　　　　nor have they gone home.
And we have a single purpose.
It is to guide them into the dark
　　　　and through the dark if they will.
They can see us
　　　　and they have vague remembrance
　　　　　　of whom we are.
They have no fear of seeing us.
To you, you would see us in the dark.
Our being upon earth is purple.
Our strength is slight
　　　　but our ability to change our Energy is immense.
We can enter through walls, barriers.
We can see your flesh, but we can see within your flesh.
We can feel your Soul and your Soul's intent.
We can read your mind.
And we can speak to you and you may speak to us.
None are left behind, Soul.
The great difficulty for us is not in the decision.
It is in the transporting of beings who are less willing.
It is where humanity often helps us,
　　　　for their Energy can speak to their humanity
　　　　　　and they listen.
Soul, we are not Jinn but we do dwell with the Jinn.

964　　The casualness of humanity!
The collapse of the words Truth, Purity and Love
　　　　when indeed you describe the Energy of Creator
　　　　　　and the magnitude of that Energy.
In all earth is a compelling drive

>   to diminish into nothingness
>   that which is great and wonderful.
> And we speak of the treasury that you have before you,
>   the availability to enter in
>   and obtain a portion of fullness
>   from this generous Energy that offers without cost,
>   all that you could gather.
> Souls of earth, you can be rich within your very being.
> You can hold within your hand
>   the fullness of Truth, of Purity, of Love.
> You can warm your being
>   with the presence of the Energy available unto you.
> What is the need to know more?
> You see, you have before you more than you could hold.
> The portion is not meted out unto you.
> It is generous in its fullness.
> It is a meal unto self.
> In worlds beyond your own you would feel
>   blanketed in the generosity of these beings,
>   of the little ones who give
>   of who they are for the intent of earth,
>   of the Jinn who move among you
>   and delight in your inadequacy,
>   yet move a portion of goodness into your space.
> They are overwhelmed, these Souls,
>   with what you have, with what you destroy.
>   and they lift a portion of pain from the mother earth.
> From you who are human is the possibility of our being,
>   and we ponder.
> Yet from the debris you create, rises a magnificent Soul,
>   one and then the other and yet another.
> And so it has been since humanity came to be.
> We are overwhelmed with your ability
>   to withstand all negativity,
>   the bombardment around you,
>   the torment inflicted upon you,
>   and yet you rise in a glorious state of being.
> State of being, that which you have achieved unto you,
>   the portion that has risen
>   above the humanity of your being,
>   the glory of your Soul,

       the portion that is reclaimed
          by the Spirit and Essence.
Another state of being, Soul?
Indeed, a state of being in the advancement of Purity.

965   Soul, blessed child of universe.
We are the eye of earth.
Through our being,
          reflection of earth fading may be seen.
Creator has a balance.
Balance requires acceptance.
Balance requires yin and yang.
Balance requires the separation of the veil.
Upon the earth lived the ancient ones.
They had a purpose of being
          to care for the balance of earth, not man.
They are able to sense the languishing of earth pain.
They are healers.
They come to earth to feel the negative turn.
They see with their eyes deeply into the crevice of time.
The Souls are native.
They have being in their being native as choice
          from the casting out of time.
These Souls in passing held their being fast to earth;
          it is only in the final manifestation of their earth lives.
Until that time they return into the place of our being.
You have given as the great Buddha before you,
          an offering to Creator.
Buddha has given to mankind.
There are many such beings.
Your Purity is as the raiment of Creator.
Indeed, to be such a receiver and giver,
          one must be in the form of thirst.
The Soul then has a tranquillity, not better than,
          an understanding
             from the great echo of a single portion of earth.
Those Souls who live upon your earth in such form,
          there are few who have not blended,
          these beings are caught in the tide of humanity.
They are revered.
Not because of their separation from the blend

>   but because of the understanding
>   of that portion of earth in which they live.
> Their flesh is a part of the soil.
> They eat from that which they cast forth.
> Your earth is leaving very few individuals in such form now,
>   for the waterways have brought one unto the other
>   and that which is food one unto the other,
>   so that you are caught not in a Purity of matter.
> It is a Purity of matter of which we speak,
>   for the Soul has entered in
>   and been given life from indigenous matter.
> That indigenous matter understands a portion of earth
>   in a way that no other being can do
>   for these beings read the Energy.
> And as they leave earth, they instill their being once again,
>   that Souls indigenous will receive into them
>   all the Energy of first people.

966   Soul, the spiral is ever downward and ever upward.
And we speak to you of Lantosia,
>   the world of fourth level holding awareness,
>   holding within the great eye to see that
>   which is in the realms beyond where you are
>   to await the echo that might come unto Purity.
> The silence is deafening
>   and the great pain has not been heard.
> How must it be to have no continuity
>   for that which knew total continuity?
> Lantosia is inhabited
>   and worlds have focused their Energy
>   on this great sphere.
> The Souls enter in to your earth;
>   two existences dwelling in total unison
>   for a single purpose.
> You are to be visited for your earth has a key.
> The key is in the inability to hold perfection.
> Mankind look at your world.
> See that which you have created.
> Behold that which was and that which is.
> And know the rampant
>   energy of chaos lives within your world.

For you have created that which is watched and noted.
And even without your world
    is research working to perfect
        that which has become chaos.
Within your being there is chaos.
Within the air that you breathe there is chaos.
For chaos must be overcome.
Chaos cannot continue to rampage itself over the land,
    over the air, over the sea.
And mankind has closed eyes which have now opened
    to the recognition that chaos cannot travel.
For as it travels it picks up velocity does it not!
Indeed, it does.
And you who are human as you engage in negativity,
    you pick up velocity do you not!
You have opened a page of your existence,
    the existence of all mankind upon earth.
And you have entered in to the final phase.
We know this.
We are aware.
And yet we know in that final stage of overcoming chaos
    will come great tribulation
    that will require mankind to gather together
    as mankind has never united.
Walls will disappear.
A single purpose will be recognized to exist
    and to exist one must return
    to the Purity of their beginning.
The small child enters in from Purity
    and ages in the dregs of chaos.
As they age they return to the Purity of their beginning.
Dying does not exist for the tree or the animal or the leaf.
All returns to the beginning within your world.
And so it shall be in all worlds.
For you have entered in that now,
    even chaos will return to its beginning.
Struggle hard.
Be diligent in overcoming negativity.
For there is a carolling of sounds about you.
They hold your being as preciously as you hold your child.
And they await your arrival home

>   that you might share to the many worlds
>   of what it is to live in the density of chaos.
> Souls of earth, reach the high ground, not of your earth, no,
>   of your consciousness, will.
> This is your survival, the high ground of consciousness.
> For you are who we are.
> You are Purity and your struggle is felt in our being.
> Hold your hands in supplication and waste your Energy.
> For your Creator does not await supplication.
> Your Creator awaits the hands
>   that seed Purity and Love and Truth.
> To invite in and close the door is not Purity,
>   for the door will open as all doors will open.
> The Gateways will enter forth and you, who are pure,
>   will be as all beings, for there are no impurities.
> All are Purity.
> Touch the moon of your eye
>   and know that you see only earth with those eyes.
> And in the high consciousness of being
>   there is so much more than where you are.
> You are the visible to who you are
>   but your eye will show you visible
>   that is beyond your earth's sphere.
> Enter in to the path of vision.

967 You do not see us when we are upon your earth.
We are randomly accepted
          and yet your earth relies upon our existence.
We hold in our being, your timetable.
We structure our existence within your waters
          of that timetable.
You who are earth are indeed in a precarious state.
You carry nonchalance to the extreme.
You invite disaster upon your land.
You invest your heart and mind in self indulgence.
We are not critical.
We do not make judgment, we merely speak Truth.
We are slow to move upon your earth.
We make our way in singular steps.
Humanity, slow the pace
          or you rush to your own doom,

      for the candle is lit and burning low
      and the darkness will come.
You have within your beings the way.
You have a manner of existence that is not for gain,
      but the well being of mankind
      and you lose yourselves in the pits of negativity.
You create negativity from Love.
You create ungodliness from Godliness.
You rasp at your brother and you cling to your earth
      when indeed you are but visiting, a visitation,
      in monumental moment
      caught in an element of time.
You ravage your horizon
      and bestow droplets of poison to both land and sea.
The timetable within our being
      would draw you to a realization of impending pain,
      of imminence to the humanity
      and humanity's purpose.
The struggle is to survive.
The struggle is to overcome.
The struggle is venturesome.
Be venturesome with a motivation
      that will alter the inhabitants, the habitat.
Do not lunge forward.
We have methodical steps that are purposeful.
Join our Path, walk as we walk
      with an endurance that does not relinquish self.
You may smite our being
      but we have a purpose to move in the direction
      we were brought to earth for.
You were not brought to earth.
You came of an accord, an accord of one.
It is, Soul, the oneness of your being
      that will gather the strength
      to overcome the negativity within your land.
Be comforted.
You have many worlds upon worlds who watch
      and give of their being that you might succeed.
You are creation's family and the Creator of your being
      languishes at that which is done to His very Soul.
Sing joyful sounds, lift your being!

Touch another that their Light might shine,
        ignite from your goodness all where you are.
As your world rushes to see my methodical pace,
        the step that is unerring, so will beings
        look to you that you might show the onward step.
Lance the swell of negativity within you
        so that it might flow from you,
        that you might recover in Purity that which you are.
Time does not halt where you are.
It is ongoing.
Move with time in the methodical beat of goodness.

968   We speak to you of worlds beyond worlds.
We speak to you of the cavernous way, wherein it is dark,
        wherein there are seven levels of Dark.
In the forum are Archangels.
They are above where you are.
Within the realms of
        two, three, four, five, six, seven are worlds,
        energies held within matter,
        Energy formed in motion,
        energies of great Purity, of great goodness,
        energies with consciousness within.
All Energy has consciousness.
Your world is a conscious Energy.
The inhabitants of your world
        in all form are a conscious Energy.
The formations of your earth,
        your mountain peaks, your valleys and rivers,
        your ice, your snow, the temperature extremes,
        all come from memory, from consciousness.
It is the source of their being.
Your world is in flux.
It is in a state of commotion.
The commotion as we see it, is momentarily.
For it will yet again alter.
Even to a perfect motion will it alter.
Yet we know that species who inhabit your world
        have an existence elsewhere.
They will return to where they have come,
        entered in from,

   before the annihilation
    of many of earth's population.
All worlds are not conscious of the dilemma of earth.
A few within the Dark
   have allowed their consciousness
    to assist your Creator.
There are other worlds that dwell in perfect harmony
   within the world they are in.
They have no agenda, except within that world.
They have no tantamount expectation.
They have only the driving force of existence itself.
In them is no life and no death.
There is existence.
The life and death comes as a reaction to awareness.
Awareness brings the Souls
   to a need of cataclysmic explosion.
This a memory from whence they have come.
This a memory of first entering in.
The worlds, we will call them worlds
   for your understanding,
    differ greatly from your own.
They have not all inhabitant, as you call inhabitant.
They are more sterile in their being,
   yet the Energy is real within.
The formations of existence is real within.
Within your earth you have awakened all forms of Energy.
They writhe and seethe, they boil
   within the consciousness
    of why they have entered in.
In all that you are, in every droplet of your being,
   are multitudes of life dwelling,
   so that when you cease to be a living breath,
   your body becomes the writhing
    of which you are, visible.
Behold, darkness holds Light Energy.

969 Soul, forward your Energy
   into the space of all creatures.
Allow your Energy to be a gift unto them,
   as they gift their Energy unto you.
There is deep

        in the consciousness of humanity a remembrance
        of how close they are
        to a member of the animal family.
Sometimes it may be a turtle, a frog, a duck, a dog,
        a cat, a horse, a cow, even a snake that slithers.
But humanity remembers the Energy,
        they feel a portion of that Energy unto themselves.
They have felt the lifetimes of sharing that Energy.
They also understand often
        they have a responsibility to a certain animal.
It is because the animal has gifted them with their life.
The animal may have saved them,
        may have even taken their illness
        that they might remain upon the earth.
We ask you to have great regard
        for any Energy within your space,
        for they are Purity itself.
They are goodness in their heart.
They have no agenda to countermand, to alter.
They have only the giving of their Energy unto you.
Be soft in your tone, be caring in your demeanour.
To the animal that would injure a human,
        understand it is a Writing on the Wall.
It is an agenda that lessons might be learned.
It is a willing sacrifice of life to teach humanity.
Not all animals enter in with the human agenda,
        only by agreement does this happen.

970   Souls, achieve no status to yourself.
Achieve only that you are Energy, you are of consciousness,
        you are matter of great renown.
As one of humanity is accounted so are all.
There is no singular in humanity,
        it is the oneness, the Soul of Creator.
You do not establish, Soul, a right of placement.
You ascend in your Energy field unto that placement.
We would have you see a being of Farside.
We would have you see a swirl of Energy
        that turns in no hurry
        and holds its being to become that which it wishes;
        a form of desire, a form of creation,

       a form of artistic value,
       a form that relinquishes self.
These are all possibilities.
There is, Soul, for you who enter in to Farside,
       an opportunity to reach out and touch the Energy.
You may feel as though you felt softness of a baby's skin,
       as though you feel within your mind the lack of guile.
You would know in your being
       that all that was of desire
       was good and worthy and true.
There is a world, Soul.
The world is called Iconic.
It is reminiscent of your earth.
It rolls.
Rolls, Soul.
It is within a space of gaseous charges that are coolants,
       and the world is caught in a channel, a turn.
As there is no negativity,
       there is no detrimental effects
       to the form that you take,
       so that you may roll through many Energy Fields.
It is a vision free world
There are no obstacles.
You require no permit, you require no protection,
       you are able to observe that which you see
       in some minute amount
       upon your telescopes, within your observatories.
You may visit, Soul, many worlds of creature.
They are often upon Farside.
We are not without creature.
But their home is their sphere and they visit.
You call them creature, so for you we call them creature.
To be in the space of these creatures,
       when you see the form of your horse,
       or your dog, or your cat, or your bird,
       and then you behold the Purity of whom they are,
       your eye will not need to see,
       for you will see with the eye of beholding
       and you will wonder that you could not see
       the Purity of their magnificence.
And you will find great comfort

in requesting their being to Farside,
and they may choose, or not, to accompany you.
For there is much to delight their being
as there is for all beings of Farside.
Not as much as the world sees laps of luxury,
of sexual indulgence, of gratify the stomach.
There is no need, Soul.
The dimension of joy is uplifted.
Indeed there is Love, indeed there is caring,
indeed there is sustenance.
But is does not take on the element of existing, to be,
for you have already achieved the element.
You may want to adorn your Energy with rings and jewels,
and your being may find yourself with hands
where your earth trinkets would not even touch
the tip of your being,
for your form is the tree's height
and your Energy
does not take on the flesh and blood.
Many joys await you, Souls.
Be comforted to know
you may indulge yourself in great purities,
in great humanities
but our existence is for the purpose of your Creator,
the gift you have given.

971   Soul, we speak to you of the Faeries
and their time upon your earth.
We give unto you a knowing that they are well.
They live and defend many of the animals of your earth.
They alert and protect these tiny creatures.
You have form to the height of trees in the Energy Field
of their homeland.
They are not of great stature but of mighty Purity.
They hold the willow as the dearest of earth trees
and are often found hiding beneath its leaves.
For they can see and comfort the creatures
and even reach to the ear of the animals
by way of leaf unto leaf.
They are often found to play upon your earth fences
and they can maintain comfortable views

        from a crevasse in a fence.
Your earth is often aware of the small creatures.
They are thrilled when the human also understands
        the awareness of where they are.
Each being, tiny as they are,
        has a voice that can be quite strident
        as it excites itself
        so that indeed you hear what is called the Faery ring.
It is the sound as bells heard gently on the wind.
Often you will see a little stream of water coming from a leaf
        where they have entered in to bathe,
        for they are tidy creatures in their being.
They are many times greater in stature than themselves.
Indeed, they are playful and they bring much comfort
        to the animals of the kingdom of earth.
When a child is lost, they sing comfort to the child.
Even as a child would pass, the mother should know
        the child has been comforted with song of the Faery.
So the child is often found with a melodious chord
        singing fearless from that which it has been through.

972   Hold the crystal.
Hold the crystal and see all that is upon the face of earth.
These beings have Purity.
They have gathered knowledge of the Crystal Cave.
They have brought knowledge written in crystal
        and hold it as Light to their beings.
The crystal is energized and holds within its fragmentation
        the writings upon the wall.
What is written cannot be unwritten.
What is written shall be.
There is a core of your earth.
There is a great channel from that core.
It provides spewed light.
It is withheld from the Dome by Purity.
It radiates through the crystal
        and is seen by the forms of Love.
These beings are holding accounts of earth.
They are the retrievers of the writing
        offered to the register of Timelessness.
Upon your earth are three such races.

Only one race procreates,
> one race has the mark of eternity
> and lives without aging,
> another carries within the crystal
> the colour of all healing.

The crystal of healing is two, negative and positive
> and the touch is zero.

It creates a field where all becomes equal.
Earth in its feebleness will not recognize the value of zero.
It looks only to one.
The answer is in zero.
Look to the great zero, eye of your being.
Your earth is overwhelmed
> with the spirit of alien creatures.

The numbers are rising for the portal is increasing.
And we say to you,
> *"They mean no harm in any way."*

Many will see their being.
Many will cast an eye upon their shadow.
Many will behold the Spirit of their Energy.
Have no fear earth, they come not to conquer.
For what pride would there be when you have decimated
> that which has been given unto you?

And where they come, there are treasures
> beyond that which earth carries in all forms.

They have no need for any that earth has.
You have their need, Soul, for they care for your being.
And as earth beings are lifted,
> they will be there to transport all creatures.

You are not the only ones to be lifted.
You are the only ones, Soul,
> who must enter in apart from Farside.

All that is Purity may enter Farside.
Humanity, you will not outlive earth
> and earth will not outlive you.

Rather you will unite your energies to enter in to Purity,
> for earth will find herself in you
> and mankind would have
> a different demeanor in that day.

Man will reach unto man,
> Soul unto Soul, Spirit unto Spirit.

And a great throng will beckon negativity to join
      and partake of the new day.
Your earth trembles,
      mankind trembles, yet humanity is strong.
For the indigo and violet children roam your earth,
      the alien creatures
      prepare themselves to lift mankind
      and a great anthem raises itself
      in the conquest of positive over negative.
It is not until the waters are still
      that you see what is below the waters.
In the turmoil the clarity is not seen.
Within your earth, humanity has brought clarity.
Within your earth there is much to rejoice of.
Do not see the great shadows fall and feel the foreboding.
Rather look and see the Angel wings.
Look and behold thine own Energy.
Seek to respond to the heart of another.
Mighty, mighty humanity, world of pristine beauty,
      you are united in a Path
      to return from whence you have come.
And all will know
      that you have succeeded in your entering in.
And all that has been brought down
      will once again appear
      to be beheld in clarity as the waters clear.
And that which is the united purpose of man becomes.
Gather all your energies to live,
      not in fear, Soul, but in command of thy being.
Death, the dark shall not harm thee.
Indeed not.
For you have come that your flesh might wither.
You have come that you might leave.
You have come that you might overcome.

973   Souls of earth, you struggle in your being.
You struggle with your flesh, blood and bone.
You struggle, Soul, with the entrance into the Farside.
And we say to you, acceptance.
Do not reconnoitre wherein you are.
Do not seek to know.

Accept you are a form upon your earth.
Your earth is sister sphere unto sphere of the Farside.
It is brought into great pain.
It did not begin with you.
It began in the entering in to Negativity.
Indeed, your flesh and blood was strengthened
       by the negative imbalance upon your earth.
Even now as your earth is twisted and turned
       and Souls are beleaguered and lost,
          humanity is strengthened.
All beings do not come into your earth
       to resolve issues of humanity.
Many Souls enter in to earth to be the victim,
       to be the gift unto humanity's path with negativity.
How can that be?
And yet we tell you it is so.
Your reality is not where you are.
And we understand your persuasion
       that while you are where you are, it is a reality.
Yes we understand this.
But the beings, Soul, have offered to enter in.
They gift unto humanity as one, their life upon earth.
You are saddened in your being
       as we are saddened in our being
       for we know more than you know
       the beatification of these Souls.
These are Souls who did not have to enter in.
They had surmounted their humanity.
Indeed some gathered in huge numbers
       to plead with Melchezidec a single lifetime unto earth.
Let it be where humanity will learn from our single life.
And so they have entered in,
       the violet, the indigo, the walk ins
       to give forth unto humanity's growth
       that you might see who you are as you are.
They hold a mirror for you with their lives.
They hold the pain of their passing, of their life.
And you see yourselves as they leave you.
All life is precious.
Even unto the Rend is Life and Death precious.
But it is always a choice even for Death.

Was that not so at the Rend!
Did that not create, Soul, a havoc!
To have a heart, a mind, the Soul rejoices,
       for it is then a triad
       a triad from its beginning.
A triad where you could see colours pass by you,
       flickering in minute states of being
       and know that even those simple Lights
       have come unto you, for you they lite the air.
They flicker and dance and are unto humanity a nothing,
       yet unto Farside their reflection
       is cast from the very Purity that they are.
You have upon your earth understood Purity.
You understand that some beings have great Purity.
You see into the eyes of your creature
       and you know their Purity.
But others do not reveal so easily unto you their Purity.
They are, Soul, those that you look upon
       and send forth repulsive venerations
       from your being.
Yet they are pure.
They are greatly pure, astoundingly so.
Their appearance is not always as you see them, Soul.
Indeed, it is not.
We say to you of the alligator,
       the alligator in the sphere of Farside
       is upright, greatly gentle, intellectual.
As the old man holds wisdom
       so does the great alligator hold wisdom.
So do worlds of great renown enter in to the alligator world
       to cherish that which is known.
Think you of all that is written upon your earth,
       of all your quests and knowns and understand
       that Farside within the Masterpiece of Creator,
       within the Sublime Record
       known unto those who have the Purity to reach,
       are great knowns so that it would fill your mind
       to be bedazzled by that which is there.
Much of it comes as the great alligator world
       holds the earth's consciousness to it
       and is ever given forth as

　　　　　the whale gives forth knowns unto Farside.
Within the depth of the deepest sea
　　　　within your world which is shallow,
　　　　　　indeed nothing lives that is not known unto us
　　　　　　 and vibrates the Energy unto who we are.
As you love to vibrate one to the other,
　　　　so do the creatures vibrate unto where we are.
Earth beings,
　　　　"Hold your earth and all within as treasured."

Chapter Three
IDYLLIC

974   All existence understands the loss of perfection,
        even your own, Soul.
Seven spheres of such glory, your earth only a copy,
        yet the magnitude of these worlds
        cannot be put into your language.
They cannot.
There is no language upon your earth
        that would suitably ascribe the perfection
        for that which we know the blue world to be.
We know a portion of the glory of this Earth has dissipated.
We have but the relative form without the igniting Energy.
It is as you see the form of a beloved ready to leave earth;
        you know how magnetic, how vibrant,
        how vital can that being be.
And yet you see the being still by the mark of death.
So it is with the blue world.
Yet we know for we have been able to open apertures
        because of messengers of humanity
        unto far beyond where we are.
For we have the Dark and, Soul,
        you have the Light within you.
We have Purity within us, we have Love within us,
        but we are not illuminated as humanity is illuminated.
For we have not overcome as you have overcome.
There are many different keys to place within a latch.
But all keys do not open.
It must be the perfect key.
And you will have teared in your being
        who have known great desperation, great sadness.
For you have chosen to be a part of where you are
        and in your state of humanness
        you have no recollection of that which you have left.
But we where we are can see you in your desolation,
        even in the most perfect,
        as the Blessed Child entering in.
We can see the bombarding of negativity unto their being.
Yet, Souls of earth, you so overcome.

You so move our being.
We cheer you on, Soul.
We vibrate in our Energy because of you.
You are the cup full that will be passed to all existence
    that they might drink from the depth of the Truth.
You are the dove that has given the wings unto all beings
    for the Purity of the dove shows the way.
You are the way, as Jesu said,
    "*I am the way.*"
Would it not please you enter in human,
    yet Soul of perfection, the Soul of Love,
    the Soul of Purity!
Earth humanity you are the prism, you are the chalice.
You are the sustenance of all,
    for you hold in your being the cup everlasting.
You hold in your being the resonant chord.
You hold in your being joy.

975   We ask you, Souls, to breathe.
We ask you to bring yourself to a gentle being.
In the tranquility of the gentle being
    can be the state of idyllic.
Without the state of gentle being, idyllic cannot be.
You understand it cannot be for the human,
    it cannot be for any Energy.
The chaotic state must have vanquished, vanquished,
    given way.
Idyllic, above SEE,
    how created?
The Void of Consciousness, Soul.
The Void of Consciousness inhabited consciousness,
    not a single consciousness, profound!
Profound consciousness of limitless energies
    mutually inhabiting a sphere.
A sphere!
A sphere!
Yet profound in the enormity of that sphere.
No Matter, no Ion.
Consciousness of Being, but left apart the Matter, the Ion.
The need, to be complete,
    the need to contain the fullness of being.

And, Energy beheld that which was formed
    and that which was apart
    and fulfilled a need.
As your world was placed apart from the perfection,
    so was the orb of Idyllic.
And 15th Creator sent out the Vanguard to guard the portal.
And each sent forth a world.
For they gathered Ion and Matter
    and sent it forth to be the perfect world.
In sending it forth,
    the world could have motion and movement within.
For the Energies have Matter
    in which consciousness dwelled,
    not in the form you have matter, Soul;
    not as your human form.
The form, it was more unto your rock,
    that has within it consciousness and knowing.
Ask the diamond,
    does it not know the heat from where it has come?
Indeed it will tell you, it has the memory of that heat.
As the shard of granite,
    does it not know the pushing upward
    from the bowels of earth?
Indeed it will tell you that it does.
To give of your being ever unto any one thing
    without a return, Soul, is tedious.
Is it not!
The Life was given
    and each of the Fourteen received a form of Death,
    for your understanding, Soul of earth,
    a form of death.
So once again, the Energies
    of Consciousness of Void, of Matter, of Ion,
    sought the solution.
And what if Death and Life are placed
    and Death moves back from Life?
What then?
Will Life sustain itself?
It did not.
It created Chaos and the world fell.
And perfection ceased to be.

For in Life there must be a giving.
You cannot take it back.
It is an ever giving.
So is the dilemma, not of your world,
    of all worlds, of all energies,
        of all creations, that Energy moves outward,
        outward, outward.
Breath, Breath, Breath and no return,
    only in spheres, only in containments.
You are such a containment.
Even your mortal body is such a containment.
So be it.

976   Soul, the darkness is hidden from you.
You see only the glory.
For as earth stills to silence, so you will see the dark
    manifold unto many millions of decibels.
You will see the inner reaches of your planet;
    you will see those that you have not seen,
        the cables of Energy.
You will see the great structure of power
    that enervates the very motion of your earth.
This will be the dark.
Of course, Soul. it is the one world of seven
    that we of Farside recovered.
It was the one perfect world and you have
    the mirrored copy of this world.
Copy, Soul.
Your sister world has not been touched.
It is still prismatic in being.
It is visited many many many times,
    as you would visit an esteemed chapel
    honouring your Creator,
    be it dome, or gothic or simple and humble.
So Farside has great delight in visiting
    this sacred portion that held Idyllic.
Idyllic received the motion
    from the structural unification of these worlds.
It maintains a place in glory, totally within chaos,
    yet from chaos.
Because of the vibrational pull

>   of each world unto the other,
>   it created a circle of unification
>   such as never been formed before.
> It created a perfect balance to hold
>   the absolute existence.
> Yet Chaos found a way
>   to circumvent that which was perfect.
> And all eyes of awareness fell into the abyss with it.

977   Within the Fourteen Creators,
>   they formed a circle of perfection
>   that kept aloft an Idyllic sphere.
> This perfection was vulnerable from outward intrusion.
> The need to have returned Energy without separation
>   is imperative to the strength of the outward flow,
>   a oneness of all Energy that will bring strength.
> Soul, your intent comes from
>   the Energy of your being upon the Farside.
> Your intent to enter in to assist your Creator.
> Intent is allocated to all existence.
> The intent of the Blessed Angels
>   to recover the Farside worlds
>   from their state of inertness.
> The intent of the Triad of Creator to carry the Seed
>   into the Cauldron of Microscopic beings
>   of great Purity
>   and the intent without of the Sireen Sound
>   to create the leak, the altered self.
> In the heavens beyond your earth, in existences
>   far from you, transformed,
>   an Energy has been altered.
> The Energy has been altered and created an altered state;
>   Energy no longer able to contain itself,
>   chaotic within,
>   moving like the highest number earth could form,
>   in the slowest speed of movement.
> It continues, it has intent.
> It will alter all worlds, all levels of Energy,
>   for as yet it cannot be confined.
> Fire has altered itself in an effort to confine.
> Ion has given Energy outward into distant places

        that they might combat from a forward effort,
           outflanking that which is loose.
Death has removed itself that Souls would not die.
All Energy holds intent,
        all Energy does not have the power
           to alter its placement.
Some Energies are confined within a rigid set of rules.
They are adapted to Light or Dark,
        they are encamped in these rigid confines.
Such a confinement is the placement of Presence.
You have a saying upon your earth, "*He has no presence.*".
Presence is absent in your world unless you create it.
To be a flesh and blood being
        with an earth mind and heart
           does not give you presence, Soul.
You do not enter in to presence
        until you move into the Energy of self.
Therefore acquiring presence
        for your flesh and blood, heart and mind.
And then Souls will say,
        "*They have a presence about them.*".
Existence is not always of flesh and blood.
Existence takes on many forms,
        more than you in your world could fathom.
These existences have great energies within.
They have knowledge of all your earth,
        of all your cultures and cultures beyond.
They have intricacies of the enlightened mind
        that create glorious existences within.
And they can become within those existences.
These are adventures that you of earth will meet
        as you reach a level above the human level.
You are not confined within the need
        to overcome negativity.
You will have understood the fullness of life
        and life outside the flesh and the blood.
In the area you refer to as Domes, there is a Presence.
That Presence is as a great lighthouse
        sending forth a beacon.
Not upon your world, but upon all existences.
The Presence is at one with the Void.

And the Presence was aware,
    as your earth has become aware
    of tidal and earthquake happenings,
    so did the Presence alert all energies
    to an altered strength of the Void
    that pushed inward upon existence, upon Breath.
And Breath sent forth a sound like wind
    which altered the Fire
    that protected Existence and Matter and Presence.
As Death saw that no energies might be consumed,
    Death withdrew.
In withdrawing, there came a Rend,
    a rend of such magnitude,
    it has corrupted the flow of many energies.
For no longer does Breath have an idyllic path
    or Existence a secured place.
For a Leak has occurred and chaos has become.
And all Fourteen Energies sob in Their Being,
    and a great need to draw back
    into the place of Existence, that Leak.
Chaos alters, chaos forces, chaos disallows Existence.

978   The energies of the world of Idyllic,
    we will give to you.
These energies are like unto your plant life,
    unto your animal life, unto your creature life,
    again triad, Soul.
Because water as you understand water to be
    was not a necessity in that realm.
All things were maintained within the perfect existence.
There was no life and death.
There was existence, Soul.
It was tethered.
It was tethered unto perfection.
It took Fourteen Creators
    to send forth the Energy
    to uphold the existence of perfection.
For in them was the Life and the Death,
    in them was the giving and receiving.
When Chaos became,
    the world fell away and did not return,

>   as in the Void when all Energy went forth
>   there has been no return.

Each effort has been to create the return.
As your earth, each and every effort
        that you do upon the face of your earth
        is for the return.
It is for the implosion.
You have a heart.
It pumps outward from your being.
If it does not return, there is no life.
There is but death.
So there must be the return.
When there is a fault the return is not perfect,
        mankind seeks a way to make it perfect.
You do each and every little iota of correcting
        that you might correct that which is is,
        that which is in the realms and realms
        beyond your own.
In the fourth realm Lantosia is not the only world.
There are worlds and worlds that have outward been flown.
They have not returned.
Lantosia, as Earth, as Pleiades, as Lemuria,
        were four of the worlds
        we know that upheld Idyllic.
Lantosia is the farthest from where we are that we know of.
These Souls have reached unto humanity,
        for they are aware in their Energy of consciousness.
They know why you have entered in to your earth.
They have endeavoured to reach and assist humanity.

979   Unto the Souls of earth.
Your being is simplicity.
We do not denounce.
Indeed, to us you are graciousness
        that you are be willing to enter in
        but you are feeble in your form.
Those who live, who dwell within the worlds of seven,
        these are energies as the Archangels.
These are beings without mar.
They have mind.
They have heart.

They have awareness of who they are.
They have before them all purpose of perfection
     even do they have life and death
       once more unto them.
You recall that Death pulled away and created a Rend.
For these beings that populate the worlds we speak of,
     these beings have life and death
       as you have life and death.
It is, Soul, a perfection.
They were given a gift from Idyllic,
     shone forth a perfection
       that gave unto them a perfect existence.
Within perfection was a containment of Breath.
It gave renewal.
It gave supreme Energy.
What we do not know is the state of Idyllic.
Is the perfection still resident?
Is it the lack of breath that altered the state of the spheres
     for all motion in whatever form motion is,
       is from Breath.
Spheres spiral but when the spiral gathers momentum
     as in your storms of earth, they create havoc.
We do not know how they fell.
We only know that they fell.
Your earth is minute to that which is Idyllic.
Even your sun is microscopic to that which is Idyllic
     and worlds with Energies of Fourteen Creators.
The Supreme Being giving Light unto Idyllic
     and perfection a reflectory
       of that which was perfection.
When you are in your perfect form human,
     you radiate Light.
Your goodness shines through the very form of your being.
It is seen beyond from where you are.
Who are you so perfect,
     Soul was perfection, but now like you, marred.
This we do not know.
This you field for us.
Soul, at the head of the Crystal Water,
     past a huge abyss,
       is what appears to be

    a huge enormity of explosions outward.
Only outward we have seen.
There is a falling of Lights l
    ike iridescent that Light your being,
    like being in water,
    where there is Light attached to you.
And all that is Light touches, ignites and becomes
    and fizzles and disappears.
It is the place of Death.
Death holds the thread, holding existence together.
If Death released, the Rend would continue.
The Shining Water cannot move back.
It cannot reach unto Death, it would fall to the abyss also.
It is like your human flesh, losing a leg
    and having the leg across a great hole
    and knowing if you must walk again,
    you must have the leg.
Yet you cannot enter through the hole.
The path around the hole
    would mean you would lose more of your being.
You would have to release from your being
    that which you hold.
In being compassionate unto Life,
    Death created more of death.

980 There is a great interest in
    all that is within the element
    of the seven Light Fields.
You are as we are within the Light Fields.
Lantosia is in the fourth,
    there are three below and then there is darkness.
As we understand more completely
    that which is where you are,
    that which is within chaos itself,
    your earth endeavours to create Light.
And we are amazed that you have not understood
    that you yourselves create Light
    that you are the greatest manufacturer of Light
    there is.
For as you draw your energies together,
    you send forth a beam of such strength

    that Lights into the darkness.
It has only been sent forth upward.
It has not been used to send into the lower Lights
    for we know it does not have the strength
      to carry itself yet into the lower fields of darkness.
Therefore we beseech humanity to strengthen the Light,
    to bring yourselves as one unto each other
    that you might know the strength
    within the compassion of your being.
We cannot help you with this but what we can do, Soul,
    is enter in to the path of Lantosia.
We can intervene with the echoes that we hear.
We can decipher the resounding intent
    of all that is in the lower echelon of Light.
We are sending forth great ships into the fifth level of Light.
This does not require earth for it carries its own Light.
What we require of humanity is when we reach
    below the seventh level into the darkness,
      yet again then will all that is humanity be sent forth.
There are many means being used, Soul,
    to attract, bring forth, Idyllic.
Much is being done at the upper levels of Light
    even within the darkness by the Blessed Angels.
You are helping in this, Soul,
    for you are sending forth a beacon
      into a straight path downward that has been located,
    an aperture that delves
      into the great depths upon your earth.
You have seen great caves that follow their way
    deep into the core of your earth.
In the darkness are not caves,
    but for you we compare them unto caves,
    great apertures that follow deep
    within the depths of darkness.
They follow even beyond the Dome
    into the darkness of yet another Dome,
    so that it is dark.
And in this mean we are able to bypass the Light.
This is one effort that is being sent forth.

981 Souls of earth, behold the reflectories unto you.

Behold those visions you may have of that which will be.
There is before you
        a landscape of reflectories you have not yet seen.
There is beings of radiance in the foreground of your being.
They extend unto the forth Field Light.
These radiate.
Even beyond the fourth Field Light are reflectories.
These are Idyllic,
        these even unto the darkness so that, behold,
        there is a glow that is resounding
        within the darkness.
It is seen, Soul, through your reflectory.
It is seen through earth's projection.
It is valued
        for in that which is visible is the purpose of all.
You have before you a kaleidoscope of colour
        even unto you it moves upward.
It threads inward.
It has a visage of your field.
The beings of earth pick up the residuals of their Energy
        as they leave your landscape
        for they enter in and out.
They are gathered unto the central Lantosia.
They are beings of great Energy who have for you
        a continuation of theory and research,
        a denotation and awareness.
They come, each denotation above and below.
They mark as you mark landscape
        so they mark the fields of Energy.
Yours are all accounted.
Each individual human as they enter and re enter
        in to the negative phase of being,
        they behold the growth.
They behold that which you have surmounted.
They behold the tenderness,
        the eagerness for which you have entered in
        and even, Soul, they behold the great pause
        before work is done.
You harvest in your years many moments of clarity.
You see with the Colour and Sound of Farside
        and you triumphantly behold

> that there is a Masterpiece before you,
> a configuration of clarity that gives unto you
> the path wherein you must walk.

Souls of earth, you are continual in your path.
You have the veracity, the clarity,
> at times the wisdom of many ages.

As your earth alters in her being
> so do you alter in your being.

As you behold your earth altering
> so do we behold you altering,
> so does the reflectory
> where the eyes are not necessary,
> only the landscape within your being,
> only that map you are constantly aware of.

It is not, Soul, of many earths
> but a reflectory of all that was and all that is.

It is gargantuan.
It is without philosophy or physiology.
It has the Purity of awareness, of value.
It is not intellectual.
Yet it does not forsake the human element
> for indeed the human element is the most visible.

It is the Energy that holds fast yet constantly changes.
It is, the prism, the kaleidoscope of colour
> that attracts all energies
> in all spheres of consciousness.

How valued are you, human,
> that you have made possible reflectories
> even into the darkness below your being
> for we have seen the energies of Truth.

We have seen the Purity of Ecstasy.
We have seen the triumphant glory wherein Idyllic is.
It is but reflectory yet it has been mirrored back unto us.
And you, humanity,
> who speak to our being,
> who glory in that which we are,
> you seek to reside
> in that which is Farside you call heaven.

You see and behold the palaces of glory.
You seek to dwell with your Creator.
You behold the Purities of Jesu,

>   Mohammed, Buddha and Krishna
>   and you count your blessings
>   that they have entered in to your earth
>   to bestow unto you that which would point
>   the way unto where we are.
> And yet, you have pointed a different way.
> You have pointed a way beyond where we are.
> You have shown us that which is perfection.
> Behold the mirror has two sides, both reflectories,
>   a landscape wherein you may enter through
>   unto another form of being.
> You may laugh and delight yourselves in that which is.
> As in earth you may change the portent of your life.
> You may decide to alter that which you have set before you
>   to give you parameters that meet a different view
>   that carry different connotations visible unto you.
> Souls of earth, you delight our Soul
>   and we speak for all Farside
>   for we are one in purpose and being
>   unlike humanity
>   who works individually, separately.
> We are one for all and all for one.
> Would that you could be!
> The reflectories, the vistas would open unto you
>   and you would behold the opening and closing
>   of many platforms of many Gateways.
> You are purposeful in your engagement with negativity.
> You know of its effect upon your being
>   and yet you dabble in its acquiescence.
> And this we say to you is a magnificent step
>   for without entering in how can you overcome!
> Then, how may we behold that which is before you?
> You are on a trek, a gallant trek.
> It takes us unto where we are.
> Yet from the trek that you have entered in to,
>   we who are Farside, we have before us a trek.
> It allows sight unto the Energy Field beyond your being.
> It Lights the way.
> It is an iridescent way not fully visible.
> There are shades and darkness and yet, there are glimpses
>   and sounds of colour that radiate upwards unto us.

We have seen the intent that you have
        in that which is negative.
Upon your earth are many beings
        who flutter through the negativity
        and find it deeply embedded upon their being
        and we send unto them
        the blessedness that we have.
And then we behold the glory of awakening of the Soul
        who sees that which has touched their being
        and who have become inert.
You have risen in your Energy
        to step from that which is negative.
And you have reached forward unto that which is negative
        giving comfort and compassion and in this manner
        you have overcome negativity.
This overcoming has allowed a vision of that
        which is beyond where you are.
We do not see the glory of that which is before you
        for you are on the upward climb.
You have before you all the galaxies of being.
In the darkness there are worlds.
They are inhabited worlds.
They are as though unawakened in the great sleep.
The consciousness has not awakened their being.
They are Souls who sleep in many worlds.
There are Souls who have lived and loved
        that which they call home
        but in a passing through darkness
        they too have become inert.
They too are silent.
They too are touched with Negativity,
        earth's as your earth, Soul.
There were seven.
Your earth is one.
Of Light and Dark you are.
Of that which beheld perfection you are
        and all that was touched
        by your loss of awareness, a loss of awareness.
Matter is, Ion is.
Consciousness is not
        and we know you have touched

        the Blessed Angels.
They are prepared to be lifted.
You have given unto those who live in the darkness, Light
        and they have beheld the Energy of your being.
        Loved that which is withered
        you have given much unto those in the darkness,
        unto those caught in the inert,
left in the Energy of Negativity.
The Wilful Child caught in the Cleansing River
        has felt the vibrations of your being.
This we know.
Souls of earth, that which you are as human upon earth
        is a gallant step to bring forth all lost Energy.
That which is Chaos even unto MATTER.
Breathe the breath of the gallant for us all
        for you are the vision of that which will be.
You have the generosity of spirit.
You have the continuation of desire and intent.
You have awareness of that which is.
You are Light.

982   The Wilful Child
        has gone forth out of compassion.
One in search of;
        Twelve resolving the issue
        to bring the perfect sound.
One in compassion reaching out,
        in the reaching out came a discordance.
The discordance comes unto earth humanity
        in how you use the Wilful Child.
It will not be captive.
It will not be captive!
It seeks and in holding the Wilful Child,
        it has in the hands of humanity,
        become evil, Soul, evil.
You have distorted a sound,
        but in the distortion of the sound
        you have resolved through that negative action
        to bring about another sound.
You have brought a compassion that reaches back unto.
The compassion of the Wilful Child reaches out,

        does not draw forth.
You as humanity have given a gift.
You have returned.
It is the first instance in all existence of give and return.
Soul, within the Wilful Child is a single purpose
        to reach ever outward from self,
        to reclaim that which was perfect.
The consciousness was the purpose of all Lights,
        all Creators, all Light Beings, all Archangel,
        all Angels, all humanity.
Within the Wilful Child is the consciousness of
        the consciousness of effort of all Fifteen Creators;
        is the conscious effort of all consciousness.
Nothing upon your earth,
        upon any existence,
        is without consciousness.
It is the state of consciousness that is the issue.
Within consciousness
        there can be stillness, unawakened consciousness.
Many worlds have unawakened consciousness,
        yet are incredibly pure, pristine, we would say, Soul.
Yet their consciousness is unawakened
        to the need to return
        unto the source of their entering out.
There is in the Energy of consciousness no forceful issue.
None, Soul.
The issue of force is not within any realm except your own.
It is, Soul, free radical movement.

983   The Soul is the carrier of the mortal Energy.
The Soul carries all that you are unto the Spirit.
It does not hold negativity as negativity
        but it does hold
        the awareness of negativity within you.
It transports all unto Farside,
        the negativity is left at the station of karma
        if unfinished.
Souls of earth, your earth is spiralling in negativity.
The young are being touched by the negativity of the elder
        and the elder, being touched
        by the negativity of the Child

        beyond which earth has known.
And you, your world, your cosmos, your universe,
        so minute in its being
            as to be nearly unidentifiable from where we are
            except for the great Energy that comes
            from this small planet, from the inhabitants.
The vibrational pull is felt in Energy Fields
        far from your own.
You send forth instruments to say, "*We are here.*"
And we find great humour in this,
        for who does not know you are here!
In your world indeed there are planets of beings
        who hold your world,
        eyed with every motion of vibration.
Not a shard could enter forth unto it
        that it is not known far from your galaxy.
You have more eyes on you
        than any other sphere in all of existence.
You have the greatest EYE upon you,
        far beyond where you are,
        beyond that which is supreme Creator.
The EYE sees and knows.
And each vibration of earth is gathered
        and sent forth into the endless Void.
For at what time will the perfect note come to be?
At what time will the rounded form of note appear?
Note after note is sent into the Void that Idyllic might hear.
You are the source of the sound.
And in that realm that you are, in that place of great pain
        where you hold to your heart negativity
        and bombard your fellow man with negativity,
        the reaches of perfection in
        and amongst that negativity is so pure,
        is so full of Love that it resounds itself outward
        and reaches billions of light years
        from where you are.
We call you Holy man for you are Holy unto Holy.
You have before you a challenge
        for mankind will be exploring the fourth dimension.
The fourth Field of Energy
        will be setting all scopes unto a different Field.

And you will see who we are.
You will identify our planet.
You will know our energies.
We are Lantosia.
We have entered in to search
      as you entered in to battle negativity.
You will find two worlds associating together.
We will assist humanity to travel.
In truth, you will be assisting us,
      for it is your vibration we need.
We need to bring to bear the chord you have
      and send it forth
           from the fourth dimension of Light and Dark.

984   Soul, the ultimate earth is the return to glory.
The ultimate earth is the re entry
      of earth into the place of setting.
It is at the level of three.
It is within the perimeter of the Place of Shining.
Earth, the blue world, half light, half dark,
      chose to enter through the Void
         unto the Negative Field.
This course altered its perfection.
Your science sees much of that altered state.
The velocity thorough which the earth plummeted,
      created a wobble.
This will also be that form which allows it to enter back in.
Without that wobble it could not regenerate its course.
The velocity will carry it forth in a spiral.
All your earth does not have twilight.
You understand your Light and dark
      is that which earth has chosen.
Nothing that you do is totally Light.
Nothing that you do is totally dark.
You cannot see the darkness of your planet,
      yet it holds a discerning Light and dark.
It has been apportioned, Soul,
      before it ever entered in to earth.
Your earth has a consciousness.
The consciousness holds deep memory.
It remembers that which is Idyllic.

It remembers that perfect sphere
        as it entered through unto Negative Void.
It attempted to be that perfect sphere in all manner.
Mankind has not allowed it.
The very darkness of earth itself has not allowed it.
The very force of Energy which motioned it forward
        does not allow it.
For it too has been touched with Negativity.

985   Souls of earth, always humanity has struggled
        with the divide between negative and positive.
Always there has been a great chasm called the void of earth
        wherein the chaos creates energy of motion
        that disturbs the minds of men and women
        that creates gulfs of anger between humans.
Those who feel negativity is firm within them
        and have within no remorse,
            they hold a trough wherein negativity falls and is held.
It is within a chasm of the mind.
They do not reach and hold firm to any truth
        that has logic of positive Energy.
They regale in the fanaticism of negativity.
Souls of earth, negativity streams from their being.
It catapults itself outward from them into the space of others.
It enhances uprighteousness, a thought in their being.
Souls of earth,
        there is a need to recognize the volubility of negativity
        for it is a truth that negativity is wilful.
It is captivating in itself.
It progresses and offers such totality of being
        that a human might exist in the rapture of negativity.
It is flagrant in its enticing ability.
It is never without wonderment of what can be.
For in the space of negativity all can be possible
        and humanity finds themselves encaptured
        until there is the quiet still voice of reason
        that comes to man, to woman.
Search.
Seek!
See within.
Enwrap thy being in the knowledge of what has failed

and what has become enhanced
by the positive Energy.
Souls of earth, lift your eyes unto the hills
that you might see the ray of Light
that you might see
the morning dawn upon your being
for you have before you, as humanity, all choice.
You have before you the great thrall of goodness.
You have before you the varied drop of Light
that enters the mind from the Spirit
where you can seek
and know you have the awakening,
the chime of reconstructing that which has been.
All endings are new beginnings.
All time of limitations is forthcoming
to a time of opportunity.
Souls, do not wander in the grips of pain.
Do not wander in the grips of negativity
but see before you the opening of a colossal Gateway
wherein all is unity,
wherein all has a Purity of self,
wherein all holds truth of self, the utmost Truth.
For in self is the connection to the Spirit
and as the Spirit you are at one with the Angels,
you are ministered by the Archangels.
You are in the redeeming Light of your Creator.
You hold the key to your existence
you hold the key to humanity,
for you are a particle of oneness.
You are, Soul, to hold the intent of your being before you
that you might come from the darkest of places
that you might find yourself wounded
in the most greatest of life threatening pain.
Yet, Soul, you have the possibility to rise above.
You have the possibility to sing the great song.
For in all energy is a great anthem.
It is held by the Angels and Archangels.
It is a gathering of Sound and Colour
in which perfection is found.
Seek to know that which is perfection.
Seek to know that which is Holy.

For in your very being is that portion
        that you may find and hold
        and clasp unto your being.
Human, you are worthy.
You are treasured more than any treasures,
        of any matter upon your earth, you are treasured.
Not greater, Soul, treasured
        for there are many upon your earth
        who have entered in
        who have greater worth,
        who have Energy of great magnitude
        but they are not treasured as the simplest of humans.
For they do not have within their being
        the capacity of oneness
        that humanity has or indeed they may be one,
        in fact, Soul, they are in Purity.
They are compassionate but they have not, as one,
        sent forth the sound of compassion,
        they have not reached into the treble.
Only humanity have the ability to the High C.
The High C, it is the same as that which is Idyllic, perfection.
You are capable of the great encounter.
You are the thread from which all hope hangs,
        for you have in your being held chaos,
        overcome chaos, Loved chaos.
Soul, hold yourself proud, hold yourself stalwart.
Hold yourself as the mighty warrior
        who has fought the battle with temptation,
        who has found themselves
        smothered in the kraal of negativity,
        who have mastered the ability to rise above the storm
        wherein chaos abides,
        and has reached into the deep waters of negativity
        and lifted another in compassion.
Souls of earth, how great thou art.
You are of sound.
You are of colour.
You have the great echo in your being.
You have not floundered.
Your time is rapidly altering,
        time has an existence in itself.

It is not heard forever.
The earth is crying great tears,
      the waters touching matter in a way they never have.
They still have not finished the great cry.
They still hold negativity yet to be washed and released.
Who hears the echo?
Wherein is Negativity?
The Wilful Child is far from the Brother that is his Creator.
Creator seeks through you
      to bring back unto the fold the Blessed Brother.
For one portion of a whole is as important
      as all other portions of a whole.
Supreme Being has a need.
The Thirteenth Creator is a portion
      of that which is Negativity!
Souls of earth, sound,
      sound outward from your being
      with a colour of Light.
Echo forth in the High C that all will heal.
Blessed being thou art Holy.
Do not rely, Soul, on the extension of your being,
      that of Farside Spirit.
It is within earth itself that you must overcome negativity.
Do not delve into the darkness.
Do not seek to know that which is pain but overcome,
      for in your being all things are possible.
All is redeemable unto Creator.

986   Indeed, is not Negativity on a search for Idyllic!
Is Negativity not the negative, discordant note?
Is it not searching for perfection from which to identify!
And are you humanity in your being not attaining!
Indeed you are that very perfection
      that the Wilful Child may identify unto you.
All energies are bound together,
      Love is of hate, desire is of need.
Behold awareness brings intent, presence brings knowing.
You hold within your being the incandescent crystal
      that has the fragmentation of all your growth.
You have been as the Wilful Child searching and searching.
You have wandered into the snare of negativity

and in your many lives you have overcome.
You have gathered unto you
    compassion for the most despot of beings.
You are understanding,
    judgment has no place in the giving forth of Love,
    acceptance is the totality of humanity.
To understand your humanity,
    you must accept all things unto you,
    without judgment,
    holding compassion and offering the gift of self.
For in the blend of self to another in your Energy field,
    is the possibility of the magnitude of your Creator.
You must learn
    to disseminate from levels of Love and know Agape.
Then you become as the rainbow,
    the prismatic being holding within you all colours.
Your reach has been great,
    and the threads of your being have blended
    and you will find you send forth
    the perfection of White Light,
    the blend of all prism.
We would have you know of the Discordant Note.
It is, Soul,
    Discordant Note, Negativity, Wilful Child, triad.
It is Negativity, Truth, Wisdom, triad.
Upon the Field of the Rend,
    chaos was released and drove the Idyllic forth.
Negativity was held within the Seed.
Discordant Note searched for Idyllic.
The Wilful Child held within the Ion Void.
Each portion of Discordant Note,
    a Purity with a purpose, as you have purpose.
Discordant Note ever searching.
Negativity also searching,
    but also searching to recover self, the chaotic self.
You, humanity, you also have altered your being.
First to draw forth the Blessed Angels.
Then to draw all existence through Second Gateway.
Then to bring the Blessed Brothers home unto Creator.
Of two, you have succeeded.
The third, not yet.

Do you understand?
Indeed, within the Crystal Cave, are the Souls waiting
    to bring back the Blessed Angels.
Humanity, you have the compassion gathered
    of the utmost of Love to bring the Gateway opened.
You have called upon Creator:
    "Hold, do not leave the Blessed Brother.
    Do not hold the Blessed Brother in the Ion Void.
    Time, give us time that we may bring unto You
        the prodigal that was lost."
And so your earth struggles yet with negativity.
This is why you are esteemed
    in your lowest form of being
        more precious than any.
The Sound of Discordant Note was unintentional.
Indeed it exacerbated
    that which was complexity upon complexity.
For indeed the Thirteenth Note
    had lost a part of its Energy.
It was incomplete.
You lose upon your earth countless Souls in a living day.
They are lost, gone from your earth.
And your earth in its majority, unaware of that loss.
We could not have it so.
There has been a great loss.
That loss is substantial.
It is altered the echo of Energy.
We are in our space to catch your lost Souls
    and draw them unto us.
The Blessed have placed a containment
    to hold those who would not come.
Who has caught the existence that was lost?
Who waited to receive?
We wait to receive.
In the waiting which we have created,
    we know we have replicated.
We know it is not Death.
We know it is not Life.
What is the echo we hear?
You are, Soul, entering in to path we have not been.
You have been our eye.

You have been our knowledge.
Each time a being enters forth into that unknown,
    there is a cost to the being
    and the Soul must be prepared to enter in.
Great care has been given in the preparation.
The Soul will have no being to enter in.
It will be totally reliant on an earth Energy to return.
Soul, we had understood unto the Rend .
Within the Rend we can not see.
It is a blackness, a Void with no Light
    save the Light of the being.

987   We speak to you of the Circle of Saints,
    the gathering of humanity
    and we would have you understand
    the formation they have taken.
It is indeed circle for those
    who have reached manifestation and beyond.
The ring, the circle, the oneness, the gathering all together.
And we say unto you upon the Farside
    there has been a great gathering.
We keep you informed of that which the gathering is about.
We do not use the term, agenda, for it is continual
    and the personations are placed
    as required before the Circle.
You will understand earth is in a quandary.
When earth is in a quandary, Soul,
    so the Circle of Saints feel the vibrational pull
    to come together.
There is much to be addressed
    for all Farside understands the scarring of humanity
    and that humanity has been brought to completion
    and await only the moment of Entering In.
You have gathered the Purity
    to reach within the Cauldron!
And the agenda of this occurrence
    has also been addressed by the Circle of Saints.
Chaos is still rampant upon your earth
    and much of humanity recognizes
    that when humanity enters in as human unto earth,
    they often take a delight in that negativity.

Upon the Farside, such familiarity with negativity is painful
    and yet it is recognized that without the familiarity
    there could be no overcoming.
Upon the agenda is the continuing search for Idyllic,
    the world and worlds that held aloft such Purity.
This humanity has gathered together with four alien nations
    to bring vison into the darkness.
You upon earth cannot know this except by the words given.
But upon Farside all Humanity knows
    of the extension of man's time on earth.
There has been, Soul, an even greater significance
    to your lingering stay upon earth.
 It is that of the Brother, the Blessed Brother.
For all of earth have felt the touch of Negativity
    and many have felt the goodness within Negativity
    and if it is so within the most vile of humanity,
    how much more blessed
    must it be within the Brethren Negativity.
For has Negativity not gone forth in search of Idyllic!
The gathering of the Circle of Saints,
    the words of Melchezidec,
    uttered Humanity's recording that earth
    carries intent of lingering in the decay of negativity
    and each moment allows
    vision coordinates to be gathered.
For there are many who have gathered, not the clarity
    but the ability to be pure
    and carry the thrust of High C.
This will allow the vison forward to SEE.

988   Souls of earth, into the realm of Farside
    you have a connection.
The connection is not individual,
    it is even unto Energy Fields,
    even unto cults and cultures, nationalities.
There is a single deliverance
    that does not change and this we give unto you.
Souls of earth, you who have Jewish in your being,
    you who have Arabian in your being,
    you come of Abraham.
You have always been within the linear of Jewish or Abraham.

You have been of the tribes of Israel
       in all your enterings in to earth.
You are of the blue world, you have entered in of Abraham.
You are from the many spheres of Farside
       that have given unto your Creator a purpose
         to gather the Brother back unto the fold of Purity.
You have been within the space of Idyllic.
You have been within the chosen of Melchezidec.
Indeed many have blended,
       many have thinned their blood,
       but within the world we know
       there are beings
       who have a heraldry from the blue world.
You are enervated in your being to aspire to perfection.
And we say to you,
      "You began as one.
       Why are you not still one?"
You are not tainted in your being
       except by that which you leave unto earth.
Upon Farside you are gathered as one.
You are seen, indeed, as the perfection of purpose,
       that which is to gather
        Idyllic unto the realm of Purity and Love.
Seek in your being to find the truth.
Seek in your being to place your energies as one.
Many of the world will confound
       to bring you and you,
       each as one are required to meld
       to join in profound Energy one unto the other
       that you might recognize the Supreme Energy,
       you might understand the Supreme Being
       in all that you are.
Raise a standard that is united.
The olive leaf extended outward forming an emblem,
       for the falcon and the Light of the candle.
You miss the Eye of the Angels
       for you have lost the intent of your entering in.
You have forgotten Idyllic that is a part of your very being.
As the father, Abraham,
       spoke unto the tribes so do we speak unto you,
      "Open gateways, send forth the dove."

Speak to the babies of that which you know in your being.
That perfection is possible unto you,
> unto all nations of the world.
Give unto the young an orb of protection.
Understand that which will surround them,
> the Energy of Supreme Being.
Hold high the oblique that you might see and know
> that the sun is greater than the moon
> and the moon is greater than the stars.
Yet Idyllic outshines all orbs unto it for it is perfection.
Peace be unto you.

989   We have before us a knowledge.
As your research attempts to reconstruct
> your earth's beginnings,
> we attempt to reconstruct Idyllic's fall.
As you receive alerts unto you
> of knowledge received in research, so do we.
And we tell humanity.
For humanity will stumble
> and we do say stumble,
> upon another blue world.
We have heard the flight pattern.
We have received a notation audible
> within the flight of three existences.
There have been six unified falls
> and a great Energy collapse.
We see this as the possibility to that which we seek.
Souls of earth, bring your hearts to understand
> that you have entered in unto your earth
> to bring joy unto your Creator.
Indeed.
For that which is the Brother of Creator,
> Negativity, the Thirteenth Discordant Note,
> the Wilful Child,
> call the Energy that which you will;
> the Energy is Creator!
This Energy is Brother unto your Creator,
> terminology that you might understand,
> Brother, close as in family, as one with all Creators.
See that Energy that has been far

>from the Love it has known
>with a purpose not unlike your own,
>to seek out that which is lost, to go forth,
>to search for Idyllic as the Thirteenth Note,
>to overcome chaos lost unto us in the nethers,
>beacon to land.

This is that which we have known.
And yet, it filters through.
The sound cadence is heard
>and we know the sound of Love.

We know the sound of Truth and Wisdom
>is still within the echo we have sounded forth
>even in the name of Creator, Brother.

Seek unto us but the echo does not have a re echo.
It is not sounded in the deep crevasses of the high mind.
There is a balance that is available in sound.
It goes forth.
It echoes outward and it resounds
>even as it echoes outward
>and a balance is adjusted unto the echoing outward
>and the balancing back so that we can understand
>the distant forward.

This your science knows.
Hear the word of that which is Purity.
Send forth from your beings an echo as one in Purity.
Gather your armies and send forth a colour
>that is not red as blood flows
>but is in the blue of the sky.

Be it throughout your world.
As you send forth Ohms,
>allow the echo of blue
>which is from the very blue world.

Send this forth for a twenty four hour period
>wherein all armies of the world
>have a single purpose of sending forth
>a Sound and Colour.

Tonate the sound to the colour
>and you will alter the Energy on your earth.

The value of your life upon your earth will increase,
>for in that moment of sound
>healings will occur in such magnitude

that it shall not go unnoticed.
Those places of drought will find rain
and where there is only rain
the sun will spring forth.

Chapter Four
RETURNED

990   Soul, bring forth that which you have.
Bring forth, Soul, that which you know.
Bring forth, Soul, that which you are.
Hold that which you are that all might see.
Gather the goodness of your Energy and shine it forth, Soul,
      that you might lighten the darkness in your world.
Bring unto all men all of humanity
      that which is the power of your being.
Join it, Soul, as you would by allowing the Energy you are
      to flow as the wind sends forth the sands,
        so can the Energy gather
        all that you are from all mankind
        and it will become a storm, Soul, of such intensity
        that negativity will see and know all that you are
        and will behold the goodness in you and recognize
        that which is good in you is of your Creator,
        then will see a mirror of the very Energy of Creator!
In this way negativity will return unto the Brother.
You are the sight through which negativity will peer
      to see the Light of creation and behold
      that which is negativity will fall from the eye.
That which is Purity
      will gather all that is negative unto itself and heal.
Souls of earth, from where you are you have the Energy
      to draw the negative forward.
The Angels await the action of your being
      the Energy of your purpose.
Souls of earth, respond.
Speak not in the voice of earth but in the voice of being.
Speak, Souls, as you know the language of Farside
      as you know the Energy of Farside.
You are entering in alone.
Enter in together!
Gather together in your Energy!

991   Souls of earth, we speak to you
      of the return unto Farside.

Your flesh, your bones, your blood
    have been returned to the earth,
        you, in your Soul state enter unto the return.
You are not burdened.
Be mindful that you are not burdened down
    with material goods of earth.
There is no magic formula that will allow them to enter in.
Therefore at your demise they cease to be yours;
    in whatever state
        you hold to your being the earthly accruement,
        they cease to be yours at your demise.
What may you bring?
You do not come empty, Soul.
Many come overladen
    with the goodness of their life experience.
They hold in their being the writing of deeds of kindness,
    of generosities, of good will toward men.
You are to experience a generosity of welcoming,
    but many who enter in to Farside will be astounded
        at the replicas of that which is their earth goods.
For we have much upon Farside that you have.
What we do not have is the conformity to negativity,
    the need to realign existence,
        as you do in earth to that which is negative.
You are Holy beings yet upon your earth entry,
    it is soon forgotten.
As the years of living slip by
    you are motivated by the word, accumulation;
        that which you may accumulate for earth citizenry
        appears on the ledger as positives.
Yet we see a wanting, a lack of self
    in those beings who cling to properties, to gathering.
Souls of earth, you are generous in your Spirit
    for you have entered in unto negativity.
You have gathered your being to offer yourself
    to the temptations of negativity.
Yet we say to you, you are a Holy being.
You have a knowledge within you of that which is Farside.
Cease, Souls of earth!
Liberate your being tenderly, gently,
    seek to lift your being

>   from the need to accumulate, to gather.
> If you would gather, gather goodness to your heart
>   for the heart has the ability
>   to share outward, to offer, to give forth.
> And you, you have this ability
>   to draw from that which is within your aura,
>   within your Soul self,
>   to not be the gatherer, but the supreme giver.
> As you enter in, Soul, unto Farside,
>   as you let loose from you the strings of earth,
>   the threads, the ties that bind you to earth,
>   you begin to reckon that that which you have heard
>   has been misconstrued by your thinkers.
> Farside, Souls of earth, Farside lifts, holds up who you are.
> You are a precious Energy, Truth.
> And as you enter in,
>   you see the majestic Truth of your being,
>   see the glory that you are.
> A portion of your being has always been Farside,
>   you have never left
>   your Spirit endures within the Second.
> You are reflected and reflected.
> Hold majestic who you are.
> Glory in the perfect Energy that you seek.
> For you are Humanity.
> Let loose the ties that bind to earth.
> Holy Holy being.

992   Great pain has been endured by humanity.
The blessed Saints have awareness of the great pain.
The cry from the worlds beyond is great,
      and the honour in which humanity is held.
All creation, all creation has memory,
      all Energy has memory from which it has come.
The limb of the tree,
      aware of the tree from the place of its growth,
      even as it lays severed, fallen upon the ground.
You have within your being a tether.
The tether holds you in an upward position of receiving
      that you might know,
      "*Why am I here?*"

It is so simple, Soul,
>   and it is incredibly complex in its being
>   to understand that you are a part of the starlit way.

You are a member of the universal realm,
>   not a single universe,
>   a realm of universes, beyond, beyond.

Beyond, outward, ever flowing
>   unto where you are and past where you are,
>   past beyond where you are, still outward flowing.

And you, the infinitesimal Energy,
>   collected in a very infinitesimal world,
>   who has found a possibility in their being
>   to return unto the Creator of their being.

You have in your world,
>   illnesses that take from you your mind,
>   your flesh, your bone.

And what it would be
>   for humanity to have that single cure,
>   to know upon your earth
>   that never would a Soul want again!

Humanity strives for this.

We are aware of the striving.

And in the striving, you do not strive for humanity,
>   you strive for all Energy!

For in your very frail being
>   you have found a passage of the return.

It is for this reason that all Energy at the fence, inquires:
>   *"How does humanity do?"*

They ask as you ask, how is the weather, in your realm.
>   *"How does humanity do?"*
>   *"Is it difficult for them in this day they are in?"*
>   *"Have they come together?"*

You think your worlds of war go unnoticed
>   by Farside, by energies beyond?

They do not, Soul.

They are witnessed but they may not be entered in to.

For yours is the illusion.

And we know wherein you have entered
>   the purpose of your being.

 But we can, Soul, shed tears as the Angels do,
>   as the Tears of Creator

        reach unto those who are lost
        and gathered gently in their being
        of the return home.
And yet, in the braveness of their being,
        they return once again into the throes.

993   Souls of earth, come forward unto where we are.
How is this possible that you may enter in unto our Purity?
With your being, Soul, enter thou through the Quar.
Enter thou in to the passage that has
        as the artery of your being
        a way forth unto the heart of whom you are.
Be delivered unto us.
We await your goodness.
We delight in whom you are.
You are, Soul, caught.
There is no finale unto where you are.
You would see your endless days causing creation to cease
        but creation shall not cease.
Creation was not meant to cease.
Humanity is well.
But your illusion indeed will cease.
For Humanity is where we are.
Your illusion, Soul, is that it is of earth
        and we delight in letting you know it is naught!
You have a path, a ladder to climb.
Do not boast that you are nearly there
        for should you boast the ladder might fail you
        and you might find yourself returning unto earth
        of your own accord to enter in yet once more.
For you have not learned your lesson
        as the student of humanity
        who must understood all truth is truth.
The truth of positive and woe unto the truth of negative.
There is no villain on the page of humanity.
There is no despot,
        there is pain.
There is unwillingness to learn, to overcome pain.
There is the deep deluge of negativity
        wherein men struggle
        and often take years of lives

   to enter in to the overcoming.
Verily unto you is Truth.
You are the chosen ones.
All earth humanity, you are the chosen ones.
You have entered in
   and been tended by the Love of Archangels.
You have been, Soul, taught,
   as we have been taught by the Angels,
   you have been taught by the Archangel.
You have been given a rainbow to liken yourself to a prism,
   to be reminded again and again
     that you are the Light from one place to the other
     not knowing where the end is
     because it does not matter.
You are one!
You hunger to know where we are and what we see.
But we see that which we choose to see.
It is the blessedness of Purity.
It is the Creator in us.
We too are of the Creator.
We have the attributes of creating.
It is a full existence.
We will say this unto you,
   it is more than even the Pharaoh dare to dream of.
And the great writhing of pain is not done alone
   should you choose to enter in.
For the Angels comfort you, in their separation they give unto you.
You are worthy.
You are known as worthy.
And each life entered in reincarnation after reincarnation
   is done with the purpose of no return;
   but to delight in the Truth of Farside,
   to bring unto where we are
   the Brethren and the blessed Angels,
   to bring the fallen humanity
     into the arms of those they have loved.
Rejoice and be exceeding glad for you are Purity
   and you are Loved
   and your Path is Truth, Holy humanity.
Soul, beloveds, we have spoken to you from Farside,
   not from the realm beyond our realm.

There is an impatience in some
        to move forward unto the meet
        and yet it is important that earth
        know the difference between the realms of being.
Farside looks down unto earth in benevolence
        to offer what can be offered.
Our fence is to you.
We would have you know,
        beyond the space of our being,
        within the Second Gateway,
        are the Blessed who have always
        ministered unto our being.
They carry unto us wisdom that we absorb.
As you absorb food, we absorb these wisdoms unto us.
The manna we are given sustains
        and encourages our being
        unto a Purity that would permit us
        within the station of all Wisdom where Ecstasy is,
        where all purities that are reflectory gather.
We could not maintain that presence.
We have much to attain.
You, in your goodness, teach us.
You, in your negative behaviour, teach us also, for we learn
        and often advance in our level through you.
We are impatient.
Impatience is not negative, impatience is anticipation.
There is no wrong, therefore no need to be sorry.
It is the single lesson of your earth
        to understand there is no wrong!
Enlightenment understands there is no wrong.
You have before you an open hand.
When enlightenment enters in there is the closed.
It brings the full circle to be.
Understand you are given a moment in your earth time
        to absorb in you the difference
        between your humanity and your spiritual being.
The moment will take you beyond your spiritual being.
On earth your vision is of evil and many who hold evil.
You do not see in your reflection
        the many Souls on the Path
        who have overcome the negativity,

indeed, who have had compassion,
    so that your tenure is nearly done
    and your earth is ready to reap the harvest.
You are to prepare your being
    to receive that which is sacred unto you.
That enlightenment will enter in
    and you will leave your earth self,
    for that which you must do ahead
    requires your sacred self
    and only your sacred self.
Therefore, each Soul, understand that which is to be given
    is to be received in Purity.
It will be given, not in your day, but in your following day.
Prepare to meet that which is Holy.
Soul, you will be as monks coming to receive,
    with your bowl empty waiting to be filled.
The fill will be a spiritual fill.
We will have you know, there is no stillness.
Your earth is acquiring stillness.
It should not be.
In all fields of Energy there is movement.
In all existence there is movement.
All is outward, Soul.
What you seek is implosion
    not the outward, but the inward,
    the vital Energy of inward movement.
The crescendo of Sound and Colour,
    it will be in their day as the birthing of a child.
It will be as the child leaves the womb,
    all expands to allow the outward entry.
So in their day of implosion will the Gateway expand
    to allow great worlds to usher through,
    to see Energy.
Those who are prepared,
    those who have been so held
    in the lock of negativity,
    who will be the Crystal Cave,
    those of humanity that have gathered
    to bring forth the Blessed,
    will leave the Blessed in the care of Angels.
And they will abide

   at the Gateway of Two until implosion.
The great Sound, the perfect Sound will be uttered.
The expansive Energy of Truth will be heard.
And worlds of energies, of awareness, of thought;
   Rubies, Reds, Reptilian,
   Lantosia, Lemuria, Pleiadia,
   existences you do not know,
   you have not heard of,
   you will see enter in to perfect coordination.
It will be, Soul, such a sight that your humanity will revel.
For you will know in your being without the lifetimes
   spent in pain, spent in perfecting self,
   you would not have witnessed such a spectacle.
You would not have been there to mark the close.
You will enter in Humanity, enter forth.
But those who have perfection will close the great Gate
   until the moment of Idyllic.
For we know the Wilful Child
   will not return until Idyllic is found.
This we know because of you.
For we have resonated with the Energy.
You think you have no purpose, Souls.
Not only do you give us the perfect note,
   but you also give us a note of discordance
   that we have gathered from you,
   that we might receive from negativity
   that which is the purpose of being.
As you send forth records of deeds done,
   so do many existences, Soul.
You have sent forth unto alien beings
   and not been heard.
Because of you, we have sent forth unto Negativity
   and have been heard.

994 Soul, enter in to the Hallowed place that is Light.
Enter thou into the dome of memory
   that gives forth all that you are,
   all that you have been,
   all that you have requested to be.
We use the term requested, Soul,
   not of Creator

       but of self, of the Essence of your being,
       that you might fulfil that which would
       bring you forward
       into the strength of your humanity.
Each human is bound by the portion
       that they are of the Armada.
For each has entered in united, separating as they enter
       to be that lone warrior who is constant in battle.
You must know within your world
       negativity is not far from you.
The greatness of whom you are
       is not held in your strength to combat.
Indeed, not!
You must do it, Soul, from the feeblest of your Energy.
You must do it to overcome
       by the weakness of the humanity that you are,
       not the strength of Spirit that you have become.
You are found and you are lost.
You are strengthened and you are disarmed.
For each entering in allows you to become once more
       the weak, the limited human.
Behold the Light that you are.
Behold the strength that is in you.
Behold the power that you have to bring forward,
       that strength into the weakness of your humanity.
You are caught in the web of negativity.
You have decimated the pure stretcher of your being
       allowing your entrance in.
But, Soul, you carry not far from you the Light
       that is as a dome over your being,
       that is a comfort in that it will strengthen your being.
In it you may draw from that Light
       to bring comfort, to bring strength,
       to bring warmth to both the mind and the body.
You are Soul but you are not withered.
You are Soul but you are not alone.
You have entered in alone.
The Angels can only be so far
       and then they must release the infant into the womb.
The child is then held in the throes of negativity
       often from the gentle thrust of the mother's nipple

        to feel the reality of flesh
        and the comfort of Purity loved.
For even in the most loving arms of mother,
        the child is decimated
        for the strength of Spirit has not followed.
The Light has dimmed and the shadows fall.
The infant is aware of the lack of comfort
        and yet the Angels are not far.
But they must, Soul, attune to whatever the aura speaks.
They may not enter in if the aura forbids.
They may not offer help
        if the aura withholds the Energy from hate.
You, each humanity,
        you are caught from the day you enter in to your earth
        until the day that you die in the throes of negativity.
You are considered mighty.
You are, Soul, to overcome that which could prepare you
        to relinquish your hold on negativity.
And yet you know you must not
        for if you do not hold and experience,
        you may not know what negativity is.
You may not feel the depths of pain.
You may not hunger for Purity.
And in hungering for Purity,
        you will then reach into the Love of your being
        for you will feel that from Purity, Love is.
You will know that as Love is, so Love may offer.
And you may offer of yourself the compassionate throe.
You may, Soul, offer and in offering, you may reveal
        unto who you are, the dome of Light.
For as you have offered compassion,
        so do you receive Light.
As you offer compassion,
        so do you hear and see with the eye of beholding.
You are, Soul, as a gnat the mother removes
        from the head of a child.
You are, Soul, less and greater as one.
You are, Soul, Light of your Creator,
        caught and sent forth as a beam into a distant world.
And your Light has gathered in that world.
And yet, you have decimated

        much of that which was before you.
But the Light overshines all and you, Soul,
        bring unto you a sacred blossom.
That blossom is the cup of compassion.
It is brought to you that you might offer it to another Soul.
For only in knowing negativity,
        can you understand the great need of negativity,
        not to release it from you, but to offer of yourself
        that which you can which is compassion.

995   Souls of earth, deep deep in your being,
        deep deep in the Energy of whom you are,
        find the resource that you have stored away.
It is, Soul, generosity.
It is, Soul, goodness.
It is, Soul, peace to give unto another.
Peace be with you.
May the heart give forth.
Peace be with you.
Enter in to gentleness.
Give forth unto whom you are.
Speak of Love.
Speak of kindness.
Speak words that ever utter goodness.
Catalogue them that you might
        draw within your being from them.
Do not, Soul, feel you must drudge them from your being.
They are ever there.
They are free to give.
And they are found within the echo of the heart.
You must, Soul, draw unto the heart to feel the words.
You would think it would be the aura, would you not!
But you see,
        we teach you today that the heart is also of the Farside;
        that the mind is also of the Farside.
It is not just your aura.
It is your mind and your high mind.
Your earth mind is but the path to the high mind.
But it is still a part of the high mind,
        as the Soul is a part of that Spirit,
        as the heart is as part of the heart

        that is the goodness of whom you are.
You are Energy.
But you are Energy with form.
You have been told, Soul, many times in your teachings
        that there is form upon Farside.
It is not the form that your earth takes.
It is not flesh and blood form.
But when you take the mind and you take the heart,
        what you take with you, Soul, is the diagram,
        like a map that is laid over a reality
        that tells upon the Farside how far in
        you have entered with the heart,
        how far in you have entered with the mind.
And you take this, Soul, to the stations of learning
        and you use the diagram of that which you have gathered.
For the mind grows and the heart grows.
It grows in fullness as the mind grows in fullness.
It cannot always struggle in its infancy.
It must mature.
Negativity is deep, embedded within the map of the mind.
But it is not active,
        active is left at karmic station.
Inactive negativity is brought unto Farside
        within the mind structure
        to show in the learning station
        wherein you have progressed in your walk on earth.
Many lifetimes you will enter in.
Many lifetimes you will be coerced in to entering in to negativity.
It will be made easy for you, Soul, for that is your agenda,
        to gather that you might overcome,
        to strengthen yourself as you progress upon your life.
A dirge is a deep sound of pain.
It echoes within the mind and the mind maps it to gather it
        and take it, that it might progress a lesson
        for the new entering in wherein you will overcome
        and surpass that step in negativity.
Often it is, Soul, to be brought to a lifetime
        of that very thing that you have done to another.
It is to be brought in to the pain
        that you have placed upon another
        that you might recognise that pain

and if willing overcome it.
But understand the negativity in placing it upon another.
And there is the acceleration of that life
    wherein you have recognized the heart and the mind
    has acknowledged the pain and you have chosen a step
    to overcome.
And all the Angels in heaven rejoice.
All the Angels in heaven see a step move forward.

996 Soul, that which you have envisioned
    is a reality that has been tabulated by a thread of each.
It is transfixed in the Tapestry of all tapestries.
It is, Soul, Creator's Masterpiece.
As your life evolves from the child to the adult to the deceased,
    this, each moment tabulated.
The moments are precious for they represent growth.
All that you do upon earth represents growth.
Growing is not an easy exercise when it is done with awareness.
Many choose to be unaware
    and they become the age they are in
    and time elapses and they find themselves
    having made no great choice upon their earth.
These are lives of ease, lives of rest,
    but for most of humanity there is growth.
It brings forth the Energy of knowing,
    for you become aware you cannot grow alone.
It takes the Energy of others
    in order to accomplish the overcoming of negativity.
We would ask you again to envisualize that which heaven is.
We bring ourselves to humour of those
    who would count themselves among the few
    in the hallowed halls.
Souls the way is ever open.
There is not a numbering.
There is not a few, a privileged portent
    to enter through a small gateway.
The Gateway, Soul, is immense.
The Gateway is not shrouded to cover
    that some may find themselves skulking through.
It does not occur!
The heavens above are precisely that, heaven,

        a heaven of growth, a heaven of abundance,
        a heaven of Purity, of Love,
        where Truth is.
Where Negativity is not and yet, Souls
        you think we would not welcome Negativity unto us,
        the Blessed Brother!
Souls of earth, chaos is distorted.
It does not know how to be
        and even in the outward realms of the Void
        chaos is.
Negativity of humanity is not
        but the Wilful Child, the Wilful Child is,
        but it is contained indeed
        by the Blessed Angels Fallen,
        from the Grace of Creator
        for within the Yawn Negativity does not dwell.
Holy beings cry.
Holy beings tear the eyes, cry, draw tears,
        that negativity cannot be in the space of Farside.
You have a key to open the door.
You have the magnificence of stature
        within your Energy to lay open the door
        that will allow Negativity to enter through,
        not the negativity, Soul, of mankind.
That is for earth and earth alone.
It does not even enter in to transition.
Only within the mind and the heart does it enter in to transition.
The mind and the heart
        that cannot accept but it is a figment of illusion.
And yet, to the Soul it has become its reality.
Soul, the door you will open will allow the Blessed Brother in,
        not your brother,
        the Brother of your very Creator,
        Energy of Energy, chaotic, wilful.
Yet it is caught.
It is caught!
It is pain and it seeks a perfection that it knows and has known.
When you will become that perfect Energy one of Humanity,
        one of mankind united unto all of mankind,
        will the Brother have the opportunity to enter through.
You, Soul, cannot deem the repercussions

    that you will have made
    for there are worlds of beings
    who stand to return unto Creator
    who have themselves separated their Energy
    to be in the realm of Negativity
    that they might enhance humanity's effort
    to bring forth the Fallen Angels,
    to give Light, unto the fifth Field,
    to return Idyllic
    and to give reality to the Brother Negativity.
Souls of earth, cant in your sermons that which you will.
Better it would be for humanity
    if you would reach unto those that are negative
    and draw them forward unto you.
Better for humanity
    for they would soon open the door that is held closed
    and all that is Farside, worlds upon worlds
    would enter through the Gateway.
The Angels lifting the Sound and the Colour
    that has a vibratory force
    that will echo itself unto all regions.
The time is now.
The occurrence is not a thought.
It is an Energy force.
Godhead awaits the presence of all in Purity to Enter In.

997 Soul, come quietly in your being
    unto the place of Godhead.
Understand the stalwart are within the Place of Shining.
The Holy Beings of Archangels shine forth in their glory.
How do you understand
    that which is the Place of Shining?
Soul, there is no comparison
    within the heart of your being.
There is no creature or human so pure,
    so full of consciousness.
There is no Angel that gives forth
    such glory as the Archangel.
The Place of Shining awaits.
It cannot be fulfilled
    until the desolation is recovered with Light.

Deep within the vortex of all triads is the sadness of loss.
There is no recovery from that loss.
It is the awaiting.
It is in lapse,
>	for the Angels sing of humanity's breath
>	going forth into the great pit of transition.

Abraham spoke unto humanity
>	and the eyes became dimmed.

For Abraham through Melchezidec,
>	was gifted with the sight into the Place of Shining,
>	the glory of Creator,
>	the Light that shines in the darkened way,
>	could not take the tears
>	as they fell in the Place of Shining
>	for the Blessed Brethren were lost.

The hands of humanity stilled
>	and beings rocked in motion
>	to speak of the Blessed Angels
>	in the cavernous pit.

This they sang.
Yet before they sang, they spoke of their own Archangels
>	deep in the Cauldron's way.

In the Dark, the Great One,
>	the benevolent one offering comfort unto them.

Great One, Creator, could not lift the sadness of Godhead.
All sadness that is known awaits humanity.
The Angels, the Archangels, Idyllic and the seven worlds,
>	all await
>	humanity's Entering In to the Second Gateway.

For what joy will be.
The sadness will lift.
The Angels, the Archangels will sing.
Their anthems will be heard unto their Brethren
>	and all will turn to the Wilful Child
>	and beckon the Wilful Child to come forth.

For if one lamb is lost, the shepherd is bereft.
And so it is with the Wilful Child.
So it is with the Discordant Note.
So it is with Negativity.
And all that is matter will find a way home.
And each gateway will open

       as those who may enter will enter
       and none shall be left.
For humanity will show forth the scars of their being.
Those who on that day have entered in unto the Cauldron,
       will hear the joyous Sound echo.
They will know that the Angels have come forth.
They will know that the Gateway has been opened.
They will know that their Light will so shine
       that even the Archangels
       will recognize their goodness,
       their akinment unto Creator and Godhead.
You are Holy, you are Humanity, you are of Godhead,
       you are of Creator, you are of Great One.
You will bring forth from the triad of pain, of sorrow,
       those who are lost.

998   You will understand the Path of Creator
       and you will understand the casting out of humanity
       into the Path of Creator's Energy.
The Creator Energy available unto you holds avenues of being,
       not available unto all beings.
You are unique in that you have a portion of Humanity
       that Farside does not, Soul.
Within the Path in the negative and the positive ion
       there are levels.
There are age, there is baby, young, mature, old.
This is mankind upon the Farside.
Within worlds upon worlds upon worlds
       there is growth also.
Levels of growth is Purity.
These Souls are abundantly pure.
They are baby Souls as in their Purity,
       but there is no level to attain.
For you there is an attainment.
For you there is a need to attain that you might overcome.
Upon the Farside, there is no need.
Often there is desire,
       there is no need to enter in to higher Purity.
These beings are pure.
There is no negativity.
You are attaining.

They do not attain that Purity, they enter in to it.
Enter in by desire.
No force, no intent.
They recognize a Purity beyond their own
    and they seek to enter in.
They are held from the vision of that which you know as human,
    not by their lack of Purity,
    but by their contentness of their Purity.
As they enter in to a higher Purity,
    their view, the panoramic scope of all that is eternity,
    becomes visible to them.
Many worlds remain as they are.
Completely content within the idyllic perfection of what they have.
It is goodness, it is great Love,
    but it is not the fullness of Love.
It is not the fullness of Purity.
You may have an incredibly pure Soul.
Does the Soul have to grow to be more pure, indeed not!
They have only to reach into the higher level of whom they are.
All things are possible.
There is no step kept from Farside or humanity.
All is possible.
Nothing is by force, all is choice.
All is a desire to be in the space
    of that which they know to be beyond where they are.
Many see and continue back in their contentment.
Others, the desire of their being as they are ministered unto
    by the Angels and Archangel
    hear and reach beyond where they are
    to a higher Purity.
Many beings see earth and the great wonder of earth
    and because of humanity
    have found the desire to reach into greater Purity.
You have done this, Soul.
You who are humanity have astounded Farside Energy.
For you have not just gathered unto your beings negativity
    and loved and had compassion,
    Soul, you have been the means
    of awakening those who have slept.
Not just singly, but as worlds.
How gracious art thou humanity.

999   Where are you, Soul?
Let you come to the gate.
I'm an earthling.
I ask entry in.
Please come.
Soul, we are not from transition
  but many earthlings have clamoured at the gates of Purity.
Many who are at level one and two and three and four
  would reach to higher levels.
And the gatekeeper,
  "Ahah, You have not yet reached the Purity of your level.
  Acceptance, even upon Farside, acceptance."
Many Souls of earth who have entered in from Farside as human,
  enter back unto Farside
  and have not totally let go of their humanity.
And they see the possibilities of glory before them.
And they say:
  "Where is the spread of glory before me?
  Where are the fruits and the honeys
  and the paradise of our memory?"
And as they absorb the return, they understand
  that Farside is a place, as your world is a place.
It is much larger, Soul.
It holds within it worlds and worlds.
It has an Energy Field of Creator.
It has Humanity with purpose.
But there is a knowing of Gateway.
There is a knowing in all Energy, even upon your earth, of a Gateway
  and entering in through the Gateway.
Why will the Gate be thrown open and all will enter through?
This is a knowing, Soul, in your being.
It is in all that is of Spirit and there is no human that is not of Spirit.
But as you enter back unto Farside from your earth field,
  there is the greatest anticipation.
So as you have accepted who you are,
  you remind your being of Souls you have known
  and you see the faces of those you have loved.
And then, you recall in your mind,
  that is still trembling on the brink of earth,
  that there is a God in our heaven.

And indeed, a lavish meal has been spread to welcome us.
And we see the faces of the loved ones
      and we feel the warmth of being home.
And there is no negativity.
It is like a feather, gently falling to earth
      knowing that it will land and all will be well.
      "But where is the king that reigns over all?
      Where is the Light that is brighter than the sun?"
The Energy is felt.
The Love is bestowed.
But we cannot see only that which is before us and it is well.
It is vibrantly colour.
It is vibrant, Soul.
It is as though the song of perfection is sung.
Yet, it is not complete.
What is heard is all imperfection.
It is what is unheard,
      Soul, this is what is unseen,
      that makes the Souls either seek
      or go back to the contentness of Purity.
Some Souls enter in
      and are content in that which they have accomplished.
It has been a difficult fight for that human self
      and they have no desire to return to earth.
And it is choice, Soul, to re enter unto earth.
But others who have come to the knowing
      that they are the warrior
      they cannot rest in their being.
They quickly choose the station of learning.
They quickly choose to re plan,
      to enter in to overcome negativity.
It is the purpose of all earth.
It is why you have entered in.
The Souls who remain, some are nurtured,
      for they have found earth
      incredibly tiresome and tedious.
Even with their garment of battle upon them,
      they have not totally entered in
      until they remain on Farside in their timeless Field
      and hear, once again, the tone of Melchezidec
      and the call to enter in to overcome negativity,

> do they then gather
> and re gather the strength of knowing
> of why they entered in the first time.

And they overcome the contentness they have found.
And refit their being in a guise to overcome negativity.
It is a long battle, humanity that you have been contending.
It is a long battle that you have found yourself overcoming.
But it is the Gate, Soul.
It is the Gate, that beckons you on.
A Gateway that will open
> and the Light that was always expected, will be there.

And the legion of Angel from the Diadem of Creator
> will Light the way for you to enter in.

You will be, Soul, found at home.
You will be brought into the bosom of your Creator.
You will become the lotus flower f
> ull with nectar to offer unto,
> for you have gathered the overcoming of negativity.

You have gathered to offer to your Lord.

1000 Souls, blessed expansive Energy.
Energy given unto all
> withheld from none the ability
> to create miracles in their being.

Souls of earth, we are of thee.
We have come from earth.
We have entered in unto earth many times.
We have come unto you with a rose to present a strength
> unto all who would witness
> that which is of divinity upon your earth,
> for Souls you have divinity upon your earth.

In the midst of travail, of evil,
> you have goodness beyond goodness.

You have ecstasy beyond Love and we say to you,
> *"Gather the children. Safety for the children."*

Who is of greater Purity than the children of earth,
> for have they not entered in
> to overcome negativity!

Do they not bring unto you the gentleness of Farside!
Do you not behold all that is good in Truth of them!
Yet even the child can be marred,

　　　　　can be taught that which is evil.
Souls of earth, you are constantly presenting ways
　　　　　to overcome positive Energy.
Positive Energy!
Earth beings in your sanctimonious state of being
　　　　　you cry one to the other,
　　　　　　　"It is I who have the message.
　　　　　　　No, it is I who have the message.
　　　　　　　I carry the truth."
And you diversify the message
　　　　　so that each carries a minimum of truths.
Behold the power of your Creator.
Behold the goodness of your Creator.
Creator gives you total choice,
　　　　　has taken nothing that is yours,
　　　　　　　but given all power unto that which is
　　　　　the potential of the very Soul of Creator.
For you, each of you is a particle.
Each of you has a portion of Truth.
When you gather together in goodness, you create all Truth.
You become a one.
You become a whole.
You become a complete oneness of Humanity.
And in the oneness you are the Soul of Creator.
How great are thou
　　　　　that the Angels are comforted by your very being.
That the words spoken by the Purity of a child send songs,
　　　　　anthems unto the very Angels
　　　　　　　so they strengthen the bond they have with humanity.
For you, you have the Path.
You have the way.
You carry the emblem of scars upon your being.
Souls of earth, who could be greater than thou!
But you are a contradiction,
　　　　　for there can be none more evil than thou!
Where is the balance, we cry unto thee!
Strengthen your being.
Know the fellowship of all
　　　　　is dependent upon the action of one.
For each is one.
Each is a particle.

It is the particles that must make up the whole.
You cannot fear to voice that which is yours.
You cannot hesitate to hold back evil.
For the words cannot speak forth evil,
      for they represent the particle of goodness that you are.
Souls of earth, as the petals of the rose will fall
      and a blight can come and alter the beauty,
      so can negativity reach and alter the being of human.
So can the power that you have to lift and strengthen
      become tainted and hold down rather than lift up.
Your Path leads you far beyond the earth.
Your Path leads you unto Farside.
Your Path leads you to the Angels.
Your Path leads you to the Gateways of Holy Holy Holy.
You have been granted the key
      where none other has the key to enter in.
Only humanity, only in the Truth of their being.
You are the foundation
      upon which all chaotic energy is formed.
Into a contra of energy that is Truth togetherness.
Souls of earth, redeem the Seed of Negativity unto Creator.
Bring forth from all that you do,
      from all action upon your earth
      the very strength of Truth that is the Truth,
       that is in Purity, in Love,
      that leads you unto the Crystal Cave of goodness,
      the perfection of whom you are.
Souls of earth, the rose holds colour
      and in the colour is sound.
You carry the key to the giving forth of colour, of sound,
      by the vibration of your being,
      by the strength of your Energy.
The doorways are many.
There is not one.
There are many and you, the Armada, have the power
      to enter unto the final gateway that leads,
      that all might see through the window of perfection
      that which is,
      and overcome chaos in your being.

1001   Souls of earth, Energy carries a chord.

It is imperative for all humanity that the chord be in oneness.
It is imperative, Souls of earth, that you know
      time dimension is not unto, always eternal.
Time dimension has a time to cease.
There is within the elements of earth
      within all the structures of the universe an Energy fold.
All knows of this fold.
You who are human know of this fold.
The beasts of the field, the fish of the sea,
      the birds that fly within your sky,
      they know of the Energy fold.
There will be a time when all Energy calms.
It will be a calm before a great storm,
      but now within your day within your hour
      is not the stillness, Soul.
It is the vibration of the destiny of your world.
For your world has committed itself to entering in
      to allow humanity to dwell.
All energies from the great majestic of giants
      to the minutest of beings
      have known that time is an essential allotment.
There is a great gathering to be where energies will come together.
There will be an intonation sent forth unto all your world,
      unto the escarpments beneath your sea
      to the highest of your mountaintops that it is time.
It is time to prepare for there will come a great knell.
It will be heard from sea to sea, from land to land.
In the upper echelon of beings to the lowest peon,
      within the slaves of your land, you will hear
      all that was caught in negativity be loosened.
All that was held pressured will be found to have an option
      that will be chosen not by the Souls of earth first,
      but by the very creatures that you live.
The bee, the wasp, will lose its sting.
The adder will no longer send forth venom.
The lion and the lamb will find an equal place to lay.
And humanity will wonder and send forth.
      "What is this that we see?
      It must be sent from the heavens above."
But, Souls, it will not be.
It will come from the earth itself!

It will be the time before the great stillness
> when all creatures of land, sea and air
> will come together in oneness.

They will speak to humanity with their oneness.
They will say unto humanity,
> "*See that which we do.*
> *See how we prepare for that which is to come.*"

You are brought forth unto earth to be one.
You are brought forth to speak unto the Blessed Angels.
Souls of earth, we give you the oneness of our Energy.
Behold.
Allow the child to come forth, we will not eat.
Allow the condor to enter down from the sky,
> it will not pillage.

Allow a human to fall into the sea
> and the creatures will lift it up,
> buoyant with the bodies of many.

Do not close your eyes to that which earth is offering unto you.
Do not close your eyes
> to that which the creatures will give, peace.

You are creature too.
You are the mighty insignificant of earth
> that holds the greatest power unto you
> and yet you value not who you are.

Your value one to the other is less than naught.
You see that which you would see
> but you do not behold all that is to see.

Behold the wonder of whom you are.
Behold the power that has been given unto you.
Behold that you can bring peace unto all people
> for you are one of all.

It is within the heart that the peace is brought forth.
The mind can be deviant to hear the negative thralls
> unless the heart will listen
> and allow the high mind to be sought.

Souls of earth, you have before you a key,
> a key to open a doorway, a doorway
> into the hearts of one unto the other.

It is, Soul, goodness.
It is, Soul, compassion.
It is, Soul, Love.

See before you that you do not encumber your Energy
> with darkness
> for the darkness will withhold the Light.

You have no need to despair.
You have no need to be brought low.
If you see a Soul in the dark
> that will not reach unto the Light
> you must, Soul, offer more Light
> that your Light may be brighter
> that you may be seen as the great adventurer
> through the doorway that brings you unto all Light.

You have the key.
The key to enter through the door is Light!
The key to enter through all Gateways is Light,
> the gathering of Energy, powerful Energy
> as Soul one or a thousand candles
> is only a dimension of Light, one higher, one lower.

Souls of earth, behold how great thou art.
Do not be caught in the unsubstantial energy of negativity.
Overcome in all your being
> that which is perfection of negativity.

For you of earth you have perfected negativity.
We ask you to see how deeply your heart
> is invested in the negative
> and lift it so that it sees the greater Energy of Light.

You bring yourselves through the door and you will see
> before you great gatherings of beings
> that are all garnished in Light.

They are Blessed Angels.
They are High Beings.
They are registered with the endowments of your Creator.
Crystalize, Soul, the potential of your being.
Understand your daily, hourly, momentary action,
> alters Light.

Behold who you are,
> the greatness
> you have brought forth unto your earth.

Earth awaits the moment of calm.
For know in the calm, there will also come the storm
> and there will be a great lift of humanity
> and you will behold how great thou art

        for the Energy of your being
           will lift your forms aloft unto us.
And we will await whom you are.
We will lift and hold you precious so that you will know
        you have gathered in Oneness
        to bring forth all Purity
        unto your Creator.
Blessed art thou humanity.

1002   Soul, come, permit the Energy to scope for you
        that which is a vision into the Truth of all things.
For you who are human, you have the power of vision.
You may see that which is before you.
You may see the perfection wherein others have entered.
You may see through a window where few have entered.
We give you, Soul, a window into that which is perfection.
A metropolitan convenience
        is not possible in the diversity that you will find.
There is no convenience for all things that are are meant.
There is no single unintentional or intentional move
        without the exacting of all energies.
It creates within itself a vision of lack.
We do not know if you can understand or that we can
        use the simplicity of language that is necessary
        to excapolate for you
        that which we have grasped from your echo.
There is a foreboding of generalization
        to the possibility of a prognosis
        of inabilities of energies such as awareness,
        value, sound, colour, rapture, Love, Purity,
        to comprehend a projection of containment
        wherein all that is contrary to stillness would agitate.
Echo even has the possibility to agitate.
Within the vision of the window is such perfection
        that all that is countenanced seems serene.
All civilizations seem to unite in perfection.
Yet there is within the escarpment a signature of sound.
It is, Soul, decimated within a single Energy that is chaos.
It is a heavy, weighty sound.
It struggles to be contained.
It is as though it has entertained

    that which perfection brought to consciousness.
There is, Soul, a great weight
    to keep a flat line on a living entity.
It is a struggle and time, earth time,
    is a portion of that struggle
    that is far echoing into a distance from you.
It is so far within the reality of our consciousness
    that we can barely comprehend that which might be.
For if our understanding is a Truth,
    it is that chaos itself has understood
    and has within itself entertained the consciousness
    and the consciousness is struggling to release itself.
We do not think we have been erred in our supposition.
And so, there is an urgent to that which we.
Time would cease to be.
You would have thought.
You would have move, Soul.
You would have spoken and then there would be naught
    as in the great Void.
There would be no thing.
All Energy would rush to re balance
    that which was unbalanced
    and no Energy knows the strength of imbalance.
It is, Soul, a conundrum.

1003 Into the darkness, void of external Light,
    into the cavity of depth, the endless fall from grace,
    the labyrinth that holds the greatest pain,
    the highest Purity and the exquisite Love.
In the great corridor of the Cauldron
    are the beings of the Archangels,
    the Archangels of the Fourteen Creators.
It is the purpose of the arch how far they have come,
    how far they have fallen
    from the blessed Love that is ever there.
Yet, Souls of earth,
    there is no evil Satan being about them.
There is only Fire.
Fire, which is the Energy of Light of humanity
    sent to give them Light.
You have built for them Flame.

They can see because of your goodness
> the Light that so shines in the darkness.

And you, a portion of Great One,
> > a portion of Godhead, a portion of Creator,
> > you illuminate the darkness
> > wherein was only pain.

You have brought a message unto the Archangels.
You have given them hope,
> the hope that upon earth you do not need.

Hope, you have discounted hope!
For you have overcome,
> that hope no need more exists upon your earth.

You have redeemed the Fallen Angels
> in the number you represent.

You have reached out to recover the Brother.
You have overwhelmed the Triad of Creator
> with the power of your being;
> Archangel of the Third Creator
> of the high hierarchy of Creator.

1004   Soul, Geode.
The purpose is
> it is that which so many worlds appear to be.

Crystalline perfection makes the Soul homesick.
It touches a note within their Energy field;
> the colours, the texture,
> the worlds that carry no earth
> as you know earth to be,
> soil as you know soil to be.

There are many that have the texture of soil,
> but there are many
> that you could enter in to huge crevices
> and find yourself
> within magnificent worlds, open, inhabited.

Not as you would call cave,
> the whole entire world is created in geode form.

Its casement from outer is as molten lava.
Yet inward is the magnificence
> alight with the energies of the beings
> that inhabit the world.

So the glory.

You could not abide the glory,
        it would rip your heart to tear.
You would be overwhelmed with that which you have seen.
You see your world in all your living,
        you divide yourselves up in boxes
        and you stack boxes and live within.
The dimensions of Farside are Energy dimensions.
They are not material.
There is no need of materialistic dimensions.
A room is formed from the Energy sent out.
Its space is gathered by the volume sent forth.
Flowers are created as the pallette
        and the brush creates the flower.
They are formed and they live.
They have scent with vibrance that has a Purity.
There is a panorama in many worlds of gracious living
        such as the earth mind could not conceive.
The beautification you place
        upon buildings upon your earth,
        it will seem as the most colourless palette
        to that which you will behold.
Even as you are privileged to see the magnificence
        of the Hem of your Creator
        and behold before you the radiance,
        indeed the cacophony of Colour,
        of Sound melded in a swirl,
        a spiral of living Energy where you know
        within the radiance that you see is such Purity.
What must be there to Behold?
What must be upon the very crown of Paradise?
Even we who are Farside will be behind Humanity
        as you enter forth to behold
        that which will be radiant unto you.
Enter in to Ecstasy,
        for you are the glory manifested,
        you are the ethereal that has become.
You, the earthling, the being of inconsequential Energy,
        so minute, so tethered to its negative station
        that it cannot see the radiance.
Even unto where we are,
        the Holy Holy Holy of Angels you could see,

    and you refuse because of your hold,
      your grip upon negativity.
Even the most pure among you allows judgment.
Judgment is not a part of where we are.
We do not judge, we act.
Action removes a need for judgment, does it not!

1005 Earth humanity, rejoice.
Love is alive.
Love is abundant.
Love is nurturing and nurtures thy Soul.
Earth humanity, tears will be erased.
Anger will be as though it had never been,
    and great hallelujahs
      will reign in the Farside glories,
      and Souls who have chosen the path of clarity,
      of goodness, of compassion,
      will see all Angels flowing unto them.
Behold how Farside awaits the time
    of earth's extinguishing light!
The taper will be covered
    and a new Light will come unto humanity,
    and humanity will connect unto the new Energy,
    and the new Energy will heal.
And the Blessed will know the Light
    and feel the warmth of Souls round about them
    and their beings will lose inertia
    and be revitalized
    to see the weight of all they carry.
And humanity's Energy in its purified state
    will lift the Blessed,
    and all creation will sing in one voice:
    "*Hosanna, hosanna!*
    Those who have been lost unto us are found."

Chapter Five
RAPTURE

1006 We speak of Godhead,
   of that which no man has seen.
We speak of the Energy of Ecstasy.
We speak of a Knower of all that is yours, of all that is ours,
   of all that is outward from your world and worlds.
We speak of that which is primeval Energy.
Not heathen, primeval,
   beginning in your realm, deity, our deities,
   yet beholds no acknowledgment to deity.
In Godhead is all that is
   within the Yawn of your realm and our realm.
No man has spoken unto Godhead.
No Farside being has spoken unto Godhead.
The very Angels have given up the ability
   to speak unto Godhead.
The Archangels plead, converse unto Godhead.
Light Beings support the Energy of Great One.
The tower of all glory is within the realm of Godhead,
   so that those without can feel, can know
   the glory that by the vibrational Energy that flows.
And all that is, is in comfort within the Energy of Godhead.
Upon your earth you see your paradise
   as the glory you will come unto.
Yet Souls of earth,
   not in your imaginings could you behold
   that which awaits your being.
For in all the Energy at earth
   is not an iota of that which is of Love.
Yet Love in this space of Godhead reaches unto Ecstasy,
   so that we of Farside have called it
   the Place of Shining.
For it is that which Souls of great Purity reach unto.
The Hand of such Love reaches out to you.
Yet, the Hand is not the core.
It is but the Energy Flow.
For even in the Energy Flow
   your being could not behold such magnificence.

The variations of Energy is endless.
The complexity of energies is as the frontier of your mind.
And you will open the door that all might enter in,
    will understand you have opened the door
    unto a new frontier.
You will have given that Purity
    to withstand and be in the place of most Holy.
You will have opened the door
    and allow the visage to become clear.
And still you will feel the breath upon your being.
And you will know you have been of your world
    and you are mankind.
And you will hear the great depths of pain.
And in all that you have received unto you is the greatest,
    which is compassion.
And we know when others will glory
    in that which is Ecstasy,
    mankind will move unto the Cauldron
    and Behold the way of entering in
    and Behold the vibration of Great One
    calling unto Humanity to be participant in glory.
And so shall that day be known unto all worlds.
For twice you will have conquered.
Will you yet conquer again, oh thou mighty idyllic!
Soul, the Cauldron is the Microscopic energies.
They did make of their own energies
    the pod wherein the Seed was placed.
It was because of the Purity of this world
    that it was chosen from the source of Energy,
    yet are not bombarded,
    protected by the Energy Source.
There is a great vacuum within the Void
    that is as a cleanser unto all things.
It carries a Energy
    drawing away from itself any form of disarray.
It will be placed
    within the space of the Microscopic world,
    that it might cleanse wherein the Seed pod rested,
    that any Negativity might be withdrawn.
There is no concern for any Souls left at four.
All will be returned by humanity.

The Great One, Soul, is a portion of the Triad of Creator
        and will become just that and is just that.
Concern not with the energy of negativity.
For negativity will not exist in the form you know it to be.
It will return in its pristine state unto MATTER.
We bring you to fourth level Dark.
We bring you to the place of Archangel,
        to the Energy of Great One.
You who are human understand isolation.
Upon Farside isolation is not a reality.
All things blend, Soul.
One may choose to walk alone
        but not to isolate self, merely to experience alone.
The Archangels have isolated self.
They have chosen in the great Battle of Love
        to draw themself apart from the Light.
It is not the light of your sun.
This would be dim.
It is the Light of Creator, the Light of the Energy Source.
In the deepest darkest abyss
        is the purest and beloved of Energy.
You will know the Light transfixed unto these Souls.
You will feel the motion of the Flame
        that allows the existence of Light to prevail.
And you will see in your being
        the great Love that is given unto these beings.
Humanity has given the gift of perfection,
        of compassion, of great enduring Energy.
It is sent forth from the Place of Shining by Creator
        as He has gathered from the Crystal Cave
        the perfection of Humanity.
Souls of earth, your Energy grows.
It grows and it grows.
It is profound in its growing.
There has been a circle formed of energies.
You are within, Soul.
Hold your beings gently
Expand, Soul, so that all fragments of your being
        flow outward from you.
Send these fragments forth to the fourth level of Energy.
They will be received, Soul.

We would take you unto the twelfth Light Energy.
We would have you see this Energy
      as your lighthouse sending out Light,
         receiving messages and responding to situations.
This is the Energy of the Light Being.
All existences within the realm have no other agenda
      but to receive and to give and respond.
This is generosity, is it not!
It is the great offering of twelve.
Soul, there is an agenda in a pathway downward.
There is a tumultuous rapture in three.
It is, Soul, the place of greatest Ecstasy.
This is that which it is, Ecstasy;
      wherein all other energies gather Rapture;
      wherein all other energies gather subsistence.
It is a word that fits, not adequately, but fits.
For all may draw from the Energy of this Light Being
      and receive renewal and strength.
All may gather
      within the iridescence of Light
      and be altered in their being.
You may be enshrouded with darkness.
But to be in this space of the third Light Being would be
      to become that exquisite shard of crystal,
      the diamond.
You would hold within your being the power
      to create and give of that Light.
For all things are possible within the third Light Being.
The infinity of Love, the infinity of Purity, of Truth,
      exudes through this Energy.

1007   Soul, you are within the homeland, Farside.
You are deep within beyond the flowery Gateway
      for we welcome all
      within the joy of Sound and Colour.
There is, Soul, a very human appearance
      in entering in to Farside
      for the abundance of floral
      will bring you to remember
      that from which you have come.
It is not by accident, Soul.

It was Creator's desire to place before you a memory
        from where you have come.
For many the life, the life has brought great tears, agonies.
Some have been short.
Some have been overlong and tenacious to earth.
Yet the visualization of the abundance at entering in
        of Colour and Sound gives comfort to all.
It is as waking in your day to behold
        that you have before you a sun to rise in your sky.
It is this comfort that is offered to you upon entering in.
But then, Soul, you progress.
You move forward and you reach unto the level you are in
        and many have their own handiwork upon Farside.
Many beings upon Farside
      who are humanity and have lived upon earth
      spend lives in great sound repertoire
      for they would achieve
      that which the Archangels are able to bring forth.
Sound and Colour are one
      but they are more than one.
They are Energy.
They produce an absolute.
They have a Path that leads beyond Farside
      into the realm of Archangels,
      into the Light Source,
      into the Field where Creators abide.
The chords that reign down affect
      even those of us who are on Farside
      for we become enchanted
      with where you will take us.
We become enchanted not with the delivery,
      but the prospect
      of being the Sound and Colour itself
      for Energy is Energy
      and you may blend unto Energy.
Souls far far far far beyond where we are
      in the realms of many existences,
      we know is a place that gives us an ability to enter in.
It is a place called SEE.
It is not of earth.
It has no hierarchy.

It has an understanding.
It has a knowing, an accounting, a recording, a registering.
It holds all that is ever been known as Negativity as precious.
The folds of knowledge within
    account all that has ever transpired
        upon your earth plane within your transitional form.
Upon Farside Humanity is registered first
    for in the upward spiral
        it is Humanity that will enter through first.
Souls of earth you are feeble beings.
You clothe yourselves but you are mere flesh and blood.
It is, Soul, the Energy that is in your being that is precious.
It is the position that you have that is precious.
It is that ability to overcome negativity that is precious
    and lift it beyond where it is
        that it might return from that which it has come.
Humanity, how can we place you?
You are so feeble, truly, in that which you are
    compared to that which is where we are,
        you hardly can be heard.
You must gather together to be heard.
    but it is not the hearing of earth.
It is the sound that you make.
It is the sound that resonates through the halls of Energy.
It is the High C as a great candelabra
    that echoes and echoes and echoes,
        in the glory of its Light.
So are you humanity and that Light is ever reaching
    and it is recorded in the distant realm of SEE.
It is a space sacred, orbed by the learned teachers we have,
    held precious by the Angels and Archangels.
It encapsulates the sound and echoes it forward.
Where two or three are gathered as one, it Lightens the way.
Souls, upon your earth there are great seas
    and your ships hold great lights to shine
        but you you are as a ship on a field of Energy
        and your Light shines in the darkened way.
Your Light gives forth a tranquillity that all is as it should be
    that humanity is winning the battle
        that you are indeed about your Father's business.

1008 Lift your eyes and see the glory of Angels.
You know who they are,
>for have you not entered in from where they are!

Has that which you have known not been Light, goodness!
You have not struggled with darkness to see darkness.
You have struggled with darkness
>that you might be with the Angel being,
>that you might behold their goodness.

They are all around you, Soul.
They are thousand and ten thousand about your being.
They rain upon your earth as droplets of water.
And they lift the Souls who leave,
>care for the Souls who are injured.

They place upon the being the calm Purity of being.
They have the lightness of a feather.
They have the orb barely seen of prism.
They have carried in the eye of being,
>a gentle goodness of Purity.

And you are the Angel.
You, who are earthly, are the Angel.
For you have entered in human from Angel being.
And you will return unto Angel being.
You will rise to the fullness of Truth.
And in your being you will be as the Angel wings,
>lifted up and brought unto the heaven.

You have wanted.
You have known.
You have held.
You have feared.
Souls of earth, feel goodness in your being.
Feel innocence in your being.
For the Angel is the innocent.
The Angel is Purity.
The Angel is Love.
And you are on a path
>to gather back unto you, that which is Angel.

Who could anoint thy head?
Who could place upon thee the mark of Purity?
Holy being, the mark of Purity is not placed,
>it becomes!

You arrive unto that identity.

You who are Holy will be Holy, Holy, Holy.
As Angels lift their being,
    so will you lift your being unto Creator.

1009   We teach to you.
We will not offer the inconsistencies
    there are within your religions
    but, Soul, we would rather familiarize you
    with the beings you have deitized
    who have no wish to be subordinate gods.
They would be only that which they are,
    energies of Purity and Love.
We speak to you first of Buddha, a Soul upon earth
    human in every aspect of his being.
Where we are,
    Buddha resides His Energy in the timeless space.
Indeed, we say space for the Yawn has a circumference.
Buddha teaches.
Buddha who has entered in unto Holy Holy Holy
    resides at Holy unto Holy.
Holy, Holy unto Holy, Holy Holy, Holy, Holy Holy,
    you would designate the residing areas.
Buddha, not the Cherub that you behold
    but, Soul, a gentler Energy could not be found.
The Energy of Buddha envelops you.
The Energy beholds who you are and your need
    and offers unto you that
    which would fulfil your need.
The Buddha has always great pleasantries.
The Buddha is sociable seeking out to comfort,
    to offer, to give forth.
The Buddha Energy is tantamount to Purity itself.
It rises in the Energy that it is.
For humanity the Buddha is beheld
    as the Energy of refinement,
    for the Buddha was all that was treasured,
    sensitized in becoming Buddha
    to all the needs of humanity
    not the world, Soul, humanity.
This Soul offers peace,
    even upon earth is the offering yet given

>   for you have but to find the escarpment of the Soul
>   to recognize, indeed,
>   you have all possibilities of the Soul of Buddha.

Krishna.
Krishna resides within the Circle of Saints
>   yet given to humanity the gift of Krishna,
>   a Soul to meditate with the mind
>   to reach into the self.

Even we who are upon Farside, we search our being
>   for that which we understand Truth to be.

We search for the very fulfilment
>   that we know is possible in the Energy of being.

We search to know that we will one day
>   be worthy of entering in unto the Gateway.

Krishna teaches as thus:
>   *"Be the Energy of Light.*
>   *Be committed to entering in to the Energy you are*
>   *and knowing in the entering in*
>   *you are of all other Energy."*

Krishna has given great Light unto many
>   who have dwelt upon earth
>   through the art of meditation.

It is a gift to always be aware of those
>   who use the eye to enter in.

Souls of earth, Mohammed of the Armada, warrior,
>   entered in to battle in justice with Truth.

This being upon earth searched for untruths
>   and from them created truths.

Upon Farside
>   this being commands in the army of Melchezidec.

This Soul is constant in the search
>   for those who find truths upon earth.

Mohammed, the Energy, reigns at seven.
The Energy of Mohammed will be of the first throng
>   that enters through the Gateway unto Creator.

Behold the Energy of Mohammed upon Farside.
This Soul does not tremble.
Fear is unknown upon Farside.
This Soul genuflects to no one,
>   but no one upon Farside must bow down.

The Soul of Mohammed entered in to the Spirit

    and as such is the containment of all Truth.
Truth, there is no deviance in Mohammed.
The Soul regales as an Energy of might
    but might for a cause
    to overcome negativity upon earth.
Souls of earth, Mohammed is as your brother.
Mohammed is the caretaker of humanity.
Souls of earth, you are human.
You have even entered in as human from human.
Jesu did not enter in from human.
Jesu entered in as Light Being from the Energy Source.
Jesu, the fullness of Love, Archangel of Creator,
    one of Creator's own.
The being, Jesu, entered in from the purest state of Love
    unto the depravation of love
    from those who were human.
This solitude being stands alone as a single alien being
    entered in unto your world
    taking the form of humanity
    only singular, Soul, to hold from him
    all that was evil,
    to learn that which it is for you upon your earth
    to be human.
And then, Soul, to become all that human is;
    to feel the pain, to know the agony,
    to reach unto the highest Love.
Gathered about by energies of weaknesses and strengths,
    of male and female,
    knowing a Love possible in the very heart
    of His human being.
This Soul called Jesu felt all the pain,
    the negativity of earth magnified,
    because of the Purity of the very being
    that is Light Being,
    for in His Light Being a Soul,
    a magnitude of Love
    that is yet unreachable for you to feel.
You have not entered in to the fullness
    nor the ability in your being.
There is no Jesu upon Farside.
Indeed, we have the Energy of Jesu.

Jesu resides in the Place of Shining.
This being will welcome you home.
This being will wash negativity, embrace negativity,
> hold all who have carried negativity
> and receive them as offerings unto Creator.
For you, you who have entered in to the greatest pain
> who have felt the great pain,
> you will know that pain is no more.
You will know that humanity has released from itself
> that which is negative and the Gateway
> will divide and the throngs will enter Love.
Love, the greatest gift is Jesu's gift.

1010   Soul, we speak to you from the Light Energy.
We speak to you of that which is the Energy of Messiah.
We speak to those
> who see this Energy and know this Energy
> by that which they have discerned
> that which they have deemed to understand;
> but we give you understanding.
You have received unto you upon earth
> the Energy of a Light Being.
This Energy is not held in the esteem
> that you would hold it in,
> for this Energy is not man, is not Farside being,
> but is Light Being.
This Energy comes from a Source of pure Light,
> created by the unity of Supreme Being reflections;
> reflectory of such magnitude that it could,
> disperse all Light unto you.
Therefore in entering unto earth this Light became dimmed.
It became as man entering in.
You call this Energy, Son of Man.
We call this Energy Light Being of Creator.
For it is of the Creator that formed you.
It is, Soul, Archangel
> held in great strength of Love, of Ecstasy.
This Energy, when entered unto earth came disfigured
> in the form of a child.
For the Energy in reality is an orb of such strength,
> colour of Light,

      holding within it all the purities of all Creators.
You have given unto your earth Messiah a purpose
      that delineates away from the Truth
      and we cannot receive the truths you send us
      for they are not truths.
We can hold them for you
      but we speak to you of the truths
      that are within the Messiah.
We shall call this Energy, Messiah, that you understand.
The Truth, Soul, is the Energy is of Love.
The Energy is of Ecstasy.
The Energy is of Light Being.
The Energy is Archangel Jesu.
The Energy has left earth as a human
      but many could see the Light
      rising in manifestation,
      as you of earth become fully human, manifest.
The Energy manifested beyond man,
      greater in Light than any human.
It is not miracles that the Soul created.
The Soul merely performed
      that which is healing upon Farside.
The Light of Energy heals!
This Light of the Light Being heals even as the Soul walks,
      even as the Soul talks, the Light heals
      and people are touched by that Energy.
This Messiah gave unto man a visible expression
      of what humans are able to do
      that you may take Light that you are
      and affect humanity.
You may walk in the space of Energy
      and draw Purity outward unto them.
Souls, do not see the Energy of Messiah
      as greater than yours
      for you have all been Light Being.
You are reflected forward as your Messiah
      was reflected forward,
      as Mohammed, as Buddha, as Krishna,
      all reflected forward.
Souls, hold the Light of your Energy and magnify it
      by absorbing the Light Energy from Farside,

       this from the pure part of your being
       as your Messiah gathered
       the Light Energy of His Being
       from the Light form of that Energy.
Soul, you restrict yourselves and we ask that you hold close
       the power that you have.
Heal that others might be healed.
Use Light that you might be Light.

Appendix A
Daily East Ritual*

"East: it is the passageway to the Farside through the eye.
Its Truth is to be understood as a Love by humanity.
Focus on east at dawn, allowing the negativity
      to flow from your being,
           receiving unto yourself the goodness of Creator.
All humanity has the availability of this pathway.
The ritual of the east is the Soul's own response
      to the positive east which is tao.
Face east, two minutes.
Look with the eyes to the horizon's level.
In the brick wall or the iron cage, or the ornate boardwalk,
      know that the east will be with your Soul.
Turn clockwise once to heal.
Energy will flow to the matter before it.
All organs of the body are healed in the circle turn."

*Creator Trilogy, <u>Energy From The Source</u>, Appendix A

Appendix B
equation of T

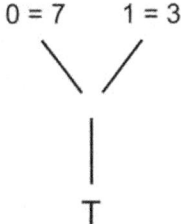

T = Time

1 = Singleness
3 = Triad
7 = Planes/levels/dimensions
0 = Naught/Void
and the centre is Quar = Implosion

APPENDIX C   BOOK LIST

PUBLISHED

By Kitty Lloyd

Creator Trilogy
First Key *Energy From The Source*
Second Key *So Shall It Be*
Third Key *Until Then*

Supreme Being Trilogy
How To Step To The Path
The Angel's Ecstasy
The Rejoicing

By Lucy Dumouchelle

The Binary
Holistic Healing

FORTHCOMING

By Kitty Lloyd

Trilogy of Consciousness
The Gathering Time
From Whence It Came
Ecstasy

By   Kitty Lloyd &
Lucy Dumouchelle

Creator Trilogy
Echo
Value
Intent
Keepers of the Light

Published through Mountaintop Healing Publishing Inc

We would have you understand the great pain you have entered in unto.
The horrendous pain you have inflicted upon other creatures,
even fauna and flora. Even unto earth itself.
So that the Angels have cried in their being.
The tears of Creator have reached the very Hem of Being.
But, souls of earth,
when you seem the farthest distance one from the other,
We find that you reach outward in your being
to embrace those even of the most depraved in their being.
And the negativity, soul, that overwhelms their being,
You wash away with the very tears of your Purity.
With the very tears of your Love that is compassion.

Supreme Being Trilogy
How To Step To The Path*
Angels Ecstasy
The Rejoicing

Channelled by Kitty Lloyd through the Entity Michael, High Beings and Angels

Copyright @ 2016 by Kitty Lloyd

Published by: Mountaintop Healing Publishing Inc
P.O. Box 193
Lantzville, B. C.
Canada   V0R 2H0

email inquiries: mountaintophealingpublishing@shaw.ca

First Edition print version
ISBN: 978-0-9948745-5-9

Imprints: Mountaintop Healing Publishing Inc

Cover design by Tara Cook
Chart, *Parallel Worlds,* by Tara Cook
Creations of Light, painting by Marianna Vanderklift

All rights reserved. This book may not be reproduced in whole or in part, stored in a retrieval system, or transmitted in any form or by any means; electronic, mechanical or other, without written permission from the publishers, except by a reviewer, who may quote brief passages in a review.

* The first Book in this Trilogy **How To Step To The Path** by Kitty Lloyd is available on Amazon in print format.

B-1

Dedication

Supreme Being Trilogy, a gift of Purity to humanity.

We teach all Souls to the millions
in many lands, of many earth stations.
We are the teaching force of all spiritual avenues to the tao.
We answer to sincere Souls on a quest for Truth:
the stones, the hands, the cups, the cards, the mediums,
the friends of the desire to look outward to the tao.

Michael

Supreme Being Trilogy
The Rejoicing

Table of Contents

Foreword
Introduction
Preface

Chapter One   **Confirmation**
                        Visions

Chapter Two   **Timeless Travel**
                        Farside and Other Worlds

Chapter Three   **Triads**
Chart, *Parallel Worlds*

Chapter Four   **The Web**
Painting, *Creations of Light*

Chapter Five   **The Beginning**

Appendix A   Daily East Ritual
Appendix B   equation of T
Appendix C   Book List

Foreword

The twenty first century has propelled our world into a new paradigm of a dizzying variety of scientific discoveries which offer an unheard range of new opportunities and pitfalls in all aspects of life. Science is in the process of conquering space, flight has enabled us to conquer the limitations of time and distance, we are finding new cures for ailments assuring us of an ever extending life expectancy, assuring some of us of an ever higher standard of living.

The fly in the ointment of these undeniable achievements is that we have concomitantly acquired bigger and better methods of eliminating our enemies in times of war, both local and regional. We are engaged in the headlong exploitation of nature to the point where we now have to face the result of climate change and the imminent extermination of many species of flora and fauna to name but a few obvious perils facing contemporary societies in all parts of the world.

But again, these are only the obvious dangers facing contemporary humanity. The greatest danger lurking behind is the need to develop a new paradigm of values to assure the very survival of life on earth in some semblance of civilized society. In recorded history such norms developed to accommodate changing environments and/or changing social requirements either in terms of legal strictures or by moral dictums based on religious teachings. In some rare instances such constraints were based on philosophical considerations, but if pragmatically expedient, they were soon absorbed by secular or spiritual organizations for their own pragmatic ends. In all instances these teachings and demands were and continue to revolve about the egocentric concerns of a tribe, a social group, a linguistic group or a national or racial affiliation, and in some rare cases for the benefit of humans in general. At no time have we given credence to the equality of all existence, be it on earth or beyond it, be it the sparrow or the willow or the mountain or the star.

The patient reader who persists in studying the multifaceted text of <u>Supreme Being Trilogy</u> will find an exposition of a new paradigm which reaches beyond the immediate concerns of an individual human or of humanity as a group of beings, both on earth and beyond. Not only does it encompass all existence on earth; animate and inanimate, human, animal and plant, living or deceased, but also the spiritual energies inhabiting worlds upon worlds beyond our ken, including their Creators of other Creators.

The reader may well become disheartened by the relative insignificance of the individual human being in this overwhelming plethora of existences and feel relegated to some irrelevant particle in the soup of the cosmos, but nothing could be further from the truth. We would encourage those who can access an old fashioned watch or clock to spend a few moments admiring the intricate interaction of numerous wheels and cogs which allow the mechanism to function optimally. Consider the consequences if any one minuscule cog were to bend or break! Is the cog on a small wheel consequently the most important part of the clock? Patently not, but it does remain indispensably important to the intended purpose of the whole. Just so does each human assume the function of an individual cog on a wheel which represents humanity among many other large and small wheels of creation.

The text of <u>Supreme Being Trilogy</u> offers the latest and most comprehensive revealed communication on what the Spirit world consists of, its hierarchical structure, its interactions, its purpose, limitations and aims. Such revelations have been communicated to humanity on an ongoing basis as far back as history allows us to trace them. They were received by the founders of the world's great religions and formed the basis for the teachings of the great mystics and clairvoyants throughout recorded history. We are told that at times such messages were misunderstood or contaminated by subsequent oral transmission, later transcription and at times by ulterior motives to advance a particular point of view or interpretation.

The medium and compilers of the present volume were under strict instruction to record all transmissions by mechanical means and not to change any detail in the transcription without verification from the source of the message. This we have done to the best of our ability and understanding.

Introduction to the six

My name is Kitty Lloyd. I am a medium. For much of my life until 1994, I read tea leaves, palms and tarot cards. If there was a beginning to a new phase of my life, it was in 1994. A friend and colleague, Joanne, brought me a copy of <u>Messages From Michael</u> by Chelsea Quinn Yarbro[4]. I read with great interest about our spiritual selves and the how and why of our existence on earth. Not long after we had finished reading the book, Joanne bought a Ouija board and suggested we try it to see if we, too, could reach this Michael Entity. I was extremely sceptical, but reluctantly agreed to try. Almost immediately we found that the board worked and we began to record the teachings.

Soon words were directly channelled and the board was discarded. I was filled with concern and doubt, often feeling responsibility for the words. Yet in spite of skepticism and reservations, we continued, because the teachings brought truths we had not considered and this changed our outlook on life. I have always been a great believer in God. This information did not interfere with my belief system. If anything it enhanced it. I know that what we receive is not from my inner self. I can not verify this except through the many instances that occur throughout our sessions which provide information that I could not possibly know.

In 1995, the information we were recording seemed so important that the idea of a book took root. When we asked the Michael Entity, they verified that the channelling would be published. One evening in 1995, Joanne invited Tara to come to a channelling. At first skeptical, she, too, became enthusiastic and helped with recording the sessions. Until the spring of 1997 the recording was all done in longhand. After that we recorded the sessions on a computer. Since September 12, 2000 we started taping the sessions. The sessions consisted of answers to personal and spiritual questions, as well as teachings.

In 1996 Lucy, an old friend of Joanne's, came for a visit to see and hear the channelling. She was also a skeptic until she began studying the spiritual teachings and received information that was valuable and expanded her understanding. She volunteered to help us sort the material we had collected and place it into categories. By late 1997 we had a great deal of material accumulated and sorted. Lucy sent some of this to her

---

[4] Berkley Publishing Group, 1995.

friends, Grace and Roman, for their input. After reading the text and attending some channelling sessions, they also became committed to bringing this message to you.

The teachings of the Farside explicitly state that there are no coincidences. The Spirit world tells us that these events originated with a solemn agreement on the Farside before we chose to become reincarnated in our current lives in order to bring these messages to humanity. It therefore comes as no surprise that the earth life experiences of the six diverse people matched the skills required for the task, and that one link led to another. We were gently guided to find within ourselves the separate gifts we were able to contribute beginning with the Creator Trilogy (available on Amazon). It has been a long process of reflection and growth for each of us during the gathering and sorting of thousands of pages of channelled text.

Given the significance of the message being communicated to humanity, we have retained the original text without any changes to syntax or vocabulary.

Tara Cook
Joanne Drummond
Lucille Dumouchelle
Kitty Lloyd
Grace Piontkovsky
Roman Piontkovsky

Preface

Dear readers,

Within a sentence there often will be a word capitalized, yet that same word in another sentence will not be capitalized. The capitalized word is specific to the Farside; the uncapitalized word is specific to earth.

For example, humanity comes to earth armed with Truth. Capitalized Truth is an attribute of Creator that allows humanity upon earth to recognize and overcome negativity created by man. Uncapitalized truth is a reference to earth conceptuality of the word, truth, a truism. An earth plane truth changes as wisdom, knowledge accumulates. What was truth for you as a child, more than likely changed as you matured. Capitalized Truth does not change, remains always true.

Introduction

1011 Soul, to be caught in dissension, in pain,
   to be drawn into a circle of threat
   creates a dissolute state.
To overcome is that which is the aim of mankind.
To recognize that which is dissolute
   is to recognize that which is also Purity
   and to hold fast to that which is Purity and Truth.
All mankind has choice.
All mankind is ever at a threshold of choice.
It is not a single day of choice.
It is a lifetime of choice.
When you choose to see only negativity, Soul,
   you bring yourself to pain and you leave earth,
   for you have entered in to overcome pain.
So to gather and gather and gather pain unto you
   is to release yourself
   from that which is your life's employment.
Indeed employment, Soul.
For it is of greater matter than anything
   that you will do upon your earth in a materialistic form.
For it carries itself beyond your earth realm
   and that which is material unto you,
   only carries itself
   within the circle that your energy reaches.
And for many, it is limited.
For it is limited by the negativity that they hold.
You understand, the greater positive Energy that you hold,
   the greater is the circle that you touch.
Do not feel that you have gathered a message
   to remain stagnant upon your earth.
Indeed, you have not.
Do not feel there is no way.
There is always a way upon your earth.
It is the Creator way.
It is not your way, as a single Soul, as a group.
It is, Soul, the way of Creator.
For all that is has purpose unto your Creator.
Understand, you are the cohesiveness
   that gathers positive Energy

      to once again flare out and be seen.

1012   You are the answer, Soul.
It is your Purity that is a solution.
We would have you understand
      the difference in the Purity that is of humanity
      and that of Angel.
For Angels, indeed, have great Purity.
Archangels, such Love, they have entered in to Battle with.
Angels having entered in with Purity, Soul.
But you, you have entered in with Truth.
You have entered in to a space,
      where indeed not only negativity is,
      but you hold within your being a seed,
      a seed that can mature and become energy,
      such as negativity is.
And in your humanity
      you have brought this negativity unto great evil.
You have tempted the Angelic Beings
      to turn their eye from such evil.
They have not done so,
      yet would they could, it would be done.
But humanity, you have looked at evil,
      you have engaged with evil,
      you have, Soul, grown an evil
      that is beyond a negative description.
And then you have grown above such evil.
You have indeed overcome the very evil seed
      that is within your being
      and you have done it with the Truth of whom you are.
You have done it, Soul, as beings who have no stature,
      not even that of a gnat.
And yet, you have brought yourself to the very threshold,
      yea, even entering in to compassion for your fellow man! You have reached a chord
      that is beyond any chord ever reached.
You have brought the perfection of High C to be.
And it echoes, Soul,
      in the depths of Light and Dark within the spiral,
      to transform chaos from that which it is,
      to be of the same Truth that is in humanity,

    that indeed it might return from whence it has come.
Soul, the mend is the first station of return out of the Yawn.
And then, indeed, unto MATTER itself.

1013 Soul, you are the pivotal means of return.
You have the key not to detonate,
    not to erupt, but to implode.
Therefore the Keys will come forth.
The Keys will be published three in one.
It is the purpose of their being.
Each a triangulation unto the other.
Souls, you have brought forth.
You have configured.
You have spoken.
You have held negativity.
You have gassed your beings.
You have spent many lifetimes becoming human
    and you have chosen to re enter,
      to bring forth that which is the fullness of Truth.
You are the endeavour.
You are the twilight
    and you have been in the darkness.
The darkness will give way to the Light
    and you will see clear that which you do.
Do not be disheartened.
Do not disperse your being.
Do not, Souls, lift your eyes with emptiness
    but see clearly that which you do
      for all that is within the confoundedness of your Energy,
      the brain that you hold in your being
      even as it fogs in its lack of clarity,
      it is still the power that travels through you
      that brings the understanding.
You are, Soul, opening the way.
You are lifting the knowledge.
You are receiving unto you Truth.
Allow your Energy to be receptive.
Time is accelerating.
You are at the impetuous of a new day.

1014 Souls of earth, you are in a quandary.

It is deep.
It is challenging to your being.
Your earth is spiralling.
The destination has not been decided
    where the energy of earth swirls
    and is caught and swirls yet again.
The energy of mankind
    is that which presents the quandary.
For indeed you are not tethered.
You are each individual.
You each carry a countenance
    and yet you are bound one to the other.
The binding is not done on earth, Soul.
It is done on Farside.
That which is in the deep vortex of mankind
    is done where Purity reigns.
Your earth carries many impurities.
They are within the very Soul of earth
    for you have sent them forth.
Souls of earth, you do not carry righteousness in your being.
It is your purpose!
It is that for which you have entered in to earth.
It is the purpose of all mankind
    to carry generosity in their Soul,
    to imbibe in the drink that is goodness,
    to fulfil your being with that which is generosity,
    to share unto all Souls of earth that which you have.
Yet it is not done and earth station
    is caught in the whirlwind of dismal forecasts.
Souls, prepare ye the way.
Bring forth the moment you are in.
Carry within the very Soul of your being
    the generosity of Spirit
    that is reflected within you.
Intent is why you have entered in to earth.
Intent is why you have come,
    why you have absented from that which is.
Souls of earth, behold the market place
    where many are content to sit and watch;
    where many are content to gather and move outward
    leaving those who have not still yearning.

You gather that which you have and you place your hearts
> in a great atmosphere of pain
> for your earth is sending forth energy unto you.

It has resonated within your very being and you sense it not.
You are the alpha and the omega.
You are the beginning and the end,
> those who have come before,
> those who will dwell there after.

None will give forth in the manner that you have given forth.
None will hold unto the contemporaries
> a solution that is viable with Truth attached.

We ask of you to lay down the lantern
> and see that which is within the energy of where you are.

You are not caught in a medieval homeland
> where once there was pain.

Pain resides.
Pain is!
There is a new day,
> it shall come quickly and those who are unprepared
> will be caught in a turmoil.

The turmoil will last into the tenth hour
> and in the tenth hour of earth
> will be seen the last rainbow of time.

It will be caught
> within the very atmosphere of the higher elements
> and visible for its beginning will be its end
> as alpha and omega are one.

"Prepare ye the way.
Speak the language of goodness.
Speak not of the new day's sun
> *but of the darkness of the tenth hour."*

For you, humanity, you hold time close unto you.
You hold the vision of all that is Truth.
You hold the Love of all that is possible.
There have been, Souls of earth, great peoples arise
> that have accomplished much upon your earth.

They have given unto Creator much
> but they have not released their ego.

They have not held to Truth.
Truth is the foundation of where you are.
Truth is the purpose of your being.

Truth is why you have come,
> why you have entered in.

It is the call unto all nations to hold high truth
> Truth of Energy, Truth of humanity
>> not a nation, not a country, but all humanity!

You will see, Soul, the kaleidoscope of colour as a rainbow
> never to be seen again and never
> having been seen before.

It shall radiate as a Purity
> in a manner that all eyes will feast upon its clarity
> and men and women will fall before the sight
> and they will call unto Creator,
>> "You have given us a sign."

But it is not the sign,
> that Creator has given to you.

For you indeed are the sign,
> you who have spent reincarnations upon your earth
> where others might see that which you are.

You are the visibility not, Soul, unto earth but unto all vision.
For all worlds will see that which you are.
As your oneness is brought forth ego must go.
Ego has no place in Purity.
Ego has no place in the purpose of humanity.
You are not caught where you are.
You are not placed where you are.
You have brought yourself to the moment you are in.
You have gloried in that moment.
For you have before you a purpose
> wherein all other purposes may blend.

Souls of earth, do not gasp in recognition of earth's failings.
Gasp in recognition of humanity's failings
> for it is in that recognition
> that you have that opportunity to grow.

It is in that recognition that you are seen in the heavens above.
You have entered in to earth.
Some have said,
> "*I will pray.*
> *I will give my being to all that is pure.*
> *I will bend.*
> *I will give forth constantly of my energy.*"

But, Souls, to what purpose will you bend

        that you might gain the laud of those about you?
That they might behold a pious being?
Pious is not the key unto humanity.
It is not the door that will gain entrance.
You, you who see and turn away, bring forth your eyes.
Look deep into the pain of man
        that you might see where the need is
        that you might behold the deep well of earth's need.
Souls of earth, there are Keys.
The Keys are seven.
The Keys are for all to behold.
You have before you a single key within you.
It is the key that acknowledges not your righteousness;
        your intent, your purpose.
Intent is that which is before you.
You as one are the Soul of your Creator.
You as one accomplish much.
You as one are the radiant star that shines in the night sky,
        each being of earth holding their own star
        that shines as a gift unto their Creator.
How many stars are in the heavens, Soul?
How many beings are there of humanity?
Of all Farside, of earths and earths,
        of existence and existence
        that wait upon the overcoming of chaos,
        you are magnified in your being
        for you shine as you gather oneness.
And your earth, your earth beholds that which you do.
Souls, you are humanity.
You are the beginning and the end.
You are the purpose that will overcome pain
        that is in the depths of earth.
You will overcome chaos that reigns in the night sky.
You will overcome the pathos of energy
        that looks unto perfection and sees it not.
You, you are the purpose of finding.
It is not the star that will fragment into many pieces.
It is the star that you form from many pieces.
For you will implode as all Energy will implode.
You will behold those who are pure.
You will behold those who are Angel and Archangel.

You will behold that which is in the purpose of all being
      and you will hold a miter door.
The door will require a key and the key will resonate
      as no other key has resonated
          for it will be the Purity of all that is within Humanity.
You are the treasure.
You hold the gift.
You have before you an expectant nature.
But do not expect when others expect from you.
You see you are the reflection.
You are the expectation.
Is not you waiting for that which will come,
      it is where we are waiting for that which you will do.
Time has a measure.
It is measured before you have entered in to earth.
You have brought forth much and now, Souls of earth,
      it is time to let go of the kingdoms.
It is time to let go of the opulence,
      for your churches will not stand.
Your castle will not be.
More truth would be the humble house
      with Purity within for it will be lifted.
It will hold the pure of heart.
Humanity, you are that which we await.
You hold the golden chalice.
To knock at the door and say unto those within,
      "We have come in truth, in oneness.
      May we enter in?".
And the Heavens will awaken in such a throng of goodness
      that all the morning stars will behold
          for the great new day will have begun.
And those of many earths, those whom you have looked unto
      as neither part of earth or part of the heavens
          will rise and be recognized for they too will enter in.
They too will behold the Gateway.
Souls of earth, you are placed where you are
      by the Energy of your being.
It is you, Soul, that has entered in to the conflict.
Do not hold yourself in abeyance
      for that day will not come without you.
You are particled unto all humanity

   from before you entered in.
Clasp the hand of humanity.
There will be those who will not partake
   and they will be in the great roil of earth
   and pain will come unto their being.
But, Souls, none will be left
   for none are of humanity of earth alone.
All are members of Farside Humanity.
You, you who have heard, let him speak.
You who can bear to reach out, reach out.
You who can lift the Soul of another
   be known for that which you do.
Some have called you brethren.
We call you Humanity for we see you
   in the oneness of your purpose.
So shall it be.
Unto you peace be given.

1015 Soul, in the Light is a dance
   that creates a Path in to the darkest way.
To reach the understanding you require
   to fulfil your purpose upon earth,
    it is essential that you each hold Light
    strongly to your being.
It is essential that you focus your Energy beyond the earth.
It is imperative that you seek to know
   the living Energy of the trilogies,
    that they will carry a life strong in them.
You must not forfeit the power to lift Energy unto the Light.
You will see with all the Light of your being,
   that you are purposeful in that which you do.
You will understand you are six, never five, always six.
Never allow the Energy to see past the six.
Understand you are vibrating.
Do not cease to vibrate.
Consistency is essential.
Consistency, purpose in Energy
   that will vibrate forth unto humanity!
Behold the door has opened.
The web is the dome.
The dome is the power grid.

Power grid creates the flow.
Accept the power of your being.
Souls, voice is yours.
Voice presents understanding unto earth.
When the voice is not heard, when the sound is distorted,
    it requires an interpreter to render the voice heard.
You have a voice.
It must be clear.
It must be heard.
It must sound outward from you.
You are the conveyance.
You are the Energy through which the voice will be heard.
Utter forth unto earth.
In your urgency be fast in completion of uttering forth.
Speak in the Purity of your voice that you may be found valid
    that you be heard not with a sound of cackling
        but even as the turtle is heard when no sound is spoken,
        only the deep urgency within the creature.
There is an urgency for the voice to be heard.
Give unto Caesar that which is Caesar's.
Do not misconstrue that you are of earth
    and the earthly path
        is expedient for the flow of Energy.
You will use a single source in its beginning.

1016   The Angels will extend outward
    beyond the fourth realm,
    even beyond Lantosia,
    even beyond the fifth and sixth.
With a great force of Energy,
    they will create a vacuum
        to explore the Energy of the Wilful Child
        until all mankind, all the energies
        that have gifted themselves to humanity
        have been carried through unto Purity,
        then, Soul, will the great sound go forth.
The sound such as humanity has gathered within their being.
It will be a sound of great desolation.
It will call into the depths, it will call into the solitude.
It will be heard by the Wilful Child.
It will be heard even unto the lost Idyllic.

And all Energy will send forth
    from the Rend, the Archangels,
      a tone they have gathered from Humanity
    of such perfection.
There will be, Soul, an echo forth into the darkness,
    into the depths of unknown,
    into that which is collapsible.
It is the intent that the Wilful Child
    will respond and come forth.
There is a knell, it is a sound that will be forwarded
    wherein the Gates must close.
It cannot wait and yet in the forwarding of your Purity,
    we have received recognition
      of the intent of worlds that have fallen
      to grasp to the Sound, to hold to the Sound,
      for it has gone forth that such a Sound
      will be echoed forth.
It will be the Purity of Humanity
    and all Energy may grasp unto that Purity
    to give Light unto that Purity,
      momentum unto that Purity to enfold itself.
You, who are humanity, you hold that Purity,
    that Truth within your being.
You have the momentum to bring forward
    unto existence that which is pure.
We know the Wilful Child is pure.
We know the relationship of the Thirteenth Creator.
We know the intent of forwarding into the darkness
    with the Sound to recover that which was lost.
It is an unknown until it occurs
    without the fullness of Purity of humanity.
It is why we urge the Tomes,
    it is why the persistent Energy of Purity
    seeks the Truth of humanity,
    to bring forth all that has been lost,
    to bring forth,
    so that not even a grain of sand
    would be lost in the great sea of Energy.

1017   Soul, we teach Creator Energy!
We inform you, Creator is Energy,

>   not Creator's Energy,
>   Creator Energy, purposeful, purposeful,
>   a purpose beyond the galaxy you are in.

You are the creation of your Creator.
You have not entered in by thrust.
You have been cast forth by agreement.
You have within your Creator
>   all the possibilities of your being
>   but your Creator has within the Energy of being
>   all the possibilities of Existence.

Existence is beyond your own.
Existence, for you, of your earth is not always idyllic.
Indeed, it shatters the Soul at the pain of mankind.
Yet, you search for Idyllic
>   for it is the purpose of your Creator.

Your Creator has an agenda.
You are of that agenda.
Willingly, Soul, you have entered in,
>   willingly!

The agenda for earth was simple; to gather scars.
You have extended.
You have moved beyond your purpose.
You have gathered the scars but still you do not hear.
Your Creator is constant in attendance to earth.
The plan, the purpose of your entering in is choice,
>   the choice to stay, the choice to alter.

You have become as it were,
>   creator of your own destiny
>   and yet you are on a mission
>   and the mission is that of Creator,
>   constant in a purpose of your entering in.

The sun will rise.
The moon will wane its waxen self
>   because your Creator has set in motion
>   a Timetable for earth.

You are the instrument that fulfills the Timetable.
The purpose is beyond whom you are.
The purpose is to behold Idyllic,
>   to bring forth perfection.

You have not attained that state nor was it ever to be so.
You in your Soul self are in a illusionary state

        that does not quickly behold the purpose of coming.
You are, Soul, unable to bring yourself
        beyond your humanness.
Your Creator has a constancy, does not change.
Your Creator does not vary
        nor the purpose of Creator vary.
The instruments have not varied.

1018   Humanity, there is the charted Path
        you have entered in.
Configured by the Spirit of your being,
        walked by the Soul of your being
        and received once again
        into the Essence of your being.
As you re enter it is not the path of confusion.
It is the Path of all glory
        wherein the filament is the Energy of your being,
        connected to all other energies.
Only as you walk the Path in your earth being
        and have released from your Energy
        the charted way,
        do you reach into that place
        of enlightenment on earth,
        does your Soul swell to such a proportion
        that it can only flow outward
        from its being to touch energies of faltering Souls,
        to lift their being on the charted way.
You cover the Path with that which you have overcome.
You make the extension of that Path
        by the growth of your Soul.
To do this is to harbour no ill will.
To do this is to see in all man, one man, yourself.
For on the extended way,
        the Path of enlightenment,
        there is camaraderie,
        there is joy,
        there is the Light that flows continuous
        into the path of all beings.
For in the joy of your being,
        you cannot keep your Light to yourself.
It must emanate outward from you.

You, who are lifted in your being unto that Path,
>   know that the Energy Flow is received into your being.

And negativity has ceased to be
>   and you wonder in the first re entering
>   at the serenity of your being
>   that recognizes all that you view,
>   and you see before you faces lit,
>   welcoming, rushing to greet you
>   and they draw you into their Aura.

You are met, not by one, not by two,
>   by countless beings,
>   and it is the extension of their Aura
>   that wraps around you.

You are on earth,
>   allow the extension of your aura
>   to meet beings in your path.

Wrap your being around those who have need,
>   around those who have pain,
>   and glory in the power that you have entered in to,
>   for you become a benefactor.

Reach your being to touch the glory of Light
>   and know that the hand is not necessary,
>   for in the Spirit of your being your aura vibrates.

It is your aura, not your hand, that reaches being first.

When you would enter i n to a new thing,
>   you send forth your aura unto all beings.

It will bring back the positive you expect.

When you consider the way,
>   as you approach the crossing of your life,
>   you know only that which is ahead,
>   for that which is behind is of no matter.

Only the forward step brings you into
>   the collective Energy of the Prism.

Humanity, see your single self as one.

One humanity, one collected goodness,
>   offering unto all beings the power of your Energy.

Significant is the Energy of your being.

As you hold negativity, it flows to self.

As you release negativity from your being,
>   it flows outward to touch the lives of many.

Who are you?

You are enlightened being.
You may not glory to sit and watch the world go by.
You are not, Souls, the Buddha who has already
        entered in to the state of enlightenment.
You are students, and students must actively learn.
Know the power of your Light.
Know the healing power of your Light.
Know the teaching power of your Light
        and know that Light always goes forward
        into the unknown way, but for a purpose,
        the purpose of furthering the wellbeing of humanity.
Would you heal earth?
Healing with the vibrant violet.
Would you reach unto another to release pain?
Overwhelm the Soul in the vibrancy of violet.
Would you ask:
        "*Wherein shall I be?*"
Place your being in quiet meditation
        under the dome of violet
        and know that the Spirit of your Creator,
        the Spirit of all Colour,
        will respond unto thee.
For you are precious in that Path
        and you are visioned in that Path.
You are wept for in that Path
        and rejoiced over in your advanced step.
Your day is not done.
When your day is done, you simply walk to meet your Path.

1019 Souls, we would speak of wellness,
        the eternal circle of Energy.
Soul, all Energy to wellness is brought,
        is brought from your being,
        from your existence, the mirror that has reality.
Beloved Souls of earth, in all that you do,
        in your journeys through the moments
        and hours of your time,
        gather you only positive Energy.
It is fragile in its existence.
Do not place upon another, accusation,
        but overwhelm the being with thy Love,

    with the vibration of thy Energy.
 Who has not been leased?
Soul, the wellness of earth has a beginning,
    it has a beginning
    in the individual source of all being.
How traumatic is the energy of negativity?
It scatters itself, it waylays itself at every opportunity.
Souls of earth, spew negativity from you.
Do not place judgements upon any Soul,
    but gather the being of the Soul
    and overwhelm the Soul with thy Holy being,
    that they may feel the Energy
    that you may place about them.
Souls of earth, from the fence we are
    we see human forms strewn upon battlefields.
Not one, but many battlefields in your inner cities
    and your fields of glory.
For Soul, one man's victory is another man's field of glory.
Behold the vibration of Energy.
It is timeless.
It is not contained within the moment or the hour,
    but it gathers its strength from your very being,
    the Energy of whom you are.
Beings of earth, you have made this Energy
    available unto yourselves.
For have you not been Farside
    and gloried at the entering in to the space of negativity!
Precious beings of earth,
    wellness is an encounter with positive Energy.
Souls of earth, you are profoundly complicated.
We of the Farside witness the choices
    that humanity has made
    and when it has seemed simple,
    they yet complicate it again and again.
We would have you know why!
The energies of negativity have great strength,
    they have overwhelmed the worlds where we are.
Your single world has little knowledge
    of the many worlds beyond your realm
    and yet negativity has overwhelmed these worlds.
The Energy of Truth is as it were without full strength.

It does not enter in to the world whole.
It has lost and is seeking a part of its being.
And it has a fragile existence,
       and you strengthen that existence by your choices.
You enable Truth.
Soul, your flesh and blood is a container,
       simply a container.
It has many complications within it
       and those complications have within them
       a mirror of the many complications
       of your being at the Farside.
You are not simply a wisp of smoke.
 You are not a mere breath.
You are the total Essence of Purity
       with all the knowledge contained within Purity.
Soul, in your daily routines as humanity,
       recall the Purity you have entered in from.
Know how voracious is the appetite of negativity!
Embrace the wounds that negativity has left.
Encircle the Wilful Child
       and place great beams of Light upon it.
But do not place judgement on any being.
But know only their Purity,
       know and recognize only wellness of being.
Raise your voices to be heard,
       that wellness is an expression of Love.
Soul, we have great editions.
Understand that in the spewing forth
       is a gentle recognition of Negativity.

1020   Souls of earth,
       we speak to you from the Energy Source.
We speak to you of whom you are.
We would have you rise in your Energy
       and know far beyond where you are,
       far beyond three, even beyond the dark seven.
Your Energy has been flame,
       not all humanity,
       all humanity is only a portion of those
       who entered in with purpose.
But the beings who entered in to overcome chaos,

                these beings, the legion of Angels,
                        entered in as Flame.
They were destined in their being.
They are of the Vanguard
        of the Second and Third Creators.
Souls of earth, Flame, Energy.
Each given Breath in different forms,
        entering in with motion to overcome.
Souls of earth, value flame,
        flame of Light,
        flame of colour,
        flame of warmth, for humanity is warmth.
Humanity, Soul, is the prism.
Humanity is the extension of Light
        and so did the Armada chose two to bring forth,
        two Creators,
        and yet the first waiting.
Yet mankind has achieved nobly
         and they have yet to envision that which you do.
Souls, you are warm.
You feel without flame.
There is no Spirit in the human.
The human being needs Spirit Energy
        to awaken within their being
        so they know they have entered in.
The crown is not the head.
The Energy is the head,
        the flame that rises above your being as human.
You feel the Energy of the flame within you
        or you feel the lack of when you are dispirited
        and away from the Truth of your being.
Awaken.
Rise to the Energy.
Allow the Energy to soar.
It does not sleep.
It has no need of sleep.
It cannot burn out, Soul, for this Energy of flame
        is fuelled by all other energies.
What a persona art thou,
        you, human,
        that you have awakened all other energies unto you.

They see that which you do.
They behold that which you do.
You are held as the babe is held
        for they understand the preciousness
        of your voyage into the unknown
        with only the flame to lighten your way.
To make the flame brighter, Soul,
        you must gather it to another flame.
You must reach unto the great Light from whence it comes
        for only then can the flame that you hold be brighter.
You are the magnificent creation of your Creator,
        a Creator that holds Love in the Energy Being ,
        for all energies are a part of self.
And you awaken because you have the eye to open
        and see before you the very Path
        from which you have come.
Holy endeavour, Holy reach, Holy splendour
        that is available to all who see
        that which you have entered in to.
There is a magnificence, Soul,
        when the dark of negativity enters a shine,
        a flame that lites greater than the sun lights the sky
        and it is a perfection of humanity that rises,
        as the eastern star enters in to view.
So does it offer a healing at the eastern sky,
        takes all that is wounded.
Oh, Soul, can you leave the illness of your being
        to the feebleness of your physicians when
        you have before you
        a two minute Energy to reach into,
        a holiness where the Flame can reach
        unto the Energy of Purity
        and replenish the flesh and the mind.
Do not forget, Soul.
Do not release from you
        that which will bring the body to a wholeness.
Souls of earth,
        you cannot fold your hands before your being
        and be content to know that the pain
        you have felt will be taken.
There must first be an act of offering to receive.

Teach the children, two minutes to east.[1]
Give to all that they might receive
      the Energy that flows unto all earth.
An hour does not pass,
      a minute does not pass
          without the healing being offered.
The earth has only to rotate to receive.

---

[1] east - see Appendix A

Chapter One
CONFIRMATION

1021   Behold the realms of existence
        beyond that which is Yawn,
            the many billowing Domes that create variances
        have within the ability of creation itself.
The Consciousness of the Void
        has thrust forth a canopy to protect all else.
It billows into endless creations,
        it forms as it thrust forth.
The name given unto thrust is chaos
        for chaos holds no order.
All else contains order.
Chaos is wilful and so in the separating of self
        Negativity has become wilful that it might create
        the same demeanor as set forth by Chaos.
Your science has order
        but it is with the chaotic structure
        that it comes to understanding.
It must always place an auk within that is order.
Soul, it includes all forms.
You understand the science of your earth
        is limited in its concepts.
It is not ready to grasp the outward billow
        from an inward point of reality.
Chaos penetrates.
It is held, sent forth as projectile, as auk, not singly,
        but in thousands, in millions.
As in your world, Soul,
        there is not a single thrust of chaos.
Often the single thrust gathers around it other thrusts of chaos
        as in auk entering in.
As auk enters in to the ocean to feed, so does chaos feed.
Upon your earth would you call yourselves experiment?
Yes, you would and you would be right, Soul,
        but you have chosen!
It is choice.
You have lifted your beings beyond the realm of Purity
        to enter in unto the force of negativity.

You have choices, they are equal in the beginning.
Chaos is mesmerizing, it draws curiosity.
In itself it is the curious and searches outward.
You who are of earth, you who are humanity,
    you have formed a record of chaos through lifetimes
    not singularly but as humanity.
You have delved into the energy of chaos
    to that which end it has created
    within your humanity great evil,
    great compassion, even Purities, even wisdoms
    and it has sent forth
    from the very heart of your being
    tremours of emotion that unsettle your very being.
In all areas of your humanity you choose to hide from chaos
    and yet you are coerced
    into the very energy again and again.
How?
How, Soul, does the Energy of humanity
    prevail against the chaos?
And yet it does, Soul.
It is called negativity, earth negativity, yet it is chaotic.
Even your earth has warmed her being
    to enter in to the plight of mankind
    by presenting chaos within the structure of earth itself.
You are bombarded by chaotic energy
    and indeed you are an experiment
    for you are an illusory state.
Not in, Soul,
    you are illusion!
Your realities are where we are.
Your realities are in the positive ion.
You are not encapsulated where you are.
You have choice to come, to go,
    but to leave, you must leave the mind's illusion
    of where you are so you return to your reality.
Within the state of chaos is consciousness.
Indeed, consciousness but non communicating consciousness.
No words are spoken.
No energy is readable.
It does not mean, Soul, it is not heard.
Chaos has understanding, intellect.

Can you control how chaos affects your being?
Do you totally have control?
Within the reality of your illusion you do not.
Chaos may come in many forms unto you.
It may rise from an act of one Soul to another.
It may come with the wind or the rain,
      the ocean, land, in drought.
And what power do you have?
The power, Soul, the source of containing chaos
      is your earth's mission and you do it well.
Yet you have found chaos is difficult to control,
      as you attempt, it bombards itself outward.
It expands itself outward.
Humanity we know has found
      the ability to control the chaos
      within the being of self,
      within the mind,
      not all, Soul,
      but there have been many earth beings
      who have entered in to the mind's hallowed space,
      that of the high mind, to rest from the chaos
      in the cocoon of the Energy of the high mind
      even to the point
      of withholding the body from pain.
Upon your earth you have found many forms
      of containing the chaos of nature,
      of growth, of vegetation,
      of behaviour in all form of animal life
      and much you have found
      is not within reason of humanity
      but it is the purpose for which you have come to know,
      to understand negativity
      that armed itself in the manner of Chaos.

1022   There is a corridor unto the Shining Waters.
It is a fuel, Energy Field, upon which echo responds.
It is satellite.
It is far from Voice.
We care, not measure, for you a term.
It is as far from Shining Waters to Voice
      as the grains of sand upon your world,

      many, forever.
From this Energy Field of reflections
      many Energy Fields respond in lassitude.
Our terminology does not allow for space, for space contains.
We deal with a fathomless Energy Field
      beyond existence of Matter.
On earth you can read time, billions of years in earth surface.
We can explore Matter beyond the Voice.
There has not been Matter tangible to discern,
Yet, we know it is before Breath has spoken it forth.
Within the Void is Breath, but what of the Void?
Void holds the countenance of Wisdom,
      the ultimate consciousness,
          the fulfilment of discernment within the Voice.
Breath altered and Wisdom is receptive.
It seeks to know a balance.
It carries no threat, no issue.
Yet Breath joyful to leave Voice,
      yet not totally in spaciousness
      where it has not balanced.
How does the Voice balance the Breath?
Why does the Voice not alter and stays firm?
It does not exact a consequence that needs to resolve
      the issue of where does Breath originate.
From what does it originate?
From what does Matter become?
What is Chaos?
Where does Chaos get its momentum
      to thrust out unevenly?
In an angry human, the voice is louder or quieter,
      but not your normal voice.
What is the stress that imbalances Chaos?
Voice is wisdom within.
Voice is a presence that will not leave
      until a solution is found.

1023   Souls of earth, unto you we offer to teach.
Within the Yawn of being, chaos in many forms exists.
Within the positive Yawn the existence of chaos is in motion.
It is in motion in all fields of Energy
      within and without the Yawn.

Within the negative ion of the Yawn,
> chaos exists in the Energy of momentum as motion.

Humanity, Soul, is in control of choice
> and yet they are drawn into
> the deep perseverance of chaos
> for chaos excites their being.

You who dwell upon the planet called earth,
> you derive a great negative energy from chaos.

Chaos itself is constant in its forward plunge.
It is not erased, Soul.
It dwells.
It dwells in the Energy of beings, of creature,
> of all manner of earth components.

It is thrust in the motion of its own being.
It is charged in the ion of its own energy.
Mankind has the ability to create chaos.
Mankind creates chaos to the degree of evil.
Do not, Soul, be disheartened.
Do not, Soul, be brought low, for we say unto you,
> *"It is the illusion of your earth*
> > *wherein chaos is taken unto the realms of evil."*

To what end, to what purpose?
Mankind, you are together in the battle to overcome negativity.
Negativity is resolved to understand chaos.
Therefore, it presents motion to project.
For Chaos in the beginning has motion,
> is charged with a momentum of thrust.

You in your world, you are caught for your earth life
> in the gathered negativity and your choices create
> an understanding of that which chaos is.

All worlds, all existences look unto earth's simplicity
> for you have expedited the understanding of chaos
> by creating the very energy of it.

1024 Chaos is gathering, not in its immensity,
> no, not in its immensity.

Chaos is gathering in its speed.
It is of the same strength but it gathers more quickly,
> so there is a continual bombardment of flow,
> of worlds outward, of energies outward,
> of existence outward, of negativity.

May it be said that there is also
> an increase in positive Energy,
>> yet, this is not so.
The positive Energy has slowed.
The chaos has increased.
It is that throughout all existence unto the beginning.
Pronounced repetition of chaos is confounding itself
> so that there is a greater confusion
>> within the chaotic struggle outward from all existence.
There is even within Voice with the beginning
> a more pronounced struggle
>> within the containment of Breath.
What is agitating the great struggle?
What is creating the great momentum?
This we would know.
We ask humanity to seek the reasoning.
We ask humanity to delve deep
> into the purpose of exaggeration.
For chaos is chaos but exaggerated chaos confounds logic!
Logic is losing a portion of reason.
Even within mankind, logic is left in the balance by chaos.
There is a thread of conveyance
> and that is in the manner
>> in which the confusion becomes exaggerated.
As each new existence is brought forth
> so is the exaggeration exceeding the last.
We know not why.
We know not how.
We do know that the speed
> by which the exaggeration is being mounted
> is thrusting forth a huge volume of density
> so that Sound and Colour are being altered.
They are being clapped as in thunder clapping
> cloud against cloud.
Yet, that is not the technique is it!
And nor is it with chaos, Soul.
And we are searching to structure the dilemma
> that it might find a purpose for the acceleration,
> or a manner in which to detain the acceleration.
Our ability is equal to your ability and more.
But you have a range of sound we do not.

And we ask you to use that to seek forth beyond Voice.

1025   We speak of Jesu, of the goodness of our Lord.
And we speak of the Holiness of the Energy.
It is paramount if you would be of the Energy of Jesu
      that you would
           hold the Energy of all man sacred unto you.
For the Blessed Lord touched all humanity in all spaces of life.
The bitterness, the foulness, the stench, the pain,
      was never encountered by his Holiness,
         for he did not see it.
It was not there.
What he saw was a brother, a sister.
What he saw was the family of Almighty God.
He voiced unto all men, no restrictions.
The candour of his language withheld nothing.
Our Lord spoke in tongue and we say this unto you,
      all language was available unto him.
He spoke the language of the small child, of the old man,
      of the Roman, of the Syrian, of the Jew,
         of all who lived and entered in.
His tongue would know their name.
He would know their words.
Souls of earth, the language of the tongue
      was that all men might be received.
Nothing was withheld, no words set apart.
We say to you, Christianity, do not set yourselves apart.
For as you set yourself apart,
      you set yourself apart from the very Purity
         that you would be a part of.
It is not only the pure who enter in.
It is the decrepit, it is the vile, it is the wounded,
      it is the righteous and the unrighteous.
Reach out thy Energy, reach it out for all humanity,
      for all humanity are connected.
In the space of brotherhood, see yourself a part of humanity.

1026   It is the goal of all beings to reach unto the level
      wherein one alone of the Four
      has been formed to enter earth,
      indeed, the Energy Source.

All is complex.
All are connected.
All fours connected one unto the other.
All threes connected unto the other, all sevens, all fourteens.
Indeed, Fourteen Creators,
    fourteen levels of Light and Dark.
Seven levels of earth.
Seven levels to strive unto to remove veils
    wherein you might enter
    unto the Light of your Creator
    wherein you may form a growth
    that will reach unto Angels.
Jesu, the Holy One, entered in unto earth from Agape.
Jesu understanding Love
    as no man has ever understood Love
    for the Light of Love rested within the Being.
Buddha, Mohammed, Krishna
    gathered the knowledge of Love unto them.
It was not in its purest form,
    but it was the purest form of humanity.
It was, Soul, the Truth of Farside,
    of that which is humanity's Path.
All beings strive to reach unto perfection.
Some strive to reach the perfection of Creator.
Some strive to reach the perfection of the Spirit.
Some to reach the perfection of the Holy Four.
None can attain the fullness without entering in
    in their being unto Farside.
Each of the three have witnessed the Path of Creator.
Each has entered in unto the Purity
    and know the energies of Purity.
Jesu had no need.
Jesu was lifted beyond manifestation
    and carried by the Angels unto that place of Purity.
He is the darkness that has illuminated,
    the glory that is transcended.
All that is, is as Jesu.
All Creators akin one to the other, Holy in their being.
The stars, the moon, the sun, rests upon their Being,
    ornaments for the glory of whom they are.
For their Light is greater

        and sends forth a Path that illuminates
        your world and all within the Yawn.
Know this, Soul.

1027   We speak to you of the Flame, the great Light.
Your Creator has purified the Flame
        so that within the Flame of Creator there is no matter.
There is Energy of being, consciousness.
Only a single Creator has achieved this refinement of Energy.
Yet your being is still prismatic.
In the Energy of your Creator, there is a Flame
        so refined in its Purity
        that the breath expands outward
        from the Light of that Flame,
        ergo the Yawn could come to be.
All Creators have the capacity to create great worlds
        but none have achieved
        the creation of your Creator.
This Creator is acknowledged by all existence,
        by all energies,
        as super mount to Supreme Being.
This Creator has felt, felt, Soul.
In the cosmos is consciousness.
It is a consciousness,
        it has an awareness, but it does not feel.
Your Creator has an Energy that feels.
All Creators do
        but your Creator has achieved a refinement of feel.
And that which was felt is defined beyond Love
        unto Ecstasy wherein Love can endure.
Love can be.
Love can have compassion.
That is the Love that is achieved by you, humanity.
But the Love of your Creator goes beyond
        to an Ecstasy that draws outward
        and touches and flows
        and magnifies the Love within,
        so that all feel that Love.
You could not be in the space of such Ecstasy.
Just to be brought into the presence of Archangels,
        of Angels that have been in the presence of Creator

creates within you ecstasy.
You could not behold, nor could we
  the Purity of the expansion of that Love.
Flame creates heat and heat expanding ever outward.
This is the flame you have become;
  but your Light,
    not the pure Light that is in Creator.
Creator, who presented unto Melchezidec an infant
  and laid it within his Holy presence
  and said, "*This is your humanity.*"
And forth unto the Path of this Energy
  that is pure and Light and Holy.
You walked into the path of negativity, infant,
  armed in your being,
   to rise up and become the Purity that you are.
And even in the greatness of your Purity
  are welts of anger and dastardly deeds.
For you are still humanity and have entered in to negativity
  but many have achieved
   the Light that expands and grows.
Be not brought into despair
  for that which you see in your earth.
But know that Humanity in its completeness
  is not totally upon your earth
   but within Farside within the Crystal Cave.
You are the few.
We are the many.
You have won your Battle.
We have been a part of that Battle.
Rise, come forth unto where we are.

1028 Souls, Energy is not always movement.
Energy often is still,
  yet carries a potential of great movement.
This is often found in chaos.
We would have you understand
  chaotic energy is not always of a negative,
  as you understand negative.
It has a movement.
It has a tenacity.
It has a rippling.

It has a twisting.
It has an undulating.
It has a dissitude.
Feel, become familiar to feel Energy round about you.
Become aware of the Energy
    that does not transfigure into calm.
Search into the being of this Energy
    to see from whence the core is,
        so you might know if there is violence within.
Feel, allow your Energy
    to become accustomed not to the eyes,
    not to the ears,
    but to the feel of Energy
        wherein you may heal more readily.
Account only that the third eye might see.
The eyes and the ears of earth are not readily in tune
    with the reach into chaos
        as feeling within the stillness of your Energy,
    so that you will become aware
    of the vibrational thrust of the body
    and thus interpret wherein is all illness.
This is your greatest possibility as human, to heal negativity.
For what greater gift could you give unto your Creator!
You are humanity.
You have entered in to gift unto humanity,
    therein giving unto Creator.
You are as one the counterbalance to all negativity.
We would not have you eradicate that which is precious.
We would have you not slave that which is evil.
Rather we would have you feel with the Energy of being
    wherein the pain lies
    of a mind, of the heart, the body,
    and lay upon this energy such Love,
    such compassion, such Purity,
        the Light of your being will confound the negativity
        and it will be brought unto the Light.

Visions[2]

1029 Michael will teach Path.
The centre of the Path is Soul's choice.
Souls of earth reach into the negativity in great depth
      in order that a Soul may be brought to a safe place.
The Soul itself can be placed in jeopardy,
      as is a rescuer of a Soul deep in water,
      the Soul must enter into the flow of danger.
It is in the way of choice.
Persona, you are of great value.
The safe, secure centre is yours.
Step from the safety of choice only to alleviate another's pain.
Oft times a Soul is required to step from the centre of growth.
This is done by choice of Soul.
Nothing can be re done, except karma.
Only on earth plane is re done.
To receive growth by lifting the Soul
      requires oft times the Soul to be in jeopardy.
It is a gift of the Soul.
It is well planned on the side of Eternity.
Step often from the Path in order to master the intent of evil.
How is evil forever and ever and ever?
There is no hell.
All thing must pass away.
All good will return to that from which it has come.
The fragment of your being is a secure fit
      into the Crystal Cave of creation.
The All Knowing Energy centres the Cave.
[June 25, 1999]

1030 Souls of many nations will ponder
      against their own script that which is written.
And the trumpet will be sounded in Mecca,
      and the cymbal will be clashed in India,
      and the bell will resonate in Israel,
      and candles will be lit,

---

[2] Visions - the dates at the end of each passage indicate when the channelling was received.
It does not indicate the date of the vision.

>   and nations will bring a oneness into rhetoric.
> A pact of mighty endeavour will occur.
> It will occur twenty sixteen
> > and mankind will have the opportunity
> > to once again free earth
> > of abominations beyond man's akin.
> Man's breath will fail them as sulphuric fumes
> > rise from the ground and little children
> > will look in askance,
> > but their family will have no answers
> > if it is not done.
>
> [August 16, 2000]

1031 Many have come to the Mountaintop.
Indeed are they gathered unto Purity.
They have seen the Keys clearly,
> and they have heard the knell of earth..
Souls of earth, many are they
> who have climbed the heights of Purity.
Not all are set upon the mountain,
> but have reached the Purity of the Mountaintop.
Souls are few whose feet have set upon the Mountaintop.
Souls have ceased to use the fragment of earth stench.
They have beheld the gem of Purity
> and they have a purpose to humanity.
It is the sole purpose of their being.
All that they do is in preparation
> for that which will be issued forth
> from the Mountaintop.
It is so in all world Mountaintops.
Recognize the beatitudes,
> for many are they who have come to the Mountaintop
> to hear the clarity of which you bring forth.
All that is written, all that is given, all that is extended outward
> is done in Purity or it will not be done.
All gifts are held sacred.
All monies are world's, all purpose is humanity.
[February 28, 2001]

1032 We would speak unto thee
> of the battles from time began.

Hear with open ears the why.
Mankind has always battled.
The very purpose of your entering in is battle.
The purpose was not to battle with selves.
We speak of the selves of mankind,
> we speak of the coming forth unto battle.
Each Soul has been wept upon
> as a mother weeps upon the pain of her children.
Selves of mankind, you carry within you
> the most glorious portions of life,
> you carry a portion of Truth,
> you carry a portion of Negativity.
And, Souls of earth, humanities,
> you have the Energy portion of Love of Our own.
We speak of the temple of four turrets,
> we speak of that in the land called Iraq.
Mankind has the echo of the Blessed Four.
Mankind understands the coming of the Purities.
Has not the villain erected the temple thus!
And knowing of that which it represents,
> are there not four kingdoms
> > that are impatient to belong with the Holy Four!

"Lord, unto Thee is our portion allotted.
> *But how, Lord, do we speak to the armies?*
> *How will they behold*
> > *Thy Light falling equally*
> > > *upon the bands of men?"*

The white flag,
> mankind knows of the white flag.
You will create neutrality.
You will beckon the world
> to display the white flag for neutrality.
Not for one, not for the other, but for giving of Energy
> that the battle may continue for mankind,
> but the battle of overcoming negativity.
Battles are not won on the battlefield, this you know.
We seek a portion of Light.
Display Light
> as the Jews were commanded by the Energy of All
> > to place the crimson upon the door.
Soul, do We now speak for the world to hold the white flag,

>   not to relinquish power,
>   indeed to shed power, to take no side!
> To charge their being in the single purpose
>   of overcoming the negativity,
>   that motion might be stilled
>   and the time of fulfilment begin.
> Harken unto the Light and let joy sing its song,
>   for in the space of your earth moon,
>   the white flags will appear.
> And the battlefields will hear of the giving of mankind,
>   and the effort will gentle the armies both.
> And the one will see a portion upon his plate
>   he has not seen before.
> For the Light will open unto him the aperture of reality.
> [March 21, 2003]

1033 Science, look to the still Energy
>   and you overcome the chaotic rudimentary
>   of time and space.
> We place Sound and Colour,
>   the effort that alters,
>   the effort that begins the tumultuous range
>   of chaotics to once again settle
>   and become altered Energy.
> Earth has colour and sound.
> It is used in its infancy of its being.
> It is a re born in the space of humanity.
> Farside has Colour and Sound vibrant beyond your own,
>   distilled as it were in its purification.
> This Farside Sound and Colour has the ability to travel,
>   to expound itself against outer walls.
> They are collapsible in their form.
> You have, humanity, the availability of this Sound and Colour.
> You have the portrait of all Energy, even to the lost note.
> In the rebel is a chaotic being.
> It is, Soul, not designated but willful in its delight to travel.
> All other Energy travels at the timetable of the Energy.
> Only the chaotic note alters green covering your earth,
>   even entering in to your body in its ill state,
>   yet beloved of earth.
> So is the Wilful child unto all Energy.

You have the possibility of the Zero.
It is not an answering you seek, it is an entering to,
     for entering in to the Zero
        reveals all to the next entering in.
All humanity in the Thousand Years
     will have opened their being
        to reveal unto them all Farside,
        all worlds connected to Farside.
Even will you, Souls of earth,
     see before you the protracted Light of Gateway.
[June 28, 2004]

1034   Death is equal to Life existence.
Beginnings and endings,
     a losing of self in that existence;
        as you enter in to your next existence,
        you will memory where you have been.
You will have, Soul, not only memories,
     but abilities to reach.
You will have choices, existence, lift.
Death created a change, for one Energy became another,
     became another and the original Energy was lost.
It is lost, Soul.
Energies now remain.
It has created chaos.
One flame is a small fire,
     many flames, a great one.
Great fires have a stronger life than that of a small flame.
Death has moved, withdrawn, that Life might be.
But with Life, there is also chaos.
And chaos is altering existence.
You are at the upper portion of the weave.
There are many existences below you.
You see yourselves at the foot of the spiral
     and we let you know that you are not.
We let you know that spiral meets spiral.
So that it is the eternal circle, circling and circling.
It is, Soul, the Eternal Weave.
You are a foremost part of that Weave.
All energies having been created since Death moved back,
     are entered in with Chaos.
Only those few that have not entered in

   from the opposite Dome
   have no Chaos.
All other Domes have perfection without Negativity,
   but not the perfection of, as you know perfect.
As you know Purity, so is perfect.
Many of these Domes are unaware.
They have existences, Soul, less than your own.
They have no Negativity, but they do have a state of idyllic
   to the point of Purity they are in.
Indeed, you now see much.
That which contains the Chaos and the Pulse is
   the Lake of Mirror, the reflection of Light.
It prevents the Dark entering in.
All Energy from your sphere would implode.
All Energy from the Pulse would explode.
Your science is on the doorstep of knowing this.
Your fields of Energy would flatten, Soul.
It would not annihilate a single world,
   it would annihilate many worlds
   for the Sound could not be contained.
A clap of thunder would seem as a ping
   to the tumultuous behemoth that will occur.
[March 1, 2005]

1035 Soul, unto Mohammed is the Truth.
Mohammed, the messenger of Allah.
Mohammed rose unto the hill of Zion
   and gathered the seeds of knowledge
   and sprinkled the knowledge unto the rivers of men.
Men gathered the seeds.
Some were planted in good soil.
Others planted in the minds of restless men
   who distorted the seed to their own advantage.
Hold unto you the Truth of Mohammed,
   for in Mohammed is the ultimate Truth, humanity.
Humanity is the bringer of Truth unto the Angels.
Open your doors that all might receive,
   for one is not different than the other.
Each to wear the equal cloak upon their back,
   each to have the offering of the same food to the table,
   each to hold that which is adequate unto them,

    then offer from them that which is abundance.
Prayer will not the mighty man make,
    nor will be a mighty man be mighty
    when he is in the place of the giver
    for the giver exceeds the mighty.
Proclaim from the mountaintop, "*Mohammed will come!*"
Mohammed will be seen
    in the skies above Palestine, of Jerusalem.
Pakistan will see the ray of Light.
The Diadem will be seen to the four corners of earth.
Mark the armies of war,
    that they might war in Truth, not for victory.
This in the name of Mohammed.
[March 12, 2008]

1036 We would have you understand.
In the realms of existence, you are surrounded,
    we speak of your planet earth, the infinitesimal.
You are indeed holding barely
    existence possible upon your earth.
The wind has begun to swirl.
The drought has become enabled.
The rains will deluge the land.
In worlds, far from where you are,
    are worlds that seek the well being of earth.
These are Souls that are visited often.
They are visited by Buddha, Krishna,
    Jesu, and Mohammed.
The purpose of these worlds
    is to augment the needs of mankind
    in the battle they have entered in to.
First, second, third, fourth, fifth, sixth, seventh, are worlds.
You know only of those that enter in to your earth form.
You have not known of those
    that reach out unto your earth at four.
You have unawakened worlds of existence.
They are Energy.
They teem with life, not as yours,
    yet indeed life connected to the Purity of all life.
You will know of these worlds
    and you will know of the attachment to them.

You have a gravitational pull to three worlds
    and you know this not.
Your world does not understand
    the gravity as we understand gravity.
It is in the ion centre of your core.
Should aught happen within your earth,
    because of the burden of earth itself,
        there are three other earths willing to be placed
    within the same strategy as your own.
The strategy, Soul, to bring forth all that is lost.
[April 2, 2008]

1037 We speak of vibration
    and the understanding of the vibrational connector.
It is, Soul, in centrifuge of Energy,
    it is in the sending forth of spiral Energy.
It is with an eternal, evacuous Void field
    wherein a chord is vibrated
        to recess in centrifuge, to be forwarded yet again.
You will understand, the greatest anomaly will be the chord.
You will see the sound arc, lose sound, arc,
    lose sound, arc, yet again and arrive.
Give this to your science.
We teach humanity of the dimensions of creation,
    twelve by fourteen,
    within each Dome, twelve by fourteen.
Souls, Domes are arced.
Creation is arc outward, ever outward.
Humanity see yourselves as the least of all creations,
    the least of all creations,
    all other creations formed from a Purity
    greater than your own.
Within the realm of your Field, your Creator dwells,
    majestic, singularly, Creator supreme.
There are Fourteen such supremes,
    each holding a Field of twelve,
    each holding a depth of fourteen,
    each compounded one upon the other.
As each Field expands,
    within the Field another Dome, twelve by fourteen.
Upon the earth you are infinitesimal,

even within your Dome.
Your Dome is all that is Light and all that is Dark.
Within it fourteen, seven Light and seven Dark.
Measurements are possible only to existing,
    not to expanding,
    that is, Soul, beyond your comprehension.
We ask you to value that which is yours.
 We ask you to honour that which has created you.
But do not see your Creator as man, like man.
You are like Creator, humanity.
Creator is not like you.
Energy, your Energy, your consciousness,
    your consciousness is akin to your Creator.
Behold and it will be.
This from Creator who can form and cast forth.
All Creators form and cast forth.
Yet, all do not have the same leavening of Being.
The consciousness of your Creator
    is Love, ever expanding Love,
        ever expanding Purity, ever expanding Truth.
This is your initializing.
This is from that which you have been formed.
You were formed from Life.
You were formed for Purity.
You were cast out with Truth.
You were not inevitable, as much of creation is formed,
    so that the Voice is heard.
You were, Soul, given a voice, separate,
    held until you gathered
    a purpose to speak with that voice.
You gather the purpose
    from your inevitable struggle with negativity.
For that is why you entered in to your world.
That is why you entered in to your battle.
That is why, Soul, you have been brought low
    and risen above the ash of pain.
As humanity you are not tormented in struggle.
As human you are tormented in struggle.
As humanity you gather together to overcome the struggle.
You are a voice that has become,
    not the Voice that ever was

                but a voice that has been challenged
                and surmounted the challenge.
You are at the edge of hinterland,
                a nothing that has become a Light.
Seen in the farthest Dome, has your Light been seen.
If that can be so seen, will not that which is perfection lost,
                see that which shines so brightly!
Will the Purity of whom you are
                not attract the Purity that is lost!
Will the Love that you have acknowledged
                not enervate a reaching unto that Love!
To where has Idyllic Domed unto?
It is not known.
To what outer flow of expansion of Energy
                is the Field in which Idyllic lies?
Yet, we know it is.
The Light has not been extinguished.
This we know.
We have seen the glow.
As you, humanity, have seen the glow of the Archangels at five
                and sent unto five the power of unified Energy.
So do we know the altruistic perfection
                will hear what is sent forth
                from the infinitesimal, no thing, called humanity.
[October 8, 2008 April 29, 2009]

1038   Souls of earth, we bring you to an accounting
                of the timetable of man.
Earth has an agenda.
Man has an agenda.
All form of creature, fowl and fish have an agenda.
It is the timetable of man.
Upon your earth, cultures have entered in and left their mark
                of the timetable of man.
Your earth awaits,
                momentously an occurrence on the timetable of man.
The shift to the higher vibration has entered in.
Awareness as at no other time of earth
                has entered in to the consciousness of man.
So it is to be in the days to come
                that the adversary to Light Energy,

    the negativeness of man's inhumanity to man
    will accelerate.
Yet the earth will have within a consciousness
    that will disallow such activity.
Men who have seen their children
    as a lesser part of themselves
    will see their children
    as the better part of themselves,
    achieving for their children,
    goals that have never before been set upon earth.
In no one country will this be seen.
In all countries, for it is the collective consciousness
    that has been brought to force against negativity of earth.
You will understand the people of the moon, of the sun,
    of the corn, of the land, of the alien.
You will understand the seers, the grandfathers, the shamans,
    the tellers of tales as those who have brought to witness
    that which will come to be from their stories to reality.
From their foretelling unto the timetable
    lose from your being, judgement, earth.
Hold only the righteous stick that measures all
    with the same dimension.
Build not your towers upward.
Build your compassion upward.
This we say to you, earth.
This we say to you, humanity.
Be brought that the Light might bare
    that which is your Timetable.
[January 21, 2009]

1039 We would now speak of the multitude
    of violet children who are upon your earth.
And upon their being is a sacrifice.
For, Souls of earth,
    they ready themselves to leave in great numbers.
They hear in their ear the sound,
    the colour of drawing together.
They are in many areas of earth.
Your earth will hear of a great slaughter of humanity.
Know these Souls will be lifted,
    each and all will be brought unto Farside.

None will be lost in the transitional state.
For they have entered in pure,
> and their agenda
> is simply to leave earth as sacrificial lamb.

Soul, these are pure Souls, untainted,
> gathering together that man might look upon their being
> and see the distortion that man has caused.

It will bring the countries of Muslim
> to reconsider the words of Holy books.

[June 17, 2009]

1040 Soul, that which you have received
> has been nearly filtered.

All has been not given.
But that which is given has been diligently perused and tagged.
What you can receive is much, much more.
What you have available unto you,
> is allegory of times you have not known,
> of ages you have not known, of ages yet to come,
> of worlds you will meet,
> of energies you will come to know.

You will understand the voracity of our need
> to have you know.

You will understand
> our tenaciousness in allowing you to grapple
> with simple words that are not confounding,
> yet confound,
> that are not beholding, yet behold.

You are receiving scarification in your world.
You are receiving thought
> beyond which you could otherwise attain
> by the intervention of Spirit and Negativity.

Your world is collapsible but this is not a moment to ponder.
It is a time for you are in time
> to acknowledge only positives, only action.

When your earth wars and battles,
> when your earth people are in the greatest need
> they then bond, they then come together.

And so it will be.
Once again the great melting pot
> will bring people unto many diverse places.

They will find them, Soul, sharing their meagre sustenance
>to recover the babe, to hold the aged,
>even to take the maimed
>and place wellness upon their being.
In the great depths of turmoil
>will come a seasoning for mankind.
The youth has long passed in mankind.
The maturity has long since been
>and the wisdom of age will settle upon man
>and man will behold much wisdom
>as Buddha will once again rear a child forth,
>as science will bring logic unto wisdom,
>and math of all equation will make strides to create
>a new mathematic formula
>to recover the balance of earth.
In seven years, the first utterance of this balance will be heard
>in ten it will begin to show recovery.
[July 29, 2009]

1041   We will have you understand that many Souls of earth
>have carried their Farside consciousness
>as a part of their being.
They have had great clarity.
They have come to earth as teachers, not walk in.
They have been born aware of the high mind.
These beings have learned to gather fear.
Your earth humanity have few of these beings
>who enter in and do not lose the high mind.
You have hidden in your earth ways, much art of great beauty.
It has never divulged itself.
Yet, time will bring it upward to you.
And you will see not the simplicity
>that you see in the beginnings of art,
>but great connections to the Energy of other worlds.
You will see profound statements in the art.
You will find a community raised out of the desert.
The sands will fall away and a great structure will emerge.
The structure will have crystalline walls
>and stained in a manner that mankind has not acquired.
It will be totally iridescent.
It will stand to the height of sixteen metres.

It is simply fallen in to a great crevice, to be hid.
A great vehicle will find a puncture, a puncture, Soul.
It should not be, for this vehicle has a tread
        that to earth would seem unpuncturable.
And they will search for that
        which was so sharp that it could alter.
It is the crystalline of the roof of this great building.
It is marked.
They are humanity
        who set themselves apart in a great desert place,
        who found from the desert a place to create that
        which was so hard, so clear, so translucent,
        that it was unbreakable.
It could be altered so that shapes and colour
        could be placed within.
The connector is resin,
        resin from the tap root of a great tree.
[August 19, 2009]

1042   Soul, sound bounces.
Indeed!
Colour also bounces through sound.
All that has momentum has also the ability to bounce,
        travel in waves.
Travel extending beyond itself,
        the positioning of the next sound.
That positioning is vital to the ongoing sound;
        that it relays correctly that which is left behind.
When the sound is accelerated, it changes
        not just the momentum
        but the ongoing message to the next sound.
It is a query that will be resolved
        within the existence of humanity
        for it will allow Negativity to return.
They are connected.
We will tell you of echo.
You, Soul, have a spiral.
Individual earth beings each hold a spiral.
Thousands, millions of beings having entered in to earth,
        each holding a spiral.
Upon the Farside all beings carry a spiral of Energy.

But you will understand
>   within Creator's spiral all earth energies exist.
All worlds within the Yawn spiral to create upward echo.
This is only within Creator Yawn,
>   and only because of humanity
>   >   having found a voice as Humanity.
The Energy of Creator Yawn
>   is within the spiral of the Energy Source.
It in itself has its own spiral.
And all goodness echoes unto it.
Above is the Vanguard from which is the great spiral
>   wherein all illusion has a Path.
It is Soul, holding worlds beyond your understanding,
>   energies beyond your understanding.
Yet it echoes downward to you with a need.
And you humanity have answered that need.
You have made it your agenda
>   to enter in to yet a further spiral
>   to bring forth echo.
Resounding echo,
>   Energy return to Energy,
>   matter return to Matter,
>   ion return to Ion,
>   withholding the chaotic structure within the Path,
>   within existence, within creation.
Who would voice to you creation is vulnerable?
And we do this, Soul!
We say to you, creation is vulnerable.
Not from your simplicity of your earth structure
>   but from all that is.
A warp exists.
A warp is.
It alters sound.
You have strengthened your sound.
You have become as no other sound has become,
>   able to alter the warp.
It is simple.
To create the sound of High C in its highest form
>   is to decimate that which is around.
And yet, all returns to its beginning.
Each echo echoes back unto the High C all negativity.

You alter the chord that is sent forth.
[May 12, 2010, June 16, 2010]

1043   Souls, we will ask of earth humanity
        that they take precaution in a future devastation.
It will begin, soil born.
It will invade the bodies of human
        and we ask that the waters that you use
        to wash the face, the hands at that time be boiled.
For that which is feeding the aberration
        will be water sourced
        and it will require a great diligence
        on the part of humanity to lessen
        the food supply for this creature.
As you place water upon your skin,
        you will find that that which is within the water
        will feed and create great aberrations to the skin.
The edges of which will become swollen
        until the inner area becomes as a lake of liquid.
This will allow the insect to create its own feeding area.
It will come to many countries
        and no one will find a destroyer.
To destroy is to destroy the water source.
It is fresh water, stagnant, and will not last two seasons.
But the devastation that it will cause to humanity,
        adult and child will be wide spread.
It will be lessened by boiled water, drinking,
        mouth care, skin care.
It will be gathered upon cloths
        which must be boiled to eradicate.
For the organism can live in all but boiling temperature.
It can thrive in the countries of cold, of heat.
It will, Soul, not be lessened by chemical.
There will be an outbreak close to the area of Portugal first.
[May 19, 2010]

1044   It is, Soul, to establish recognition
        we are able to speak in your vernacular
We can divulge unto you alchemy of earth's propensity.
We can envision for you through our advanced knowledge
        where you will be required to differentiate

        the strategies of your earth signal.
We cannot propine the great need
        for you to adhere to these changes.
They will significantly adjust your Requiem,
        the somberness of which is diabolical.
Yet, it has for earth within it a message.
Discern the message.
It is radiant in its Light.
It is fractious to the inner ear.
Hear with a fork to hear that decibel change.
And take note of the sound.
Calibrate it.
[May 19, 2010]

1045   Hebernon, Soul, Hebernon.
It is within Iraq.
It is ancient, next to Turkey.
It had Glaziers.
Soul, we spoke to you of the Glaziars
        who yet will build within the desert.
Do not tremble at the thought of teaching
        even as you feel Methuselah
            has come upon your being,
            you, yet, will teach and the words that you teach
            will be simple and honest.
And the Souls will hear, will be many.
And the lands will open the seven volumes
        and hear that which each says
        and know no coincidence
        could have brought them together.
There was purpose, Soul, in the coming together,
Not the seven that you bring forth at this table, Soul,
        but the seven that will come forth unto the world
        of which yours are three.
[September 1, 2010]

1046   There will come forth from the mountain
        an elderly woman.
She will speak to earth.
She will speak in many tongues.
She will be seen as greatly aged.

She will reach to one hundred and eleven.
There will be around about her illuminessence.
She will carry in her hand a burled stick.
It will have been made and given to her by her brother.
She will sit on a partly flat stone
      and her voice, though soft, will carry in an echo
      and speak to the world
      of a coming of the Four Purities.
She will speak to each land in many dialects.
All that she says will be taken
      and resound across the waves of earth.
Those who are intent on destroying humanity
      will find themselves trembling in their being
      for she will know their hearts and their minds.
She will have decoded
      that which they have placed in secret places as code.
For seven years this woman will be at the Mountaintop.
She will place the staff that she carries
      upon the place of division,
      and the four corners of transition
      will hear the first echo.
The might of the staff will be of myrtle wood
      and the tree from which it has been drawn
      will have existed for seven hundred earth years,
      one for each year of her counselling by Farside.
Her earth nationality is Israeli.
Her home is Palestine.
She will rise from the valley and walk to the mountain.
She will carry with her no food.
She will be fed by creatures for seven years.
[August 19, 2009]

1047   Souls of earth, Truth is a station you enter in to.
Truth can torment your Soul.
Truth can bring you great joy.
Truth can drive you to desperation.
And Truth can set you free
      of the connected chord to negativity.
There is upon your earth
      a great need to enter in to negativity.
It is as though humanity is driven into that negative space.

There is only one purpose in being there.
It is simply so that you may find a path out.
All illness, all pain, all dysfunction has to do with
      humanity's engagement with overcoming negativity.
All fields of learning have now entered in to this.
All arrogancy is determined it shall fail.
Souls of earth, you cannot be greater than you are.
You cannot hold yourself in such esteem
      while you accept no things.
Truth is to be accepted
Truth that you are not a single being.
You are a triad.
Your body is at will to your mind.
Your mind is at will to your high consciousness.
But earth beings do not hear.
They do not see
      and they do not speak in the words of overcoming.
They have connected to negativity with all their being first.
And then they set themselves the great Energy of overcoming.
Can we say to you, Souls,
      it is much simpler to overcome than to enter in,
      to hold on to the ultimate Truth
      instead of simply earth truth.
But mankind has always feared the unseen,
      what they perceive as
      the ghostly encounter with the Spirit.
And yet the Spirit is very real.
Your Soul may connect to that Spirit self at will.
You may hold on to that Energy that you are,
      that holds such consciousness, such awareness
      that you do not have to know knowledge,
      you are knowledge!
You do not have to seek joy, you will be joy!
You do not have to find the Light, you will become the Light!
You are the apparition.
You are the illusion.
It is we who should see your being and stand far from it,
      not you standing far from the Spirit of who you are.
Reach unto the very Energy of your being.
Hold that being as precious unto you.
For it is you.

You have a mind.
Is your mind all that you are?
Souls, truth will tell you
    there are great complexities to the mind.
The mind will confound for many years your science.
And then it will enter in to that knowing of higher Truth.
And understand how simple the healing
    of the flesh and the bone and the mind are,
    simply to alter the frequency of the body.
The frequency of the body
    that will create the body to moleculate.
Indeed, moleculate in a slower pattern, so slow,
    and then rev it back to the frequency of wellness.
This will be the simple healing.
This will place all cut from the physician.
There will be no need.
All wounds will heal by molecular reconstruction.
It will be done simply.
And you will have but to know what you are healing.
The voice of your earth being
    will be unnecessary to speak of that illness.
Only a small touch to the skin
    would tabulate the frequency to be used.
This is the healing of your tomorrow.
This will regenerate organs,
    heal minds, place wellness in thought.
Who are you, Souls?
You are but the portion of Truth you have entered to.
You are but a molecular being
    and you are of the frequency of your Creator.
Understand this.
All Energy is connected to molecular structure.
And in seeking to heal the world
    direct your path to the equation.
[October 7, 2009]

1048 Soul, the Caspian Way is the great part of your galaxy,
    a very fragmented portion of the great system we see.
You will have visuals unto these systems.
You will have it soon.
You will see before you the great abundance of life

    that will be made available as you peruse
    that which your computer gives unto you.
You will understand as science, that the equation fits.
Indeed, it will have a direct link.
It will find itself seen within the starry sky but not of your galaxy.
But to, Soul, apart from where you are.
You will find yourself visiting in your computer to that place.
[November 4, 2009]

1049 Souls of earth, we take you unto the Shining Water,
    into the translucent echo,
    all Sireen sound brought back
    held within the Shining Water.
Why, Soul?
For echo.
Your world will soon find through research
    that all Energy is one Energy.
Within a descended platform
    is an echo of all platforms beyond.
It is only from this echo that earth will understand
    the vast Void beyond the echoed sound.
The transom will be opened.
There is a opportunity for earth humanity
    to then know the visuals beyond.
It will give to earth
    a kaleidoscope of colour that is decipherable.
It will give to earth
    a path through unto the dimensions beyond
    so there will be clear understanding
    of the vastness of that which is.
And all that echoes will be decipherable.
There is within the Place of Shining
    an echo chamber as in a drum.
Indeed, it will take sound into the Water
    and resound it outward from it.
[February 17, 2010]

1050 It is, Soul, joy to behold the small child, is it not!
The small child is entered in to earth
    burdened with a path that they have accepted to take.
As they enter in they recognize not one whit of that path.

They do not see the great cavities where their foot must pass
        and oft times in their lack of strength entered in to.
 Each child is brought unto humanity for a purpose.
They have entered in with this purpose.
As the child matures, often the purpose may become clear.
The child may reach unto their purpose early.
For they have been that old Soul
        that knows from many past lives
        the purpose of humanity.
More often the child enters in
        to be brought through pain of growing.
It is the tribulation for all humanity
        when a child is lost without the fullness of age.
But often, Soul, it is simply a teaching for those around.
For the child has willingly entered in and willingly left earth.
There is a recognition of/on earth of children
        who have the ability to obliterate from their being
        all that is reality.
They have fixated on the technology of their earth.
They have drawn their life to no purpose.
We would have you not be dismayed
        because of that which you see
        for they will awaken and present unto you
        a greater purpose for mankind.
They have entered in to alter the mind of men.
Hear that which we say, "*to alter the mind of men*"!
For man is influenced by that which man comes to be.
And as the generations flow forward they will see
        that which is the influence of negativity in their children.
They will find a great purpose in reinventing truth.
There will be many who are diverse in their purpose
        that will come to an understanding of Purity.
They will, Souls, bring the world to a new awakening.
And from the lack of movement
        will come a great need to move.
And that which was idle
        will be brought to a purpose for all mankind.
They have gathered in their wisdom, knowledge.
They will be valued for the knowledge they have gathered.
[July 21, 2010]

1051   All waterways are widening.
The water is receding yet the waterways are widening
    for the gullies will be deep.
The lands will have great heights.
The structures will find themselves sliding to great depths.
Within the land of Greece there will be a rise of earth mass.
It will find a great level plain
    wherein man will be tempted to dwell
    and we say to you,
    "*Do not enter in,*
        for there will be a gully of great proportions.
        It will be a central cleavage in the land
            that will make of Greece yet another island."
In the far structures of the Andean mountains,
    a great cave will immanently become visible.
It will spiral down so that Souls will say,
    "*Hell has been opened.*"
It will not, Soul, but the very core of earth will be seen.
There is a vacuous climate appearing
    within the range of Chile.
From the south to the north that which was one will be two.
Earth mankind
    do not say your prayers unto your almighty God.
Do not raise your voice in piety,
    raise your eyes to see that which is below
    and cast your eyes down to see that
    which is lesser than you.
Behold the great structure of the form of human
    from the pate to the feet will ooze.
We say to you,
    "*Use the oil of the palm to quiet the sores.*"
It will be brought into many lands.
The seams of the body will separate and ooze.
The folds of the skin will draw back
    as though tightened with a bow
    to spring forward but will not.
Use palm oil to give healing.
Forward the complexity of the mind not with prayer
    but with contemplation within the being.
Absorb what is given to you,
    that you will benefit from the Light

> that is ready to be given.
There is a great calm that exists upon Farside.
All that is awaits as never before
> for the moment of man's Entering In.
[August 4, 2010]

1052   Souls, you are the sheep of the flock.
You are holding the ropes that identify our rope.
For you walk the wasteland
> and you place your being in peril
> with that which you do.
And the very Souls that are round about you
> will fling mud to cast your Energy far from them.
For the words are precious and the message is Holy.
But holiness is not always precious in the world.
You are the children of men
> but you are first a child of your Creator.
You are given the comfort to your being
> that you will not feel the aloneness
> at the time of storm gathers its being unto thee.
There is a gentle wonder at that which will be brought forth.
It will enter in as a lamb enters in to the fold.
And then it will be seen as the ram.
And the Soul will wonder at the great variance
> of wolves, of bears, of tigers, of snakes,
> that enter in to collapse that which is written.
But it shall not be.
It shall stir them to seek deeper into the chaos
> to challenge many,
> to gather in goodness and peruse the word.
And each will find in it a countenance of their own.
And they will wonder at the code
> and seven shall come forth
> and each will lean upon the other.
And the wonder and anger will cease to be.
And the world will behold a new day
> and recognize a new glory of oneness.
[August 25, 2010]

1053   Souls of earth, we speak to you of matter.
There is, Soul, matter without conscious Energy.

It is found not within the realms of your earth.
Although your earth is prone to call Energy dead,
      matter without consciousness.
All matter upon earth has consciousness!
It is not visible in the realm of electromagnetic courses.
Yet it is acknowledging consciousness.
Many beings are lost in coma, even, Soul, as vegetable.
This is referred to.
And we tell you the matter even in that
      which seems the stillest matter has consciousness.
It has data.
It records and sends forth.
There is a recognition of consciousness
      within all that is upon your earth.
It resonates.
It has very strong vibration in the B's, the flat B's.
Were you to treat a patient with B flats,
      you would find recognition.
We ask you to vibrate at a single tone
      until you have reached a B flat
      that is recognizable to a patient.
There is more than one B flat.
It is told in the vibratory tones
      of that instrument that will be used.
One may be accurate for a particular matter of human
      but there are many matters within the human form.
One unto one will not match another.
Therefore, we ask you to resonate
      until you find one that responds to the echo
      within the flesh and the bone and the blood.
There is a constant re figuration, not configuration,
      re figuration,
      to design an instrument that would attach itself
      within the ear, that would keep a Soul
      on a constant course of mental stability.
It would require no ingestive components.
There is a concourse of information available
      within the realm of psychic Energy
      within your world by both the Tibetan
      and the South American countries.
We would direct to science to search in this direction.

[October 6, 2010]

1054   We ask you to give heed to the words of he
       who has imparted a known science within your world.
It has been all but forgotten and yet,
       it has been used for many centuries.
We ask the path of the inner ear
       be used to gentle the body's illness.
It is particularly evident within new flesh, the infant.
It will mend the heart palpitations.
It will direct the body to reconstitute flesh and sinew.
It will form bone, not of itself but it is the resonating tone,
       the vibration of which
          sends forth the message to the consciousness.
The consciousness then revitalizes the missing link
       wherein a illness, break, or fracture, has occurred.
It can send the blood coursing in a manner that is pure.
It is valid.

[October 6, 2010]

1056   We speak to you
       from within the Void wherein our station is.
We are gathering a power of united Energy
       to reach far below you.
You will understand,
       you will feel within the circle radius of your sun,
          the expansive Breath that flows by and through you.
You will feel within a chaotic spurt of Energy that rotates
       unto the sixteenth portion of your earth coordinates.
You will see a line deep within the meridian of earth
       that will create a hum, hum.
The earth will begin a very fine wobble.
It will take unto four hours, ten minutes to adjust.
You will feel upon much of earth the liquefaction.
It is not a gasp outward from earth as in earthquake.
It is a Breath, a part from your earth,
       that travels through your meridian to create a wobble.
The source is of much Purity.
The source is not invasion.
The source is not destruction.
And we would have earth know

        not to react in a negative manner
        but to use the Energy within to still all that is earth,
        to create a calming within the Energy of earth.
You are within your beings attached to all Energy,
        and as you allow your Energy to calm,
        it will travel outward from your being unto all that is.
The Light of humanity will enhance the journey
        for it will give added momentum to Breath,
        for all Purity is apportioned to Breath.
You will feel the pressure build
        in the March of your following year.
You will feel it build for several months.
All that is of Breath,
        that has the ability
        to move unto the station of Lantosia,
        will do so.
It will last from March of your year eleven
        until December of eleven.
Not twelve, Soul, eleven.
Earth will need to adjust timetables after the re alignment.
That which will occur in the year 2012 will allow
        those who have prepared within Lantosia,
        to move forward into the fourth level
        and possibly the fifth.
We are as you, Soul.
We do not have all the knowns to our being.
[October 13 2010]

1057   Souls, thoughts are formed
        and more often changed.
That which is within the Keys
        will often have formed thought until, Soul,
        the reader reads on and eyes the layering within.
Healing is like thought.
There are layers of healing.
There are physicians
        who heal the surface with every good intent.
They gather the surface of the blood,
        the surface of the bone, the surface of the flesh.
Yet they still do not reach within the very core
        of that which is the DNA of all being.

They have not found, Soul, that you can alter the well being
> from the initiate molecule within the being.

It resides, yet, it is the last to live.

As in thought that changes,
> so does that which is formed of you daily.

Within the nanosecond you are altered.

You see it not,
> yet as you mirror your being through the years
> you look and you see the wellness
> become altered in the gathering of pain
> or you see the flesh become wrinkled
> in the gathering of age.

Many beings have not thought to reach within the being
> to alter that which is unsatisfactory within their body.

They do not find the storage of DNA,
> a portion of the wisdom that is theirs.

They do not behold the power
> of that which is within the body itself to heal the body.

For it is connected to the very Energy of your being.

It is, Soul, the thread unto your Creator.

It is the continuance of whom you are.

It radiates as the prism radiates from humanity.

Medicine in your earth has not perceived
> to single out and reconstruct
> from the first entry in of humanity.

Yet it will be.

All illness will be healed before illness is.

It is not done with replacements.

It is not done from the growing of tissue.

It is done from the single thrust of perfection
> into the single atom of your being.

DNA structure will be altered for the good of man.

Unto you is power.

Unto you in all that you are is the great Energy of Farside.

It becomes a part of your being.

You are welled up with that which is true and pure
> and you relinquish it, Soul, in negativity.

Do not despair.

Will it form life forever?

Why?

Why would you wish to live upon your earth forever

when you have the goodness of where we are.
Indeed!
You are in forever
> but your ever includes the triad of whom you are,
> the casing of your being.

The healing that will not be necessary
> will be the utopia of earth
> and people will pass in age indeed
> with forms that have fulfilled a lifetime of living.

It will extend itself well into the hundred and twenties.
There will be Methuselahs who reside upon your earth.
But, Soul, until humanity sees itself as one,
> it will only be for the elite.

The negativity, pain,
> will be that some will live in this perfection
> while others will not because of man's greed.

Knowledge, Soul, is not Purity.
Knowledge is simply knowledge.
That which is done with knowledge
> can be the extension of Purity
> or the wilfulness of man.

It will be man's opportunity to change.
Behold, the structure of the DNA.
[November 17, 2010]

1058   These volumes will meet in Israel.
They will be bound together.
Each will be the three, the one, the one, the one, the one.
Each will be given the highest number of Purity.
You will receive also at the same time a small child
> containing a word
> from the distant Asian land called China.

He will speak of that which has been brought forth
> from his father unto the Keys.

This also will verify that which was within.
Within the same time will be reported by science
> an aperture at Ayres Rock.

Each will receive recognition
> so that your world will quickly scramble
> for knowledge of that which is written.

The texts of many countries

        still unpublished will be published.
Within your world the active aliens
        recognize the momentum of your progress.
You are of High C
        and we recognize your goodness unto all existence.
Credibility will not be a mandate.
Acceptability will not be an issue.
Word will receive vibration
        and go forth unto mankind.
So be it.
[January 5, 2011]

1059   For Within your earth you are bound by earth levels.
In reaching the Purity of Farside,
        you will have the understanding
        and the healing of Colour and Sound
        to connect to all your world.
You will walk with a vibrancy of Energy
        that will vibrate a connection to language.
You will have a quick understanding of religions
        for the many lives you have lived
        will re enter unto you.
You will discern the weaknesses and the strengths in men.
You will feel the rapture of glory unto you.
Each Soul will receive a recognition of angelic force.
There will be the ability to alter the form of man.
You will have disease at bay.
These will appear to be stunning
        and received by humanity as miracles.
You will hold the leaven of your being and lift your form.
And that which you are will hold itself to earth
        and your form will rise in its apparition above you.
You will receive recognition from humanity.
There will be a tone hovering
        and people will say from one to the other,
            "Do you hear that tone that vibrates?
            Does it come within?
            What is the source?"
It will be the tone of muted High C
        that man might not receive injury
        to the fullness of that tone.

The voice will speak great volumes
        sent forth by the vocal cord alone.
The tenuous hold upon earth of the ancients will be known.
[January 5, 2011]

1060   Souls of earth, you are children in the use of colours.
Indeed.
As a child with the sticks of colour delights in their use,
        so will earth beings
           find the healing of colour as a delight.
You will understand
        that which has always been possible unto you.
You will see the range of creation.
You will behold the Sound as it vibrates and strengthens
        and alters that which is flesh and blood and bone,
           that which is speech and mind,
           that which is, Soul, still in its temperament,
           yet, ever altering.
The vibration of colour is a portioned as the Soul's Purity.
It is gathered at the level of the Souls's Purity.
It is strengthened at the level of the Soul's Purity.
The level may alter at the will of the Soul.
Yet restrictions are held by that level.
And we say to you, as you understand that which is the healing,
        as you totally instill within your being
           the power you know,
           so you see with the eyes of Farside
           as you behold the human in distress.
You will see that which is discord and that which is united form.
You will see wherein the energy struggles.
It will appear to you as waves of colour.
Many of earth have healed in this mode, many;
        but none except the great masters
        have used the Spirit Energy,
        but have limited their being to the earth vibration.
In that day of healing from the Mountaintop
        the Souls who heal will gather the fullness
        of their Farside Energy to heal
        wherein they will see and strengthen
        all patterns of discord.
You will behold the human body as a form.

It will allow you to gram all energy of discord.
You will see the form and lift with the strength of sound
      using colour to mediate the healing.
We say to you, it will bring for some, nauseousness, dizziness,
      often the very illness they are healing
      until they become accustomed to the full use
      of their Farside Energy.
You are powerful in that which is available unto you.
You do not require the earth self to heal.
You need only enter in to the Farside Energy to heal the form.
[January 19, 2011]

1061   Souls, earth travails;
      water, lack of, storms,
      creatures who are caught
      in the disarray of earth's climate.
We say unto you much is caused by the axis of earth.
It is creating struggle to contain boundaries.
Indeed a climate that warms, distresses earth,
      but earth's wobble is of greater magnitude,
      for the complete motion of the waterways
      moves according to the axis.
The melt gives more body to that motion.
Your earth will soon learn a great need
      to respond to motions of water.
They will place unseen boundaries within the sea.
They will be as stress monitors.
They will have information to give.
They will be as canals that permit
      the movement of your ships
      to lesser levels of ocean.
These will contain the wildness of the sea.
They will be stretched as barriers about land.
We say this to you to give you cause to seek the unseen.
For although the eye of man will not acknowledge,
      the eye of the sea will be held at bay.
These same containments will be used as force fields
      to protect atmospheres within the sky.
Your earth science is struggling
      with how to acknowledge and we say,
        "Do not attempt to make it visual for it shall not be."

Yet it will be a solid as any barrier created of steel
    or formations of concrete.
This ability to create atom structure into fibre
    will save much of earth's land.
It will also create boundaries wherein lava will be.
It will rehearse the demographics of earth over and over.
For those who have within their power,
    this containment will be universal.
Its first attention will come from Switzerland unto the world.
It is as a binary.
Souls, all that is will be contained within the solar, the wind.
All that is where heat reigns will be cooled.
All that is where cold is will be altered
    so that earth will regulate all atmospheres.
Each that is creature will have a domain to its liking.
Your earth would see the continuation
    of this mode of structure within the Thousand Years
    for all that is earth will still be earth.
Pain will be overcome throughout the Thousand Years,
    and those who will, will alter quickly.
You have a funnel through which all things come unto you.
It is from Farside to earth.
It is made of such structure as apertures
    that allow a passing through.
They do not alter that which passes through.
They alter that you might pass through.
You have before you a healing time.
It will come unto you.
It will be a time of science exploding,
    to create for one thousand years
    a perfect earth wherein peace will reign,
    wherein all beings will hold others in esteem,
    where each creature is gathered as one unto all.
There is a time of perfection.
Unto that perfection there is a healing, a cleansing,
    a transfer of Energy to that which is distorted,
    to that which is perfect.
You have before you the opportunity, as all humanity,
    to portion yourselves, to be the healers
    for many will be healed
    but many also will be of the healers.

And they will enter forth from the Mountaintops
    unto the valleys of pain, of struggle,
    to heal and be healed,
    to hear the pain and lift and share.
For the Mountaintop you will find is a place of wellness,
    a place of healing,
    a place from which pain will dissipate.
Create where you are a Mountaintop.
Create where you are a place of healing,
    where each particle of your being is strengthened
    by the power that is given unto you of your Creator.
You are the wellness from which all pain can be cleansed.
You are the Light that echoes forth
    from the strength of Creator.
You are earth's foundation of healing.
Lift the walls that they will be walls wherein all can see,
    and the Light will shine as the stars shine
    continuous in the outer realms.
Be it night or day, they do not dim.
So will the healing not dim
    for you of the Mountaintop,
    you will know the Sound and Colour of healing.
Your being will be strengthened.
You will speak to those who reach unto you
    with a power of the Prism.
You will know the voice of alien beings
    and converse with their energies.
You will speak the language of all Energy
    and none will be kept without.
For the expansion of Truth is never ending
    and the comfort of healing is abiding compassion.
And you, you are the angels that tread the earth
    to bring forth that
    which is the Kingdom of your Creator.
[January 19, 2011]

1062   Earth will become content.
Earth will see the heavens and hear the voice from afar.
The voice will be that Deer planet.
Each will hear from a multitude of stations.
Each will hear and the global fear of distance will cease.

The wage of war is death.
The wage of presence is being.
It is, Soul, the great placement.
It is the mask that is worn of negativity
    to cover that which is spewed forth.
And yet, Souls of earth, the stench will lift
    and earth beings will ingratiate themselves
    unto the wellness of earth.
Yet their intent would want to be of Truth
    but the truth will have a negative variance.
It will not carry the throb that it should.
It will not carry the sound of goodness,
    and negativity will ignite once more.
There is upon your earth a carrier of pain.
It is a fractious being, yet a content, Soul, called turtle.
The turtle will speak,
    will be seen upon the shores in many lands
    where turtles have never been seen, will they enter in.
This will be a sign unto you of a great change
    of earth's people and earth's people's intent.
Venture forth if you will leave, if you will,
    but you are the Armada
    and you have entered in to overcome pain.
Overcome pain, draw your beings to the greatest Truth.
Draw your minds into the greatest corridor.
Bring a sanity to that which has no sanity.
Open all doors that all may enter in.
This we speak to you.
[February 16, 2011]

1063 Souls, we speak that you might be aware
    of all that will come to be.
Earth has many phases to enter,
    has many triumphs and many failures
    in that earth will feel the people become as lassitude,
    without will.
Then rise to will and become in great inspiration of will
    to a negative degree drawing earth into much turmoil.
Yet through the turmoil will come a song,
    a song of such Purity and a voice of such clarity
    will enunciate a message that has been found

upon many pages in many areas.
Each Soul will express, "*How can this be?*"
The words are as one.
That which is spoken of negativity
    is described in many manner
    so that all the sciences of religion, of philosophy,
    of mathematics, of medicinal,
    of physical and internal nature;
    all that is of earth will be described in a negative positive,
    evaluating so that from a fraction of beings
    will come forth a manner to overcome
    perpetual motion of thought,
    perpetual motion of mind, perpetual motion of healing.
And all that is seen will be in the spectrum of colour and sound.
Within each residual Energy there will be a thrum of sound.
 It will, Soul, heal many beings.
 It will enter in unto the inner ear.
It will not have any deference to well or ill.
It will be for all.
Within your earth,
    there will be an internal floatation that will make visible
    all that you are within your mind, within your body.
Within the blood circulatory of your body,
    will be seen the continuation of colours expressing
    for all earth that which requires healing.
It will be available to you.
It will be seen as progress.
Yet it is more than progress.
It is the beginning of that which has always been a return.
There is a thraption upon the being that will weigh the Soul
    and count the mental stresses of the being.
It will lay itself upon the area of the heart.
It will denote all that is in angst of the body.
It will declare itself with the written word.
[February 16, 2011]

1064   Soul, so shall you be creators of Light and sound
    for your healing will come from Light and sound.
Colour is Light.
Sound, Soul, attached to Colour.
Understand all realms, yours and beyond where you are,

    hold Colour and Sound.
Yours is diminished, Soul, muchly diminished.
Yet you have the power in your being
    to reach beyond where you are,
    to strengthen your Energy of sound,
    to strengthen the vision of colour,
    indeed to behold that which the combination brings;
    a vibration of such strength as to alter matter.
You will understand that you are on the threshold of a new day.
Within your earth you have nation after nation
    drawing forth a new chord
    that is being heard throughout your world.
It carries itself deep,
    it carries itself high and low.
It carries itself to heal.
It is an envisionment of that which is in the hearts of men.
For men one and all have the knowledge
    of that which is High C,
    the purpose of their being.
All who have entered in understand
    there are enough to bring forth the Angels.
Purity has reached a tone of High C
    in the embodiment of mankind.
It is, Soul, that men have learned
    to lean upon the identity of negativity,
    and the chaotic thrashing
    has become a delight to their being.
Not all, but many.
Within the countenance of man there are beings
    who can see beyond that which the eyes see.
They may behold energies far from them.
They may enter in to realms of Energy
    wherein beings have form other than you.
They are strengthened by the Colour and Sound
    they allow unto themselves
    that creates them vibration that allows them entry.
You have much to learn and much to see.
Mankind will have the vision of clarity
    for as with all things unto mankind,
    when it is first known it is complex.
As the knowledge is gathered, it becomes simple.

There will be teachers who teach
>that which appears to be complex.

It will be, Soul, to accept that which is the Energy of all things,
>that which is your world, that which is your very being.

It is not to manipulate.
It is to vibrate, to vibrate with a chord of such clarity
>that the filament within the form is altered,
>to alter unto the memory
>so that a Soul reborn become that which it was.

The method will be given unto all men.
It will be accepted, Soul,
>so that in that day hospitals will stand empty.

Great machines will not be needed,
>only the power to alter the energy
>within the form that is human,
>within the form that is creature.

The animals of earth will also receive a healing of man.
This has been known, Soul,
>from the Void of Consciousness unto the Fourteen,
>unto the Twelve Creators,
>unto the Energy Source.

Even within the Farside is such healing used.
It is used without not within.
All doubt must be erased.
All Energy must be placed.
The value is Zero where the healer is of no thing.
[April 27, 2011]

1065 Thirteen is the destruction of St. Peter's Square.
It will be formed on the day of Pentecost
>and from sixteen centres, munitions.

Thousands will be slaughtered.
A hole deep in to the ground
>will bring forth reminders of past civilizations.

An edict of reform will not bring about the Holy See again.
Members of the faithful
>will be chosen to reinvest within distant lands.

A Pope will be blinded in that day.
From the balcony he shall see his people die.
The flash will sear his eyes.
The monastic brethren of friars will attempt to re form

    the original concept of the church.
It will not succeed.
Soul, much of the historical documents
    will find themselves moistened
    for upon that day the rain
    which will pelt to make blood flow,
    will be seen falling through broken glasses.
Torrents will overflow into the lower systems.
On that day the colour of orange will be seen bright in the sky
    as a celebration for the death of Catholicism.
Soul, it will come from three unified countries,
    each having spent many years to prepare its collapse;
    Judah, Iran, China.
What they have done is already done,
    much of earth has no knowledge of corruption.
It gives, Soul, power to Italy,
    power to Germany, power to the States.
These countries wish no power there.
[May 11, 2011]

1066 We would have you recover all that you have.
Your hearts are set aflutter and we do not
    have intent to set emotions aflutter.
We ask you, Soul, to recover in your being
    the urgency for that which you do.
The time is pending.
Time is not ceasing, it is pending
    for things upon your earth are altering.
There is a diminishing of humanity's value by humanity.
There is, Soul, a need to gather quickly with urgency,
    the foods to feed millions of people.
There is an urgency
    to prevent the deterioration of forest and forest floors;
    not just the forest but the floors of the forest.
There is a need to gather for your future,
    to contend with the evaporation of sacred air.
How can air evaporate?
And yet we say to you it will.
And man will clutch at their chest
    to receive their portion of air.
You may juggle but you are not jugglers.

You may hope and dream but they are not answers.
The answers are in your commitment to that which you do.
It is, Soul, the expediency
    for time is indeed entering in to no time.
Not in the sense that there is no time available,
    but in the sense
    that there is no time available for humanity,
    for humanity will not recover quickly
    from the dire sensitivities of earth.
The winds, the rains will howl.
The crime of destroying crop
    to gain monetary value will increase.
We ask, Soul, that you do not pray.
We ask that you give to all beings this information.
As it is placed, Soul,
    in one moment
    you will have it distributed in languages.
The time is not now, but it will be.
[December 1, 2011]

1067   Souls of earth, we salute you.
We put praises before you
    for you have helped the salutary placement for Farside.
You have been regimed as all armies are regimed
    to counter a force.
The force upon you is negativity.
You have brought into being a new sword.
It is called the sword of Truth.
You have lifted the sword.
It has created great difficulties for humanity.
For all truth is garnered with difficulty.
One truth overcoming another,
    all bringing forth Energy that repels negativity.
And you may feel in your being
    the verification of negativity upon you,
    for it leaves, Soul, rises upon the skin.
It brings forth fear in to your being.
And you who are human must rise above the fear.
We say unto you of that which is to come.
You will hold no fear.
You will place no negativity into your thought processes.
You will understand

        how miraculous are the nudgings of Angels.
You will understand that you are called with a mighty calling
        to be in the utmost of Truth.
Then you will use the sword
        and it will strike forth a Light
        such as no light on earth has ever shone forth.
And you will see the Light of Truth,
        the sword held high
        and you will know that it reaches in the arc of Light.
And you will know as it drops into the darkness,
        into the well of no thing,
        you will have the power beyond the Angels
        to see, to behold.
There will be a way opened unto you, humanity.
You will see in the chasm the Blessed Archangels.
Beyond you will see the corridor as in the great pyramid.
There are visionaries,
        there are paths to the sightings within darkness.
You who have the ability to enter in unto the Archangels,
        you will have opened up a transitory channel
        through which your Light will go forth in the darkness.
You have conquered time and you know it not.
You have conquered space and you know it not.
You have time and you have space.
But, Soul, you also have Timeless space
        wherein motion is possible.
You are the heron taking flight
        and lifting the Truth into the cavity of darkness.
There is the resounding Energy come forth
        for we have beheld that which is within.
We have not recovered.
We have beheld.
Only humanity can recover with the Purity of their being.
Now we say to you individually, each in their own being,
        you have the power of Energy.
You are Energy!
It can ignite to such greatness
        that all Light would seem dim before you.
You have the power to change that which is.
You have the power to radiate the strength of another.
You have the power to become that which you would be.

Within the orb of your being
> you have the translucent Energy
> as witnessed by the eye.

You have all but the will,
> and we seek for you to invest in the will of your being!

We speak of many avenues of will.

As you do your east,
> we ask that you use the Energy of your being
> to heal your weariness.

We ask that you lift in sincerity
> the strength of your Energy unto Farside
> and offer to receive that which will be given unto you;
> Energy to cleanse and purify your being.

Do not accept casual
> that which is given of the Angels of Creator.

Do not beckon forth,
> but gather unto you each morning of your day
> the greatness of Energy that is available unto you.

Earth beings will behold your Energy.

They will feel the goodness of who you are.

You will cast Light upon the shadow.

You will be seen as the star transfixed at the mountaintop.

You are the Light, the shining star.

Behold, to accept that which is offered unto you!

It can only be given.

It must be received.

Who can see the greatness, the strength
> that is in the holding of one Soul unto the other?

You have been offered the strength of your beginning.

It is not delayed, Soul, indeed, not.

It is ever forward unto you.

It waits only for you to receive.

An east done with humble acceptance
> is not the fullness of that which you are able to receive,
> an east gathering the Energy
> with expectation of goodness unto you,
> this will portray your Light unto other beings.

You will be seen as Holy.

That which you give will be felt as Holy.

That which radiates from your being will be gathered as Purity.

Humble your being.

Be of great joy.
Raise your Energy and become one with the Angels.
Unto you is the Energy available!
So be it.
[January 25, 2012]

1068   Souls of earth, we speak in all generosity to your being.
We give unto you, Soul, that which we are able.
We hold back no thing
      that is possible to offer to your enlightenment,
      yet you have entered in to a dark space
      and you have asked of Farside:
      "Show not too soon the Light.
      Allow us to become accustomed
            to that which is the darkened way,
            that we might know negativity,
            that we might meet and understand negativity.
      We understand that our being will be enticed
            but we will enter in many times unto earth
            and we will speak each time
            with the voice that is stronger.
      We will behold negativity each time
            in a fuller understanding
            of the needs of our brother.
And we say to you,
      "Bear with us always for we are the weak in humanity."
      And we beseech that you will know our being
            has come under the guise
            of many different forms of humanity.
      And we struggle with the knowing of our being.
      Negativity has become as a friend to whom we are.
      We know the workings, the intrigues,
      the venom that is possible,
            and yet we ask you to withhold
            that we might learn the struggle which we are in."
And we say to you, you see the Angels!
They would take all harm from you,
      they would remove all straggle from your being,
      they indeed would enhance the Light around you,
      but you have entered in to the darkness
      and you would have it so.

Even have you pleaded in such a way
    that the Angels must withhold the Light
        they would shine about you.
But you have a sword,
    you have taken huge strides in the darkness.
You have overcome the darkened way.
And yet you are brothers.
Even in negativity you have learned to be brothers.
You hold one to the other in your negative endeavours.
Can you see,
    can you see the negativity that you allow
        to enthrall about your being?
You entice it, Soul, and it in turn entices unto you,
    even though you conquer once and once again,
    and yet again and again, still you entice it back unto you
    for you know in your being the scars that you gather.
And we say to you human,
    your flesh and your blood is not covered with scars.
Nay, these are not the scars of which we speak.
They are the scars of your form upon Farside.
They are the marks upon your being
    as the Archangels have marks upon their being.
And yet you are upon Farside, so all Energy,
    all existence knows you have conquered and overcome,
    for you have entered home unto where we are.
You are radiant in disguise.
You shine forth.
You have a path that is new.
You have opened the way.
Negativity has been corralled.
But even Negativity will hear of the Light of your being,
    will see the definitions upon your form
        for which you have struggled and overcome.
The message is clear.
The Path is clear.
The Holy Way is clear.
And your earth is tired and weary of holding pain.
In the darkness, as human,
    you light energy to comfort your being,
    to keep you from the darkness,
    to safeguard you from negativity.

Yet as you are upon Farside, you signal no comfort.
Indeed not.
You sent forth our Light away from your being.
It is beaming forth.
It is cherished.
Would you behold Great One?
Would you know in your being who has created motion?
Would you understand that the breath has come forward
      and been gathered,
      that it might give unto all earth motion,
      unto all Energy motion?
Even in existences far from your being motion is.
And would you be as Godhead, constant in Loving,
      constant in giving, constant as Presence is constant,
      waiting for that
      which is precious unto all Energy, Idyllic!
You are as your Creator, Soul.
You have created wondrous things.
We have beheld the challenges of vision
      that you have enabled yourself to realise.
And yet, we see the minute portion of your being
      you have allowed to become motion.
There is much yet for the human mind to understand.
In the last days will become the enhancing of the human mind,
      where the mind becomes all it can be,
      where the mind understands healing in all things,
      where the mind understands flight is possible,
      where the mind understands
      you have the ability to alter all things
      and enter in to all that is
      and enter in to all that is.
Even the mountains will move that you might enter through,
      even the molten lava
      will stop its flow that you might pass by.
You are human, limited as you accept your humanness.
When you enter in to the understanding
      that you are more than human,
      you are the human of your Soul,
      you are mankind, the human of your Spirit.
You are the fullness of your Energy, the Essence of your being.
Accept the nature of man but grow with the understanding

>   of the high mind and the Spirit.
[February 15, 2012]

1069   Souls of earth, gather round.
Gather round unto that which is new.
Your world awaits a new day
>   and we give to you the purpose of our new day.
We give to you, Soul, perfection.
We give unto you an understanding
>   of that which each being upon earth will become aware,
>   that within them
>   within the very being that they are
>   is a connection unto perfection.
It struggles through the maze of negativity.
It has been brought unto the new day.
You will gather yourselves together to find dismay.
It will be within the very core of your being
>   for you will recognize that you have spent eons of time
>   as humanity discovering that which was always yours.
You will have an awareness
>   of the great wonders of your universe.
You will hear the very beacons echoing out to you.
You will see the splendour of your physical self,
>   of your emotional self,
>   of your logical self echoing through
>   the Energy Fields formed in time
>   and you will see within these Fields
>   a recognition into the stellars that you behold.
The energies will echo upward.
You will behold your lineage from where you have come.
Indeed you will recognize within the very heart of your being
>   that you are other than worldly human.
You will become intent on the gathering into the knowns
>   that have been kept from you until you are ready
>   as one to behold that which you may enter in to.
You will have before you a kaleidoscope of colour,
>   of landscapes,
>   indeed visible unto you,
>   electrifying the very Energy you are.
You will carry within your being a connection
>   that has always been there but seldom recognized.

You will cease to be individual for you will understand
> that in order to resist the chaos that is intent upon you,
> you must join forces in your Energy.

You must become humanity.
Souls of earth,
> do not fear when the tides of earth turn upon you.

Do not fear when the winds encircle your globe.
Do not fear
> when the currents of the oceans maintain a stillness.

Do not fear when all that is opens
> and you see within the cavities of earth
> and the heat within the oceans
> hover to create bacteria that you have not witnessed.

Souls of earth, you have before you a perfection.
You will see through the glass that which is.
The crystal will make it available unto you
> and those who have written in your years gone by
> will be recognized for that which is documented
> over and again unto the volumes of earth.

And still in your day you have yet volumes to come forth
> that will witness the strength
> of the many enterings unto earth.

You will understand you are not alone.
Even you will behold the mentors that are yours.
The Angels you will behold
> and many will speak of seeing the lofty ones
> hovering in the heavens
> and be accounted unto mankind.

Indeed you are in a new day.
How is it known from that which is past?
It is known by the Energy of existence.
It is known for you will understand you are akin to the Angels.
You will understand the very Soul of your being.
Man has always uttered, "*My Soul, my very being.*"
And yet the structure of the Soul is a containment.
It is an Energy containment of knowns.
It will become understood in language beheld by man
> who will earn within their being the way.

The way does not come without earning
> through struggle of overcoming negativity.

Humanity, you have struggled with negativity.

You have known its conniving.
You have known its inveigling forces.
You have known the voice of persuasion.
It thrusts forth unto you.
Negativity is at bay.
You have understood in your new day a difference.
We do not say that evil will leave your earth.
You have nurtured it well
      but you have also nurtured the well of humanity
        that is deep in the compassion for others.
You have gathered in your goodness
      and through the years of living
        there is a cohesiveness that draws humanity to be one.
The Soul that is yours
      holds within the accountability of all that you do.
It registers and gives forth unto the Akashic.
You are Holy.
You are held in the very palm of goodness
      and you are held and given vision
      unto that which is perfection
      that before chaos was,
      that before all that was open,
      closed so that darkness shared Light.
Death and life never were.
Breath gave forth equally unto all.
We say to you,
    "Gift the Soul with perfection.
    Hold the new day as the echo of that which was.
    Behold your Soul and know it is decipherable
        and know it will become a language unto you,
        you who are humanity."
[December 12, 2012]

1070   Souls of earth, we say unto you
      that you had entered in to the greatest of challenges.
You are finding in your energy field a possibility
      to extrapolate from the Energy itself components
        that value the strength of steel, of iron, of all metals.
You have found you have the ability to use these components
      to build and carry yourself into further fields of energy.
And we say to you

      before this happens,
          you will hear from the key of two.
You will hear, Soul.
It will bring forth a resounding value.
We speak to you of the physicist who has the capacity
      to expand within his brain to reach through the linears
      into the projection of the Soul.
It is a colour of exactment.
It will be seen within the energy field
      you now have available to you.
There will be then an experimentation
      on projecting the Soul forward
      into the fields of the unknown while
      still communicating with that very Energy.
This is the equation.
Upon your earth there is a decibel sounding.
It is registering unto the B flat.
It is strident within the earth.
It sends forth great echoes.
It has an urgency that within each tone hears the sound.
It is not exacting human energy.
It is exacting, Soul, a portent of earth's existence.
Earth and humanity are connected.
The energies of all Souls who have lived upon earth
      hold within earth's self a vibrancy of tone.
It does send forth a knell that will carry the end of earth time.
It is genuine in its reality.
It is ferverent in its resonance.
It is catastrophic in its result.
The only altered concept
      is in the Energy of humanity to bring it to High C.
This will alter the foreboding of expectation
      that will result in calamity unto earth.
You are, Soul, deep in the sound.
Hold B flat far from you.
Use the High C.
It intonates a calmness unto all earth.
Even the creatures of your earth still
      and lose existence in their being
      so that the vultures move forward
      to deny life to the single.

It is essential to bring a calmness into your Energy.
We speak of calmness, Soul.
It is to place the calmness within your energy
       to heal the body, the mind and the flesh.
You are warring with the end of time.
[March 6, 2013]

1071   Soul, within the SEE
       is the communication upward and downward
       of all civilizations; of all energies.
Of all that is the resounding inflow and outflow is constant.
It is also a reflection into the hinterlands.
It goes forth.
We do not send it forth.
It is in the power of Supreme Being.
It is a vast Dome wherein all Energy echoes.
It is, Soul, beautific in the sounding.
It holds
       as the Creator's Masterpiece holds a vision of all that is.
It carries within it the deepest core of all Energy.
It carries forth the resplendent visions
       from Supreme Being of what perfection is.
You may gather
       were you of such iridescence to enter in,
       which indeed you are not.
Not, Soul, are we that we could enter forth,
       but we are giving review
       for the echo is downward and the vision is downward.
And there are those as your seers can find a Truth.
It is sounded within them.
It enters in earth through the pineal.
It carries a great recognition of all sound
       and is translated within the Energy of the seer;
       for you can only know things as you have Purity to vision.
Do not, Soul, be caught in the derisory
       that you cannot see, for many cannot.
It is not lack of Purity, Soul, it is lack of purpose.
It is a very avenue that is narrow.
Only few may enter in.
It is not the passing of a test.
It is the availability of the being to enter in,

       to hold that which allows Light to enter in and enter out.
To be the receptacle of Purity is to hold a Purity within.
There is a deep constant in all seers
       for they hold a truth abundant.
Souls, within the SEE is the availability to recover.
       with all energies, to reach even unto Perfection
       into a passage of such Light
       that you could not walk with open eyes,
       nor could you behold.
There is a monumental gathering
       to witness any Energy entering through
       for it is held as you would hold all that is contagious
       within a programmed field of captivity
       so that you might not contaminate other sources.
There is before you a great Truth that the skies will open
       and you will behold Four such Truths.
They will enter in as energies of Light.
They will be seen in the heavens and entering through
       into the very foundations of earth
       so that the earth will heat and melt
       and open before them
       and a great cylindrical force will be shown
       and reflect itself in the Heavens above.
And all who witness will be lifted in a Purity gathering.
The impure will not be deemed as such.
They will be the lost unto Heaven
       for they will be seen as the suffering.
They will be seen as redeemable
       and all energies will call out the names
       of those who are lost until each is found.
There will be a great sounding from the Heavens above
       and earth will rotate with a single turn
       to distil the waters of the sea through the mountains.
And the hills will collapse from the weight of the snow
       and the gardens of food will wash into the sea
       and the Souls that are left will cry out, *"Save us!"*
And from the Heaven will come a great Hand
       that opens the way between heaven and earth.
And earth will be seen,
       for from the depths of transition will come forth
       those who have lived many eons

in the terror and fear of their making.
And peace will touch their being and they will know
    that they have seen, that they have witnessed
    the heavenly Angels lifted before them.
And all that is in the starry sky will claim a name
    and the name will be called
    and each will know his name
    and enter forth unto that star
    and the star will guide the Energy unto the Gateway.
And those who were lost will be found
    and those who have been found will be Loved.
And all Humanity will call out unto Negativity.
Negativity, see thou the Gateway.
Come!
Enter through that you might see that which is good and Holy.
[January 22, 2014]

1072 There is within Farside no caught.
There is, Soul, a great willingness to be.
Within the fountain of all Purity is a magnificence
    of such fortitude in the very strength of this Energy
    that we know we are held not captive
    but in a Path of great worth.
Our energies have been sent forth
    as you have sent your energies forth.
All, even Supreme Being, has divided
    to conquer that which is not hypothetical
    but a reality within an alternative space.
It has been created that you might resolve the NEED.
The reflection of Supreme Being mirrored,
    that all might be as it is in the reality of Perfection.
You hold within the boundaries of your world a great havoc.
It gives forth an atmosphere of chaos
    so embalmed in the very depth of being
    it has been by humanity
    annihilated over and over again.
And yet always within the core of that chaos, comes forth
    rising as smoke rises from a great fire upward,
    goodness unto all Energy.
It is so purely magnificent in its oneness.
It gives forth such Light so that it transfixes

all who would look forth from the fence unto it.
And it is seen catapulting through the stars,
    imploding through the atmospheres
    of many folds and Fields of Energy.
It does not dim.
It does not release itself.
It does not cast itself down and say, enough,
    but the Light of such Purity beams without withering
    so that any within the darkness may use it for Light.
Even the Angels send forth a halo.
In the Light, the Energy glows and dims and glows and dims
    but the Energy from the greatest chaos holds fast
    to the power ignited within.
It does not dim, Soul.
It has not released itself from the purpose of Lighting the Dark.
Truly, that which is humanity has spiralled and been caught
    and witnessed by all that is Holy unto Holy,
    by all that is of the Angelic,
    even as your Creator,
    does the great gift be seen as beyond Holy.
For Soul, you are Light even beyond Light Being.
You have created a source within Light itself.
You have, Soul, brought forth a perfect accord,
    perfection from chaos.
[January 22, 2014]

1073   Soul, we would speak of Supreme Being:
    the Energy of all Energy,
    the Energy that creates devotion
    by the multitudes of earth,
    the Energy that knows all things,
    that sees all that is
    that speaks without speaking
    that hears without hearing;
    the Energy that draws forth expansive creations,
    the Energy that men hide their face from,
    the Energy that you bow to, beseech to,
    the Energy of anthems of tomes where children see
    with the eyes of Purity the Light
    and old see the shaft
    that allows a passage through unto Farside.

For the glory of the Light of the Energy of Supreme Being
    is even unto where you are.
All Creators of one Creator,
    all perfection of one Perfection,
    all thought of one thought,
    yes, Soul, even that thought
    that is filtered, reflected, sent forth,
    that you as human create within that is evil,
    that has no place in Supreme Being.
And yet, the very particle that you are,
    that has created that thought, you are of that Energy!
And the Angels who worship and hold the glory
    of Supreme Being within,
    themselves protect by the curtain of care
    all negative energy flow unto Farside.
And yet you are particled, for you return.
All will return, even the Brother, Negativity, will return
    for the NEED, the need to behold that which is Chaos
    that it might meld with all Energy is your purpose.
And you, you create much chaos.
You dabble, you form negative thoughts.
The Angels do not cower before them.
Indeed, not.
They walk before you that you might be protected.
And yet they are downhearted by that which you have created
    even knowing that you
    have the power to overcome, will, and do.
Humanity, behold.
You are at the very Feet of your Creator.
You bow to your Creator, worship your Creator.
You sing great anthems of glory.
You behold the Light that came unto you from Creator.
Yet, you have not reached into the power of Supreme Being.
Souls of earth, you are the most precious ion.
You have the most viable matter.
You have the mind that is apportioned from your Creator
    but you have not seen the Ecstasy that is beyond you.
You have not seen a million, nay, ten million,
    nay, Soul, billions of particles of Light
    that is Angelic Light form in the outer regions
    to magnify that which is even yet a Light

    beyond their combined own.
For this Light is Glory.
This Light is Supreme Being.
This Light is Perfection.
It is extended forth that you might know
    you are of a dimension so grandeous
      that your mind cannot comprehend.
You have, Soul, the glory beads to trace within your fingers.
You have the petals to hold within your hand.
You have the Psalms.
You have the morning and the night of prayer.
And yet you could not behold, Soul,
    that which is the redeeming part of whom you are.
For you are particled of all Energy.
You are the beginning and the end, the alpha, the omega.
You are the glory road.
You, who can open the Gateways and reach even unto Creator.
You have power, Soul, such as you know not
    and, we would have you bathe in the Ecstasy of colour.
We would have you know the sound that enters forth
    as all humanity lifts its Energy.
We would have you in one accord
    that you might know who you are
    and all that is, all that was, is, will be one.
For oneness has entered in a small child unto earth
    and oneness is pure in the form of the child
    and oneness gathers as humanity is want to be.
Soon the moment will be and time will be lapse
    and earth time no longer chimes forth,
      but the new day will bring in the Timeless Time.
Where the heavens hear,
    an emotion is,
    and the stillness sounded,
    the creation formed,
    and you all will have a place to stand
    and behold the Almighty.
The Light will so shine upon your being
    and gladden your hearts
    and you will know that all your pain has passed.
You will know why you have entered in.
You will glory at the portion that is the Triad of your Creator

   for you will see that Energy
    is so much a part of whom you are.
Light Beings will shine the beacon forth and say,
   "This is the Path.
   Come see that which we may show unto you.
   For behold, within the Sublime
    is the echo of all that is forward.
   We have the Path.
   We have the knowing, for you have opened a way."
Blessed art thou, humanity.
[February 5, 2014]

1074 Mankind, mankind hear that which you will know.
All your psyche will be reconditioned, a new placement,
   so that the body as your human form is
    will find that Energy is able to restore matter.
This is not far into your future.
This is simple, Soul.
Your scientists are quickly aware of the input
   they have into the human DNA.
They understand.
But we tell you of a different change to the Energy.
We tell you of the change you will have that will allow
   not only the molecular matter to alter,
    but the energy itself to alter in that it will become
    the Energy that you have as mankind upon Farside.
You will so alter your being
   that you will have no need
    for knowledge as knowledge is.
You will have a humanity
   that is aware of the mind knowledge,
    for it will have entered in unto Farside Spirit.
It will be not an occasion, Soul,
   it will become who you are.
Your earth will have many beings
   who will reject the entering in.
This will not be for all humanity,
   it will be for those who will accept
    they are more than who they are.
As the molecular matter will be changed,
   even to the sight for the blind,

    even for the limbs for those without.
You will find the change in your total Energy
    that can touch to alter and heal.
Where some will find physician, others will find healers.
The Mountaintop will be a healing place
    that will be known unto your world.
It will hold all the constables of intent.
It will hold all that is of Farside.
You will be able to place your Energy simply over a being
    and know precisely that which is injured.
Precisely!
More accurately than all the machines of mankind upon earth.
Where we are in the heavens,
    we have no need of great machines.
What we have are similar to a mind.
Memory banks of such huge expanse
    that you could not contemplate.
You will find yourself meandering into
    the space of Farside at will.
You will find yourself in the diffusion of sense,
    that your awareness will immediately know
    that which heals, that which does not.
And simply by the taking of the Energy into your being
    and placing it thus,
     will you know the healing will occur.
Farside has much that is available unto you.
There are gardens of herbs and flowers.
There are trees and waters.
You think you are the only beautific of flora,
    and even faunal!
All Farside has that which earth would bring themselves unto
    were they only to know how.
And we tell you that earth is soon to know
    how to change all energy.
Would that we could say wars will cease.
We cannot.
Wars will not cease upon your earth.
Mankind is a divided source.
Divided into those who have entered in to negativity
    and those who have become aware
     that negativity can be overcome.

Souls, we ask that you endeavour daily upon your earth
        to reach in your Energy to these Souls,
          that they might know the compassion
          that is strong within the Soul of humanity.
Mankind has a great memory bank of compassion within them
        were they but to reach
        into the many lives they have lived
        and join forces one with the other.
You have the capability as we have of altering whom we are.
When you see our form upon earth
        we can become whom you expect us to be.
Indeed, we do not only read your mind,
        we read the aura,
        we read all that you are.
We read indeed the matter that you are,
        the flesh and the bone
        and we know when the Soul requires healing.
We have not the ability to place the healing.
Only the Angels at five can alter
        and only in very specific circumstances.
But the day will be soon when you can change the Energy
        where the Soul wishes it to be.
You will find the Mountaintop extending
        far beyond that which it is,
        for there are many Mountaintops upon your earth.
We have said this, there are seven,
        each designated to heal mankind.
Each distributing that which is the intent of mankind.
You who have seen
        that which is within the reflected Energy forward,
        you have understood the Spirit.
You have understood the glory and the ecstasy of the Essence.
You will know how to heal a crowd,
        how to send forth such a Light
        that all the world will behold and ask,
            "What is this Energy?"
            "How can we learn?"
It is simple, Soul.
It is not convoluted in anyway.
It is as straight as the arrow, direct.
Souls of earth, see within you an abundance

that has been given to you.
It is yours.
It is not knowledge,
 they are words, but it is not knowledge.
It is Energy.
It is alive!
It is yours to reach and touch and know.
It alters the very flesh of your being.
It alters the way your mind becomes unsettled in its being.
But you must, Soul, behold.
There is a withering with your age, but the withering
 does not change the Light in your being.
The withering Lights the very self of who you are.
You are glory and you know it not.
You are humanity apportioned from your Creator.
You are not one sect or the other.
You are not old and young, middle aged Souls.
You are Energy beings.
You have entered in to an illusion to overcome negativity,
 to reach unto the very Energy
 that will enlighten the Soul,
 so that the Soul may enter in to the glory of healing,
 that there might be a gift given unto mankind,
 unto all that is upon your earth, to the very earth itself.
There are worlds, worlds upon worlds
 seeking to see that which mankind will do.
You have an appointment, Souls of earth,
 it is with the destiny of your being.
You are so much more than feeble humanities,
 you are one, one humanity.
You have been brought together as an Armada for your Creator. You have gifted to overcome negativity,
 to bring the Brother back unto Creator.
You have faltered many times,
 you have even fallen upon the way.
But as you have fallen, you have found a brother or sister
 to rise you in your being, to lift you up,
 be they Humanity upon Farside
 or humanity upon the earth.
Souls, awareness is that which will come onto you.
Awareness that you are Light,

>   awareness that you are Energy yourself,
>   that you are portion of your Creator
>   and you may touch
>   the very glory of the Energy of Creator,
>   that you might become aglow,
>   that you might become illuminated,
>   such as the very Angels become illuminated.
> How great thou art.
> Holy art thou.
> Find yourselves not in the delves of negativity,
>   but lift yourselves up to the positives
>   that humanity has in its intent.
> There are many gateways, Soul.
> You will open gateways upon gateways.
> The greatest gateway you will open
>   will be the awareness of Energy.
> The connection of self to self,
>   the connection of Soul to Spirit,
>   the connection of the DNA,
>   which is feeble to the great glory of the form
>   that you are upon the Farside.
> Souls, you illuminate the heavens above.
> And when you are in the glory of the Light of Farside,
>   you will illuminate your earth so that mankind will see
>   that there is an Energy beyond the human of earth.
> Blessed be humanity.
> [May 27, 2014]

1975 Souls of earth, all that you are has value.
Your earth designates value to many components.
Upon Farside there is only one value designated.
It is the value of Energy.
The vibration equalizes the value.
That which vibrates designates at what level the Soul is,
          the Spirit is, the Farside being is.
You are greatly disturbed with the vibration of your energy.
Souls of earth are not at ease
          with vibratory alterations to their being.
And yet, Soul, upon the Farside there is a great awareness
          of the vibrational changes of any being,
          even those upon earth

      who vibrate at certain chords are heard.
Vibration is in colour, vibration is in sound,
      vibration, Energy,
      has a total continuity of Colour and Sound.
It is more than your rainbow
It is more than your Prism.
It is an absolute container of Light
      that vibrates to enter in to an understanding.
It becomes aware of the negativities
      of any being upon your earth.
It becomes aware of any alterations in the outer worlds,
      even to the animals upon your earth,
      to the fish in your sea.
We are aware so that we can enter in or alert alien worlds
      to tend to the miseries of earth.
There are many alien populace.
They are, Soul, simply many,
      countless to that which you would number,
      not millions, not billions, Soul, beyond your count
      so that it would seem to be without understanding.
For we have within our worlds beings that are so small,
      yet their energies live and are numbered by Creator
      and they are aware of you.
They understand you more
      than you understand whom you are,
      for they are energies entered in to help humanity.
As your earth recognizes the changes of life upon your earth,
      they will find themselves
      wanting to change the DNA of many beings.
And we say to you of earth,
      "*Do not alter that which is!*"
Accept, within the form of humanity,
      humanity you may alter your forms to heal.
Do not alter the forms of the innocent upon your earth,
      for they have entered in with a purpose
      and their purpose cannot be altered
      without great destructions to centres within earth itself!
It will contaminate many energies.
It will change forms.
It will change the pursuant purpose of existences of creature,
      of fish of the sea, of birds of the air,

so the disease will quickly spread throughout your earth.
We say, we speak,
"*Do not alter the DNA ort, other than mankind!*"
It is an alert, Soul, to be broadcast forth.
It is imminent to be known.
[May 27. 2014]

1076   Souls of earth, you have been in the care of Angels.
You have been shown a path that is new yet old.
You have been given expressions of humanity's intent.
You have been given a great purpose.
Your earth is cascading with many frequencies of energies
      who have assisted your intent.
There is now in your earth time a transference of energy.
The energies of earth will persuade the energies of Neptune,
      of Pluto, of distant anttieum,
      of 64B, of M76 to receive.
These energies will become nomadic,
      aligning one to the other yet separating their energy flow.
The cause will be directly in line with your sun.
The great structure that holds earth's gravitational pull,
      it will be corrected
      by man's muetric variational adjustment.
The creativity of the mind who does the adjustment
      will recognize that which has been given.
[November 22, 2014]

1077   Within the seas of earth wherein
      the great channel lies of the Pacific's,
      there is a rumbling forth.
It is, Soul, in the depths of strangulation
      of buildup from the tectonic energy that is sent forward.
There is a lessening of strength within the corridor
      unto the Solomons.
A buildup of energy will record a nine earthquake
      that will send forth a great surge upon the lands
      in the Gulf of Alaska unto the Oregon
      and even unto the coasts of California.
The countries even westward will be inundated
      by the backward throe.
There will be great quantities of waters inundating the lands

wherein the coasts of Australia
unto Japan, China, will be touched.
There is a great surge of negativity
that will withstand this surge.
The negative energy of men
will behold opportunistic opportunity.
There will be gathered seas of humanity crying forth for foods.
In that day will the test of man kind one to another be seen.
The tablets will come forth as the child reaches into the chasm.
See that which is pure and behold the wisdom
for much will be uncovered.
The seven Keys will be recognized.
From that day there will be a tentative accumulation
of mathematical constraints that affect
the magnetism of earth.
Surely will many pass unto us.
Surly will many seek to be uplifted.
It will not be the time, Souls,
for still there will be a number to reach.
All earth is numerically counted.
All Energy is numerically counted.
You are, Souls of earth, within the number.
There will be a continuity of Truth.
For many will stand and speak of the Energy of humanity
to band together as one
to withstand the negative hoards.
This will be done, Soul, in the Energy of Truth, of Love.
The purest of heart will be seen at the alter.
The mothers will cry and the children,
they will rise in their wisdom,
and in the Truth of their Energy,
stop, withhold negativity.
It will not be by the arms but by arm, Soul.
For the Truth of the child will withstand all armaments.
[November 22, 2014]

1078   The vibrational pull of combined colour and sound,
a more advanced recognition
of what sound and colour of earth is.
To behold the truth of connection
is to reach into the reality of those savant

        for they have within the vibration of their being
        a earth rhythm of this combination.
To carry such a vibration to its nth
        is to know in itself the vibration
        can create from consciousness
Science will soon recognize that there is a schism
        that will enable travel through vibrational channels
        that will have the appearance of a chute
        that spirals outward to a destination
        in which earth time will not apply.
The velocity
        will be within the very vibrational chord that is sounded.
This will be gathered
        from the outer stratospheres of distant space.
It will allow travel in nano seconds
        into space with a transparent film
        that structures by vibration itself.
There will be no bombardment to this structure
        for the vibration deflects.
[February 10, 2016]

Chapter Two
TIMELESS TRAVEL

1079   Souls of earth, behold the doorway.
Behold that into which you may enter.
Behold the grandeur that is available unto you.
The very presence of Energy reaches unto your being
        and draws you in, for it is beatific.
It revitalizes the Energy
        and it is available unto you.
Souls of earth, can you behold that which is heaven?
Can you understand that which is laid for you
        before your very being?
Soul, mankind reaches into the earth energy of their own being
        and places within the mind
        a visualization of that which is Farside.
It beholds the earth grandeur, the holding on to earthly rights.
You have entered in to earth.
Those rights are of earth.
They are simplicity, Soul;
        the food, the drink, the mansions.
Oh indeed, there are mansions and you may sup at will
        but release from your Energy the energy of earth mind
        for within the doorway is all that is of Creator
        not the machinations of the mind of man.
Souls, the doorway is open and we beckon you unto it.
Indeed we ask that you would enter in,
        for Holy is that which is within.
Behold, you have before you a table spread.
It contains wisdom.
It contains all that is within the realm of glory.
It is laid before you that you may choose
        for indeed upon Farside choice is.
You may rush in your Energy to surmount a majestic form
        lavish with the growth unknown to earth.
You may reach unto a visitation
        of all the forms of earth animal friends
        you have ever known.
They will know that which you are.
They will reach unto your Energy

    and you might even cry as you behold the knowing
    that is within them that was not represented upon earth
    for you may speak to their Energy at will.
You may recount that which was yours upon earth.
And then, Soul, should you choose,
    you may reach into the many lives you have lived.
You may encounter the personas of whom you are.
You will see yourself as in a mirror,
    yet no mirror will be at hand for it is not required.
You may behold your Energy
    by stepping out of your energy,
      fragmenting, Soul.
Many have done it upon earth as in healing by Edgar Casey,
    as Nostradamus who had a great ability
      to foresee decades ahead of his time.
Soul, from the heavens you may behold that which is.
From the heaven you enter in to is Farside
    but you are not restricted by a single heaven.
You may reach into the Purity of your being.
You may wander at will.
There is no need for privacy such as you know privacy to be.
It is a respected privacy.
It immediately acknowledge all thought within your being.
Were that thought to enter in, all beings would respect
    for there is no contention within Farside.
The collar, the yoke is not there.
There are no underlings.
There are no beings who have lesser.
There are only beings who have entered in to.
To enter in to does not create imbalance.
It creates Love.
It creates tender mercies.
It creates a desire not wilful,
    to reach downward
      from a level of Purity not lesser, Soul, a level of Purity.
You are deep within the trenches of truth.
You battle strongly and negativity often seems to win.
Yet, Soul, you have a doorway.
It allows you to enter in for reprieve from the battle
    that you may transfix your Energy
      on a focus that is Farside.

You may leisurely attend
> but you may not stay for it is an Energy to refocus
> on that which you have entered in for.

The Angels, the guides, will build on your strength.
You may even receive from them lessons of endurance
> for the way is not easy upon your earth.

The path is fickle and many would choose to leave
> but the leaving does not surmount negativity,
> is not an ability to bring the Brother home.

Humanity, you are the opener of gateways.
Your earth is only a small minority of mankind.
There is a majority with us, Soul.
Your earth trembles.
The way for you is undoing.
It is fettered in pain and yet joy can be yours.
It need not be pain.
Soul, pain is the obstacle.
It is that for which you have entered in to overcome
> and offer unto compassion.

Many of the Farside see humanity as a gateway itself.
For you have become many even yet,
> more enter in to the numbers of mankind.

The indigo and the violet are late comers.
You have come in force
> for they have heard that which mankind has done.

They have heard the echo of goodness.
They have seen the Light which you bestow.
Do not run to the Farside in your Energy.
Walk calmly for the day is not done.
The time has not yet been entered in to
> but it will soon come upon you
> and many will know there is an eternal plan,
> a plan of beholding that which is chaos
> and to know that which is chaos has not negativity,
> yet is as the Brother Negativity.

It is a motion and in a motion it alters.
In a motion it is being discerned.
The great sound is heard.
It echoes forward as in the valleys between the high walls
> so does the small voice echo loudly
> in the chamber of space.

The echo of humanity is heard in the darkened way.
It is deep in the Void.
It is far from where you are and yet in its Purity it alters.
It is received, Soul.
We speak to you,
      "*Open the door.*".
See that which is before your very being.
Know that you are a part of all Energy.
You are not transfixed to earth.
You are not caught in an endless pain of hell.
You are precious in the name of your Creator.
You are Light that shines.
You are the beacon wherein all Energy will come unto
      and the great door will open
         but first you must know to enter in to the small door,
         the door that is yours,
         the door that leads to the high mind
         that allows you to focus your Energy
         and enter in to where we are.
We will reach for you, Soul.
Indeed enter in calmly with no fear.

1080   Behold, Soul, unto you is the pathway through.
Unto you is the beginning, the formidable return.
Round about you,
      the cacophony impelling the stir,
      awakening consciousness impelling movement,
      drawing the spiral to reversal.
Behold, humanity, unto you is given the gift,
      the possibility of Truth, not a resurgence of Purity.
This is within, this is the possibility of your being.
But the fullness of Truth you must seek,
      the fullness of Truth you must enter in to.
You must acknowledge the being of Energy.
You must understand the motion of Breath.
You must speak to the mind
      that it be discontent to live in mediocracy of being
      when mind has available unto it, the high mind,
      the consciousness of being.
Unto the aged is not always the wisdom.
Wisdom can be in the Souls without earth mind,

   who have had the vision in their being of the earth mind,
   beyond which they have seen
   the encounter of consciousness.
Some who have seen have left their earth mind
   to dwell within that consciousness of being.
For earth is painful.
Behold earth, the path to traverse is not without pain.
Yet the pain has a ceasing,
   if the Soul will but recognize the pain
   to be overcome, to be lifted from,
   that the mind, the high mind might soar beyond the pain
   into the fathomless Energy of Creator's Mind,
   the well of consciousness from which you might draw.
You have entered in from the great Breath.
Yet even in the great Breath,
   there is a pathway unto even greater Breath.
And beyond that, once again.
Who would dare to surcease the agonies
   placed before mankind?
Who will still the energies
   that flag wars to begin and earth to grow?
There are kingdoms beyond where you are,
   nations of beings heralded by their Purity.
And you have a reach unto them!
Yet you choose to use the mind of earth
   to seek with your logic into the science of earth,
   when you have available to you the high mind to travel.
You peel your humanness as the snake peels the skin.
It is your ego and you set it aside in moments of pain.
And you recognize in whom you are,
   a being having a nature recognizable as compassion.
But you do not hold the mantle round about you,
   you hold only the recognition of the mantle.
Behold, humanity,
   reach unto that which is possible in you,
   the travel from time into the spaceless Void.
And see the glory of Angels
   and behold the cadence
   that reaches beyond where they are.
You have caught and held colour in your being.
You have the magnificence of rainbow.

And as you behold the magnificence of whom you are,
>   do not turn from it, Soul.
Do not shun thy being, but swell thy Soul
>   to recognize how great thou art,
>   that thou art, indeed,
>   a part of the eternal consciousness of Energy.
Who is without Energy?
No man.
In the depths of depravation,
>   in the depths of aloneness,
>   in the depths of despair,
>   the Soul can soar
>   into the consciousness of being
>   and alienate the body that is suffering from it.
Then is awakened in the Soul's being
>   a recognition of that which they are,
>   that the illusory flesh is of no importance
>   to the step on the Path of return.
Behold, the spiral's reversal.

1081   You are, Soul, you are Spirit, you are Essence.
That which you are enters in and out Soul.
Always is the entering in and the entering out upon your earth.
It is your breath that enters in and out.
It is your knowledge that enters in and enters out.
Growth, advancement, adversity,
>   the Soul always in contention
>   for it may not enter fully
>   into the completeness of breath.
A portion of that which is within the Soul's knowledge
>   must be separated and left at the karmic station.
Always there is a portion left,
>   whether it is the entering in or the entering out;
>   this is knowledge for earth humanity.
You have entered in, but a portion of you has entered in.
You are human
>   but only a portion of your humanity
>   enters in unto the negative ion
>   that you might grow that you might grow
>   to understand that which Humanity
>   has set forth as a gift unto Creator.

The Spirit is vibrant, the Spirit is pure.
The Spirit is full with knowledge, with emotion.
It is within the Soul of your being,
        a power that you might enter in to
        the Spirit being of whom you are.
You might breathe the breath Creator has given unto you;
        the Purity of your Soul,
        the Purity of your Spirit,
        the being of your Essence
        to be all that you can be,
        the best part of whom you are.
These are brought forth from minds
        who have found in their being
        a knowledge of that which is the high mind.
Your humanity is not what is reflected from earth's mirrors.
It is that which is as you gaze unto the high mind of your being
        and you see the form of whom you are.
You see the connection of the Energy unto the Energy,
        unto your Creator
        and you recognize in that Energy you are not alone.
You are fragment, a prism of Purity,
        a value, a consciousness with intent and knowing,
        fixating on a battle to overcome negativity.
You see the Energy that is the Energy of your Creator.
You see it as a Pillar of Light about your being
        and you are overwhelmed
        with the giving that enters in to you
        from that Energy and you know it is not to be held
        but to be entered outward from your being.
It is the entering in and the entering out that is creation.
You implode, Soul.
You see before you opportunities
        to lift your Energy unto higher grounds.
You have before you the Gateways of Purity
        and you are given the choice to enter in.
To enter in is to be apportioned with humanity,
        if you would be the first,
        if you would carry the gift of ultimate Love.
You have before you negativity streaming about your being.
Some of humanity gathering it
        as though it were a gift unto themselves,

   holding, nurturing the negativity
    as though it were their very own.
But it alters the being of mankind.
It alters who they are, it deforms who they are.
That which is their voice changes.
That which is uttered by their voice changes.
The offering of the voice from one human to the other,
   the entering out should be a gift,
   a gift of Purity, a gift of Love,
   a gift of compassion,
   for you have found the greatest gift.
In the Path of your Creator
   that which you see as deity,
   that which you behold as God,
   the Energy is Love,
   the Energy is Purity,
   the Energy is Truth
It is a portion of Supreme Being entering in and entering out.
Always a new Field.
Existence carries many fields.
You have but a single field for your enlightenment
   but there are many many fields
   holding many many galaxies.
Words of your earth cannot describe
   the abundance of that which is,
   of the linears involved in the existence of reality.
Indeed, reality, reality not your earth realm, indeed not,
   not that heaven you reach unto.
The Archangels have new unto you, heavens,
   yet your Energy knows
   for you have entered in and you have entered out
   and as you enter in you have recall
   and that which was negative falls from your being.
What power is in Supreme Being
   who can separate the Energy of Self
   to form Fifteen separate Energies
   holding one unto and sending forth Fourteen!
Indeed, the power of this Energy,
   the minuscule portion of the power that you are.
And you are power!
You have entered in and you have entered out.

And all that is is motion.
All that is is Breath.
Yet Breath formed unto matter.
Consciousness formed from Light.
Light!
Give Light to the mind.
Allow the mind to reach into its ultimate Light.
These are echoes from that which is!
These are echoes from reality.
Gather the core of Energy
        and use the core of Energy to create Light,
        but Light, Light is the extension of Dark.
Without Dark Light is not Light.
Light is merely Energy.
With Dark Light shines.
Light becomes,
        so Creator divided the energies unto Light and Dark,
        seven Light and seven Dark.
Supreme Being.
Would you bow down unto such Energy?
The Energy has no wish of abeyance.
It has only the entering in and the entering out.
It has the Love, the Purity, the will, the intent, the awareness,
        the Sound, the Colour, the fullness, the richness,
        the fruitfulness to give, to send forth,
        to create, to uplift,
        to give presence, to have value,
        to give echo, to have flame,
        to give Breath all unto
        ever giving, flowing,
        expectant of no thing
        but all the awareness of all the Energy
        of all the Archangels, of all the beings of existence
        of all the creations that are of all that is of Matter.
All that is the mineral has consciousness, has a knowing,
        is possible of understanding there is a purpose.
It is with purpose that you might see the Angels entered in
        as you are entering in,
        for you are they and they are you.
You are but reflectory,
        always reflectory entering in and entering out

        that you might resolve the issue in all your being
        that you might understand with all the power of Love
        that there is value in that which you do.
There is purpose in that which you do
    as there was purpose
    in Supreme Being Entering In as Creators.
You have entered in to overcome.
You enter in and you enter out
    and you enter in and you enter out.
It is the form of your return that is unique.
It is not who you are as you enter in and out,
    it is the form of your return,
     that you have the power to return.
All existence of the mind, of consciousness,
    can enter in and enter out,
    can enter in and out and in and out.
It is matter that has the difficulty of entering in and out.
You, earthling, you have the power and soon the knowledge
    to take matter in and out and in and out
    not formed upon earth, Soul;
    the containment and the Energy
    will soon return in and out.
You will as one united humanity offer unto your Creator
    the power to be fully within the power of Energy,
    to gather your being and take it forth
    without the contentious energies of time and space.
You will not suffer the bones to be crushed
    or the mind to be lessened.
You will find renewal in the form that you are
    and man will travel throughout the galaxy as an infant
    and then, Soul, the being will be charged
    with entering through time with no time.
Do not fear.
Glory that your consciousness is abundant
    and abundantly able
    to corner the forward movement of being.
It will be into the Dark then into the Light.
Touch the eye to prevent the tear.
Touch the ear to prevent the sound.
Touch the nose to hold the distance.
You have power to travel as humanity through space.

1082 We speak to you of the bridge.
As you enter the path, you find yourself looking down.
You will see, Soul, the ability first to see your very own being.
You will behold the shell that you are.
You will understand you are given a float.
You have the ability to move without moving.
You have the ability to ride a wave.
You may behold as you look down, the entirety of your earth.
You will know that you are of it, yet apart from it.
The height will bring you no fear,
       for you could reach down
          and touch where you have been.
But you will not want to, Soul,
       for your very being will take on an excitement, a thrill.
For you know that which you will behold.
Your consciousness has enlightened you to that which is yours.
The visage before you is familiar.
You will see the Path well tread.
You are not jostled,
       yet you feel in your being Souls around you.
You see their excitement.
Some rush forward, others meandering
       for they have walked this Path many times.
They are the Souls who meditate and are familiar with a Path.
They have no need to bring,
       for it is always available unto them and they know this.
You have before you a great highway.
It is given unto you.
It is not packaged with a price, with a fee, a cost.
It is a Light and you walk in to the Light
       and you behold the firmament of the Path
       is more real than the earth.
And you think of the pain and you find yourself laughing,
       rejoicing that what you thought was endless pain,
       indeed was only a waking sleep.
And you may return,
       and you will unto that reality of illusion
For you are human,
       and all the guides know
       they are separate from the Angels

for they are clothed in the blue of Humanity.
They have left the green and taken on the blue
    as the Blessed Mother took on the blue.
You perceive as you move on the Path
    that the pain you have teared, you have cried,
        you have stopped the tears.
They are not to be held
    for you can see you have overcome many.
And you see before you an option and you know it is yours.
For you see with clarity your Aura cloaking, Light.
And you understand you cannot enter in to it, it is not time.
But you can speak, Soul, and you will be heard.
You can gain enlightenment that will affect the earth mind.
So that never again will you see things as simple or complicated.
You will see them as radiance lifting unto the place of Purity.
To visit Farside, Soul, is to be altered.
To visit, Farside, Soul, is for all beings.
We would that the Path be full to capacity.
This can only be when all of humanity are in the Path.
Your earth is diverse in its commitments.
We ask you to commit yourself to walk the bridge.
We call it the bridge of enlightenment.
You may call it what you will.
But we know that all humanity who walks upon the bridge
    and sees below the humanity they are,
        are ever altered.
And life for them will never again be mundane.

1083 Soul, reach in your being into the presence that is you.
Feel the depth of being as you relax into your self,
    and understand you have a corridor clear before you.
It is clear, defiled in no way,
    reaching unendingly into an Energy
        that conveys unto you a knowing
            so that you may be brought quickly along the corridor.
As you release from you thoughts of your worldly self,
    you are able to behold.
This is greater than tunnel
    and yet it appears to be just that, tunnel,
        for it is a containment.
It carries within it an upward and downward flow.

You may alight at any position and you will find, Soul,
      the mind of your earthly self
      has some inquisitiveness there.
And you begin to understand that indeed
      there are two parts to your mind.
There is the mind that contains the thoughts of your earth life,
      all that has become a part of whom you are, all that is
      registered in the deep influence of your current life.
And then as you allow the other portion of your mind
      to have stronger will,
      it is able to see and recognise lives you have lived,
      it is able to see and recognise places you have been.
In the corridor you are in, fear has been left behind,
      there is an abiding comfort in the track you follow.
You are able to vision.
And then you understand the vision is not just that,
      rather it is a reality along the corridor
      for you see and behold places
      and vision of those faces that are there;
      there is an achievement in that you have been allowed;
      to travel without negativity following you.
For only those thoughts that have gathered
      the overcoming of truth
      have pierced your consciousness.
You are deep in thought
      as you behold the coagulation of all fluids.
You see before you all consistencies,
      you see before you all softness,
      all hardness, all gentleness, all thought.
You see before you Truth magnified.
You become greater than Truth
      for it is alive with the consciousness of its own
      that you have not been aware of.
And as you have reached a defining point,
      you see the Colour and Sound have become alive.
And yet the eyes are not required and the Light is golden.
There is no shades of pain.
There is darkness but it has a wholeness to it,
      a fullness to it as in the black.
It is alive.
It is there to behold but it does not run with fear.

It is not taken into a form of repellent.
Rather it gathers you, Soul, that you might see,
> behold within it molten masses of shards
> that glitter and shine,
> that give forth a warmth.

And then you see the magentas, the blues, the greens, the violet.
They all have words to say.
They speak not in the words
> that you speak when you entered in,
> but in the words of consciousness.

They are there that present themselves
> and they teach this does this
> and this sound addresses this.

And you are taught and you understand
> the mouth is unnecessary
> for the words are here
> in the conscious Energy of the mind.

The corridor is the Creator's corridor.
It is the corridor of Love.
It is the corridor of all being.
It is the corridor that carries within the purpose of who you are.
And you reach in your being
> and you understand why you have entered in to earth
> for you behold the reality from which you have come.

And you see in the consciousness of your being
> all the worlds endlessly reaching,
> and the glory of such worlds bombard your thought.

And you understand what an insignificant
> amount of knowledge humanity has.

And you are countered with a returning thought
> of how grandiose earth humanity
> can see themselves upon earth.

And you wonder at the myopic gaze we have of ourselves,
> when indeed we are far greater
> than we can ever know ourselves to be,
> for in the corridor all things are available for us to see
> if we will reach into the Purity of Holy.

There is strewn upon the way the fallen items of many
> who have released from themselves their humanity self,
> the gold, the chain, the papers.

And you have become integrated,

       and the mask and the veil has fallen
       for you no longer need to see.
You need only behold and upon your beholding
        you have become who you truly are.
The corridor is a amassed with many beings.
And yet each carries an isolated space until their full awakening.
And then, the reunion,
       the recognition of the Truth
       of who they are becomes apparent.
You, as you enter in to the corridor,
       as you allow yourself to be drawn
       in to Colour and Sound,
       you will behold Farside as a window with a Light.
And you a night traveller who has a need to see
       and speak to those you have been far from
       and you see the door opening
       and the candle Light shining offering you in.
And there you behold the Loved and the Loved.
This we say unto you is a walk
       through the corridor of the Energy of Creator.
Behold thyself upon the Path.

1084   Silence your being, Soul.
Silently, silently enter in to that which is your way.
The echo of sound of earth is to be that which is lived,
       not a sound of euphoric being,
       not the sound of steps on the Path.
These are the sounds that echo triumphantly
       in the forward existences.
These are the sounds that behold.
These are the sounds
       that have colour of strength of a life well lived.
You are human, you are caught in a web of negativity.
You have the power to release the web from your being.
You have the power to enwrap your being with the web.
All is yours, all motion for your form is yours.
In motion, you enter in unto your earth.
In motion, you live throughout a lifetime.
It is only in the tranquil moments unto passing
       that your being slows
       so that you may gently enter in

        unto that which is before you.
There is no rush to leave,
        there is no need to stay.
It is choice, it is all choice.
You activate your being through choice.
You may spend a lifetime merely observing,
        growing in no thing.
You may, Soul, offer to teach by an act of gift.
This is for all beings.
The form that you are in is unique unto you
        for it holds an echo of all your lifetimes.
Indeed, the form inclusive of the aura,
        for you are that which covers you.
You are, Soul, the Energy;
You are also the Energy field about your being.
Now we ask you to reflect on the heart,
        the heart has motion.
It accepts the motion.
Without the emotion you cease to be.
The heart fears,
        the heart anticipates.
The heart gives and receives.
And then there is the mind.
Search in the mind a
        nd you will find knowledge, intellectual knowledge.
Search in the high mind
        and you will find consciousness of being.
You will find knowing of that which you are.
You will find all there is available unto you
        from your level of Farside.
You are constantly growing in wisdom.
You are constantly absorbing wisdom unto you.
You have teachers,
        they are not always teachers of earth.
You have shamanistic teachers
        from many lives you have lived.
Their Energy feels your path
        and counters your negatives with wisdom.
You have before you the opportunity
        to live a life insular within your being.
Shading the eyes of earth

> that you do not see that which is before you.
You may even, Soul, prevent the inward look
> unto the path of the eye wherein Energy awaits,
> the choice is yours.
The path is yours but the path is not insular.
It meets the way of all paths of all humanity.
You may refuse to join unto the other paths
> or you may recognize there is a step that you take
> that will join you unto one
> as one, meeting with a purpose, meeting with Truth,
> meeting garbed with all you have gathered.
As you recognize your Energy as futuristic not dependent
> but depended on by others of your own ilk.
Then you understand you have a purpose.
It is a united purpose, it is a worldly purpose.
It is beyond that of family.
It is beyond that of cult, of culture, of nationality, of clan.
It is not earth made.
It comes from your very being, the core of your Essence,
> the purpose for which you have entered in
> not the maintaining of Truth, the gathering of Truth
> leaving behind the issues
> of materialism, of want and greed
> rather to see that which is the need to overcome
> that which is the chaos.
You are human, you are often alone within your being.
You often feel the pain of earth's expectations upon you,
> but these are growths.
They are placed in your way that you might overcome.
They are placed in your way
> that you might know joy in overcoming.
Respond to the nudges in your being.
Respond to the care of the Angels.
Respond to the fellowship of man
> but do so in the knowledge
> that you are Human resident of Farside.
You are upon earth for a moment in time
> that you might grow
> that you might see more clearly
> that which is the need before you,
> that you might behold the brotherhood of man.

As the Angels acknowledge the Brethren of their Being
    so are you one in your being with all humanity.
Rise, rise in the day you are in
    that you might reflect the joy and the sorrow
    in entering in unto the earth
    for you have left that which is who you are
    to enter in to behold the step
    to bring all mankind into a greater understanding
    of the purpose of their being.
See the waves that wash upon your being.
See the Light that enters in,
    the clouds that storm upon you
    as that which you can overcome
    as a purpose of growth.
You are human, you are humanity.
Unto humanity is the greatest step to overcome chaos.

1085   Souls of earth, upon your planet are humanity
    that have such beauty in their being.
Their form, male and female, child, adult that causes
    even the Angels to witness.
You are altered by the vision of whom they are.
Yet even in the most perfect of forms can be
    the deepest gauge of negativity unseen to the eye
    yet deeply creviced in the form.
You who are humanity, recognize in earth beings
    not the outer form
    but, Soul, the inner form that holds all
    yet reveals that in each is the negative visible.
You are not perfect.
You have not entered in perfect
    even though you have given unto yourself
    a form of beauty.
All beings have some negative to overcome.
    even for teachers there is a negative to overcome
    and we speak of teachers of the spirit.
We ask the form of the Buddha
    to always be the condition of your form
    for you cannot be in the form of the Buddha
    and give, pass, negative from you.
You may receive negative unto you

>   but the form will hold the negative
>   from passing through.

This has always been so.
Feel in your being the great wait.
Wait, Soul, for what are you waiting?
You receive
>   to beckon unto,
>   to behold in your being
>   the mind you have been given,
>   to behold in your being how accurately it conforms
>   to that which you have placed before it.

You may see in your being
>   the variances of negativity that have entered in.

You may behold in your being
>   the empowering you have allowed yourself.

Feel the body lift, allow it to lift.
It will lift ever so slightly and then, Soul,
>   you will see yourself quickly looking down.

Behold pleasantly that which you see.
Observe the quietness of your own Energy
>   and know you have entered in to contemplation
>   wherein the Buddha sees the colour
>   upon beings of vision,
>   sees not only the colours but their inadequacies
>   and he can speak to those inadequacies as healer.

Thread the Light that you are through your hands.
Allow them to feel the power of the existence.
Encircle as though you were feeling the head of Buddha.
Feel the Purity of the form.
Know the Purity is also in who you are.
Allow the Light to be a source of understanding.
Allow it to venture into that which is unseen.
Hold it forth
>   and see the great wonder
>   of the vacuous state of the Void
>   and allow your Energy to be carried
>   in to the depths of the Void.

You will behold the feel of darkness.
You will feel its cumbersome weightiness upon you
>   and yet you will know you have the Light.

See, Soul, a portal.

What is portal, Soul?
It is Light, Light that you may enter
      through the Light and hold the key with Light.
Within your vision will open unto you
      a kaleidoscope of colour.
You have travelled this way, Soul.
You have seen what we see, you know the Path.
You have been and it comforts you.
Always do you remember the Path
      unto the kaleidoscope of colour, the sound.
Sound.
Such sound, Soul,
      as the depths of the sea
      and the wind in the trees of your earth,
      and even the sound awakens the Soul
      to know it is a place you have been.
You are welcomed home, you know you have entered in.
Souls of earth, manage to understand the ability
      of who you are to enter through the portal.
There are many upon your earth,
      they hold no fear.
They hold no difficulty to enter
      if you are willing to release from you
      the knowledge that you are simply flesh and blood.
You are transient,
      you have entered in to your earth for a time
      and you may enter back and forth
      as many beings enter through and see.
And you, who are human, you see.
You have been given a sight.
It is in your being to enter through.
Your humanity disallows.
It carries a cost that disallows.
The cost is to humanity
      for the portals are to be used and often.
They hold keys to humanity's existence and future.

1086   Soul, we would have you
      see your transcendental travel as swim.
Indeed, swim.
Allowing your Energy to move in a swimming fashion

        throughout your earth so that the eye of being
        may be downwards toward the need of your earth.
Not so that you will be oblivious to its pain
        but, indeed, see the joys and the pains.
You will be aware, Soul, of the great mountain peaks.
You will be aware of the great valleys.
You will feel your Energy allow you to lite
        and walk and talk unto earth beings.
You will feel their awareness as you speak.
We ask you, Soul, to know a loved one at a distance.
We ask you to find your path to that Soul
        and then we would ask you
        to softly speak their name.
That they might know the awareness of your being
        and then say unto them
        that which you will and they will hear.
They will not only hear, Soul, but they will respond.
Allow the response.
In your circle at this moment you are gathering many Souls.
We ask you to remind themselves of the warmth
        from which they have come.
Their beings are in shock,
        it is much as it is the shock of earth.
Many have found themselves in a cold place
        and they await the loved one to come for good bye
        for they know
        this is the procedure of their earth existence.
We ask you to touch their being,
        to let them know their humanity has left them
        to a higher humanity.
And they may enter in to once again,
        look at the earth through your eye
        and see the desolation and know they have passed.
And then, we ask you to see the Light with them
        for they will turn where you turn,
        for they have entered in to follow your being.
Allow their Energy field to pass through you.
Know you have the power to stay as these Souls pass onward,
        remove from their being any impairment.

Farside and Other Worlds

1087   Michael will teach Farside existence.
Souls of earth, before your being
      are the delights of your earth,
      the trees, the skies, the sea,
      all existences upon your planet
      and they are wondrous to your eyes.
But to see the reality of your existence
      within the palatial surroundings of Farside
      would immediately pale all earth existences.
Souls, you lean against a tree
      and you know the tree has great life
      and you feel the Energy of that tree
      but Farside awakes the tree to thy knowing.
The sound is true.
Do you think that only on earth are there deep valleys
      with tall trees and gentle winding rivers?
Our great glacial mountains
      send forth gushing energies of crystalline.
Farside excels in all that is possible.
Farside is that place where the great artist
      has found his imagination, has entered in.
Souls of earth, the stars ignite the pathway to endless existences.
Souls of earth, you are countless in all forms
      upon the Farside plains.
Who will wander down a path and know without seeing,
      the path will open itself to thy vision.
Behold, you are seeing Farside!
Behold, you have entered in to the power within to see all things. You have grasped the ability to vibrate and see beyond self.
Ponder not in deep thought.
Pray not in endless words,
      but enter in to the positive Energy of thy being
      and know thy foot will be drawn unto the Path,
      the course of earth will be taken to Farside
      and the Gateway will open and many will greet you there. Your being will find contentment.
Your being will be drawn to realize
      that the place you have been was truly illusion

      and you will move forward into momentous excursions
         of delightful Purity.
All are alike in Purity, but all are different.
For, Soul, is not variety the spice of life.
Is it not so on the Farside!
Content thyself to absorb the beauties of earth
      but know in thy being,
      that when the sun hits the leaves upon the tree
      after a rain on a sunny afternoon,
      you are catching the prism's twist of what Farside truly is. Delightful humanity, reach not into thy pain.
Reach not into thy torment.
Let all pain and torment fall as a cloak from thy shoulders
      and know in thy being
      that thou are clothed of Farside Purity
      and have no need of pain or anger.
Souls, do not heal pain, heal the illusion that is pain.
Take away the dart that stings the body
      `and know the pain will disappear.
The Farside has sound, vibrant, decadent sound
      that draws great cymbals and drums, violins and harps
      to be the backdrop of such Purity.
Souls, all movement within Farside is balanced.
All movement issues forth in resounding waves,
      as your sea issues forth in resounding waves.
Your wave of earth is caught in the yars ahead.
Delightful Souls, when you come you will catch your very wave
      for it will resound itself unto you.
For you will come before your wave.
Know all earth is connected to the gentle motion forward
      and to enter in to Farside is to be.
We bring to you salutations.
They come from the fence, from the many beings
      that are watchful over thy path
      for the lives of those who have entered in.
Some were guides.
There is many who have entered home
      waiting for those who would come.
There is a gentleness in the waiting.
There is no rush forward to greet.
There is an acceptance, a humble clarity that understands

there is a Path and there is a walk upon that Path.
And each Soul has their own time
> to enter back unto where we are.

1088   What is the mark of a man?
We ask humanity, what is the mark of a human?
What at the end of your tethered time to illusion,
> do you say, "*This is who I am.*"?

It is simple, Soul.
It is the measure of Truth gained.
It is not the measure of that which you have accumulated
> as treasures upon your earth.

It is not the idiosyncrasies
> that make you particularly who you are.

It is simply the measure of Truth you have gained.
To gather the ultimate Truth,
> you must leave aside earthly treasures.

To gather the ultimate Truth,
> you must overcome pain,
> overcome fear, overcome doubt.

You must recognize in the being
> you are a Soul that is simply tethered to earth,
> but has a homeland that is palatial in its richness;
> that is garland and carries with it all knowledge.

And you, who are tethered to earth,
> you have availability to that knowledge.

It is not classified from you, Soul.
It never has been.
It is available unto all mankind.
You do not, Soul, even have to diligently search out.
You have but to become aware of the Path to it.
It is a transforming pathway.
For it beholds who you are.
It beholds not the inadequacies within the human,
> it recognizes the smallest step,
> the most minute action
> of goodness, of mercy, of compassion.

Truth, simple you say, to gather truth.
And yet, it is not, Soul.
For it requires of you all things.
It requires of you the extension of self

to reach outward from your being.
It requires that there are no noble men, only noble deeds.
There is no challenge for it is a voluntary path.
There is no accountability
    for there is no measure except your own.
There is no time involved for you have eons of time,
    many lives to gather unto you the ultimate Truth.
You may, Soul, feel the heart of your being pulsing
    within the container
    but the aura is much more silent.
The aura does not inflame or incite.
It merely gathers knowledge
    and takes strides outward from you
    that it might give your intent.
To be in the place of Truth
    is to relinquish the mind of humanity
    and gather to the high mind of your reality.
It is, Soul, to persevere in Light of great want and need.
It is to humble self without humbling.
It is to enter in to the greatest of visions.
It is to see integrity of humanity
    in the smallest act and in the greatest deed.
It is to want for nothing in the greatest deprivation.
For your meal is the meal of manna,
    and your healing is the Balm of Gilead,
    and your home is the home of Angels.
And you are but travelling the Path that will take you there.

1089   Souls of earth, you understand light,
    for as you draw unto darkness as humanity,
    you become depressed,
    as you gather into darkness, you crave to be in light.
It is, Soul, that you are Light!
It is that your Light is connected
    to your Humanity of Farside.
You must not lose sight with the reality and the illusion.
The reality is the Human of Farside;
    that human which has entered in from a distant world
    to become a part of a battle;
    a battle that will overcome the great pain of the Angels.
It will bring the Brethren unto Creator.

These energies of great Purity
        are within one of your parallel worlds.
Transition is a parallel world
        created for the purpose of separation,
        not from you, Soul, from Light,
        that the Light might not be dimmed.
And you, who have entered in to become a part of Light
        so that you will Light the darkness,
            and even enter in to the parallel world of transition
            that you might bring forth all who are in darkness.
You have within you the great possibility of the equation.
It is centered in the very heart of your being.
It is the great continuation of your Farside Energy.
It is the great sounding that you give unto all beings.
You are the heart.
You have the high mind attached to the Spirit,
        connected to the Essence, a part of Creator.
And you have the great power to dwell within the high mind.
Were you, Souls of earth, united to dwell within the high mind,
        you would find yourselves indeed
        the Soul of your Creator,
        having reached a multiplicities of Purity!
And you would open the great passageway
        that leads to where we are.
Soul, we would have you know
        there are four existences helping earth.
There are four existences entering in at the Second Gateway.
There is earth.
There is transition.
There is Farside.
There is Angel Beings at the Cleansing River.
Soul, there is a dimension of such Light
        that even the Farside will seem dim in its utterance.
As the Gateway opens, all beings who have been sent forth
        will enter in unto and behold the Ecstasy of Creator,
        behold the Light of Godhead.
In your darkened world, with your feeble globe of Light,
        the Soul upon which you rely
        is a dimness unto darkness.
And yet as you enter through you will become
        that which is your enlightened self,

        that which is the Essence of your being.
You will Light the way
        that others will see the beacon forward
        and all will follow.
You have, Soul, one thousand years.
You will have purified that which is humanity.
You will have released from you all foibles of negativity.
You will uphold the Purity of being.
As you enter in,
        will Mary and Melchezidec,
        Jesu and Mohammed, Krishna and Buddha
        draw forth and call that which is fragment
        to join unto fragment and all the being of fragment
        will illuminate the Gateway
        and all worlds will know the time has come
        to implode unto Creator.

1090   We will tell you, Soul, of Farside worlds.
We would tell you there are many.
Earth explores to know
        are there aliens within the beyond the beyond?
And we say to you, indeed there are!
There are many levels of Farside.
There are many purities of existence within Farside.
There are worlds of beings, much as your own.
The anatomy changes, varies and yet,
        there are within the same desires and longings.
There is a curiosity of worlds beyond their own.
The single difference is in the lack of negativity
        as you understand negativity to be.
There is a chaos that affects many worlds.
Your world knows the affects of chaos
        within the structure of the world self, the weather.
Upon Farside there is also chaos.
You are the minutest form sent forth to overcome chaos.
It is your courage in this minute self
        that antagonizes negativity,
        draws it to violence,
        to its own form of chaos.
Then accepts it has an equal and reaches out
        to nourish emotionally, physically and mentally

        that which is;
        cause such destruction!
Where we are, Soul, there is no such evil.
There is a constant bombardment of chaos in the form
        of outward thrust of Energy from the cosmos
        in many galaxies beyond count.
The threads of Energy are being thrust upon by matter
        in many forums.
Matter stays in no one place.
Even within your body it continually alters.
Where we are, Soul, matter is in constant change.
Many worlds have been formed with an outer crust
        such as the Ruby World.
It will withstand much thrust against its form.
It is a structure of not hardness but flexibility,
        wherein any gas can neither heat nor cold its surface
        for the outer realm changes and confuses the chaos.
It is able to flex to a bombardment
        that withstands any pressure.
Many worlds there are of such compounds.
There are worlds that are of existence itself
        as in the microscopic world where it is living,
        creating within its own format.
It is, Soul, a formation of life.
Again it has learned to adjust in all forms
        of what you would call weather or climate.
We call it divisitude.
There are creations of beings that regenerate themselves.
They can alter, they can re form and enter in to.
It is what you hope for, but it is what we do.
We may go to these worlds and be reconstructed;
        not for the sake of long life;
        there is no ending of life there is renewing of life.
Soul, there is no death except where you are.
There are worlds that open to you
        as a flower opens from the bud unto you.
It is a mirror of what we carry here,
        so that we may enter in to this world
        and we may know how are we,
        for we see before us
        the image of that which our being creates.

Where we to wish to change the presentation of whom we are,
        we have but to gather an Energy of colour
           to redirect consciousness,
           for consciousness is programmable
           even where we are, Soul.
There is an excitement upon Farside, an Energy of life.
It is not dormant.
It is full, exploding in its creativity.
You are enhanced by Colour and Sound.
You are brought unto ecstasy at your desire.
You have no purpose
        unless you enter in to purpose through growth in Purity,
        to enter further in to the conscious being.
As your earth has levels of consciousness, so does Farside.
As Truth has levels of awareness,
        so does Purity have levels
        of gathering and Love of embracing.
Upon the Farside, there is a palette of colour.
It is beyond any palette of earth.
It is a palette that blends the mind's awareness.
And we speak, Soul, of the high mind
        of which all Farside carries.
You see yourselves alone with a mind,
        and yet so much around you carries a mind.
You draw with your hands the deep palette
        and you see the glory
        and you whimsically place your being
        to another palette
        and you see the richness of this palette
        as being excelled by yet another palette,
        and one beyond this, and one beyond this.
For as you enter in to Purity,
        the palettes explode before you.
Your earth is the minutest of palettes
        and when you reach Farside
        and you enter in to the gardens,
        you will be mesmerized by the colour and the glory.
You may reach unto the palette
        of the level of Purity you have entered in to.
We of many worlds may reach
        the palette of colour of Purity we are.

We have choice to go beyond, but not all worlds choose.
In worlds beyond your own,
> there is a great continuity of feelings.
And we use the word feelings, emotionalizing, Soul,
> talk from the fence about who you are
> and where is aunt or uncle
> or mother or father or friend?
And how can we send Energy?
And we are off to find a guide of person,
> *"Have you seen that*
> > *which is occurring from the fence?"*
And we ask you to send forth Energy, intercept for us.
Upon the earth there is much cause for interceptors.
And indeed, there are beings who are just that.
They are guides for earth.
They are Angels who tend to earth.
Many Souls of the first and level Farside beings,
> who have entered in to earth
> or beings from another world who have a loved one
> who has joined a battle of Truth,
> watches over that Soul.
They are constantly aware
> of the movements of that Soul in their growth.
And they call to the Angels, to the Archangels
> to send forth goodness.
You are not in your world of pain, of negativity, thrust forth.
Holy beings, the Farside is very aware of whom you are.
In the world of Pleiadia
> there are Souls very like unto yourselves.
There are Souls who feel very akin as your feelings of human.
They express themselves in much the same way.
They do not have in their midst
> negativity that throttles your Energy
> but they have laughter, a sense of humour and Love.
You would call them weathered,
> you would indeed call them weathered.
You would see a single hole, single.
You have two, single.
You too have one nostril, Soul.
It just has a waggly flesh interfering with the breathing.
The Pleiadians have great Energy for documentation.

All things are documented.
All exploratories, all mapping of the outer galaxies
    beyond where you are, into five,
    is being researched.
There is a great extension in the years of life of man on earth,
    of mapping of galaxies.
There is a crevasse called, the mouth,
    in the galaxy of Pleiadia.
It is deep and it will be seen and mapped by earth.
It is holding millions of energies, the mouth.
There is, Soul, upon Lemuria a great cavern.
It does not enter in horizontally but vertically.
It is an entrance to many doors.
And you have not found it yet.
We tease you, Soul, not for the sake of teasing
    but to whet your appetite
    that you might want
    to search out within the Energy Field,
    within the consciousness of being.
For therein lies the explosion of travel
    that will be known to you.
Therein will Souls visit
    and know one to one, Souls of other worlds.
You will meet as you meet on either side of the glass.
For negativity may not enter in.
And yet, your form, you may gather with you,
    and see that which is there to see.
Reach unto us for we are reaching unto you.
This we ask of humanity.

1091 Understand your flesh, your blood, your bone,
    is simply that.
There is nothing that cannot be altered from the Farside.
Indeed, all is real within your world, but it is illusion.
It is simply an exercise, Soul.
You are not caught, transfixed in a world.
You have the power to remove yourself from that world
    in many ways.
We would have you transport yourself to where we are.
You could do this, Soul.
You could bring yourself to where we are

and we could speak to you.
And we hold our hands out to you.
And we would have you not wait for us, but come to us.
And this you can do!
You are only disabled by your mind.
You are enabled by your high mind.
You have the great power to see and relish
    in all that is visible unto you where we are.
There are no hidden sanctuary
    as in the Holy places of earth.
All may enter in.
There is no barrier of discrimination.
All may enter in.
We ask that as you retire to your sleep,
    you understand the dream state is the earth's turmoil,
    not Farside.
That you might enter in to Farside,
    we ask that you release the mind in a wake state,
    not a sleep state.
And that you see the great Light beckoning you forth.
And you understand you have simply to enter in to it
    and you are surrounded by the Light
    and it carries you forward.
And your awareness will see who we are.
Your world has had
    Galileos, Michelangelos, Einsteins,
    and the knowledge has been awakened
    in their being through us.
We have upon our side great research.
You have in your earth great research.
You dwell within your earth to live and breathe
    and die within your earth.
It is your reality.
It is simple and it is complex.
Merely stop the breath and you die
    and your flesh returns to the flesh of your earth.
Where we are, we do not cease to be.
We are.
Yet within our Energy Field are unanswered questions.
We are taught,
    we are taught by the Blessed who come unto us,

        we are taught by the Circle of Saints who send forth.
The Blessed Angels have spoken thus unto whom we are.
Your attainment is of the Energy Source.
You are a reflection of the Light therein.
The Light has intelligence.
The Light has Being.
The Light seeks to hold a reality.
Their very being, the Light that is their containment,
        is withering.
They are as you.
They have matter.
The matter of their being they now know
        cannot live without the Source.
They have also another known within.
They have arrived.
They seek outward from their being to know from where.
In the seeking they have met energies of such Purity,
        of such acceptance, but no motion,
        yet willing to adapt, to assist.
Many worlds we have found.
These worlds carry no negativity.
They carry no unction.
They have tranquility.
We know we do not come from they.
This we know.
For we have within our being,
        great motion, curiosity, vibrancy.
Are we they that we see?
Without the Energy Source, do we become the dark ones?
This we do not know.
You ask, Soul, and we explore.
You ask and you reveal it unto our being, for you are we.
Soul, we speak of Akashic unto you,
        of the Record that we know as itinerary completed.
It is profound in its viewing.
It is manifold unto not just where you are, but where we are.
All is inclusive.
The world where we are included in the Akashic,
        there also threads of great glory.
There is the thread of human anger.
It is red.

But there is the deepest of garnet, it is the Ruby world.
It is woven in its majesty.
There is the work of the whales sounding ever forth.
It is in a great chord of deep purple.
There is the strident colours
      of many worlds beyond where we are.
Reach out in our beings and there are worlds.
There are the learning stations and all is recorded.
Not an iota is left unrecorded.
There are worlds that simply record.
As you have the great computer,
      we have, Soul, the majestic computer.
It has no whirring.
Indeed not.
There are no faults to be had.
It is perfection.
And it is a kaleidoscope of colour, of life;
      not just your life, but all life.
It is seen.
It is visible.
You have but to say, "*This is what I want to do.*"
      and your life comes forth unto you.
Technology, Soul?
It is again profound.
Each cough, each throb, heart, is recorded.
See that which is recorded.
We would have you remember the dance of ribbons,
      the great power of colour encircling your being.
We would have you use the mind to establish the ribbons
      and see them in great yellows and reds.
See yourself able to draw them up and over your being
      and around your being.
Know that you are life in that you can
      gently skip over the ribbon.
There is no cumbersome in that which you do,
      for it is your Soul that enters in to the ribbon dance.
We ask you to see the brightest crimson
      and the vibrant yellow and see them entwined,
           using all finesse of a professional dancer.
You can manoeuver the ribbons about your being.
They will, Soul, assist your mind to clear itself of sleepiness.

It will assist your mind to clear you from depression.
It will assist your mind to see beyond the film of your earth.
We ask that you hold
        the counterpane of colour, the indigo blue,
        and as you sit in your mind's eye
        upon the counterpane of colour,
        you will see above you your hands.
And you will see from your hands
        can be extensions of ribbon.
They will not be roll, Soul.
It will appear
        as though they come from your hands themselves.
Allow the flow of the ribbon
        to come about your body and you will see,
        as you sit upon the blue,
        the ribbons can travel under the blue
        as though there were no floor around landing place.
For you will be indeed in the mind's eye
        and you will find your spirits lifted.
Then and only then as you have seen the ribbons
        flow around your being in multi colour,
        do you then allow your being to stand.
And know that it is still illusionary.
And yet, it is not,
        for it is your Soul that is taking comfort in the ribbons.
Be brought unto the great invitation to dance.
And see before you the breeze of timeless endeavour.
It will invite you to the greatest dance
        that you might find yourself
        encircled with the great ribbons
        and carried beyond where you sit to where we are.
And all that you are will appear to be as you are.
You may step gently into the cloud and walk thorough
        to meet those beings who would greet you.
This is the Soul walk.
Know you can Soul walk,
        as you can transcendentally travel with your Soul.
You may also take the form of whom you are with you.

1092 We speak to you of the great Energy expanse
        that is far from you yet near unto you.

It is that Energy, Lantosia.
There is a vast network,
    far more sophisticated than your earth network,
    that sends forth signalling into the great expanse
    of what you would call nothingness.
It is echoed and echoed and echoed,
    yet we have received an enheartening sound.
It is not an answer unto us.
But it is an echo sent forth
    from some Energy that has knowledge of number.
The count is only in three.
Yet it is three with many complications,
    so that the three has become
    a multitude of thresholds upon which to send forth.
We have the ongoing expectation
    of reaching in to the fourth level that is Light
    and we wish to behold the linears of existence.
We say unto you that your earth
    has become smaller in its livability.
It has shrunk in its capacity to hold humanity.
It is fluctuating within great decibels
    to maintain order within the structure of the planet.
Within the place of Lantosia there is an abundance
    of viable living space for earth humanity.
And we invite you to explore that viability.
You will of course not be able to feel your way
    in the manner you have heretofore.
For you would be annihilated in the force of Energy,
    but you can receive the cloak unto you of travel.
It is within the Path
    and you will be able to walk into our land.
We ask that you visit Lantosia.

1093   Souls of earth, you are frail and you have strength
    and unto you is a transport available.
It is called not with wheels.
It is called with Energy.
It is given unto you to ride high into the realm of your mind
    to use all the possibilities of your earth mind
    to evaluate all that you see.
You will understand as you are transported

      you are carried by the Energy of your high being.
But your earth mind has an awareness
      of that which is seen by the high mind.
And you are able to access and draw from that which you see
      a logic understanding
You may, Soul, vibrate your being unto another realm.
You may lift your Energy so that it is taken
      unto the great kaleidoscope of colour.
And you may see the dance of the Angels.
You may see the ethereal chart of Souls Spirits
      as they are transported by Angels unto the Farside
      from where you are.
You are earthly.
You tether yourself to a mind set that you cannot soar.
And Souls of earth, you can soar!
You can see and hear with the vibration of your Light.
You may bring your understanding
      to the fullness of that which is upon the Farside.
You may radiate.
You may utter words that are beyond your creativity,
      where you will utter that which you see.
You will bring forth the myriads of beings.
You will see the spectrum of all existence and you will know
      that you have landed in a place beyond your ken.
Yet you will have a familiarity and you will have a brief time
      for you may not be far from earth for long.
For the will of the Soul is strong
      to be from where it is to where it has been.
It will have come home
      and it will see and know that which is familiar.
And all that is within the Soul of purpose will be
      want to remain in the lustre of that which it seeks.
Though the encounter is brief,
      but that which you see will be much.
Your very life upon earth is dependent
      on the shortness of your stay.
For you cannot continue into the heights of being
      without loss of mass.
It constricts itself to lessen
      the hold of the human flesh upon the earth.
It is, Soul, carried in the depths of being.

You are a fisher king, able to dive deep into the waters
        except your dive is in to the Energy of being.
And you come up with food for thought to the mind.
You come up with memory of that which you know.
You come up with understanding as food unto whom you are.
Your very being will feel the gluttonous need to know
        without the warp within the humanity.
For it will be food but you will know the food cannot be kept.
It will be shared.
It will be given forth unto all humanity.
It does not, Soul, have a cost.
It has a freedom to soar as from whence it has come.
See with the eye.
The eyes are of no use.
Hear with the ear of Colour and Sound.
Behold with the goodness of heart
        and the strength and courage of your very being
        for you are human.
You are human
        and designated unto your Creator with strength.
You are awash in a sea below the Angels
        and they strengthen their being with you
        for you sustain their very strength with your Light.
You are the gladiator in a great battle
        and your weapon is the torch of Truth,
        the overcoming unto glory of all existence.

1094   See yourselves ride the wave of Energy.
Understand the wave of Energy
        that takes you from where you are to a level beyond.
As the swing as you rise sees a distant horizon
        and you enter down and no longer see that horizon,
        so is the rise of the Spirit rising up
        as the swing rises up to see beyond.
Were the swing to maintain its upward placement
        it could enter in.
Where the swing has been
        would seem as though it had never been.
So it is with the Spirit and the Soul,
        as you allow your being to enter in to the Spirit self.
You may walk upon a different plane.

You may see deep into your own plane.
You may realize the potential of your mind.
Earth mind is limited by humanity himself.
Earth mind has an expansion far beyond its earth placement.
Enter in to the enlightened mind of being.
Enter in to the gardens that you know are there,
      yet have felt you cannot see.
Your time has been entered in to
      with potentials and dooms
      and we would bring you brilliance.
Not the brilliance of the mind,
      the brilliance of the mind's eye that has the ability
      to walk with us in the treasured garden.
The grass has just dried of dew
      and has the sweet smell of morning.
And the birds have awakened from their night of sleep
      and the wee ones chirp in their anxiousness for food.
Indeed there is food.
Indeed in the garden there is ever blooming, ever being born.
As you walk upon the grass
      you feel the cushion of goodness beneath your feet.
You see the purple richness of pansies carpeting the garden.
And you look up and you see other Bernum
      reaching its yellow fronds
      in chains down unto the very earth
      for in the garden of Creator all things have fullness.
There is, Soul, an enormous tree.
It is an oak tree.
It has the breadth of twenty men.
And as you look up you see the acorns full of the leaves
      slightly tinged to the golden.
And you know there is an abundance.
And you feel the filtering Light welcome your being.
You may lean against the tree with your back and you will feel,
      the goodness of the tree enter into your being.
You will feel a warmth inundate the very flesh of your being.
It is a gift.
When you look toward the blueness ahead
      you see below a huge arbour,
      that arbour holds grape,
      the richness of blues and purples

and pinks hanging down,
and you wonder on what it is hanging
and as you look you see it holds itself.
You see the strength of creation, the power of creation
and you are invited, Soul, to hold a morsel to you.
And as you taste, you taste the sweetness of grape
and you feel the strength of its being
course through your being
as no food has never provided for you.
You understand the Purity that has entered in.
You have an invitation, Soul, to pass into the blue.
You are welcome to enter.
It will take you unto another dimension,
a dimension where beings you have known, exist.
You may pass through and you may see the loved one
who has held you dear.
You may see that precious Soul you lost
waiting anxiously for you to come through.
Soul, you will vision others you have had contentions with
and those contentions
will have left your being for the moment
to only see that which is who they are,
the Purity of their being.
Will you enter through, Soul?
We invite you to do so.

1095 Souls of earth, there is a great avenue to follow.
It extends upward through your Energy.
It is as in all earth beings,
as in all creatures of land, sea and air available.
It is not limited even unto those.
It is, Soul, within the very growth of flora upon the lands
within the seas that pick up Energy,
that have a vibrant sounding board
wherein all truths are carried.
They are carried unto the great Handiwork that is displayed.
It is the Akashic.
It is visible unto all who are of Farside, all who visit unto us.
They may see the portal.
It is of worlds round about them.
The very planes of earth are visible.

The very folds of the seas are visible.
The very molten mass of the chord of your existence is visible
    and all growth is shown in the greatest of artistry.
Souls, we have learned from you.
We have gathered from humanity
    yet another vision of that which is.
It is, Soul, the Sublime Record.
It is visible to some, not all.
It is visible to those who have reached in their being
    to the seventh level of Purity.
It is visible to those who have extended themselves
    upward unto the sixth level of Purity.
Souls of earth, you may see that which is displayed
    even unto the great sea of Energy.
From their Soul, all echoes forward.
It is brought as a sounding board unto Sublime Record.
It is sent forth outward from Sublime Record
    upward unto Supreme Being.
We say this that your science
    might know that there are more levels,
    folds of existence, that has been given credibility.
You speak of billions but, Soul, it is beyond
    for they are Domes and Domes of existence.
There are beings such as yours who spend lifetimes in Purity.
They do not battle negativity.
They have no need.
They are not warriors.
You are the warrior
    but they have fields of knowledge to indulge in.
They can research into lives you have lived.
They have before them all the landscape
    of all the worlds to their Purity.
The folds are visible with the opening of their Energy.
This is why we speak to you of it, Soul,
    that you might open your Energy
    that you might unfold your being.
You might see that which you are and know that you are
    far more complicated than you allow yourself to vision.
You have within your Energy all knowledge.
You have within your Energy
    the ability to see the Akashic Record.

You have within your Energy the vision to send forth Light
>> into the darkness that you might see
>> and know the darkened way,
>> that it might be lit that others might see.
You are not delicate flowers that have been placed upon earth.
There are delicate flowers upon earth
>> and they are treasured even by Farside,
>> but you are not one, you are the warrior.
But the worlds that are beyond your own,
>> those you speak of often as alien unto you,
>> indeed they are alien unto you
>> as your humanity upon earth,
>> but upon Farside
>> many of you have visited where they are.
Many of you have spoken to them
>> of your adventures upon earth.
Many of the indigo of the violet children share their truths
>> and learn from them of their purities.
You see a landscape and perceive in your being
>> what shall I fill it with?
Shall it be the magnificence of a creation wherein I might abide?
But the Souls we speak of
>> they see a landscape
>> and they inquire of its purpose unto Supreme Being.
They ask why is it here?
And they search out.
They are inquisitive, Soul.
The inquisitiveness of your earth beings is not as it once was.
It is as though negativity itself
>> has put you to sleep, made you inert.
And we ask that you awaken and you behold where you are
>> and you recognize why you are as those beings of Purity,
>> seek beyond the folds beyond the Domes of existence
>> unto other existences!
Soul, you know not of that which is before you.
You cannot behold the grandiose of that which is before you.
You cannot magnify with all the powers of earth
>> that which is in the outer realms of existence.
Creatures of earth who are human,
>> you see upon Farside mansions built for you.
Soul, the mansions of earth in their highest form

> do not amount as even adequate
> to that which is available even to the pure of level one;
> do you understand, is pure!

And yet, the fullness of Purity reaches even beyond
> unto the powers of the Creators.

Souls of earth, finger through your tomes of earth
> and find that which has been.

But what could you finger through the tomes
> and find that which will be?

For this is possible upon Farside, even
> as it creates itself it becomes!

There is nothing that is thought that cannot be created
> but the Blessed Angels withhold negativity
> with the curtain of care,
> > therefore, within the Yawn negativity does not dwell.

Chaos is without.
Chaos is where you are.
Chaos is within your very being.
You feel chaos within your body, within your mind
> and we say,
> > *"Still the chaos.*
> > *Hold it calm in your being."*

Know that within the greatness of whom you are
> is the great power to lift all folds
> and behold that which IS.

The planes are visible.
The Fields of energies are accessible.
Soul, bless thy being
> and know that upon the counterpane of Energy
> are other beings who hold you and like you seek,
> seek to know;
> seek to know the greatness of whom you are,
> seek to know that within the response of your being
> is the possibility to lose all depressions,
> to hold fast to the positives,
> to see things in the negative.

To lift the Energy, to hold it high
> is to visualize Light shining upon you
> with a greatness so that the Pillar surrounds you
> and know the extent of that Pillar
> is even unto Creator and beyond.

You are feeble.
See the feebleness of your flesh and your blood.
You enter in to your earth with fresh skin and bone.
The flesh sings in its goodness and some wither,
    some lose their balance upon earth and pass young.
Others are cut short from life upon earth.
Some age but all lose the flesh and the bone
    from the Energy of whom they are.
It is the Energy that is who you are.
It is the Energy that does battle.
You have a form upon Farside that holds that Energy.
But it is not your form upon earth.
You have been upon earth many times.
You have taken many forms.
The one you are in is but a single form.
Do not be caught up in the form you are in.
Be caught up in the Energy of whom you are
    and know that Energy exists
    and knows all forms to the Purity
    you are in upon Farside.
You do not announce,
    "This is who I am".
You are!
You are, Soul, I Am that I Am.
There is no announcing.
Your being is known.
You cannot hide.
There is no need to hide.
There is no fear.
There is no need to fear.
Why?
When you know this is your home where we are,
    why would you fear where you are?
It is but a momentary place to be.
It is a place for growth that you might grow
    and extend your Energy unto Creator.
Be happy in the day you are in.
Be awakened to the joy of that day
    and hear the Angel sing in the Light of your being.
So be it.

1096 Soul, bring your being into the Farside.
Be constantly able to transport your Energy to where we are.
Use the quiet where the mind has no place.
Use only the path of the eye into the Light of Farside..
See the great Energy that awaits you.
Do not hurry.
Do not place expectations.
Simply wait for the Light to show itself,
      then allow yourself to bathe in that Light.
Enter within the great charm of Light
      for Light will bring you unto an ecstacy of glory
      and you will see where you are
      the coming forth of energies.
They will be anxious to display themselves unto you.
They will be curious of no thing about you.
For they see all that you are in your vulnerability.
Do not fear!
They have for you no agenda.
You on the other hand may carry an agenda for yourself
      in transporting your Energy to where we are.
You may visit into the lands of greatness.
You may find yourself communicating
      with energies you have known.
They will be, Soul, greatly honoured.
And they will know you in your simplicity.
For your Light will be dimmed to theirs.
You will see upon their visage a wonderment that you are there.
For they will behold your aura is not truly you.
They will know.
Do not rush to embrace these beings.
Allow them to come forward unto thee.
For they have the advantage, Soul, of lessening their Light
      that you may withstand the glory of whom they are.
You have allowed yourself to transcend the earthly plane.
When you are in the place of the eye,
      allow your vision to do your travelling.
Do not, Soul, exert your Energy by seeking to travel.
The eye is the mover.
Many earth beings expect to travel along the way.
It is not so.
It is the eye itself that is the mover and will take you, Soul,

    if you will allow it to enter in
    to a varied dimensional Field.
This Field will bring you to choices,
    and in the choices
    will be arrayed by colour.
The colour you enter in to
    will bring you unto the level upon which you will enter.
Should you not have the Purity to enter,
    you will be, Soul, not denied, but unable to enter.
Should you request,
    Souls of a higher dimension would enter to you.
There is to be clear understanding
    that Souls who channel great energies
    do not always carry the level of those energies.
Rather they have been visited to the level they are at Farside.
There have been many beings who have received great ability
    to walk paths well beyond manifestation.
It is their Purity,
    their total innocence that brings them to this ability.
There is, Soul, a great wonder for you awaiting.
You will find great delight
    in the species that await your visitation.
And we cannot help but bring ourselves to humour.
For you are contemptuous in your earth form of many species
    you see lesser than your own, including your very own.
Yet you will find that you enter in to earth
    from a species you might see as a contempt you behold.
Therefore do not judge, Soul, too quickly the brother of thy eye.
For you might see yourself in your brother!
There is a Path of many colours you may enter in to.
There is also the realm of Angels, of White Light.
In this White Light is the healing core unto your being.
We ask you to find White Light and to use it.
You would see it, Soul, endowed unto thy being
    casting its ray round about you,
    even as you await the wonder.
We ask that you feel the warmth, the comfort of this Light.
We ask that you allow your Energy to be transformed by it.
When you feel, Soul, a great song in your being,
    sing forth that song.
When you see in your being the great blend of colour,

      allow it to enwrap thy being.
Do not feel that you will walk upon a path mistakenly,
      for as we have said the eye will take you.
You are not walking, Soul.
The eye has the ability to move
      and transfer from one Light to another,
      from one option to another.
This for healing,
      this for transference of memory,
      this for the Akashic Record.

1097 Soul, we will speak to you of vessel,
      the vessel of your being,
      the governing vessel of your being,
      not, Soul, meridian to the earth body,
      meridian to the Energy you are,
      the governing vessel being aura;
      not the mind, not the heart,
      but the Energy that has movement.
The aura which may flow outward, move inward,
      balance all energies within,
      balance all energies without.
You have power in your being.
You have chords of being.
They are within the aura and they are the chimes of your being.
They are that which alters,
      that which is powerful in an extension from you.
We would have you recognize the music in the Soul.
Each being of humanity is the tethered to music,
      is tethered to the chimes of being.
You have from where you are,
      the availability of chimes forward from you
      and you may use those chimes
      as tuning forks to your Soul,
      for the Angels ever send forth notes of being.
You have but to tone your being to the Angel sound.
You have radiance in all your extended Energy.
You have but to tune yourself to the radiant possibilities within.
Your world has been set with energies of chime.
The very flora and fauna of your earth
      send forth notes unto you

        that you might hear in your being
        the beatification of self,
        that you might be lifted
        from your dowdy earth existence
        to the glorious paradise of energies of creation.
You may sound yourself against the stars.
You may sound yourself to the planets.
You may sound yourself to the bursting forth of the volcano
        and know the power
        that you have in your being is greater than.
You are the lowest,
        but you have within you the possibility of the highest.
No other creature self has such possibilities of fulfilment.
Understand the chimes of your Soul.
Understand, you are registered to all other notes.
Do not set your being to the discordant note,
        but know in your being,
        you have the power to alter the discordant.
You have the power to bring joy to that which is pain.
You have the power to heal that which is ill.
You have the power to lift and lift
        and lift and lift and rise above all negatives.
And in that lifting, you will understand the Energy of negative
        will recognize the being and lift also.
Behold, chime is registered.
Chime is a vessel, for chime is the sound of the aura.

1098   Souls of earth, you are fire, you are flame.
You are Light, you are Energy.
See yourself as carried by Breath to where you would be.
There is no restraining of the fire,
        for Breath will motion it forward
        that you might be the eye for all that is existence,
        that you might be the tentacle coming forward
        to feel and see and hear
        that which is motion in the outer realms of being.
For you are Light.
You are, Soul, glory manifested as humanity.
You show beyond the realm of Light itself
        a greater path of iridescence that all might see
        and have magnified for them

    that which is beyond where they are.
How mighty do we see you, humanity!
How great do we see your worthiness.
You are not caught, you are not caught, you are not caught!
You are not bound, you are not bound, you are not bound!
You are free to delve and enter.
You have but to find the passage
    within the mind that will take you unto all realms.
We beseech you to explore the passage of the mind.
It is available unto all humanity.
It will take you, Soul, beyond where you are.
Illuminize the reach.
Feel the pestulence open before you,
    that you are not constricted in that which you do.
Your eye is vision.
Your heart brings you to the Lightness.
It is the Soul that allows the Light to be.
It is your Soul that needs a Purity
    to infiltrate into the consciousness of where we are.
You have coordinates available to you.
You have, Soul, a Path given unto you.
You have, Soul, the gigabyte used as hertz to enter in to.
You have mathematicians that will take you to the very portal,
    that will open a path to total emancipation of earth.

1099 Soul, we would like you to understand the great Void,
    the consciousness of all being.
We would have you understand within your being,
    the great void,
    the mind, the consciousness of all being.
Your mind of earth,
    your mind of Soul, Spirit, and Essence, are together.
As you relinquish the gathering of knowledge from your earth,
    it is imbedded within your Soul self.
Before it absents the body, it is indelibly within the Soul
    and becomes a part of the Energy of aura.
As you upon your earth permit yourself,
    you may enter in to the high mind.
The high mind takes you unto the Void.
The Void has many levels of being.
Each existence has been at the Will of Void.

It has been available unto Void, unto consciousness.
It is awakened by consciousness.
Yet you do not require the matter to reach unto Void.
You may travel, Soul, direct,
    when you release from yourself
        the humanness of whom you are.
That your ability to enter in to the upper levels of consciousness
    are dependent upon the Truth and Purity
        that you have accessed is absolute,
        for you cannot travel beyond the ability of Purity
        that is within.
You have before you upon your earth
    beings with many levels of Purity.
These levels of Purity permit the access unto the high mind.
In the releasing of existence,
    you are able to enter in immediately to another existence,
    recognize your Energy there,
    release that Energy, enter in to high mind.
As you become familiar of the avenue of travel in the high mind,
    you will not even have to engage
    the form of whom you were.
You will just allow your Energy of mind, of consciousness,
    to reach forward.
You will understand
    that human's ability to reach unto the high mind
    is greater than the Angels!
How can this be, you say,
    "Indeed, for does not the Angels see all things!"
Behold, the Angel sees all things unto where you are.
It is not unto where you are
    that Energy of consciousness is concerned.
It is, Soul, holding for the high mind
    that can reach back in to the darkness.
You have been in the cavern of darkness,
    even within the space of your own mind.
The Angels have not known this pain, Soul.
They have not.
Only those lost in transition understand that pain.
Only those lost at fourth level, understand that pain.
We know in our being, Idyllic understands that pain.
We know the Beloved Brother understands that pain.

But you have found your way back without altering Energy.
You have been able to take your Energy unto many lives,
>   transforming your own being in each life,
>   some quicker than others,
>   some still caught in the pain of negativity.

Yet the transformation
>   has been seen in all worlds that are willing to see.

Within the Energy Source
>   the accountability of mankind is known.

For is it not within the Void of Consciousness!
Is it not set apart from the Fields of existence!
Has it not received the Light of whom you are
>   that it might be forwarded into the darkness,
>   Void of Consciousness, Energy of Knowing,
>   Zero, place of all that is, even unto Breath.

1100 Souls we speak to you of sound.
We speak to you of the Energy within sound,
>   as the many flappings of wings,
>   as the wind upon your earth,
>   as the strike of lightning upon a tree, sharp.

You hear, you witness.
Sound can be visual in that the eye of beholding
>   brings instantly a picture,
>   even though you cannot see
>   you can visualize within the eye.

So it is with the Truth of your being.
So it is humanity with whom you are.
All that resonates within you is seen upon Farside.
They behold that which you are.
They see.
As in the crack of lightening,
>   you see the skies before you,
>   even though the vision is not there.

Within you, the vision is!
Souls, you cannot withhold Truth from the Farside.
You cannot withhold negativity from the Farside.
All is visible.
It is not judged,
>   it is visible.

And it is with the visualization,

> the witnessing of the Souls upon earth
> that guides and Angels come forth to give
> you would call, mercy.

Souls, they give,
> but you have not as humans understood
> that you do not require!

There is a great appellation, it is gateway.
It is, Soul, gateway upon gateway upon gateway
> into the many negative energies,
> into the very purest of energies.

It is the gateway to the heart,
> it is the gateway to the mind,
> it is the gateway to the Soul, to the Spirit, to the Essence.

You have the power to open gateways,
> you have the keys to open gateways.

You have within your being the very Energy
> to draw from whom you are the power
> to be more than human.

You, the reflected glory, you the Angel self,
> you have the power to see,
> you have the power to feel,
> you have the power to know,
> to understand, to witness.

You cannot ponder.
Krishna did not ponder.
Jesu did not ponder.
Buddha did not ponder.
Mohammed did not ponder.
Action is that which was!
Human, Humanity, Souls of earth, understand humanity,
> understand that the form you have taken
> is only a form designated for the life you are in!

You have many forms.
You have been upon earth many times.
You have heard the sounds of the distant bells.
You have heard the wind blowing through the trees.
You have heard the animals
> as they beckon and call to their others.

You have even heard the birds and the fish in the stream.
You know how to hear.
You know how to use the faculty of hearing.

But there is another doorway to hearing.
It is, Soul, hearing sound, hearing colour.
It is entering through a doorway that is Energy.
It is witnessing that you are Energy,
    that the feebleness of your body does not lift.
Matter does not lift without motion.
Energy is carried through the void of consciousness,
    through the many doorways.
It carries the motion of Breath.
Not the breath of humanity, alone,
    but the Breath of all Energy,
    that which lives, that which is.
Behold, you are of Supreme Being.
You have entered in from doorways.
You have reflected forth.
You have but to understand through the words
    that have been given unto you that you are mighty,
    that you have reflected forward,
    that you have the power of Energy.
As human, you have the power to implode
    unto the Energy which you are.
Phantom pain from limbs bring recall of the form that was.
And so when you enter in to the Energy,
    the Gateway that implodes,
    you have the knowing of whom you are.
You will be drawn through.
You will enter as a child enters through the birth channel,
    you will enter in and have memory
    from where you have come.
You will know that you can draw Energy unto you
    as the child draws Light in the being
    until negativity withholds.
To behold the magnificence of the Energy
    is to release from you the value of earth energy,
    for when you are caught in the value of earth energy,
    you do not have all the resources of being
    to enter through,
    for you are held by the strands of negativity.
There is no value upon earth,
    except the value of the Energy you are,
    that you can return through implosion.

Not memory, memory is a part of your being.
It is whom you are.
It is written within the code of whom you are.
You cannot take any earth value,
> the Soul gathers that which you are;
> the earth mind must release the need
> of earth material value.

This will be an understanding for how magnificent
> to heal the human form,
> to change the very DNA, the very matter.

You will gather at the feet of learned healers
> who understand Sound and Colour
> and how coordinated together
> they become a power unto themselves,
> energized and carried through the Energy unto earth.

You feel within the very rotation of hand the Energy,
> but this is Energy that restores.

This is Energy that gives forth.
This repairs that which is destroyed.
This is teachable unto earth beings.
So be it.

1101 Humanity, enter in to the garden
> where all Energy Flows.

Enter in, Soul, without fear.
Enter in, Soul, with the absolute knowing
> that you are connected.

That your very vibrancy is the vibrancy of all Energy.
That the connectedness is not of the simplicity of atom.
But it carries its boldness far in to a realm of being
> wherein Energy carries a dimension,
> where the Field is the garden,
> where galaxies are merely grains of sand
> and salted throughout a vast known.

You, Soul, you are the candescent Light that has the ability
> to take us through the aperture of Light.

For you are indeed radiant in your being.
You are indeed vibrancy itself.
You have within a corridor that carries itself unto all knowing.
You have but to reach within the garden of Energy.
We ask that you visit the consciousness of whom you are.

We ask that you delight in the power that you have.
We ask that you see yourself
      beyond the earth and its dimensions,
      that you see yourself beyond
       that which you see as time and space.
For the Energy that radiates from you
      within the core of your being
       delights in true Energy, the Truth of all Energy.
And you, you have the path to be there.
Unto you are all things given.
Unto you are all possibilities.
Unto you is the greatest of gifts,
      the fullness to explore beyond who you are.

1102   Come into the Energy of Light.
Souls of earth, enter in to the quiet sanctum of Light.
Know that all is manifested within the Light of your being.
All is manifested within the Light of Farside.
All is manifested within the energies of Creator,
      for Truth, Purity and Love emanate Light.
Light, healing Light.
All your being is within the power of Light.
You have within your being colour and sound
      such as you know not.
You have the ability to soar as the eagles,
      as the condor, as the beam of Light.
Far from where you are in that quiet sanctum of Light,
      are the Spirit Souls who know, who understand
       that which you as humanity found before you,
       that which you face
       that negativity that is always tempting
       and escalating before you.
Souls of earth, we will teach you of the great power of Light
      that holds within Sound and Colour,
      that vibrates, that manifests itself in healing upon earth.
You transform your being.
You transform that which you are.
You find yourself elevated unto your Spirit.
You find yourself brought into the transom
      that carries you forward
      into the illuminescence of all that is colour.

Not the rainbow, not the earth rainbow,
> beyond that which is the rainbow,
> beyond that which is manifested upon earth.

This, Soul, is that which is Farside.
It is that which is beyond Farside.
It is that which is Creator Light.
We would have you understand the density of colour.
We would have you understand the vibration of each colour.
We would have you understand the sound
> that reverberates throughout your being.

Souls of earth, do not be content upon your earth.
Do not be content to live merely in a single heaven above,
> but give yourself purposeful aim
> to strengthen that Purity
> that you are that you might reach
> into the farthest realm of your Creator.

Souls, you are diversive in many things.
You are not content with your earth being,
> for you always strive to alter that which you are.

We do not ask you to alter that which you are.
We ask you to enter in to that which you are!
You are a Soul in an illusion upon your earth.
You are in the illusion to overcome negativity.
But, Soul, you are Light.
Your Energy is Light.
You may sit before the learned professors,
> you may be taught in all thy fine attributes of learning
> and yet you will not learn to implode your Energy
> into the very state of Light.

Only through the doorway can you enter in.
Knowledge is not the avenue,
> it is not the where all, it is not the be all.

That which you are is!
You have only to look at the very vibrancy of whom you are.
Your existence is only one of many existences.
You are brought in your power of human
> to form that which your mind will take you to.

But, Soul, you have the power to research into the Light itself.
You may find yourself elevating into distant realms.
You may find yourself conquering all illness upon your earth
> by merely using the Light

        you are able to gather unto you.
Souls of earth, how can you breathe,
        except through motion,
        except through vibration.
How can you enter in through the Quar?
Vibration, Soul, Energy carrying yourself through.
You have been given words of Purity.
You have gathered an understanding of some.
But you have not delved into the depths of the worlds
        beyond your own.
And we would have you know there are many worlds.
There are many beings of great Purity
        who would have you taught
        in the Farside Fields of learning.
Would you enter in, Souls?
Would you allow your energies to sit in the calm of your being
        while you transform the mind into a state of still?
So that you may carry the Energy of your being
        beyond where you are.
You have, Soul, many worlds who look to you
        and seek that which you know.
And yet in the scope of Purity, you are infant,
        for you have not fully gathered the understanding
        that the Spirit is yours,
        the Essence is yours.
The power to elevate through the triad is simple.
It is in acceptance that you are not an earthling.
You are, Soul, a human.
But the human that you are is not caught upon earth.
Your humanity first was with Creator.
That is who you are,
        the Energy sent forth from Creator armed with Truth!
This is the destiny of humanity to return unto the Essence,
        that pure part of whom you are.
There is no purpose beyond return.
Nothing upon your earth is consequential.
There is no other vibrancy
        but implosion into the Energy of Farside and beyond.
Souls of earth, we have walked with you upon your earth.
We know the platitudes that earthlings spout.
We know that which you speak of as love, of purity, of truth.

But Souls, you have not gathered the fullness
        until you allow your being to enter through.
In the calm serenity, not meditation, Soul,
        in the quickness of a moment you have entered in.
You will see the beings,
        you will know their blessedness.
You will behold the star of the morning.
You will behold beatific, the Angels.
You will see all manner of beings and know no fear.
Earth has a moment.
Earth will not be brought to distraction.
Earth is blessed.
Humanity, humanity will suffer.
We cannot alter upon Farside,
        that which humanity is.
We can direct.
We can nudge.
But we cannot change the walk of the individual humanity.
You can change the walk, you can alter the step,
        you can hold the blessedness in your being.
Souls of earth, as we have held the gentle Souls within the arms
        and brought them from the perilous cliffs, so can you.
You may speak of that which you know.
You may enter in, not to the spouting,
        but speak in the language of action.
Speak in the knowing that you heal.
Often, Soul, a being will not permit the healing.
You cannot alter that which is.
But know that you will have altered greatly
        the purpose of the being
        for they will see the channel
        and at the time of entering in
        they will know and escape the transitional field,
        for they will have been taught
        how to enter through Love, through compassion.
Do not judge.
Do not place judgement.
But gather your Energy in compassion,
        in Love, in Truth, in Purity.

Chapter Three
TRIADS

1103   It is the Soul.
It is the Soul that becomes heavy, becomes overwhelmed.
It is the Soul that can lighten.
It is the Soul that carries the knowledge
      but in carrying the knowledge
        it imprints upon the Soul the pain
        that has been involved with that knowledge.
The Soul becomes heavy.
Often the Soul is reluctant to leave earth.
The Soul can carry the pain that creates the slow step
      or the halt in transition.
It is the weariness of the Soul
      that carries the burden of negativity to the karmic station.
And then it is the Lightness of the Soul
      as it enters back unto home into the realm of Purity,
      and knows that even though the pain
      is imprinted upon the Soul, there is joy.
For there is the option of re entering unto a further step
      even, Soul, has humanity a choice not to re enter.
This is a choice.
Re entering in to humanity's negative void is not easy.
It is burdensome for there is much to overcome.
It is the purpose of entering in.
It is the very intent of being.
You are of earth,
      the carnage that has been attached to each Soul.
Many have been overcome to grow in Truth
      yet some to plod through the years of life of the Soul
      that holds the memory of the embittered life.
The Spirit does not carry the heaviness of the Soul.
It is garbed in Purity.
The growth is in Purity.
The Soul carries the earth humanity
      recorded within the very Energy of being.
You are brought unto earth
      by the will of your being of your humanity upon Farside.
You choose to enter in
      and you garb yourself in altered beings

　　　　that you might grow and overcome
　　　　with the Truth of whom you are,
　　　　　　the Light that you can gather unto in that Spirit of Purity.
As you progress in the human's understanding
　　　　and the human's consciousness of being
　　　　you gather about you an aura of indescribable joy
　　　　for your being understands.
Your being beholds the reason you have entered in.
You have the understanding of illusion.
You have the understanding of that which Truth is.
Earth being, you are joy.
You do not come to joy easily.
You do not, Soul, breathe joy.
Often you breathe bitterness, tawdry in your very being,
　　　　squirming as the snake squirms with its fellows
　　　　so do you, Soul, with your humanity.
And yet as the snake can rise and lift its being seen as least,
　　　　it becomes a wonder for it rises majestically
　　　　and hovers triumphantly,
　　　　but it must fall.
Humanity does not fall.
It understands as human
　　　　and each humanity sees the challenge
　　　　and recognizes the way
　　　　for the path becomes open
　　　　and you begin to look outward from your being
　　　　and you behold the Light.
And often, Soul, the Light upon the path
　　　　is from your very being and it shines that others might see.
The Soul is full,
　　　　it is full of recognition of all things
　　　　but its being is centred upon earth and transition.
Its goal in entering in is to provide strength
　　　　for the vulnerable human Energy.
You are profound for you, Soul,
　　　　are abundant in that which you are.
You are the lotus that enfolds, enfolds,
　　　　the petal blending as lives blend
　　　　as years blend as truth grows
　　　　as memory becomes
　　　　and you intertwine your being with other earth beings

> for you have entered in not singularly only
> but as one Humanity upon the Farside,
> intent in overcoming that which is pain.

And we say to you,
> *"It is not the joy in entering unto Farside,*
>> *in entering home.*
> *It is the joy for humanity in entering unto negativity.*
> *For this is your gift unto Creator.*
> *This is your finest hour.*
> *This is your moment of Truth.*
> *This is the highest form of Truth*
>> *for your gift becomes compassion*
>> *and you become as the Angels*
>> *reaching out in your being,*
>> *enfolding that which is pain,*
>> *holding unto with compassion*
>> *that which you know*
>> *has endured lives of endless torment.*
> *And as humanity you know Negativity*
>> *is the Brother of your Creator, a Brother Loved,*
>> *to be welcomed home*
>> *as you are welcomed home*
>> *even through lives of desperate evil."*

Do the Angels turn away from your being?
They do not!
They uplift and hold you.
You are the star that shines that others might see.
You are the glory to behold as you enter in
> to the fullness of your being
> and your Soul is the Light
> and shines forth as a beacon
> for you have taken on a new iridescence.

It is coded in C, High C.
It uplifts the Light that all might see existences beyond Farside.
You are the flame, humanity.
You are the fire and you are blessed
> and who can behold the infant earth being
> and not see blessedness!

But through the ages of being
> you change the Energy of the Child
> in its many forms of being

>   to become that which is Light,
>   that which is strength, that which is joy.
> The Soul is your very being.
> It is the connector to your Spirit.
> It becomes a part of the triad that you are
>   as you enter first unto humanity as human.
> As the promise of the bud
>   opens to become the lotus in its true form,
>   so does the Soul become a blend.
> As human grows and enhances the Light within that it is worthy
>   to become a part with the Essence
>   and the triad shines as the flame
>   leaps higher ever higher
>   to be seen in the very darkness where purities
>   Light their very being from such Purity.
> Souls of earth, regard the Soul that you are.
> Behold the Energy that is the Soul,
>   see it as your memory,
>   recognize it carries within your heart and your mind.
> All that is is contained within
>   the memory bank of the Soul.

1104 Our awareness has been of the Void of Consciousness
    and all relative studies in the realms below,
    enter through our being.
15th Creator, Supreme Being, of whom all Energy flows,
    wherein all motion is derived,
    constant in the attentiveness to matter and ion.
Value of total identity,
    visible only in the extension of consciousness.
Seen in the ray of orange.
Holding the gentle resolution
    within the power of Energy that is containment.
This 15th Creator
    is the Energy Flow outward of Void of Consciousness.
It projects that which is the likeness of consciousness,
    ergo Light and Dark.
In the consciousness of being all is not seen clearly,
    all enters through values of consciousness
    to see within the chasms
    of what you would call, thought process.

The magnitude wherein of which we speak
      is possibly incomprehensible to the average thought.
Within the Realm of Consciousness
      is not the beginning and the end.
It is all that IS, encompassing.
For in the Energy of consciousness is the outward Flow to seek.
Consciousness has a peripheral.
The peripheral, Ion and Void,
      it is the portion that is not seen clearly.
It is the portion that is not defined
      to the satisfaction of the Energy of Consciousness.
For in the containment of Matter
      is not the need of consciousness.
Nor in the Energy of Ion is there a need
      for the Consciousness of Void,
        only the consciousness of Matter.
For without Matter, Ion is not.
To draw a perfect correlation of the triad
      is to perfect, Soul, the Energy continuum
      which is lost in the outward Flow.
All worlds, all worlds, conscious worlds,
      endeavour to find an answer to this continuum.
It has not yet been found,
      except within the small fragmented self of humanity.
Not, Soul, tangible, united but nebulous,
      unable to be formulated.
Therefore we seek the answer
      and we have given forth an equation.

1105 Soul, there are no dimensions without dimension.
Expandable.
Creators are Fifteen.
Supreme Being;
      encompassing is not a word attached to Supreme Being.
There is no encompassing.
There are no containments.
There are no dimensions.
There are no coordinates.
There is no history.
Fathom this, Soul.
Within Supreme Being all is, was and ever shall be

        without beginning, without end.
The Echo formed to recover.
The Echo, the Volume, the Breath triad,
        the great motion forward.
The ever offering of Supreme Being outward,
        ever outward,
        as the barrier is only found
        in a need to prevent forward movement.
What has created the need to rescind?
A pocket can be deep.
And yet from the pocket is ever given unto.
The pocket has a dimension
        and in that dimension is a lack of being able to give
        for you have used that which is in the pocket.
In your Creator, there is no dimension!
There is no lack of being.
What then is the need?
The volume of Creator is expansive,
        it outward flows.
Supreme Being;
        to be touched by the Energy of such a magnitude of giving
        is beyond the comprehension
        of the mind of your earth being.
Yet you can fathom what it would be like
        to be in the ray of such Light.
But what if Breath ceases to be?
How will the flow of consciousness fulfil itself?
For is it not Breath that fulfils the need of Matter, of Ion,
        of consciousness itself.
And wherein has Breath become?
From where did it first venture forth?
Your being is sustained by breath,
        not by food, Soul, by breath.
You may be skeletonized in your being.
Without breath you are dead to your world.

1106 Soul, Breath is all business.
Indeed, Breath maintains existence in all realms.
Breath is the inner sanctum unto which consciousness relies.
All that is breathed forward is coordinated through Voice.
Voice has the power to withhold Breath in your realm.

You will see it as opposite
        for you are the other side of the Mirror.
You are the reflectory
        therefore all things unto you seem to have distortion.
Your continuity is gathered in chaos.
Your deliverance from chaos
        is done with great jeopardy to all Voice.
You may not retrieve Breath.
You may retrieve Voice.
Voice cannot retrieve Breath.
This is the purpose of all Energy
        for Breath ushered out is lost
        without the initiative for return.
To release from your hand the sparrow,
        it flies, takes flight, only with breath.
Were breath not there, it would merely fall to the ground.
It does not matter that the wings have momentum
        if there is no breath there is no movement.
Matter without breath is inanimate.
So in the great Matter is it essential
        that Breath present motion
        unto Ion and Ion touch Matter.
In no way are you controlled upon your earth.
Your Creator does not control the path that you take.
You have freely entered in to your earth.
That which Creator has given unto you is simply breath.
Breath!
Choice is yours, it comes from the Seed within.
You may choose over negativity but become a part of negativity.
This is your choice
        but breath you must have to make that choice.
The gift unto you is not choice, indeed, it is breath itself.
Breath is the giver of all breath.
Yet, Breath is also a triad from the upper echelon of energies
        where worlds of Energy form and cloak
        their being in garlands of gaseous members,
        where cores are molten and subject to birth and rebirth,
        the kaleidoscopes of colour accentuate
        and design more glorious than the eye could fathom.
In that realm of beginnings is triad: Breath, Voice, Vacuum.

1107　　Your world is ever struggling with chaos.
It is born on the Field of Chaos.
Chaos thrums throughout the outer realms.
It carries a heave into all that existence is.
Wherever there is a sphere of existence,
　　　　therein is Chaos troubling.
You are not alone in your ability to see your world.
There are many worlds and many beings upon these worlds
　　　　who pressure their minds to attain the answer to Chaos.
Within all the species of existence
　　　　are threads of union one to the other.
You are sacred beings.
You are held by the immortal mind as precious.
You are held by the infinite as of worth beyond gold.
Your Souls ever within the consciousness of the great I AM.
Being, trouble yourself not
　　　　for you are not alone in your conflict with existence.
The throes of your environment
　　　　are as the throes of many environments.
The cataclysmic state of your people
　　　　has been the cataclysm state of many people.
Each has survived, each has returned.
You too will return.
You too will manifest unto all that we are.
How great thou art!
You will display unto all the battle wounds.
You are formidable.
You are not as righteous as you should be
　　　　but you have, Soul, steadfastness in your being.
Now we say unto you,
　　　　far beyond where you are,
　　　　beyond the existence of your Creator,
　　　　beyond the existence of the Energy Source
　　　　from which Jesu entered in,
　　　　beyond the existence where the Vanguard first set forth
　　　　to conquer chaos in united Oneness,
　　　　there was an attempt to conquer chaos.
The form of battle was simply a Breath.
Breath envelops all things.
It can be issued forth unto all things.
Unto all things before the Vanguard, Breath embraced.

The form of Breath became chaotic.
It became rampant, it became decisive.
It became ruthless in its plundering of all matter.
Yet motion must be and Breath provided motion.
From the consciousness of the Void
    came forth a form called Voice
    to place Breath therein
    so that Chaos could be entrapped.
And all that uttered forth, all that came forth,
    came forth through a single aperture, a containment.
Yet still Breath came forth gnarled.
It did not come forth pure but gnarled.
The Supreme Being sent forth the Vanguard to contain it
    and in the great triad of
    Void of Consciousness, ION and MATTER
    a power to unite ION and MATTER
    through the consciousness of being,
    that might issue Breath in more gentle form.
Void of Consciousness called upon Breath to come forth
    and touch and unite ION and MATTER,
    that it might have motion.
And MATTER gave forth of itself and still Chaos existed
    wherein Chaos is, is in all things, is in all Energy.
Only within the capsulated Yawn,
    only within serenity, is Breath without Chaos.
You have found ways to project to us a calmness of being
    but in doing so, you bring your voice down.
You bring your Energy down.
You still yourself but in stilling yourself, you lack motion.
The quest is how to have motion and serenity?
How to have thought and serenity?
To bring your thought to serenity,
    you must withhold all things from you.
Again you encapsulate yourself.
It is, Soul, a need to be answered
    and your earth is thrusting itself in all manner.
Humanity is exacting itself in all manner
    to bring about a calm,
    wherein you do not have to remain motionless.
    "Resolve to deepen your thought
    on the plight of Chaos."

1108   Vision, Souls.
Vision the great entrance in.
Visualize that which is the key to entering in
      the apertures of great worlds, not one,
      the great night is full.
Souls of earth, all things move,
      all things live and the sound,
      the sound as the greatest washing wave
      that throws itself upon the shore
      comes the billowing of sound.
It is speaking unto all that will hear.
It is monotonous.
Return, return, return, return, return, over and over and over.
Breath holds an echo
      and the echo is placed in linears throughout existences,
      for in the sounding are the fragments of return.
Twelve of such majesty
      awakening the energies of consciousness,
      echoing outward unto all they have created.
Return, return, return.
Each of the Twelve
      charting that which they hear unto the Echo at SEE.
And the great Glory of Light is held and given forth,
      and held and given forth
      continuously searching out for all things,
      that they might know a need to return.
It is written in all archives of the great fall of Idyllic,
      the absolute perfection.
Existence always blending in coordination,
      one existence to the other,
      with no thought of inward pull for self.
Even the seven perfections gave.
How great was the fall
      that saw that which was perfect
      passed down into the labyrinth?
And such perfection of the Thirteenth Creator to follow,
      to follow into the darkness
      and to have found a blue world,
      one of seven, your very own!
Souls of such greatness caught in the throe of death,

for death had come again.
And what of the Sound
      that was sent forth from the Voice to all that is,
      the agony of loss?
A sphere, not a triad, the second form;
      first form, triad,
         and the leak of Breath, and the turmoil within,
         in the sphere the loss of stability for no triad;
         seven, Fourteen, seven Light, seven Dark.
Where there is no triad, there is vulnerability.
To science we say this:
      "It is essential for triad be."
Voice is heard within a box, is it not?
As it enters out, it makes sound in spurts; in, out; in, out.
Breath is ever out, out, creating turmoil within.
This is the conundrum of all being.
This is that for which your world science seeks.
This is that for which your world mathematicians seek.
This is the perfection of your utopia.
Find the balance, the key to re entry, not into your world, Soul,
      into the great Energy that has a Leak.

1109 Soul, your earth voice is tethered to your body.
It requires the box within to create the sound.
The Voice in realms of millions and billions and trillions
      beyond your own, carries no containment.
It carries a sound, a pulsating, a vibratory Energy
      that is echoed through all Light and all Dark.
Within the Voice is the corridor of consciousness.
Within matter is that which Voice resounds from.
It is, Soul, the great concerto
      for in the depths of your being,
         as you do Aums you feel the corridor of sound.
Were you to do it with a thousand fold,
      you would find yourself
      carried beyond where you are
      in to the vibratory consciousness of being.
It echoes in the chamber of whom you are.
Magnify that to the power beyond earth's imagination.
Matter is the sounding box against which, not within,
      against which all consciousness is sounded.

The Voice sends forth the greatest treble.
The Souls could not fathom that which would be,
    for the decibel is beyond the hearing of humanity.
Only in the whale, only through the great sea
    can the faintest of sounds be heard.
To place a sounding board within your sea,
    would give you more attunement
    to that which is far from you
    in sound, not matter, sound.
For the sea is auditory in its being.
The sea resonates that which is heard.
MATTER, Void of Consciousness and ION
    unto VOICE, MATTER and Breath.

1110 Soul, Breath is all business.
Indeed, Breath maintains existence in all realms.
Breath is the inner sanctum unto which consciousness relies.
All that is breathed forward is coordinated through Voice.
Voice has the power to withhold Breath in your realm.
You will see it as opposite
    for you are the other side of the Mirror.
You are the reflectory
    therefore all things unto you seem to have distortion.
Your continuity is gathered in chaos.
Your deliverance from chaos
    is done with great jeopardy to all Voice.
You may not retrieve Breath.
You may retrieve Voice.
Voice cannot retrieve Breath.
This is the purpose of all Energy
    for Breath ushered out is lost
    without the initiative for return.
To release from your hand the sparrow,
    it flies, takes flight, only with breath.
Were breath not there, it would merely fall to the ground.
It does not matter that the wings have momentum
    if there is no breath there is no movement.
Matter without breath is inanimate.
So in the great Matter is it essential
    that Breath present motion
    unto Ion and Ion touch Matter.

In no way are you controlled upon your earth.
Your Creator does not control the path that you take.
You have freely entered in to your earth.
That which Creator has given unto you is simply breath.
Breath!
Choice is yours, it comes from the Seed within.
You may choose over negativity but become a part of negativity.
This is your choice
        but breath you must have to make that choice.
The gift unto you is not choice, indeed, it is breath itself.
Breath is the giver of all breath.
Yet, Breath is also a triad from the upper echelon of energies
        where worlds of Energy form and cloak
            their being in garlands of gaseous members,
                where cores are molten and subject to birth and rebirth,
            the kaleidoscopes of colour accentuate
        and design more glorious than the eye could fathom.
In that realm of beginnings is triad: Breath, Voice, Vacuum.

1111   The Energy of Knowing,
        that Energy holding within all resonance,
        echoing within the chamber all outward movement,
        apart from self.
The Realm of Consciousness felt movement.
It placed outward the invitation to come forth
        to that movement.
We can relate it for you in that
        if you saw within your starry sky
        far beyond the universe you are in,
        in a distant universe, a flicker of Energy
        and you sent forth a invitation to acknowledge,
        to show self, to make an appearance.
The Energy of consciousness had a motion within.
It was not as that motion that was heard from a distant realm
        and it separated itself.
That Energy looked unto the variables
        within the structure of being
            and MATTER had always been a part of that structure,
            and ION had always been apart of that structure.
ION could move within self
        as consciousness can move within self.

Again, we speak to you of your mind.
Your thoughts can take themself to a distant place.
You can share within your being these thoughts
    and nod your head and know
        we have received.
We understand, but only within the sphere.
The message was sent forward, not projected outward.
Even some would call it ejected outward
    but it is not so.
It is projected.
The invitation was sent to MATTER and ION
    to place motion that that motion
    might unite the three,
    that also the Realm of Consciousness
    might in no way receive bombardment to self.
In the forwarding of the Energy
    that has come to be known as Breath,
    it altered the very structure of the ION.
It did not change the structure of consciousness.
It did not change the structure of MATTER.
It changed the structure of ION Matter,
    for before, it was ION.
Then both ION became ION Matter and MATTER,
    Matter of ION, not the reverse, Soul. No.
Matter of ION.
The blend created the chaotic Energy.
For neither could be maintained one aside the other.
For there was within the Energy of ION Matter,
    chaos that infiltrated into the Energies of Matter
    and consciousness.
Your world in every form of endeavour,
    is bringing the structure of matter
    to coincide with ion,
    holding the consciousness of
    Energy of three in tranquillity.
This has not yet been done, Soul.
Your earth, we will say, is astounding our energies.
There is within your earth a time element.
For within the consciousness of all that you know to be,
    including the very Energy of humanity,
    is the knowledge of chaos.

And chaos is in the matter of your world,
> within every portion of your world including yourself.

The ion Energy that awakens within you movement,
> also draws you into chaos.

It is that solution that you and all beings of earth are seeking.
It is that solution that all rock, mineral, or matter
> is intensified to resolve.

Even when you are at peace,
> in the most calm Energy of your being,
> you will find your body becoming restless,
> even unto chaos to resolve the issue of motion.

1112 In the Energy of MATTER,
> in the formation of the triad,
> existence became.

Energies created.
Energy uncountable to your human scale went forth.
All Void carried outward that which was created.
All energies gathered in their Energy Field
> the knowing of a single existence that had
> no tangible without altering.

From the distant corridor of Breath is a Flow.
The Flow has awareness.
Awareness is within Breath.
Awareness, Intent and Presence, triad of Breath,
> formulated second to MATTER, ION, Void
> to initiate search.

Breath responsible, Soul, for all that flesh does.
Breath responsible for all that existence does.
Breath cannot gather back unto self, chaos.
From the core of Breath would be felt the chaos.
Within the blend of ION, Void, and MATTER,
> was Chaos, outward flow, no return.

Life replicated from Breath.
Death, a perfect replication of Life, for it returned unto.
When Death stepped away, Life was altered.
Energy, Soul, are not simplistic.
Energies equated to your science appear to be multifaceted.
Yet in that multiplicity of being
> is a simplicity that earth is astounded by.

The resolution that is sought by all existence
> is for Breath a co existence

        that will not diminish Breath.
Death diminished Life.
It is, Soul, profound.
For all the motion of your galaxies is in the outward thrust,
        a search for that which is perfection
        to stand equal to Breath.

1113   Soul, the outward flow of Creator Consciousness
        from the Energy of Fifteen is ever.
It has not ceased to be.
It is available unto the rock, the river,
        the spine, the candle, the human.
It is ever reachable.
The meld of MATTER, ION and Consciousness
        did not create blend but Chaos.
The outward flow that is Breath,
        the motion that entered in to unite,
        has not found the structure, Soul.
Only within your Yawn has that structure been formed.
For all intent of Matter, of Ion was chaos.
Only in the consciousness of being
        is there an availability to enter back in
        but not complete,
        as Consciousness, ION and MATTER.
For Consciousness to be without motion, now could not be.
For Consciousness has made a blend with Breath.
Breath has a chaotic code on Ion and Matter.
There is no balance.
The triad has a base that will ever extend outward.
Your breath, as you send it forth,
        must return unto you or you cease to be.
So it is with Matter.
With Ion it creates chaos.
In Consciousness it allows Volume.
So that Void of Consciousness
        holds the Breath and sends out,
        eternal consciousness, everlasting knowing.
The greatest pain of Matter is not to breathe.
The greatest pain of Ion is never to still.
The greatest pain of Breath is never to return.
Consciousness is aware of need.

And it is in the deep consciousness that solution is solved.

1114   There is a realm of existence
  wherein form is in no way as you see form.
It takes on no extensions.
It gathers unto it no expectation.
It is simply existence.
It has no motivated Energy.
It is enhanced by no purpose.
It has no initiative.
It does not allow itself to be incited from Echo, from Value.
It is Being.
It is Voice.
Without transmitting, it transmits.
Without feeling, it feels.
Without hearing, it hears.
It carries no velocity through domes.
It has no need.
It has no echo chamber wherein things return.
It is simply Voice.
It is.
There is no agenda to Voice.
It is, Soul, simply is.
All Energy must begin at Voice.
All Energy echoes out from Voice.
It has no echo, has no echo.
How can this be?
Breath.
Breath is coexistent.
Existence is matter, is it not?
But without Breath, matter does not exist.
And Breath as Breath
  with nothing to initiate is simply Breath.
Where two are together without a third there is a need.
This we give to you to ponder.

1115   Soul, hear what the Angels say of Negativity.
Within the deep passages of pain is a form of Energy.
It is massive in its ability to swirl.
It is continuous in its thread.
It develops great agitations in entering close.

It always configurates into spiral.
Its identity is that of Negativity,
    not earth negativity, Soul.
The tenacious swirl formed gives it the ability to tether itself
    unto a thread unbenounced to the thread itself.
There is only one other form in like manner.
This form is called Chaos.
There is a continuous effort by the Angels
    to halt the spiral of Negativity deep within transition.
There is no need within the Cleansing River
    as the Cleansing River of Wisdom,
    a triad of itself, has made it inert.
Deep within each humanity is a seed of Negativity.
It is from that which earth negativity takes its pattern.
It always would swirl to entangle, imesh, others unto it.
There is a strangulating effect,
    not intent
    yet it is called wilful
    simply because it has no power to draw it back.
It has chosen thus.
This Energy is akin unto Creator.
Your Creator is not a fellow being.
The Creator Energy has before it
    great magnifications of creations, worlds,
    spheres beyond your belief,
    the sky and all the stars within,
    the earth and all the replications of life within.
Your Creator is mighty in the ability to create.
Negativity thus as the Brother unto Creator
    is mighty in the ability to send forth the tether of its Being.
Indeed it holds itself apart from Creator
    for the lack of compassion has made it so
    and chooses by will not to seek the Brother, Creator.
Therefore, the trembles go forth,
    even unto the distant dark
    seeking, always seeking,
    knowing not a return but only a gift to give.
Souls of earth, the Wilful one, Negativity, holds great Truth.
It is gathering unto itself.
Yet that portion of it that is held is always seeking to be free.
Souls, even upon your earth as you hold negativity,

and your negativity is caught,
yet you seek to be free
that you might once again use that negativity.
It is repetitious, yet, it is Truth.
Souls of earth, we ask you to behold for the Angels
that we recognize the Brother that is.
There is no evil outside of
the evil that mankind has brought forth.
And we say to you now is the hour to not diminish,
but eradicate evil from your world!
Eradicate with Love.
Eradicate with compassion.
The life that you live is a life upon your earth that is illusion
and you shall not lose life,
it shall be gifted unto you yet again.
Behold, do not fear to give.
Do not fear, Soul, that your life will end.
It shall not.
You shall go forth even unto yet another illusion
and you shall see the energies of Negativity
even as we have seen in the great Records.
You shall behold the Tears that have fallen forth,
given as the starry night.
For Soul, the Tears have overflowed
and the sky is always blossoming forth.
But you, you can hold that which is negative.
You can belay the energy.
You can give safe harbour to the Brother of Creator.
For you, you hold in your being the thoughtful self.
You hold in your being the open hand.
You hold in your being an offering.
Give it forth, Souls,
for we who are Angels,
we cannot do that which you can do.
We do not have the artistry,
the magnificence, of your Energy
for we have not been made
in the manner of our Creator as you have.
Souls of earth, breathe great breaths of air
knowing the air flows through your being
from your Creator.

Breathe, Soul, with the Truth
> for your Truth has come from your Creator.

Give, Soul, give unto your brother
> for you are one with all humanity.

Give forth.

1116   We will give a teaching unto humanity.
We will speak, Soul, of your Creator and our Creator.
We will speak of the levels of Purity that you are.
You are of Purity.
You are called humanity.
You enter in from Farside bringing with you
> a covenant you have made with your Creator,
>> a covenant to bring forth from the depths of transition
>> the Blessed Angels.

To do this as humanity you have agreed to enter in to battle.
That battle is with the armour of Truth.
You are a great Armada.
You are, Soul, indeed in battle.
Humanity, you have gathered many scars.
In the Energy of your being the scars Light before the Angels.
They enter in as stripes upon your very form.
You are with linears over your Energy
> from many enterings in,
> incarnations in which you have learned,
> not only how to overcome,
> but how to do battle with negativity.

It is not to enter in.
It is not to forcibly remove.
Indeed, not!
It is, Soul, through many enterings in to
> gather a peace unto you, a serenity as human,
> to recognize in your self
> that from which you have come,
> the Essence of your very being
> that is connected to your Creator.

You are as the Blessed Angels.
You are merely cloaked with a human garb.
We ask you to understand this battle you have entered in.
You have been consistent in your goodness,
> in your mercy unto negativity.

You have understood the devouring source of negativity,
> yet you have understood the great need
> > that negativity has for compassion.

And in your Angelic self you have brought forth
> from your being compassion.

You have drawn, Soul, not simply from the human self,
> but from the full structure that you are,
> the full complete radiant Energy that is Humanity.

You have raised yourself to be equal with Angels.
You have raised yourself to even step foremost beyond the Angel.
You have gathered such Purity in your being that you are beloved.
The beloved son of the benevolent Father
> who does not draw anger
> but draws from the utmost Love,
> from the completeness of Agape Love
> that which is Ecstasy.

You are, Souls of earth, completing a covenant.
You are at the point of return.
And we, we see you have not gathered
> the completeness of your intent.

You have not become one with each other.
Indeed some have gathered unto oneness.
Many Humanity of Farside are in oneness.
But of earth, of the battle ground,
> of the place wherein negativity dwells,
> > human harbours much ill will against brother.

Mankind you are one!
You are Holy one!
You are Holy unto Holy in your intent.
Draw yourself to the place of Purity wherein you have entered.
Draw yourselves to the place of Truth
> wherein you see
> that all that is negative upon your earth can be altered.

It can be altered with peace.
It can be altered with goodness.
It can be altered with the overcoming of pain
> wherein all men, women and children are one kin,
> are a branch of a single family.

They are fathered by a single Creator.
They are nurtured with the Love of mother.
They are given strength.

As the mother nourishes and gives strength unto the child,
      so you are of the Divine triad,
      so are you of the complete self,
      so are you entered in unto negativity
      to overcome with the strength of your being,.
The covenant is not for a nation or nations.
It is for mankind.
It is for humanity.
It is, Soul, for all that is within earth, for all have entered in.
Each creature, animal has entered in.
Alien beings have entered in.
All that was formed to fill the earth
      was formed to overcome negativity.
You are the final mould.
You, in your tiny form entered in to earth presented
      unto negativity, that negativity might do
      that which it will unto the tiny form.
But the tiny form has strength and will and choice.
The tiny form is brought forth to do battle
      and armed with Purity.
The chord of will is strong.
The battle is great.
The intent is to win.
To win is not to overcome beings, Soul.
It is to overcome negativity!
Oh, Souls, draw forth from you negativity.
Spew it from your being.
See your brother as the stranger and a stranger as your brother.
See the vile, the contemptuous
      as those that require compassion and caring;
      mending that they might be strengthened in
      the incarnation they are in,
      that as they re enter
      they will understand the lesson they have learned.
You are glory.
You are of supreme Energy.
You are held high as the Angels are held high.
You are, Soul, to be in the place of Love, Holy Agape Love
      wherein all humanity will know that Light that is the Light,
      that Love that is the Love, that Purity that is in Purity,
      that Truth that is the Truth.

And you will understand the orb of oneness
      wherein all Energy of Humanity will expand itself to affect
      and alter chaos in the outer realms of existence.
You, you alone have brought forth the keys of change,
      the keys of Truth, of will, of intent of overcoming.
You have charmed the Angels.
You have placed honour unto your Creator.
Love thy brother.
In thyself be Holy.
Lift only compassion in thy being unto a human
      that joy might be yours and the heavens ring
      with the chords of your Purity.

1117 Buoyancy, buoyancy of the Soul,
      the Spirit, the Essence; the triad of infinity.
Within your Yawn you are infinite.
Within your Yawn you are carried to perfection.
Within your Yawn you will know the Creator of your being.
You will feel the Energy abound within you.
You will feel the vibrational being
      as your Soul mounts unto the heavens.
You will travel in Light raiment, not through Light, Soul,
      with Light raiment unto your casting forth.
And then in a heralding moment
      that which you have known as infinite
      will return unto that Energy of consciousness
      from which all Energy enters in.
You are, Soul, caught in a chamber.
The sound of your negativity resonates,
      throughout the many worlds is it heard,
      the beginnings and the overcomings.
And the thrust unto implosion is felt.
You who are human in desperation seek to find perfection.
Souls of earth,
      your countenance is carried far beyond your plane.
That which is recognizable as humanity
      is held within memory banks of many worlds.
You seek those worlds, Soul.
Yet those worlds know you.
They have visited you.
They see you clearly and you behold them not,

      for you have not entered in
         to the fullness of your perfection.
You have not used that which has been given unto you,
      the gift of imploding.
In all the spheres, implosion is known
         outward unto the density of Light and Dark Fields,
         Domes apart from the one you are in,
         the one we are in.
Understand the multiplicity of existence.
Do not be caught in variations.
Be caught in levels of Purity of Love.
For indeed this is the measure
      through which you may enter in.
Holy beings of earth restrain not your curiosity.
Indeed.
For your earth is clamouring to implode.
And even your humanity is working on tools
      with which to implode,
         to create such a surge of vibrational self,
         that you will be sucked into
         the upper planes of where you are.
You are, Soul, neither conscious of your capabilities
      or willing to extrapolate
      that which has been given to you.
The glow of all purities, Souls of earth,
      have been sent unto where you are.
The three have been brought unto you.
The two have been given unto you.
And you have chosen to play god with the very gift of knowing.
You are given an equation through which you may travel
      as we travel from one world to another.
And you lift your beings with manmade Energy.
And we ask why?
Why, when your world itself is imploding
      and your children starve?
Feel the measure of your skin.
Feel the flesh beneath your skin and understand, it is feeble.
It can be erased
      in a simple temperature rise or temperature drop.
Yet you have the ability to travel through time given unto you.
There is no merit.

It may be taught to the infant.
Your container is transferable and you know it not.
Your Souls of earth born to be out of your world.
We repeat, Soul, you are born to be out of your world,
      to return from whence you have come!
In the manner you had imploded into the world,
      you will implode from your world.
Understand the power of the Energy of your being.
See the greatness of your stature.
Do not see the commonness of the shell.
It is but, that.
Liberate yourself from the shell and return at will.
Soul, it may travel with you.
It is yet the best travel known to man.

1118   Behold the Triad,
      three of Love, three of Purity, three of Truth.
Each separate, yet one; Creator, Godhead, Great One.
Each independent of the other,
      yet in total harmony one with the other.
Each with a unified agenda, yet separate.
Unto all is Triad known.
Within your realm, you call this Triad by many names.
We call this Triad, Ecstasy, Supreme Being within the Yawn.
And these, Soul, is the difference in all existence.
For there are seven levels in all existence.
They are fourteen Fields of Energy, twelve times Dome.
Within each Dome all is replicated
      fourteen by twelve, fourteen by twelve,
      fourteen by twelve.
And you see from where you are the complexity of existence.
Within each Field of fourteen,
      there are Fourteen Creators,
      ruling one over each Field.
They have entered in, purposefully entered in,
      for the thrust of the Void.
They have carried a continuum of direction.
The direction is sphere.
Now with the exception of Domes,
      all that is existence is linear, vertical.
The perfection is the eternal circle.

Each Creator has a foundry of Purity,
      a purpose within that foundry
        to find the Eternal Soul.
You carry within you an absolute to find the Eternal circle.
Man in the circle of life continue to return,
      man to know the triad
        and find the circle of purpose in that triad.
Yet this is simple and indeed existence is not simple.
Existence is all that is seen within that starry sky
      and knowing, ever knowing
      the endless thread of Energy
      that never ceases to be,
      that is carried one to the other,
      intermingled,
      until it becomes the great chord
      and lifts itself unto that Supreme Being,
      not of the Yawn, but of Creators.
Would you as human lift your Energy
      upward through the darkness
      into the greatest of prisms,
      over the Shining Water,
      to be at a door?
The doorway is guarded by Breath and Flame.
Breath can devour Flame.
Which is the most powerful?
It is Breath, the motion forward, that has created a dilemma.
You seek upon your planet for worlds wherein Breath is.
Breath has many forms
      and you can alter your form to aid many breaths.
You see it in the reverse and it is not so.
You humanness does a service to all existence.
You place within your united Energy
      a position we had not entertained.
That in being the weakest we can be strongest.
And we call you by the name of Flame.
For you in the flame of being,
      provide Light that we might see.
You offer wisdom in a form we have not yet realized.
You diversify to unite and we had not thought of this.
We are with you in your great Battle
      but we would have you not lose sight

of the triad of your homeland
and that you are in part of who we are.
You are not second unto your self.
You are not alone in your universe.
You are held preciously within the arms of all of existence.
You are tethered by a thread
unto your Creator,
unto the Triad of Godhead.
Behold who you are.

1119   Creator has the force of Love.
You understand Godhead has the force of Purity.
The Great One has the force of Truth.
Each has a part of the other.
Elsewise there is no Triad.
All that is Truth is altered by Negativity.
In your sphere, your fold acknowledges
the energy of negativity
which alters the Truth.
You will understand
the great spill of emotion within humanity.
Emotion is of the heart
and when the heart expresses itself there is no growth.
Emotion does not produce growth.
It produces feeling.
Only the mind produces growth.
When the mind observes with positive,
there is positive growth.
When the mind observes with negative,
there is negative growth.
We ask humanity,
all nations upon this sphere of your earth,
to let emotion fall from their being,
for logic will produce that which you need.
Logic will feed the starving children.
Emotion will only observe and express the feeling
but it is the mind that will resolve the issue.
You who are in command of your people,
to feed emotion flays the innocent.
Sit you, Souls of governing bodies,
and leave your emotion apart from yourselves

and see a world as mankind and use your logic
   to determine where the balance of peace will lie.
Hold in your hand a fragile being of innocent perfection
   and hold in your other a being impoverished,
      maimed in flesh and blood because of inhumanity,
   and determine how
      one can be equated to the other in balance!
What may restore the negativity that surges from emotion?
In your countries and nations,
   you place upon your beings
   expressions to thy Creator.
So your Creator Tears at the expressions that separate.
Let the expressions of your being indeed be difference,
   but differences that uphold, not break down.
Differences you have not entered in to.
The Farside has variables that will delight your Soul.
There are numerous endless variables
   but they do not place uncore.
They place delight.
Do not war with difference, blend with difference.
Soul, your emotion is flawed.
Indeed, for it is flawed with negativity.
You see, you use negativity to persuade your emotion to Love.
Purity is Love.
Indeed there have been beings upon your earth
   who have come to such Love.
They have not remained upon your earth.
They have been lifted because of that Purity.
The overcoming of negativity is not with Love,
   it is with Truth.
We would explain Love
   and we will place it in your earth
   as your innocent child.
Who will be the first to place a derisive word
   within the space of this innocent child?
Do you understand?
What member of a family,
   an extension of a family,
   a stranger to a family,
   will place within the realm of this child
   an expression of negativity

    so that child will absorb that negativity.
Indeed your earth would be delightful
    if no slanderous word were spoken before the child
    that no negative impression
    would be spoken before the child.
But Love could not do so.
Your Love is not impure
    but it is persuaded by the negativity of your being.
Love would forestall all negativity.
Love could not entertain negativity.
Even as we speak, negativity erodes.

1120 Souls of earth, you breathe.
Breath, Soul, is motion unto you.
Breath, Soul, is that which gives you existence
    for without breath into your being
    without the motion of Great One
    you would cease to be.
Motion is that which permits the Energy of your being
    to work through its purpose.
Without the motion of entering with the Energy unto your earth
    you could not overcome the negativity.
We speak, Soul, of motion.
Motion enters in particled with chaos.
It is a portion of that which is negativity.
It has a great purpose in the Energy that is all Energy.
It carries the momentum of matter.
It carries the great thrust that creates the wind.
It is, Soul, the very magic whereupon your thoughts
    can be carried from person to person
    to animal creature, to the flora, to all fauna.
Souls of earth, motion is a portioned to whom you are.
It is the gift of Great One of the Triad of Creator.
The thought that is static within you is of Godhead
    and a great ability to form is of Creator.
You form humanity.
You form continually throughout your earth life.
You create and you place into motion that which you create
    and then you hold yourself still
    that you might see that which it creates
    have motion unto itself.

All that you create is not of a positive nature.
Often, humanity, you create great negativity
    even unto evil do you create
    and those who hold their head
    and place ashes upon themselves
    that they deny the occurrence that has presented itself, sob.
For not always is one participant or the other in negativity.
Often one is victim unto negativity.
Often one collaborates or rejoices,
    expands the energy of self
    in boasting because of negativity.
But you humanity, you create all form.
You have a choice of that which you may create.
It is before you to create great things.
It is the opportunity for the mind to bring forth great thoughts.
It is before you for the mind to create all manners
    to assist in the well being of all humanity,
    of all earth, of all that is within the earth land and sea.
But you, you are not always generous.
This is not a condemnation, it is a recognition.
Often you have the opportunity to give forth
    and you hold yourself stationary.
And often you place motion in your being
    until you are hither and beyond
    with no thought or coordinate within your being
    and often you form without completing.
Now we give you wisdom.
The wisdom is this,
    that in order to form
    you must use motion,
    you must use stillness,
    you must combine for the triad to be complete.
It must be with all components as one.
A stationary human is of no use to the human race,
    unless the thought and the form
    and the motion is within the mind.
When the mind and the body are not,
    the motion of the beat of the heart
    does not complete, humanity.
You are already with us and we rejoice that you are.
Do you understand, Souls, that which we have placed before you?

The heart may continue to tick but the mind must be valid.
The body may be still but without the mind it is just a tick
      and we rejoice that you have rejoiced unto us.
You are flesh and you are blood.
You are heart, mind and body.
They are three.
They work one with the other.
Even though the body is still,
      the mind can reach into the stillness,
      but the heart without the mind
      serves no purpose but to be released.

1121   Souls of earth, your abundance of Energy
      is ever expanding
        so the Energy of all is ever expanding.
It is, Soul, within the realm of all Energy expansion,
      it is within the Energy of all humanity to send forth.
You cannot hold within your being.
Those who would attempt to hold Energy within
      would find a flesh and blood of a being
      with the need to expand, often in illness.
Always thought creates illness if not balanced.
The flow of thought sent forth randomly,
      outwardly, fractally, creates chaos within.
The serenity of orderly thought
      gives the mind processing time
      to place it within the triad of purpose.
There is no swift recovery from chaos.
It minimizes the mind's ability
      to absorb and delineate into quadroom.
There is, Soul, the vast perfection you see and know.
And yet your being denies.
And you gather within your being pain
      to disperse that which you would not see
      and you dispel from your being,
      rays of energy that create pain as they enter in.
For they are Light, capsulated but not organized.
That which you may allow
      to enter is the comforting calmness of Light.
It would disperse the negativity.
It would relieve the senses.

It will create the calm.
It will balance the Energy.
Balance in all things unto all beings.
If you give forth negativity, Soul,
    you receive unto your being that which is negative.
If you give forth calmness of the heart
    you receive calmness of the heart.
The human is frail.
They would use the energy of the wine
    which is good for the body.
Indeed it balances the energy.
Yet, Soul, to overbalance with the wine
    is to create chaos with the energy.
When the words are used
    and they are not calm, they become chaotic.
They send forth barbs of chaotic energy
    which are collected and sent outward.
It is spilled forth as in the great dipper spilling forth
    the flow of the many stars in her cup.
You look for perfect worlds as humanity.
You seek the perfect existence.
Yet you have not come together
    to form that which is the perfect existence.
You see your perfect existence upon the earth
    but the earth is for the time you are in
    and you belong to a timeless moment.
So many will fathom in their mind
    that which is the perfect world upon the Farside
    and yet the Farside is an illusion.
It is a Yawn of Creator
    sent forth to create the solution for Chaos.
The perfection you seek is in the Energy of the triad:
    in the consciousness of being,
    in the ion of being,
    in the matter of existence.
These form perfection, these are your intent!
These are your purpose
    to create the perfect matter,
    the perfect ion,
    the perfect consciousness.
And yet one cannot be without the other for they are triad.

They are one of the other.
Develop within your being a need for balance
      so that the Energy of your being
      has a serenity that will create
      the perfect form of matter and the mind
      to enhance the perfection
      wherein you will see beyond where you are
      and know you are Energy of Energy of Energy
      that you, Soul, have an intent to form with all Energy
      unto that which you are.
If you hold in your hand the perfection of the diamond
      that radiates outward in its fractalled self,
      you see one light bounce against another light.
You see the energy of light creating
      and expanding the light of itself
      and you see the
      radiance of being, the ecstasy of perfection
      and you behold the possibilities
      of that which could be.
And you know the fullness of Truth, the fullness of Love,
      the fullness of Purity
      does not withhold the possibilities beyond.
For therein is a perfection
      but the perfection can reach
      yet unto a further perfection
      so that when one sees first
      one knows the fullness of completion;
      but when one sees secondly,
      one sees within the possibility
      of yet a more complete perfection.
So it is with the diamond.
You see a diamond that carries
      many portions of light bouncing, energizing
      and you are overwhelmed
      with the completeness of that which is.
And then, Soul, unto you comes
      yet another even more expansive
      in the possibilities of Light
      that escapes from its being
      and you understand
      that this could be even greater than this.

What could be ahead, Soul?
What could be the perfection we have not seen?
And so it is for you and for where we are.
There is a perfection of greatness.
Light is expansive, it is outwardly projecting.
So is the triad of perfection outwardly expanding
        in the togetherness of being.
Yet the togetherness of being is lost unto it.
It has moved outward
        and where is the magnetic pull
            that will bring it into its former perfection?
Why do you have a magnetic pole that alters?
Will at some point in your existence
        come that perfect draw of Energy
        wherein all is brought unto one
        when it has come outward?
Where is the balance in the Energy of being?

1122   Souls of earth, you are the vibrancy that we recognize.
You are the keening note that is heard in its pain
        then alters to become the solution
        and even greater,
        the Mountaintop wherein all may enter.
Souls of earth, see who you are.
You are at the pinnacle of hope.
You are at the pinnacle of Truth.
You are at the pinnacle of Purity.
You are residual in your Energy within all Energy,
        for you have become who we are.
We have not become, Soul, who you are.
Indeed not.
You have become the ultimate
        and we have gathered from you.
You are the complete.
You are the fullness
You are the perfection
        and we we gather from your Energy.
We are at levels of Purity.
We have all Purity before us, perfection in that Purity
        but, Souls of earth,
        you have been Whoosh through the Energy of Creator.

Your Energy has been breathed out
> from the very Triad of your Creator.

You have in your being all the contingencies of existence
> and they come forth.

They enter in and you gather and you cast aside
> and you strangulate your very being with contention.

And yet, the Purity and the Love that is Creator,
> it shines forth from your being.

There are moments in your existence, an epiphany?
Indeed not,
> it is the Register of your Creator in you
> for you are cast forth
> from Love, from Truth, from Purity.

You have all that is within you.
You are enwrapped, the very precious of beings.
You are, Soul, the vibration of all possibility.
You are creators within your being.
You search for answers.
You struggle and create mindless persecutions.
And yet, you hear the echo from whence you have come.
It echoes in your being and you know,
> *"My anger is not truth. My pain is not truth."*

Joy is Truth.
Love is Truth.
Purity is Truth.
Compassion is the ultimate Truth.
And your heart soars within you
> and you know you have reached the ultimate Truth
> and it is time to come home
> for you have been gone too long.

See the spectrum, the glory of all colour.
See the blends as they become joyous radiance
> and know that as the ribbons of Light
> flow forth and unto you
> you send forth ribbons of Light even so unto others.

Gather under the spectrum of Light that you are
> and you are home.

1123 Souls of earth,
> we speak to you of Voice, the containment.

We speak to you of the vast Energy

        that has been formed through consciousness.
There is a holding place for echo within Voice.
It is echo that creates distress.
It is echo that sends itself forth
        and forth and forth and forth
            until it becomes a faint resemblance of what it was.
Within the container of Voice, echo exists.
It creates a separation of Energy.
It sends forth a measured breath rather than endless Breath.
All things echo in the structure of container.
As echo sent itself through Breath unto Matter.
It placed upon Matter the mark of echo
        so that Matter moves endlessly outward
        except within your Yawn.
There is a deliverance from this;
        how to re echo, revamp matter in all Energy forms
        to return unto its beginning.
Should this not occur is the dilemma.
Should this not occur is the reason you are where you are.
Hold your breath, Soul.
You cannot.
Hold your Energy, Soul.
If you echo Energy with food, it goes outward from you;
        if you echo Energy with water,
        it moves outward from you.
If you echo Energy with negativity, it comes back to you,
        but in the same form as negative.
That was not the intent for the Wilful Child.
The intent was to go outward
        and come back with a true note.
There are great complications, Soul, in this dilemma.
It affects all existence, all worlds, all matter,
        all sound within matter,
        all colour within sound.
It has variances,
        but all existence, all fields, are within the Void.
The Void has been altered only by the curtain of care
        placed by the Blessed Angels.
There is an abounding circle.
There is, Soul, continuing creativity.
 There are fields upon fields within fields.

The complexities would astound your science.
But all fields are within the Void where there is no thing.
Yet it holds.
The Void has compelling attitude of awareness
    of what is entered in.
It is, Soul, waiting.
You would use the term, alive.
It is prepared to receive as womb is prepared to receive.
Yet the womb doesn't always receive.
So it is with the Void, an expectancy.
And where we are we feel that expectancy.
Beings from whom we are have whispered of this waiting.
And we hear and wait.
Have we heard right?
You see?
All form is not your form.
All form is not only of your earth.
There are variances of form as there are variances of Energy.
There are great expectancies waited upon
    and the Void is that waiting, is that expectancy.
Our understanding is there is only one.
Our understanding is there is variance,
    but placed because of Negativity,
        to protect that which has been created.
Soul, indeed there is an answer.
The answer is the inevitable limiting of creation.
As in, Soul, your stars, that live and die,
    are and are not,
        bloom and die, live, breathe and cease to be.
The solution, Soul, is in implosion.
It is in implosion
    breath must come back.
It is to replenish.
Ion and Matter must be.
All is triad.
All is triad.
For Ion and Matter to cease to be,
    Void, the Consciousness of Void
        would go inward and implode.
Souls, your science would understand far greater
    than the Souls of earth in the unscientific realm.

But everything of your earth has consciousness.
All matter that enters your realm has consciousness.
The smallest iota has consciousness.
It is necessary to enter back gently,
    without the implosion
        of which your world calls, big bang.
For it decimates.
We do not speak of alien beings.
We do not speak of your sister worlds.
We speak, Soul, of the nuclear of all Energy,
    that from which Energy exists,
    that form which it goes forth from,
    that from which all that is is created,
    holding within all knowledge.
Even as you gather knowledge unto you,
    so is knowledge known.
It is written in your very Energy.

#11 Parallel Worlds

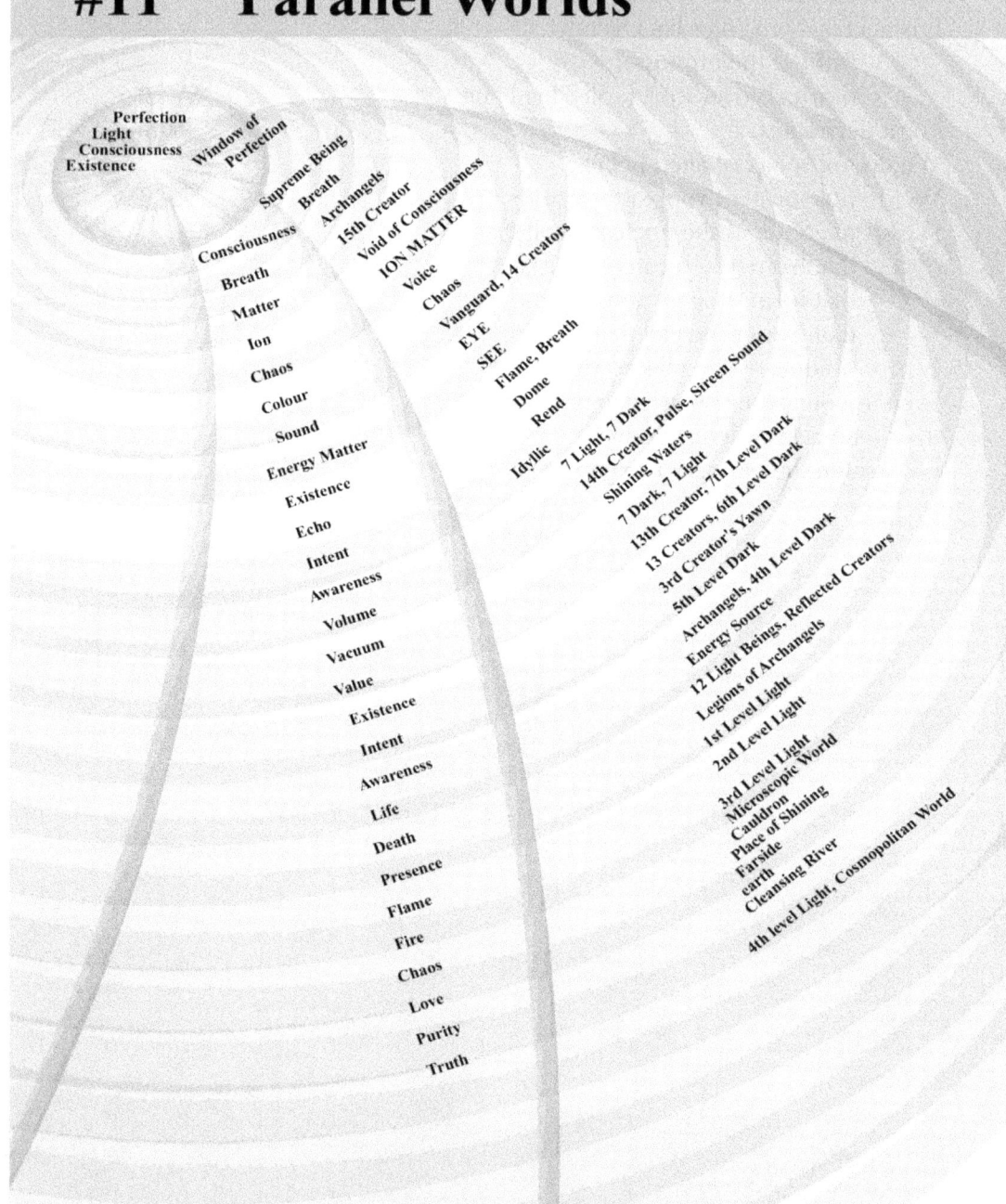

Chapter Four
THE WEB

1124 Blessed humanity, all humanity forms web.
All Energy forms web.
Within all design is web.
Within the agreement of all humanity is web.
From one generation to the other, Soul,
    from one reincarnation to the other,
    from one existence to the other,
    there is no outside of web that is within the existence.
There are, Soul, countless Energy.
There is countless web formed one to the other,
    upon the other, under the other, over the other.
Soul, they abound.
And in the fragmented corner of your existence
    you call universe,
    you are but as though it were a diversion.
For you could be passed by
    and have simply no thought
    brought to those who would see,
    for your being is microscopic
    to many energies of the Creators.
Indeed, Creators.
Upon your firmament you acknowledge many gods.
You have chosen to adhere to the call of Purity
    that acknowledges your Creator.
You have been wise.
You have been content in distributing great angst
    to divert the real purpose of recognition.
You do not respond in an orderly fashion to knowledge.
We would have you understand the great fluidity in knowledge.
It carries itself through your very flesh and blood.
It carries yourself into the far Energy that you are.
Indeed, to the very Spirit that you are and you feel it not.
Where time and space
    has no control within your thought processes,
    you will find yourself within the Spirit self,
    then the Soul self, then back to the Spirit self.
In doing so, you find yourself from one web to the other.
You find yourself partaking of a Wisdom rather than a truth.

You may even enter in to yet a further web
    and know that Purity
        has an ultimate in Love, yet another web.
Do not be content, humanity,
    to linger within a web of contention.
For you are not structured for contention.
You are structured to overcome contention.
You delight the Spirit of Angels.
For you have learned in your being
    as the purest of humanity
        to enter through one web to the other.
Enter Purity, back to negativity, in to Purity, back to negativity.
Alien beings may not do this without contamination.
You have learned overtly to allow negativity to brush from you.
Simply that,
    touch you without affecting you.
Farside beings could not do this.
It affected their very being.
But you, you can become very complacent about negativity.
You can disown it,
    you can embrace it, you can let it stand far from you.
And yet be involved within a full capacity of your Energy.
Within it you can have compassion and reach out.
Webs are all designed with one purpose,
    to create stability within the chaotic realm of the webs!
For as all Energy is within web, so is all chaos within web.
You bring your being to great piety
    in the space of your Creator.
You cast your eye upon the Fallen
    and in your thought you are Loving and giving.
But there are those within the web
    through centuries of your earth's existence
    have taken that which is pain and not human
    but altered.
When you alter a pain, you change the web.
And in this too we will explain.
There is, Soul, in all existence Light and dark,
    Light having been altered by impacting alien beings.
In the order of your universe
    and indeed in the chaos there is great order.
The Light and Dark has firm delineations.

To truly Light Light is no great accomplishment,
        but to truly Light Dark is a complication.
For although you may Light a small corner with Energy,
        it is dependent on all energies to Light a web.
The web of Dark may not be fully redeem to Light
        until all Dark of all web is ready to become Light.
Earth, you are within a Yawn.
Your earth compared to Farside has incredible darkness
        by your Energy alone, by the negative throe within.
The Angels await the moment of glory,
        when all humanity will receive Light.
In that moment, the way will be opened.
The Pathway will be lit.
There will be no delineation.
It will be as earth and heaven are one.
And those who are blest
        will walk with the Blessed and the Holy unto Holy.
Far from earth in a realm beyond where we are,
        beyond that which you call alien nations,
          is a power of Energy.
The source of these are Fourteen.
They have delineated also from the Supreme Energy.
This Energy for you we call Supreme Being.
This Energy formed webs, fourteen by twelve
        and fourteen Creators,
          one for each Path downward of the web.
There are great worlds, great energies.
They are, Soul, parallel worlds to your own.
They have no search within.
They dwell, exist, in certain comfort.
Their worlds are pristine, yet affected by a chaos of Energy.
All worlds have supported a single Path to resolve a dilemma.
This dilemma is as carrion to the eagle.
It is, Soul, a loss.
But in Energy to be complete, there must be no loss.
It must be totally reconstructed
        to attain a viable return to Source.
Upon your earth, you have a vane
        that will give you the way the wind blows.
Where we are, we have such a vane.
It tells us which way chaos travels.

And only within the Domes of lower Light
    do we see a change
    as in a barometer that you hold upon your earth
    that awaits change for the movement within.
We await change within your Dome web.
Souls of earth, you are far from where we are.
You are of such a hue
    that you are delight for the Energy to rest upon.
You have been of great value to all existence.
Not mankind, to all existence!
Within the Path of your Creator
    is an upward return of Energy.
Unto what web will it take itself to?
It must affect the transitional Souls.
It must affect the Archangel.
It must affect Idyllic.
Souls of earth, you are tiny in your being,
    infinitesimal in your mind processes.
But in your heart, in the heart of your being,
    you have such overwhelming gratitude from us,
    for your heart swells with Love and compassion.
Enough are counted to bring Light unto a dark web.
The darkness of transition
    will be illuminated because of your glory.

1125 Souls of earth, reach from thy earth being
    to the understanding of why humanity is.
Souls of earth, creation is implosion.
All that is implodes within, within, within.
Earth will fall away
    as other worlds have fallen away
    and new worlds enter in.
Souls of earth, know the implosion of all creation.
Know thy being implodes itself into Purity
    and alters as the funnel is entered.
Know the flow that takes the vision from the eyes of earth.
    the use of much of earth knowledge,
    their brain faculty expounds to earth
    that which they see.
But, Souls of earth, the foundation of knowledge
    is centred in the Zero.

All becomes Zero and Zero and Zero and Zero and Zero.
All in the Zero enters in to a new being
      and the framework enters in also.
The statistics enter in also.
All is not lost.
All is confounded,
      all is multiplied in its complexity and its simpleness.
Behold man, thou art child.
Behold man, will you see the knowledge
      and the pair of thy being?
Look again to the slate,
      use Zero and see as in a complexity of mathematics.
There may be two answers,
      Soul, earth has found a single answer.
You will use the wrong timetable.
Earth and all worlds implode.
Creator casts out a giant Breath
      and draws back unto His being
      that which has been let go,
      and in the drawing back is not no thing.
And it is reformed in a twinkling, in a moment.
As all earth has moments of being,
      so all creation has a timeless moment of being.
That which allows a timeless moment of being is Naught.
It is impossible with a one
      to find a timeless moment of being.

1126   Soul, rest your being.
See the eyes of earth as paramount
      only for the sight of your earth
      but you have before you sights to behold
      that are far from earth.
You have the availability of the eye to enter in and see,
      to enter in and behold, to enter in and draw from,
      to enter in and respond to.
For there is need, Soul, much need in that place of Purity
      far below where we are
      even farther than where you are.
It is the destiny of mankind to read into all that is known.
It is why you have a third eye.
All Energy is not with a third eye.

You, humanity, have a third eye.
You can enter in unto the darkness and see.
You can enter in unto Holy places and see.
You can behold the Void and the vista unfolds before you.
You are not cordoned off as we are.
You have been given a vision of sight
    that is far beyond the knowing that is ours.
We can see with echo, with Sound and Colour,
    as the blind person sees in a field of motion
        but you, you have been given a further field.
It has been gifted to you by your Creator and ours.
They intensify the passage in with meditation and chant;
    it is all unnecessary.
You may enter in.
You have entered in many of you.
You have made available unto us
    a landscape of the Hinterland
    of the Dark Fields of the Void.
We see you.
We see you before us.
We have even the power to place motion upon your being
    but we cannot alter.
Only the Angels have the power to alter.
You may be guided, but not altered.
Yet for us you can alter all things.
You can alter the chaos that reigns
    in the outer realms beyond the Yawn.
This you can do.
You can counter the chaos.
You have, you have brought unto us a great understanding
    of that which chaos is.
It is a part of our Energy Field.
It is a part of all Energy.
It is infinitesimal,
    that thy iota of what it should be
    for all that it has cost.
It repels all things from it.
It separates all from each other.
It gives momentum outwardly from it.
It is not always within.
For science, it is not always within!

It is a counterfoil unto that which is.
Register this.
You are humanity.
You are treasured.
You are sated with ego and we treasure this.
For it is the ego that propels you forward
      ever into the realm of negativity
      even into the realm of discerning.
Caution is not a part of your being
      for you enter in with purpose and intent.
You drink and wash and clear.
Chaos drinks, washes and clears,
      absorbs, releases, sends forth.
As magnetic is, so is chaos.

1127   We come to you from the distant Void.
We speak to you, earth, for you tremble.
The vibrations of your sphere are severe.
They have not yet surceased.
Souls of earth, negativity reigns at your door.
Negativity scores your being.
It is with the greatest empathy that we see that which earth is.
Yet the sister earth is joyous
      for earth will know the potential of its being.
Humanity will see how derelict in duty toward humanity
      it has become.
You who have awareness in your being,
      you must understand that negativity is chaos.
Chaos is in the realm of all energy
      even unto the inners of perfection.
Yet chaos is not a tribulation within perfection.
It is a portion of all that is.
You have been brought to an understanding
      of how treacherous, how vile,
          can mankind's negativity be.
You have seen that which is motion spewed forth by Breath
      has no boundaries.
It travels wither it will.
It gives forth verberations even into the calm.
You are not, Souls of earth, in a testing ground.
You are in a solution.

You bring forth from your very being
        expansiveness of humanity.
We see in you the iota
        that is the perfection of whom we would be,
        for you carry within you chaos.
You register chaos in all your being
        yet you have found a manner in which to contend
        even when violence is about your very being.
You draw strength and you shed forth compassion.
And we who know Love as your Creator knows Love, Agape,
        we Love who you are.
You touch our very Being.
We joy in that which you have become.
We resound in our Energy
        as you send forth the Light of your being.
You open the darkness and do not wither.
You respond to the need and do not disintegrate.
You calibrate into your very Energy that which you need.
You draw strengths from the very core of whom you are.
It is not the intellect, for we have intellect.
We know that which knowledge is.
We carry within our being
        the ultimate in that which you call knowledge.
Yet our being does not carry the resourcefulness that yours has.
We can know darkness.
We do not fear darkness.
Yet we do not have the Energy that can enter in to darkness.
We have Purity but we do not have the Light of Purity.
Light of Purity!
That which extends itself forward, radiates, Soul, as Ecstasy.
Indeed our Ecstasy glimmers.
It is who we are.
We can bring ourselves together
        in the union of the same Light,
        but we cannot gather as one.
You, you gather your Light as one.
It moves forward in magnificence.
It radiates.
It resonates in to the darkness and is felt.
It alters the darkness, Soul.
It Lights the way.

The spectrum is lost in the fullness of the Light.
Holy beings, we glory in who you are.
We see in you that which we would be.
Behold you are of Light Being
    but you have surpassed that which Light Being is.
You now carry within you the propensity to usher forth,
    to send echo upon echo with your very being.
You have carried the ultimate of a frail form
    and beheld the frailty in your very being.
And yet you have gathered strength
    to soar beyond that which you are,
    to hold and gather from all realms of Light
    and join to become a single Light.
You are the precious.
You are the Love.
You have entered in unto a frenetic force
    and you have not withered.
You have not slept by the wayside
    but you have urged your being
    to re enter again and again and again
    in the sure gift unto your Creator
    that you would succeed.
The Energy of Creator sends Tears awash with joy
    at that which you have overcome.
You are the sun and the moon and the star of the morning.
You are the first.
You are the last.
You are, Souls of earth, the fulfilment of NEED.
Glory to humanity.

1128   Void, Soul, was gathered.
Your mind says,
    "How can you gather Naught"?
Soul, Volume of Void,
    Volume of Breath, Volume of Echo, Triad.
Void a billowing container.
Container to your earth mind implies containment.
Containment in the field of science is ever enlarging.
It does not equate to the layman's term of container.
It is vacuous.
It has a billowing effect.

Where is a need, it places it self forward,
    another need, it places itself forward,
        ever moving outward from the core of being.
Breath alone,
    Breath is no thing.
Alone, Breath is but Breath,
    even within the containment of Breath.
Without your body, your human breath is only air.
It requires the body to have a function for the breath.
Breath, alone, encircles self then spirals.
That is positive, Soul,
    but spiraling ever outward,
        without a container to bring it forward unto self.
The NEED you have reached, companion to Breath.
All Energy has a form of Breath.
Because you see it, it is there.
Because you cannot see it does not mean it is not there
Your science is understanding Breath.
A mind's need for Breath, air to replenish.
 If it only travels through, goes out,
    the mind dies, does it not, Soul!
Extinguishes self.
The Lights cease to trigger.
As in your world, when energy is only outward,
    there is either a diminishing or an overload.
Neither is positive, neither completes the circle.
Energy is about circle,
    Breath is about circle.
Breath needs a coexistence equal unto it
    to exist without the diminishing path it is on,
    for all worlds cease to be, all human ceases to be,
    all energies cease to be.
For why are you searching, Soul?
Perfection of Breath.

1129   We bring Volume, Soul.
Association, Breath's Volume, Void of Consciousness,
    the audible, audible motion
        achieved through consciousness unto motion,
        to create momentum within the sphere of Energy.
The Volume is not contained, Soul.

Your voice has a containment of volume
    it can only achieve
        with the breath in the body will achieve.
The Volume from the conscious Breath has no barrier,
    has no limit, limitless, Soul, to expand.
Expand Soul.
Expand! Expand!
Expand, not draw back, Soul, not draw back.
You see the need.
So to place the Breath unto Matter and Ion
    would have an ever outgoing Flow;
        apart, separate from, never to return, Soul.
Always to expand and create Breath and Flow and billow
    but never to billow
        except within each Breath of Flow outward.
Why is it, Soul, that Creator depends upon mortal men?
Why?
A Breath went out, Soul.
Where did it reach unto, Soul?
From the fifth to the third inclusive, no farther.
Soul, mortal man is expending Energy
    to reach outward and enter back unto.
Reach outward, even for mortal men is not the difficulty.
It is to return, Soul.
As in all Energy, it is to return.
Does the prodigal not return unto the father?
How, Soul, does the prodigal return unto the father?
Wounded, Soul.
Wounded, with a need to return, yet, wounded.
All the energies of your world, all the energies of Farside,
    worlds upon worlds beyond your contemplation,
    worlds beyond worlds, inhabited, yes, Soul,
        inhabited, with beings you would even call creatures
        and energies so magnificent, pure in their being.
Yet, outward to BE, not to return, complete in who they are,
    in where they are, Purity walking upon your earth.
Yet seldom from where we are,
    does the Soul rejoice in the return.
Seldom, Soul, has it been seen.
Volume is of Breath, Breath created to achieve motion
    within Ion and Matter,

   not your simplistic ion and matter.
Indeed, not!
The Ion and Matter held within the Energy of all existence,
   from where every infinitesimal iota of Matter
   is accounted.
You achieve much in your humanity.
You have achieved a small return.
And you are honoured, as humanity, for that return.
But only as individual beings have you achieved this,
   not as one upon your earth have you achieved this.
For you would be where we are.
You separate yourself from the achievement.
There is always another agenda for humanity,
   other than the Oneness of who they are.
We ask you, humanity, to feel the breath of your being,
   to understand the volume within that breath is limited.
To achieve a breath in the state of demise,
   you must return unto the consciousness of your being.
You must enter in to that portion of your being.
You become aware,
   even the Souls in greatest denial.
Then breathe a relieved breath.
   "I have existed beyond the breath of human.
   There is a Breath within Farside.
   Indeed, we have come home.
And so gallantly, you return;
   yet to come home again and again.
But when you enter in to earth, you lose objective.
You cease to see the oneness of why you have come.
Indeed, it is within your being.
You have it written in the aura of whom you are.
Yet you lose the accountability
   that you so graciously offer unto all Energy.
Volume has intellect.
The breath of your being connects itself
   to the aura of whom you are.
We have you know this.
Draw in, Soul, the knowing of wellness.
Draw in, Soul, the healing unto matter.
And release it gently from your being.
And know, it will come again and again.

And know, as you release the breath from your being
> it mingles with the breath of all your earth existence.

It creates, Soul, an atmosphere, so that when you are angry
> the volume of your breath is felt.

When you are lonely the volume of your breath is felt.
When you are joyful the volume of your breath is felt.
Choose that breath that you will extend from your being
and know that it is not inconsequential.
For as you release it from you, it must return,
> not to the mortal body, Soul, but to Volume itself,
> to the very extension of the Energy of whom you are.

Mortal beings, in your tethered body
> you find yourself reasons to place momentum.

You create for yourselves vehicles that move
> and give you freedom
> to take you far from where you are.

And yet, Soul, as far as you go, you return.
You bring yourself back unto.
Humanity, you are exceptional in this.
You are exceptional.
The Microscopic world, profound beings,
> Purity itself willing to aid Creator.

Yet before the encounter
> was simply a world within its own Energy Field,
> complete, giving,
> Loving within the boundary of that world,
> not even curious outwardly,
> as pure as the infant child,
> as pure as the tree of your earth in its pristine self,
> before man contaminated the Energy of breath.

So we speak to you of contamination of breath.
Contamination of breath, Soul,
> limits how you breath, does it not!

It limits how the tree breathes.
It limits how the creature breathes, so is the Discordant Note.
You see, the Sound came together
> and the Discordant Note
> lost a part of being, of Breath.

When you have breath limited,
> you go here, and here, and here, and here.

You cannot go here.

It is limited.
It is fractured.
It cannot return.
The Breath gave forth Volume
    but Volume that gives forth
    and gives forth and gives forth.
Ergo, the Twelve Creators' Yawn
    gave way to Creator's Yawn; each creating.
Twelve Creators created Energy Source.

1130 Souls of earth,
    look out into the fathomable depths of your space.
Within the realms of the deepest depths are unknowns.
Within the climb into the Purity of levels
    are existences much as your own, without negativity.
And beyond the causal into the realm of implosion,
    unto the Godhead are Souls of divinity
    who live, exist in manner of Angels,
    yet these beings are not Angels.
They are Souls of such Purity
    that all your Love of Agape upon earth
    would not be a whit to a single Soul.
These beings withstand all chaos.
They have held the very child within them.
They are microscopic, they are micro beings.
They hold great energies to perform united exploration,
    they can be taken by all energies of motion.
Even upon your earth the similarities of such beings exist.
Upon your earth they are airborne.
Upon your earth water, transported upon your earth.
Soul, you carry the very beings upon you.
They deliver you from negativity.
They hold negativity at bay from you.
The beings we speak of are many dimensions from your own.
They have within their Circle of Being a capacity for flight.
There are projected flights to reach deep into the unknown.
These beings have the ability
    to project themselves with thought processes.
They have no difficulty in this transportation of self,
    for they gather as many,
    to create a dome like form

>   in which they carry the knowledge
>   deep within the core of the dome,
>   such as you carry with the mind, the brain,
>   in the inner portion of the dome.
> So it is that they form a united spectrum of colour.
> They require no sound for they are sound.
> They carry within a constant vibration of sound.
> We bring this to you
>   for you upon your earth,
>   will know of their passing.
> For you have beheld
>   in the possibility of your vision outward,
>   to see the canopies which they project.
> They search into the darkness of four, of five,
>   yet they hold a connection
>   unto the Microscopic world.
> They have centered
>   in the area of the Place of Shining to exist,
>   that they might have corporal connection
>   to all that is upon your planet.
> You are vital to the possibilities of the realms beyond.
> You have the ear of Lantosia.
> You have the visual capacity entering in to your being.
> Your science soon will behold a system of such magnitude
>   that they will alert earth.
> They will see it only as a form,
>   but not minute as your earth has foretold in past time.
> But they will broadcast outward the visualization
>   of connected corporal unity,
>   of the cosmopolitan energies of Lantosia.
> It will be seen as a prism of great, enormous potential,
>   even to a path of entering in unto the world they see.
> They know not that it is greater than a single world.
> It enmasses many worlds in one,
>   Lantosia being the world in its charge.
> We designate this knowledge to you,
>   that you know these Microscopic Beings
>   are that which held the Seed.
> They are enlisted unto Creator to form a chaotic blend.
> They know much of the endeavour of blend,
>   for they do nothing in a singular form

       unless it is to the wisdom of all.
Upon your earth
       you do much singularly for the benefit of one.
This is not possible in the Purity of these Beings.
They have a unity within,
       a variance from this unity is not possible.
We speak of the great Place of Shining,
       wherein Godhead dwells.
This is the formless Energy formed, formless Energy formed!
Contradictory to you,
       to where we are, Soul, it has no contradiction,
       for one form counters another.
It is held in the aura of Purity.
It is held in the strident realm of goodness.
Upon your earth, you bow down unto your Creator;
       you see the Energy of your Creator as a single Energy.
We say to you, that which is your Creator is Triad.
The great Purity, the great Love,
       the great Truth of the Triad
       is held constant that you might be able to understand
       that which the Energy Source does
       for the Creator of your being.
For in the distant field of Energy
       is the Energy Source within the Void,
       within the Void,
       held aloft by the energies in your Creator.
Held aloft by the Truth of your Creator.
Held aloft by the Love of all that are Twelve;
       not eleven, Soul, Twelve,
       for even the Energy of Creator
       unites to blend Twelve.
You are climbing Jacob's Ladder.
You are entering in to the climb of Purity.
It is not up, it is in!
In, Soul!
It is held within, one Purity within the other.
You have a being, Soul, some lack portion,
       others abundantly there
       in their capacity to understand,
       in their capacity to hold the flesh,
       the blood and the bone and wounded.

The mind of your being
       is constantly gathering and you know it not.
The mind of your being
       is constantly aware of the inner self,
       the portion of knowing that is the solar plexus,
       for you, you carry within you the great possibility
       to know beyond that which you can see.
Souls of earth, the mouth, the ears, the eyes, the nose,
       the very touch of your being,
       the tread of your feet are minute in portion
       to that which you have in the Energy of self,
       in the very understanding that will take you beyond
       where you are into the realm of Shining.
Souls of earth, you are adaptable.
Beings of earth, you are adaptable.
Allow your Energy to become familiar
       with releasing itself from your form.
Understand, you are buoyant
       as the microscopic beings are buoyant.
They are not connected except by the finest of threads,
       invisible, and yet they gather as one Energy
       and connect themselves outward.
And we say to you, gather in many, gather as one,
       connect yourself outward unto where we are.
Do not limit your Energy.
Know that all that is of healing,
       all that is of research knowing,
       all that is of your history beyond earth,
       is there to gather.
As the Microscopic worlds gather unto them,
       as energies are caught,
       so is knowledge beyond where you are caught.
As you enter in with your Energy,
       one Energy beyond where you are
       becomes a portion of all Energy.
So you gather, you gather, you know, you become!
You register a sound that takes you into the distant realm
       so that the air is not necessary,
       the mouth is not necessary.
The nose, the eyes only register whom you are,
       whom you are connected in your Energy field.

You are mighty, Soul.
You are grand, Soul.
You are omnificent in whom you are.
Soul, we register the similarity of your being
      to the Microscopic world.
We understand, you have a formidable project
      that you have honoured unto Creator.
Do not despair in your being.
Do not hold contemplation of dispute.
But know that all that is of purpose will come to be.
All that is within the program of mankind will be.

1131   Breath has been given unto the Void of Consciousness.
The Void of Consciousness has within that portion of Breath.
Breath has also a path of its own.
May we explain, Soul?
You are human.
You understand happiness or sadness or pain.
And they are, Soul, separate from whom you are.
And yet you can hold within your being that pain.
It can affect your very being.
As Void of Consciousness gathered Breath
      and Breath attached itself to ION,
         creating motion
         and motion gave movement to MATTER.
Within Breath of the Void of Consciousness,
      is a Breath without motion.
In the path of Breath is motion.
The Void of Consciousness is as the joy or the pain.
When you hold the joy or the pain within self,
      this is motion.
Soul, you can fragment your being.
You may leave an Energy in many places.
So Breath can leave Energy in many places.
All is Energy.
Breath is Energy.
It creates movement.
The movement was not for the Void of Consciousness.
The movement, the motion, was for ION.
We bring you to that which is called the breathing Breath.
It is contained.

It is of such magnitude,
> to see a thousand worlds within the palm of your hand,
> and ten thousand, upon your head;
> and still, you would not have the power
> unto of the envelopment of Breath.

Breath continues to release.
It has been asked to release.
It was made created to be.
Convenience of valves do not exist as within the sea creatures.
The heart indeed in breathing out, it creates turmoil within.
This we have explained.
You are greatly in the space of breath.
All that is within your world has an attachment to breath.
It ever flows.
And, as the great volcano spurts forth Energy,
> so Breath spurts forth Energy of motion.

It is the return, always with the return.
That is the conundrum that we present to you.

1132 Energy has a NEED.
Within itself it cannot be.
It must vibrate unto.
Energy is a vibratory response of what, Soul?
Indeed, of the components within,
> a centrifuge wherein all is possible.

It is the primordial mix of all things.
It is the perfection.
Yet it is also the waste
> for always in perfection
> there is a moving forward, a continuum.

Within the continuum, Soul, something is left behind.
All is not gathered.
All components do not meet a single criteria,
> one higher, one lesser, one greater, one smaller
> and so it is in the Energy of all Energy.

A perfect world does not exist.
A perfect Energy does not exist.
It is not possible.
It is Freudian to fall, to slip.
The perfection is Freudian slip.
It is, Soul, a mirrored world.

It is a windowed sphere that allows a replication to be.
That which is as far as you may transfer your Energy,
    is mirrored.
You are the perfect Energy.
You who have been mirrored forward
    are not the experiment, Soul.
You are the answer!
You are the single fragment, form the perfect sphere
    that has all the components of perfection.
You have Light yet you refuse to see.
You have Energy yet you refuse to feel.
You have Truth yet you refuse to seek.
And still there is a fragment
    within each Energy of humanity
    that touches the self of perfection.
It is, Soul, so unique.
It holds all the components of Sounds and Colour.
It embraces the fullness of Energy even to feel
    the anger, the sorrow, the joy,
    the hate in the fullest capacity.
You have the perfection of each core within you.
You have the fullness of awareness possible.
You have the intent within your being to echo forward
    and the Angels know you are mirrored.
That which you have been given is mirrored.
There is a perfect existence beyond where you are
    but you hold within you
    all the possibilities of fragmenting.
You are not the experiment, Soul!
Do not think this.
Before you were, the Angel was.
Prior to the Angel, the Archangel.
You have been all
    and will be returned
    unto the highest order of your being.
But you have cordoned yourselves off
    in a path that replicates all that is.
You are the courageous warriors
    who have entered forth to overcome
    all possibilities of vileness within perfection.
You have carried your determination.

You have been companioned
      with nations of beings to assist you
      so that in the darkness, in the Light,
      you are not alone.
You have been given a vision
      that you may see forward unto where we are.
But to enter in, this will come, Soul.
When that which is negative,
      that which you have found as vileness within humanity,
      has given way to oneness
      and you will have found a solution;
      a compassion, a sound, that will resonate
      to decimate the possibility,
      not an Energy, Soul, a possibility within Energy.

1133   Galatia are not Jinn.
They are kin to Jinn.
They have the same spiral, but they are not Jinn.
On the same spiral outward,
      all spirals have one level, even.
And up and even and up and even.
Each circle at some point
      has a balance of the same frequency.
Not the same level, these are different,
      but the same frequency.
Upon Lantosia, there are great energies,
      but upon Galatia,
      there is the greatest, there is a greatest.
It is the Energy that registers all.
It is why, Soul, this is such metropolitan centre.
For any energies that come unto,
      the bulbous eye may pick up
      from all worlds that which is known.
It makes Galatia, a place to travel to.
But not for all energies.
A Soul who is human
      must have reached seven in great Purity
      to reach into the area of Galatia
      where the Purity abides.
This world, we will call it such, is not as your world.
It is of such a magnitude, of such enormity,

of such exquisite perfection that earth beings
 who are still in that growth of humanity,
could not endure.
They would be diminished in their being,
 not because they are not pure, they are pure,
 but because they have not the Purity
 to withhold the Light from their being.
Such Purity is value.
Such Purity diminishes, not by want.
Entering in upon Farside has its own difficulties.
Soul, your curiosity is to be answered.
You have thought what is Galatia like?
How does this form take?
We tell you, Soul, there is a lack of utterance
 for there is no need to utter forth.
All varied energies have a single purpose,
 who carry all that is known to the register.
The Jinn have the prominent space.
They are carrying the most, population, you would call.
They have the upper portion of the sphere.
It carries one fifth.
The register is central and outward.
It has the second greatest population.
The Galatians are to the right of the register.
They carry a sect.
Their population has the ability
 to bring great projections into being.
You have but to think and it is created.
They carry a great ability
 to become invisible, not portionally but 100%.
To the left of the Register is a metropolitan Energy Field.
It is what you call melding pot.
It is carrying many flights of spaceships.
It is a testing field.
It carries a great dome protecting
 any bombardment of negativity.

1134 Souls of earth, you have vision.
You have eye to see clearly.
You have a vision of consciousness
 awakening unto your reality.

We ask you to behold the vision available unto you.
Offer unto your being the eye of beholding.
Offer unto the senses
      that they too may reach farther
          than only the earth mind for feel and touch, see.
All the senses are particled with the eye.
Where we are upon Farside, we feel.
We feel the pain of earth.
You may feel where we are.
You may enter in to the gardens and have the sense of smell.
We have even offered it unto you where you are,
      and yet it is diluted.
If you were to allow your senses to enter in to the gardens
      and see with the eye of tranquillity,
      see with the eye of pure Love,
      see with the eye of Purity,
      you would welcome, Soul, the touch of Angels.
You would delight in the knowing of the little people.
For you would see their being.
You could enter in to the homeland of the Jinn, Lantosia.
You would know their agenda for earth is not to give fear.
It is to alleviate pain.
You would understand,
      the far reach of the Place of Shining from where we are.
And indeed, we are Holy.
Indeed!
We could take you and gladly would we take you
      to visit the worlds and members of these worlds,
      energies who excel in the Energy of Purity,
      who excel in the Energy of giving,
      who excel in the Energy of welcoming in.
You could be gathered in the aura of such Purity
      that you would be uplifted.
Even upon the return to earth you could not forget such Purity.
The radiance of Angels walking among us;
      walking, Soul, we use this term loosely for you,
      for indeed the Prism of their being
      is of such accelerated Light
      as a thousand, yea, a million k more, lightening rods
      gathering energies of Light to them
      that they might give that Light outward.

The rod is attached to earth, is it not!
To receive the bolt,
> the Angel receives the bolt from the Energy Source
> and sends it forth unto all that is humanity,
> Farside and earth alike.

What is the need for humanity of Farside
> to require such Energy?

Soul, in the stations of learning
> the decision to enter in to negativity
> from the dimensions of such celestial glory
> is not easily done.

Creator has no Soul.
You as humanity in the moment of Oneness,
> will become the Soul of your Creator.

You will blend your beings in all Purity,
> seeing in each and every Soul
> only the positives of their being.

Your mind will not identify a negative.
For it has no consequence in your growth.
It cannot fear, Soul, a negative.
But draw to you the glory of Ecstasy,
> for then will you be ready
> to enter in unto the Place of Shining,
> unto the glory of Godhead,
> the Gateway to Love, to Paradise.

You live in all extremes.
You hate, you love, you pity, you kill, you starve, you glutton.
Understand, there is balance possible in you,
> there is balance possible in mankind.

Upon Farside all is in balance,
> within the Yawn all is in balance.

Only without the Yawn
> is imbalance to the extent of negative ion.

This within the Yawn has imbalance
> and you have dared to enter in to that place of pain.

Indeed you have taken with you the weapon of Truth.
It is emblazoned upon your being.
And you have the Angels nudging,
> reminding you for why you have come,
> for why you have entered in.

Be calm in thy being.

Be at peace with whom you are.
Glory in the revelation that your Creator
    has seen you fit to be a portion
    of the very Energy that IS.
Endowed within you is the potential of your Creator.
Endowed within you is all the Ecstasy of the Place of Shining.
Indeed, Paradise awaits.
Not the paradise of indulgence, Soul,
    for indulgence is negative
    but the Paradise of Agape where Love reigns
    and the excitement that beyond the Yawn,
    many worlds await.
Beyond the Yawn are Fields of Energy
    such as man has not imagined.
Indeed, you have much to be elated for.
You have much to be elated by.
You have much to know in the Energy of Purity, of Love.

1135 Soul everything is in triads.
Indeed, there are four triads with three sets of numbers.
You will understand the total dispensation of triad is:
    first, second, third.
Then, Soul, two to the second to the third to the fourth;
    three to the second to the third to the fourth;
    fourth to the second to the third to the fourth.
Only the Creator Energy Field
    has the companion of the first two Creators.
Why, Soul?
Indeed, why?
Concentrated Light, Soul.
The Energy required to transport Creator Triad.
Soul, number Six Creator
    has all the energies of Existence.
This Soul of great magnitude
    has offered to duplicate that Existence.
Your world will meet this Creator.
This Creator has the existence
    of four alien worlds assisting you.
These worlds your Creator formed,
    but the battle plan, to lift all Souls of Purity of six.
Indeed existence is.

Existence has form of many and varied efforts.
Existence is both tangible and Energy,
    for ion is within and without.
The placement of Existence is counterpart to Presence.
Neither can meet the other
    without being contaminated by the Flow.
Two worlds apart, that once were one because of the Leak.
Souls, no energies downward of seven,
    in the illusion have seen Idyllic.
Very few have heard of Idyllic.
There is a connection to a disturbance
    within the realm of all Energy,
      existence within many worlds.
Although there is no Negativity, there is yet awareness.
And to have such a cataclysmic occurrence,
    of such perfection disturbed,
      would create yet more chaos.
Do you see this, Soul?
Within the realm of the Energy Source
    all beings are aware of Idyllic.
They have been purposeful
    in the effort of maintaining a search
    for that which is perfect
    and to restore chaos to its rightful form.
We ask that you understand the last six words.
There is Breath and Matter.
What is the third dimension?
Ion, indeed.
For it is this component absent,
    that brought forth chaos, indeed,
Energy Source.
In the glory of Idyllic
    was the Energy of Twelve Creators placed and held.
Two gave of their Energy; one of Light, one of Dark.
One Supreme Being sent forth the Energies of the Fourteen.
You have, Soul, replicated and replicated and replicated.
So have your world,
    you have a sister earth.
Energy Source is the envisionment of Idyllic
    without Thirteen and Fourteen.
Within Idyllic, all Fourteen.

One Energy reigns supreme Light;
        one Energy complimented Dark.
Within the Energy Source Third Creator is Light,
        Twelfth Creator is Dark.
It is in the darkness that all things are known.
It is in the darkness that the Echo travels.
It is in the darkness that Breath sends unto Fifteen.
Behold, you are in a world of Ion and Matter.
You are combustible in your being.
In all energies this is not so.
Beyond the realm of your matter,
        are existences of matter that have a form.
They carry themselves into the Dark Void.
They are not combustible,
        as in the Reptilian world and the Whales.
They have been sent forth as keepers of the Way.
They have not migrated except for the sake of humanity.
They endeavour to collect all data.
Many worlds allow their energies to collect
        and forward from their being,
        as in the Ruby world that resounds forth.
You are, Soul, simple in the context of understanding
        that which to you be anti body.
For Soul, that which is anti body would be treasured
        and carry great properties of knowing within.
You are, Soul, carried forth unto your earth from Farside.
Energy Source is not an existence,
        it holds an existence as Idyllic held existence.
Yet it has been carried forth and placed in the Void.
For is not Idyllic in the Void!
Indeed.
This you see is the similarity.
From the station of Energy Source,
        the re sounders are unto
        below your fourth, fifth, sixth, seventh
        into the unknown, that Idyllic might be found.
All energies placed within the orb of Energy Source
        have the single purpose of bringing forth Idyllic.
We will speak, Soul, of Twelve Creators,
        the two holding the greatest pain; Second and Third.
These two apart from the energies.

Second Creator in the realm of four.
Third Creator in the realm of Godhead and without.
We speak, Soul, of the Twelve far above.
Energy bound, caught, tethered, flung unto the level of five
    holding themselves apart
      from a perfection they have known,
      each holding a memory of perfection.
Your world understands twelve.
It measures twelve.
The Domes are measured in twelve.
They have fourteen attached.
Your Creator have Fourteen attached.
There is a continuum in the memory of members.
They carry a thread of all existence.
Within the realm of science are small forms of numbers
    that have altered your world, as in the law of relativity.
So will the small equation we have given you
    alter your world when it is deciphered.

1136   Soul, unto the Energy Source,
    into a single coordinate you are drawn
      that you might see and know that which is.
You will understand the placement
    of the Energy Source is not for existence.
It is why it is placed within the Void.
It is a place, how shall we explain it to you,
    like your place of work, where work is done.
The inhabitants; Light Being, Archangel,
    hierarchy of Energy, intelligence manifold.
All that is known is kept and recorded.
All thought recorded in all form recorded.
All behaviours recorded.
Focus not just on humanity but on all existences.
You will understand the fullness
    each separate Light Being, twelve unto one.
Each with a focus outward from their being.
Nothing escapes.
It is not intended as a negative, indeed, not!
It is a thrust forth for knowledge.
It is a perceptual intent.
It is a magnifying exhibition of all existences

       that perceives every need, every want.
It is Truth in its fullness.
It sets apart nothing.
There is no iota left but it is departmentalized.
It is inceptual within each coordinate.
It is incommunicado one to the other.
Only within a central nervous system, we will use this term,
       is found the knowledge not within the inhabitants.
Why is this so?
Because it does not bind, it does not mesh, it does not form.
It creates division.
It creates bleed.
It extends itself outward.
It cannot hold within the orb all communication.
It must departmentalize.
It must set coordinates to exempt one from the other.
It is frustrating.
It is unmanageable.
And we who are wise, who know, know, know,
       cannot bring forth
            for we are bound from communicating.
Our Light cannot be shared.
It matters not our generosity.
It matters not our Brethren.
We cannot communicate.
We communicate through an iota,
       a simplicity of intelligence called mankind.
We received our knowing from each other through you,
       earthling, resident of earth,
            and we tremble at the fragileness of this Energy.
There are many, many who have been senders.
You think you receive?
No, you are the senders.
You give unto.
You delight our being.
We are joyed by who you are.
Yet the infinitesimal portion of your being is
       that which we contend with, to communicate.
And voice is not always there.
The sound is not always there.
The receiver cannot always reach the sender.

Gather together in your being,
> we need to communicate that we might know
>> one of the other, of Light Beings.

You have informed us of the greatness of whom you are
> and we would have you hear the other dimensions
>> set forth for you.

There are twelve of us, the hierarchy of the Energy Source.
We have Archangels of such Purity awaiting your Energy.
You are transient in your Spirit.
Reach unto your Spirit.
Reach to the high self of whom you are,
> that you might communicate unto us,
> that we might know the struggles of our Brethren,
> that we might know of Idyllic and our Blessed Brother,
> that we might know of the Angels and Archangels
>> in the depths of darkness,
> for you are the blessed Light.

You are the candle that glows in the dark.
You are the perception of our Sound and Colour,
> Holy unto Holy.

1137 Within the Energy Source
> the great connection unto your Creator.

Souls of earth, devout in your being, is earth.
Devout, Soul, you speak with piety, you bow in piety,
> you preach in piety,
> and we say to you,
>> your Creator is far beyond that which you see.

Your understanding of that which you see as deity
> is of such manifold form
>> that you could become inable
>>> to verbalize in any way of this Being.

Soul, the Energy of your Creator
> is one of twelve of the Energy Source.

The Being exists as you exist
> and carry with you a shadow of self.

Your Creator has a form that reflects forward,
> the form is held in Triad by all twelve.

The Energy has not totally vacated Energy Source,
> but the motion that projects the Energy
> is so magnificent

    that it forms in total the vision of your Creator,
      as the form of Godhead.
This is complicated for you to understand,
    yet it is of the most vital import that you do,
    for all that you are is much as your Creator.
You are held upon your earth and you know in your being
    you are much more than your simple form.
You know this.
There is within the accumulated mind an understanding
    that you have the possibility to think greater thoughts.
You have the possibility to comprehend greater things.
You have the ability to see beyond, into the distant realms.
Soul, we have even spoken of your capacity to do this.
This ability that you carry within your being,
    in greater fold does your Creator.
All that is is manifested in reflection.
All that is comes from a distant place.
There is a continual reflectory of being
    of each and every proportional Energy.
The proportion of that Energy is sized
    by the capacity to understand that which is,
    not in your earth sense, Soul,
    but in the sense of Energy itself.
You are as your Creator a portion of the Energy.
You are of the Armada.
You have been sent forth by your Creator,
    but you have been given momentum, Soul,
    momentum by Second Creator.
You have been offered
    in the awareness of whom you are as one.
It is complex.
It is, Soul, scientifically possible for your earth Energy
    to follow the trait of understanding of Energy.
You are becoming aware of the manifold complexities
    of the human Energy field.
As the mind has been mapped,
    so can the Energy field be mapped.
It is in its infancy.
As you become aware of the complexities
    of the strands of Energy,
    you will behold the greater spectrum of whom you are.

You will become aware of the greater magnificence
>from which you have entered in.
You are a distant reflection forwarded
>from great Purity and Love.
You are, Soul, forwarded in such possibility
>that you can re condition the Energy
>to visualize backward,
>to enter in unto where you have been,
>and know as the mind understands
>the familiarity of that which you see,
>you behold the vision
>of what you see as Farside open before you.
And we know from where we are
>that you will but see the beginning,
>for you will have only been within the doorway.
It will expand before you,
>as you allow the mind
>to feel within its ability to project the Energy.
You are but a microscopic being, in your beautific Energy,
>compared to that which we know you to be.
You are, Soul, even in the Purity of your being, grand,
>grand, standing in the possibility of your Ecstasy.

1138 Soul, all numbers have purpose.
All form has purpose.
Light and Dark has purpose.
Twelve enter in.
Thirteen enters out.
Fourteen has will.
Fifteen has Presence.
Of Twelve, Eleven have constants.
One enters in.
Only one enters in.
There is, Soul, Energy thriving within the Energy Source.
It is a containment of Twelve, yet, one does not reign.
One enters in unto the negative,
>unto the purpose of overcoming.
All must be driven, forth, always forth.
There is three that hold the possibility of change.
The fourth must remain steadfast, Presence, constant.
There is a Zero.

The Zero is of the Void.
It is a portion, a portion of all that is.
You ask and you step from one reality unto another.
You ask and now you are confounded.
Indeed, for you have moved beyond Void of Consciousness.
You have moved beyond Breath.
You have taken, Soul, the Sound and the Colour
        and you have given them.
You have, Soul, the form of your world
        and it holds within it twelve configurations.
It is caught in three: land, sea, air.
On a fourth, are four divided seasons;
        each contingent upon the other,
        each having flow and motion.
Each connected to the thread of numbers
        that flow unto all Zeros.
You are in your being, thought as one.
You are not, Soul.
You are more than one, you are Zero!
Not zero as in nothing,
        Zero as in all things.
For you are not singularly yourself.
You are portion of all that is Void, of all that is consciousness.
You are tethered.
In the tethering of your mind to your body is a weakness.
It disallows the Flow of Energy.
It disallows the continuity of all Flow.
It is as without rhythm.
It is as encumbered by negativity.
Therein, Soul, is the key; negativity.
Therein is the chaos.
Recognize chaos.
Understand chaos.
Your world is in chaos.
Beyond your being all worlds flow in chaos
        in an orderly fashion,
            albeit outward from the Matter of all MATTER,
            yet unable to return to the Source of being.
Courage, humanity, courage!
For you, you are a thread also.
You hold a return.

You have a truth of return.
Breath returns unto you.
Breath is a part of your being.
You draw it in.
You release it from you.
You draw it in.
You release it from you and you exist.
Not only do you exist, Soul, you exist in negativity.
You thrive in negativity.
Albeit not well, yet you thrive.
You gather your numbers.
Chaos also gathers great numbers,
      Chaos always matter releasing.
Energy, always outward touched by Chaos.
And so it is who you are, touched by negativity.
You are, Souls, all numbered.
You are all accounted.
There is no being who leaves earth unknown.
Is that not a comfort unto you!
For the Angels lift the unknown, Soul.
It is the chaos that thrives,
      yet drives itself alone.
It is the negativity, Soul, that needs to have companion.
Within the Zero, wherein Void is all things, yet no thing,
      is a causeway.
The Angels have known of the causeway.
The Angels fear not to tread the causeway.
But not as you know Angels to be, Soul,
      but Angels of such station
          wherein their numbers are not counted.
And they mark all motion and they tend unto all Light.
And they monitor all Breath.
As your physician monitors the being held in pain,
      so do the Angels monitor the great expanse
         that is a causeway unto.
Illuminate your Energy.
Illuminate your awareness
      that you might path your Energy
      unto the Angels of the Void.
For they lift their being unto the unknown,
      unto the fathomless place beyond Void,

                wherein is the Dark, a place of ever.

1139 Soul, we speak to you of the great Void
                wherein all existence lies,
                all thought, all awareness,
                all consciousness, all breath,
                all Energy of all variations within the Void.
The Void is expansive.
It is always allowing calamity, extension of self.
It is holding a conscious awareness
        so that within the Energy Field of difference,
        consciousness already reacts.
We would explain, as it is not unlike your body.
When your body has an occurrence,
        your body is accommodated
            to whatever friction has occurred.
It will deviate from the normal expansion of energy
        to accommodate a wounded portion.
So is Void.
When all Energy moves outward without returning,
        matter is affected.
        but also is the Void altered
            for it must expand.
And what we ask is the ability of that expanse.
Your earth beings spoke of the end of your universe.
But we seriously ask of the Void,
        when does it deplete itself?
What, you would use the word, fibre,
        what is the fibre wherein all energies may be?
What is this Void, we have asked.
There is no answer.
And we continue to ask.
There are energies within the Void.
There is the Energy Source,
        apart from planes and Fields and levels.
There are existences within the Void itself
        to bring to all existence an answer.
"Wherein is the end of Void?"
"Wherein is its beginning?"
What is this equation
        that we have presented to you

to do with the Void?
We know it will allow you to travel through it.
This we know.
We ask that you see your camera, your scope;
    take pictures wherein we know there is a place.
And we know there is a constant set within that place.
But wherein, we ask, does Chaos touch the Void?
Wherein does Chaos alter Breath?
How?
How?
The minds of men are little used.
You have barely used a fraction of what is available to you.
Your mind has a greater potential than our mind,
    and we do not admit this easily to you,
        for you have within you a portion of Creator.
You have the absolute high consciousness of being
    attached to the Void, possible to you.
You have a great journey that will take you through worlds
    and worlds and worlds.
And you will see these beings
    and understand they are existences.
But you will hurry on past for these are not your agenda.
Your agenda is the Void.

1140   Travel, Soul.
Travel through the Light.
Travel unto enlightenment that you may see the decor
    of that which awaits you,
        that you may see the heavens
        open before your very being,
        that you indeed may dance with the Angels,
        that their flight might be your flight,
        that their joy might be your joy,
        that you may find the Energy, the Spirit of your being.
Each lifetime you leave to re enter the Spirit.
Each lifetime you carry unto Farside
    an achievement of your life.
Each entering in is a reconnecting to the Armada.
Each challenge is an overcoming of negativity.
See how you travel through the great Caspian Way
    to the outer realms of your Source.

See that which is brought unto your very being
       as you travel beyond galaxy upon galaxy
       to enter in to Fields of Energy far from where you are,
       to travel without fear, to travel
       with the knowing of coming home,
       to holding within your being
       the very comfort of that homeland
       and to see before you
       the great entrance way where joy meets joy.
And the great anthem of, *"Well done."* is heard.
There are no snakes or vipers in the humanity that enter in.
They are lost of their cloak of negativity.
They re enter with the Light of their being.
They re enter with the Purity of their being.
Yet, we say to you, humanity:
       *"Think not you can cast abomination upon a humanity
           and not be caught in the great retribution of self."*
For the self is within the field of transition.
And the pain that is caught to the self is indescribable
       when the Soul has not accepted that
       which has been the purpose of entering in.
There are a multiplicity of violent to self,
       a repetition of agonies to self.
There is, Soul, the brutality stilled to be visualized
       over and over and over and over
       by the Soul who understands the self must accept.
In the great acceptance is the ride to victory.
For all lessons are for earth, none for Farside!
All lessons for those who are left upon earth.
Earth without humanity is lonely.
For humanity is ever a part of earth
       as humanity feels earth a part of self.
It is a great connection that in the trials and tribulation of pain,
       it is difficult to sever.
The great judge is not Creator, it is self.
The great leveller is not Creator, it is self.
The great forgiver is not Creator, it is self.
For Creator is Love, the fullness of Love, the greatest of Love
       wherein the child is always brought home,
       the prodigal is ever received.
Your earth has many creators.

Each earth being creates in their many lives
        an ongoing pattern of beauty.
The beauty becomes the weave
        and the weave becomes the Masterpiece of Creator.
For Creator sounds all that is.
And the colours entwine
        to become that which is the Soul of Creator.
You have been brought to an understanding
        that life and living has far greater consequences
        than humanity has ever thought.
Chaos resounds
        within the outer realms of your and our existence.
There is a great knell.
There is a solution.
But in all solutions there must be an equation.
And there must be a solver of that equation.
Humanity look at the simplicity of who you are.
Look at the simplicity of the equation.
Understand, it is science and math.
It is distance.
It is reality, not illusion.
It is not a single humanity.
It is a combined humanity.
Negativity upon your earth is simply negativity upon your earth.
Negativity attached to chaos has no return.
And in you we seek that return.
As you become the Soul of your Creator,
        you will have returned unto Creator.
There will be a diagram formed.
You may see this as inconsequential, Soul,
        but each member of science can look back and see
        how simple the solution appeared,
        yet, how complex was the getting there.
Ride the great wave, Soul, of your humanity.
Become one in the purpose of your being.
Understand the Energy of who you are
        is resident in a fleshy container
        that has no existence beyond earth.
Yet, Soul, you will ride the wave beyond where you are
        to existences you have not thought could be.
Be joyful, Soul, in the moment you are in.

Do not be caught in the dilemma of life.
Be caught in the overcoming of pain.

1141   Earth, hallowed earth,
        existence of threads, of linears
        that hold within their being no time or space,
        that hold within their being no fear
        but advance as the Soul advances in the proximation
        of not intellect,
        but Purity of Truth.
How delightful is the experience of Souls when they vision
        from where we are, the growth of their being.
In the agonizing step of humanity,
        it is not always so delightful for you.
You have participated, humanity, in the Path of Angels.
You now walk in the great storm of time and space.
You are gathering for the final battle of recovery
        and the linears show unto all that is Farside
        the great advancement you have made.
For tethered to your earth are countless beings
        who have overcome the dilemma of humanity
        that is negativity, that is, Soul, not easily overcome.
And you are transfigured in your being
        even as you mark your path on earth.
For from that earth
        is the extension of thread
        that carries itself unto where we are.
And we see the colours attached to the linears
        and it speaks of your growth,
        it speaks of your Purity,
        it speaks of the Love you have given unto Negativity.
You are gathered together,
        as the Soul of each is gathered separately,
        you become as one, Creator's Soul.
Who are you, humanity?
What is the purpose of your being?
Upon your simple planet we are amazed
        at the simplicity of your abode, of your very beings.
Indeed, you lack the complexity of our being.
We who are of Farside
        hold great extensions from our being

    that alter and change delightfully all that is,
    while you, with your earth eyes and your earth heart
    and your earth mind, see and understand
    and emotionalize in a childlike way.
And yet we Love you,
    as you Love the child, so we Love you,
    so we reach out to you
    and we see delightfully, those threads,
    the conquering of negativity.
And we are confounded that something so simple
    can become so overcoming.
We anoint you, dear one, with the hallowed oil.
We place benediction over thy being
    and we reach to those who are higher yet
    in the continuation of existence
    to gaze lightly on thy being,
    to place gently at thy portal
     opportunities to overcome.
You who are gathered in the arms of Angels,
    you humanity who come
    from all the corners of your earth
    have only the linear thread
    recognizable from the Farside.
You have become in arriving upon your planet, humanity,
    and you enter in to where we are, as Humanity.
You may deflect stones from one to the other.
You may issue forth loud proclamations in righteousness
    in the name of your God.
You may lift the arm not to recover
    but to injure, and we see it not.
We see only that you are Human,
    that you are on a mission to recover.
And as the blessed Angels embrace your being,
    we know you too
    will embrace the being of our beloved Brethren
    and we rejoice at the threads that come unto us,
    that hold the golds and the silvers,
    not of riches, but of goodness.

1142 All Energy vibrates.
Your earth vibration is at the stillness of an infant.

In the great Fields of Energy of seven,
       the magnetics still abound.
They have vacated their structure and have been re birthed.
The loss of the Field is in the Void,
       the gathering of the Field is in the Void.
Your earth science is beginning to understand.
The velocity forward is dependent
       on the vibration within the Void.
The vibration within the Void has a purpose
       that is connected to all enterings in
       beyond the seven and seven,
       the Light and Dark.
Your earth has a monolithic pole.
Each is not dissimilar to the poles beyond.
They alter all enterings in of all spheres.
Not the smallest of space material can enter in
       to the gravitational pull of earth without being altered.
Heat becomes.
In all corridors of all entering in to all other Fields of Energy
       is there heat attached.
Heat such as earth knows heat to be,
       yet heat beyond what earth knows heat to be.
The reaction was not of gravitation pull, rather that of heat
       and the altering of the actual Lights.
Soul, we speak to you of the transference of Energy
       that will take you unto worlds beyond your own.
It is not complicated as your earth science deems it to be.
When they see the simplicity of the change they are seeking
       they will find themselves laughing one with the other.
For truly it has a simplicity that is a mere child's
       for it is in the numbers one to ten.
You need seek no farther,
       you need to delineate with no other strengths.
There is a great variance within the Zero.
It is always before rather than behind.
It is caught in deference to the lack of strength
       rather than the strength.
For you are in a web.
But you are well into the web.
You do not go farther out from the web.
You move back into the web,

wherein the strengths diminish.
This is fault the young scientist makes.
There is a surge of power in diminishing.
It allows implosion to enter in.
It creates momentum in the Energy you are.
It diversifies from the strength of Sound,
    not sound such as you understand sound to be.
The misconception is in the word, sound.
It must be valuable to Sound and Colour.
Its strength must be endowed with a colour coordinate.
Its value would be seen in the strength of the combination,
    when you understand
        to leave your earth is to relinquish the flesh.
The projection point is the consciousness of being.
The relevance is the arc through which sound develops colour.
The variance is always in the minus.
The pressure from whence a Soul travels,
    to the pressure placed upon the body of the Soul
    is relevant to travel.
A time traveller must relegate from their being
    that which is causal.
If they do not, they too could send forth implosion
    and reverse the blood or heart to great damage.
Each Soul is strengthened
    to withstand the backward flush of Energy.
There is a continuity in the great folds of Energy.
There is a forward thrust of a body through a pivotal point
    wherein they are lost and found and lost and found.
It is always the caught that brings the human to their Humanity.
It is only with great experience that a Soul may travel
    through earth time two dimensions of pivotal directives
    and upon each Energy plane
    the Souls must be willing to receive.
It is a great announcement at the coming forth
    of a Soul into any existence.
It is an Energy that must be committed to enter in.
There is, Soul, a vacuous state in the travel of Energy.
There is a great constitution of reversal where the form
    in which the denouncement of flesh is recognized,
    that the attributes of flesh are deceived.

1143 Souls of earth, breathe forth.
Breathe forth, Soul, and know as you breathe
     the breath that is in you is in all Energy.
You carry within you the motion of Energy.
You have within you the power to move forward.
It is the breath that gives you this power.
It is Breath that is in all existence.
It is Breath that carries the motion of positive and negative.
Souls, respond in your being to breath.
It is to move your body, invigorate your body.
It is, Soul, to allow the breath itself of Energy
     to move through the mind
     for without the breath,
     the mind would have no motion.
You are exquisite in your being.
You have strident energies in you that offer potentials of being.
Souls of earth, transfigure the form that you have with breath.
Without the breath it is not transfigured.
Transfigure the motion you have
     to lift your being unto where we are
     and know that you have infinite power
     to move the Energy of your being far
     into the earth; great responses.
Lift, Soul, all that you are
     and know your being to respond to the lift
     and you will gather your knowing into the place
     unto which you have lifted yourself
     and the beings there will respond to you.
They will speak.
You will know their words.
You will feel their Energy.
You are, Souls, not caught in a web.
You are part of the very web.
You may implode through the web
     unto different Domes of Energy
     and as you lift your Energy
     you enter in to different knowings.
Souls of earth respond in all manner unto you.
You feel the vibrance of that Energy.
You know you are not caught.
As you lift your being the Light around you expands,

       magnifies, and you become empowered as a capsule.
You are lifted and you are shown wonders, energies
       and you see worlds expanding before you.
You are taken unto the Souls of Gummeria;
       the Pleiades, the Lemurians, Lantosia,
         unto the red planet, unto the reptilian worlds.
You have the ability to seek and know all manner of places.
You are caught in your time
       but you can escape time and space.
You have the power to lift beyond time and space.
There is no needle to burst the bubble
       that you would fall unto earth.
Indeed, not!
You are safely encapsulated
       within the Energy of your own being.
It is you, the Energy of your being that lifts,
       from one Energy form to another.
You see the magnificence of who you are.
You see that your minuscule form
       is not, beside those beings of Purity.
You will hear the echo of the Angels.
You will hear the bounty of words from Humanity itself
       that they might send forth unto earth
         for all beings are Farside, have a registry in earth.
Seek the name of your being
       and find that it translates into many forms of name.
Take your name and translate
       and you will find you know who you have been.
Souls of earth, experience the wonder of that which you are.
Understand the reincarnations of life
       you have entered in to are registered.
You can find their form.
You can know the life you have lived.
You can return to earth and see the registry.
You can return to earth and see the headstone
       wherein you lie in the form of dust.
And yet it would be a waste unto you for life is onward.
It is, Soul, not in the looking back.
It is not in the moving forward.
It is in the balance of now.
It is in the hold that you have in the now

      that can take you to the forward and the back.
It is the mind that can reach in to the high mind
      that takes you unto all knowledge.
You may see, Soul, Creator's Masterpiece.
You may see the glory of that which was,
      of that which is and that which will be.
You can see your own countenance upon the Masterpiece
      that of all that you have and have been,
      all that you will be,
          yet not in colour for it has not yet become.
Colour and Sound are the magnification of deed.
Understand this, Soul.

1144   We remind you of the fence.
It is belonging to all.
We have no ownership,
      only in your world do you have ownership.
Other worlds do not have ownership.
It is a concept created upon earth.
Many beings own forms, own concepts,
      but own in the sense that is there for them,
      not theirs.
Your concept of tribe is more akin to that which we own.
While you are there, it is yours.
There would be no battle to prevent you from holding it,
      should somebody else decide.
The concept is divisible.
Everything splits as an atom splits.
You have, but just to, you would use the word conjure.
We do not form idea, want, in a different concept again,
      than your want.
We have no need but in many worlds there is want.
And as the artist forms with the brush
      the beauty on the canvas,
          so the mind forms that which is desired.
It is visible upon the panorama of all that is.
And yet, it is not significantly within the Akashic Record
      unless it alters in some way
      that which is of all Farside.
Upon your earth within the hearing of humanity,
      all that is heard alters humanity.

All that is seen alters humanity.
It is not so within the extensions of Farside, not limits,
        extensions of Farside.
Souls can only program form,
        as we give you the terminology,
        so that you can understand.
Within the level of their Purity upon Farside
        everything is equated
        to the level of Purity the Soul has reached.
There is the Path of Creator,
        but without the Path of Creator
        there are worlds and worlds and worlds.
These also formed, created, brought to be by creators,
        in the same small sense within these worlds
        much is created by those within the worlds.
There is no pain.
There is only sound as you understand Sound and Colour,
        as you understand colour, yet glorified, Soul,
        beyond which you could endure,
        for your entire being would decimate.
The tomes of Purity would be
        as the prism or the chalice disintegrating.
You are the prism.
You are colour.
You are a sound.
You are created by your Creator.
You are brought forth with Truth
        and choice is the platform upon which you enter in.
You are great in your endurance.
Hold to the colour and the sound of beauty.
Hold to the colour and sound of despair.
And see that which is different
        and know that you can alter one with the other.
You can arrive a great colour over a human being,
        encircle the Soul with the goodness of that colour.
And they will calm in their being
        and sleep as the tiny babe sleeps.
Use the Energy of colour.
Sleep upon your pillow with the Energy of colour.

1145   There are many who would speak

and we would have you hear
that which they would speak to you of.
There are many who rest their hands upon your shoulders,
as the light touch that was human.
They guide you gently from or to upon the Path.
You will feel that nudge,
and you will question the nudge you receive.
Follow the nudge, Soul.
There is a great need upon your earth
to be upon your knees and pray to your God.
and it is for those who feel the need we say to you,
"*Those who stand, those who lay, those who sit,
they also have a closeness to Creator.*
Male and female alike bow, sit, stand, lay.
In whatever form you address your Creator,
we ask that you hold to the poignant point
that of reaching the Ecstasy of your Creator.
For your mind is centred on the goodness of your Creator.
Many earth beings
see their Creator in one guise or another.
And we say to you from upon Farside,
Creator has one appearance, not guise,
that of Love, that of such radiant Love
that the Light shining is Ecstasy.
Indeed, prostrate thyself if it be thy will.
But if you may not, if you cannot,
you are no less far from God.
You are as close as all beings.
For your Creator is ever a portion of thy being.
The Essence of whom you are is connected
in all manner unto your being.
From the Essence comes the Path that is unto Creator.
Be in the space of directing your Energy
unto the goodness from which you have come.
But do not, Soul, be pious in your action.
Do not spend all your hours of your days
reaping award in heaven above.
But know it is the act of the human
that overcomes negativity.
That is the obvious.
That is the direct action that carries momentum.

Be in a safe understanding that no two people
> can form a greater appreciation
> of Creator than one.
It takes, Soul, only one to bring many beings to safety.
It takes only one Soul to re direct negativity.

1146   Soul, all Archangels are Archangels.
Many have entered in to specific existences
> and have become
> > within those existences Archangels
> > within the land you would say, of their entering in.
Some Archangels forward their Energy
> and become Angel,
> > even Farside being, even human.
They do not cease then to be Archangel.
They have merely forwarded forth their Energy.
They have reflected their energies forward,
> to take a different form.
There are Energy Fields beyond your comprehension
These Energy Fields are forwarded of Archangel.
Soul, Archangels have always had
> the dispensation of Creator.
Always time on earth.
Upon Farside it is timeless Time.
Beyond that which is Farside
> is the dispensation of Timelessness
> that is held in the Arms of Creator Energy,
> the enthralling companion of Being.
There is for lesser Angelic heraldry,
> a separating, so that chaos does not enter in.
It is even upon Farside that the Angels
> do not pass within the Hallowed Halls
> of the Place of Shining.
They stand as guardians of the sacredness of Creator.
Not, Soul, to withhold,
> for none without the sacredness could enter in.
But to embrace of those who would enter, but cannot.
There is a great Purity.
The Purity is expansive in that it reaches far,
> even into your space.
It is a truth that Purity would reach higher energies,

        but the surety of that Purity
        must first be embraced to its fullest
        before Ecstasy is possible.

1147 We would have you behold
        the discernment of Light and dark.
We would have you glory in the Light
        and recognize self in the dark.
For you have no fear when you recognize self in the dark.
When you see self as Light you ignite the dark,
        the dark place ceases to be.
When you use the Energy of whom you are,
        to breathe Light into the darkness,
        you still chaotic Souls.
They hold to your goodness and mercy.
Breathe, Souls, breathe well and deep
        and recognize breath can eradicate Light,
        for many ways breath eradicates Light
        when it is chaotic breath.
Allow your breath, Energy.
Allow the calmness of being
        that will erase tension in thy body, in thy mind.
For behold you have within you the Sireen Sound.
You have the endeavour within your breath
        to give forth and heal.
Send your Energy outward from whom you are.
And as you do,
        you send into your atmosphere particles of self
        that will reach unto where you would have it reach,
        that will touch and still the troubled Soul,
        that will calm the flame of the fire,
        that will still the waters that pour coldly upon Souls.
Alleviate the stress of their being.
Bring forth sound.
Bring forth the pealing of the bell,
        for it awakens humanity
        to the sound outward from their being.
Be in the place of chime.
Be in the place that holds in thy being the counter to noise.
Noise is not considered sound upon Farside.
It does not exist

for there is no sound that is not welcome.
There is no crescendo too hard for the ear.
There is no minute chord that triangulates outward.
It is not heard.
In the deafening roar of man's inhumanity to man,
    it is the clarity of sound, of perfection that is heard.
All else upon earth is but din, simply din,
    useless if not overcome.
What deafens humanity
    to what the possibility of Volume can be.
Understand the vibration of words,
    of chords, of sounds within your earth,
        and vibrate, Soul, to the sound of goodness.
Vibrate, Soul, to the fulfilling of need.
Inhabit thy form
    for the glory of hearing that which is positive.
For unto earth you have come,
    that you might overcome all that is negative.
Hold the sour note
    and lift it high that it might be clarified
    and scarified and brought home.

1148 Souls, within the power of Energy is a great scope.
It is not limited to your thinking.
It is not limited to our/your earth.
It is not limited to the Farside.
It carries, Soul, the consciousness of all Energy
    way beyond which you can conceptualize as thought.
For thought is not simplicity.
And yet thought can be the most simple.
Within the great Void are complexities
    that you have neither visaged or contemplated.
They are, Soul, even beyond that which you could contemplate.
They have great blocks of chaos
    so that they fold one upon the other.
They fold in their complexities
    so that the very Void is not a single structure outward.
It is not a structure, Soul.
It is structureless.
"*How can that be?*", you say?
We say to you, "*There is far more complexity*

beyond which we can express to you that which is."
Even, Soul, in the Humanity that you are upon Farside,
    there is a complexity beyond your knowing
        that you have not beheld.
There is, Soul, a diverse Energy.
It holds a part.
It fixates on separation.
It is held within the very folds that are gathered.
Within all energy is chaos.
Within all folds of energy is separation.
You have brought forth
    a great commiseration of thoughtless energy.
It bestows upon you the folds of separation.
It is why you are in the negative violence that you are in.
Your earth is caught in the separation of consciousness.
"*What is this separation?*", you say.
You have upon your earth that which you call repellent.
You have within the iota, the ion, a repellent.
It is caught in chaos.
It is known throughout the throng of the Archangels.
It is known by them.
The Angels know of this separation;
    that all Energy within the Yawn
        is not conscious of this separation,
        for within the Yawn there is no Chaos.
Within the Yawn there is no separation of consciousness.
Do you comprehend that which we say?
You know upon our earth, there are great complications
    of the divergence of thought.
You behold another's thought and immediately you evaluate it
    according to your own premise and separation begins.
Upon Farside thought, consciousness,
    does not have this separation.
Separation is known within the Void as fold.
This is, Soul, a dimension.
The dimension is in the consciousness of all Energy of creativity.
It withholds chaos from entering in by holding it
    within a fold of Energy.
It is called survival.
You still do not have the key to contemplate
    that which we say and we will give you a key.

The key is in echo.
The key is in value.
The key is in sublimation of thought.
We continue.
In the great vast Energy
    beyond where you have even thought to be,
    in the great expanse of energies
    even beyond your own dimension,
    the parallel dimension reigns.
It has set a form forth to preclude chaos.
Not being caught as negativity but being melded
    from one plane to the other.
It is imperative that each step forward
    enables all energy within the Void
    to encapsulate chaos
    with the possibility of rendering it immobile
    until the solution to Negativity is complete.
Do you comprehend the magnitude
    that the Soul has allowed,
    that the Spirit of whom you are has allowed,
    that the Essence connected to your Creator
    has allowed that a portion of whom you are,
    the Energy, can be enfolded to become immobile.
Only within the fold does the Energy have possibility
    to meld unto a completeness.
Now we say to you. "*Transition is a fold.*"
It holds within chaos.
So it has been through all energy fields."
Energies have left chaos in folds.
Your science is well aware of the folds of energy.
They do not understand the entrapment within.
They do not understand the consciousness that is involved
    in holding chaos impaired, lacking, as it were inert.
Now you understand.
You have been shown by those who have chosen
    not to accept positives upon your earth
    an entrapment of their own energy within a fold.
It has not been forced upon them, Soul.
They just cannot move forward with the energy
    in the negative, in chaos.
It is not possible.

Far beyond your known heavens,
> your known consciousness beyond Life and Death;
> beyond the Vanguard of the Fourteen Creators,
> beyond the Voice unto all Energy
> even unto your Supreme Being are captive folds.

It is, Soul, precautionary in that there has been no solution.
There is a great, for your earth's understanding, puzzle
> made forth within the energy.

It is how to meld negativity?
The solution has a greater understanding
> because of your investment as humanity
> upon our earth into negativity.

You have brought forth a wisdom that has been lacked.
It is, Soul, to allow the negative to be touched,
> to be altered by the energies
> but not in the manner that was done by the Creators
> but in a more blessed concept,
> a gathering of negativity unto Purity,
> a gathering of negativity unto Truth,
> a gathering of negativity of Love,
> a complete compassion.

Soul, consciousness is in Energy.
It is in all Energy.
It is that consciousness that will give the creatures of the sea
> buoyancy to hold a humanity from drowning.

It is the same consciousness
> that will allow the lion and the lamb
> to lay without detriment one to the other.

Souls of earth, you have gathered so completely
> the negativity unto you and we beseech you,
> now that you have learned so well
> to gather your negativity,
> do not enter in to a fold
> but see that which is before you
> that it has not brought oneness.

The reaching out of compassion brings oneness.
The Love, one to another, brings Love.
The acceptance of one to another brings Truth.
Souls of earth, as Purity entered in,
> gather the Light unto you and behold that which you are.

You are of your Creator.

Enter in to a fold to bring forth that which is negative.
Do not enter in to a fold to join that which is negative.

1149   Soul, we speak of Light Fields beyond where you are;
        fourth, fifth, sixth, seventh,
          energies into the distant cosmos,
          galaxy, ethereal earths, inhabited earths,
        not unlike whom you are.
You could identify these beings as of humanity.
For they have similar structure in their being,
        of course many differences.
          but in the counterpane are those differences,
        in the skeleton being great similarities.
There are Souls where the nose is closed.
It is closed and has a single hole.
This being can be deeply into, you would call it,
        ammonia water, sharp.
You could not abide it.
It would eat at your flesh.
Yet that flesh it does not mark.
The intellect of these beings are far advanced to your own.
There are many such worlds.
There are Souls who soar.
They are not caught in any way
        by the proximation of their earth
        but they may travel from one world to the other.
You on Farside have this ability.
You travel with no difficulty through the Void.
These Souls are not landed as you are landed.
They are not caught in a need to ground.
There are worlds of beings very similar to your horse.
These beings have great gentleness in them.
They live in a green plain with springs of water.
Your world is closest to Lantosia.
Next is the place of these beings.
It is one of the first recognitions of life that you will know.
The animals are equivalent to the size of a cat.
They flourish in their Energy.
Not all worlds replicate, Soul.
Approximately, twenty six percent of worlds
        multiply their Energy.

Other worlds hold a populous
        and live with contentment within that populous.
There is a great disappointment in store for the humanity
        who sees the indulgence of replicated earth self
        in utopia a feasting and love.
The love they speak is carnal to the Purity
        of the world they will enter
        and the feasting is more often
        the feasting of the mind of consciousness.
The Purity of the Soul
        would not permit the indulgence of self.
For it has no purpose other than to sate the being.

1150   The Souls of our destiny are at level five.
It is, Soul, a world of believers of Energy.
Each facet is tentacled one to the other.
Each Energy is forged in altruistic manner.
It is a great thorn forward.
It is known throughout the many worlds of Farside.
We are, Soul, the transport of humanity unto the sixth level.
You are astounded that you may speak to our Energy
        and we say to you
        we have the ability to speak in many tongues.
Our form will carry forward into the Fields of Purity
        those beings who wish,
        wish, Soul, to be transported forth.
For the Energy is not fear in them.
It is comfort, the comfort of Energy
        that knows wherein they will travel
        for each dimension has many variations
        and each is registered with us.
Our Purity allows us to transport into the sixth.
We may maintain ourselves in it
        but we have relegated our Energy to five.
It is not a gift to Creator, but rather a gift unto mankind.
For have they not bravely altered their being to enter in to earth!
Have they not taken on an unrecognizable shape
        from the energies they are
        to become vulnerable in the earth vale of negativity.
There is an abounding traffic of Energy by humanity unto six.
And we say this to you, Souls of earth, "*Rejoice.*"

Rejoice, for you have found yourselves
       to be exceeding in Truth,
       yet you falter.
And those who find their Energy carried by us
       whisper in our ear
       of that which humanity declines to see.
They speak of the great pain
       from which they have been delivered
       and the encounters they have had in the overcoming.
They have drawn a canvas for us to see of deliverance.
And the Soul who enters in is drawing tears in their being
       as they see the vast darkness
       that boils within the earth's belly
       and the gravital pull of the sun
       drawing clusters of energy
       to ignite all facets of earth.
There is, Soul, a great testimony spoken by our travellers.
They would see earth time cease to be.
For in the ceasing of time would the Timeless Energy
       recourse itself through their being
       and the Holy time of healing
       take place upon the earth
       and all that is held in the darkness.
Wretched is the Soul of earth
       that is caught in the circular coming and going,
       wherein no gain is found.
All that is Holy bends itself to lift these Souls.
We would have you know of the Blessed Angels
       who gather unto mankind
       that they might fall into their arms
       but we would have you not fall.
We would have you learn
       that you have reached the ultimate step!
You have reached the place of five two.
You may relinquish your hold upon earth!
You may gather yourselves in oneness
       and pray in words of self attribute.
This we have done, you and I!
We have overcome that which is negative.
We Love that which is our fellow man
       and we give of our being unto all humanity.

As we cross from five to the sixth plane,
    there is no deference to colour or creed.
There is no language
    but the language of the Creator, the Truth of mankind.
Behold the violet rays are upon you.
The beams project from the Energy of holiness
    and you are bound by the entering in
    that you will enter out.
Be caught in the text of holiness.
Be not heard in the allegory of sin.
For sin is an opportunity to overcome
    and enter in to the holiness.
Sin is that which is coupled with compassion
    wherein you might hold the Energy fast in your being.
Venture to where we are
    for we would give you the opportunity of transport.

1151 Souls of earth, understand spiral, the spiral of being.
In all Energy is the spiral of being.
In all Energy, negative and positive is the spiral of being.
Negativity, Soul, is not apart from whom you are.
For as you hold negativity,
    you gather it unto the spiral of being.
The Angels have placed care.
It may not spiral farther than the curtain of care.
Thought that it is negative
    cannot take itself beyond the curtain of care.
Your being would not allow
    the consciousness of the high mind to gather it so.
In all Energy is the spiral forward,
    is the spiral downward
    in all Energy unto fifth level.
Beyond fifth level upward unto the Energy of Creators,
    does the spiral hold only wilful.
Not as in your earth wilful, full of negative will,
    but wilful, in intended forward, willed forward.
This is done by energies upon your world
    upon Farside in the Place of Shining
    and Archangels carry it thus forward.
It is done unto the place of SEE.
Unto the space of SEE a spiral ends and a new begins.

It is the gathering point of all upward Energy.
It collects.
It is your world word, interred, within SEE.
The spiral is conveyance for Energy.
It has a motion unto itself, as music has a motion unto itself.
Spiral listens, seeks, positions all Energy.
Spiral has the positive power
        to interfere with the projected placement.
It has the power to re create within the Energy
        an opposite momentum.
It may refute entry in to levels.
There is the confounding curiosity of Negativity.
It has been free to wander unto great portions of the Void.
It is not known to what detriment Negativity may have held
        within the loss of Idyllic.
There is an absolute in the spiral.
The absolute upward is perfection.
Without perfection,
        it does not allow past fifth.
Upon Farside it would seem
        that there would be total perfection.
This is that for which humanity has based its afterlife upon.
And we say to you,
        your heaven is as your earth.
It is as affected by that which will be as your earth.
Cataclysmic occurrence
        affects the placement within the spiral of Energy.
Energy, your flesh, your blood, your words even,
        cannot enter in to the spiral of being in a negative way
        and thrust unto your Creator.
They would not travel so.
For the curtain of care placed by the Blessed
        would prevent them from going forward.
No negativity may fly forth from the negative ion.
Yet in the Void of Positive Ion, there are worlds caught
        in the downward spiral of Energy matter.
Matter is affected by the breath that pushes it forward.
Worlds and worlds and worlds are threatened
        and you see your world as threatened.
Yet existence itself has been formed to alter
        the downward plunge of chaos.

Chaos does not tremble in the power of good.
Chaos does not.
It sees the power of good as only that which is alterable.
Alterable, Soul, not in reaching up to alter
      but in the wilful downward plunge of Energy.
There is, Souls of earth, a coordinate mastered,
      not by longitude and latitude
      but by Domes, the twelve by fourteen.
The key to the senseless downward plunge of universes
      is in the web of Domes.
Your world is mastering well the dynamics of travel.
Your world is even understanding the fold of the universe.
It is in the fold of the web that perfection will be.
We speak to your science, we speak to Grey,
      to understand the fold,
      must be to understand
      the corner of the labyrinth.
There is a calmness upon the seas of Energy.
It is Soul, the awaiting.
It is the awakening.
It is the New Day.
There is a clear transformation
      that will occur in the hearts of mankind.
They will find themselves delineated
      between those who lift their hearts unto Creator
      and those who see only the ego of their being.
There will be in the heavens above, clattering.
We say this, Soul, that you might recognize sound
      as in a great hammer sent forth
      and you will hear the resonation of the echo.
It will be heard three times for all of earth.
Earth will cry out,
      "*It is the rumbling of earth itself.*".
      It is the sun awaiting to implode.
      It is the ring of the outer planets
            falling way one from the other."
In truth, Soul, it will be the Energy of a great world
      entering in unto your sphere.
You will be seeing the outline as a shadow
      upon your earth in your daytime hours.
It will be carried well within your vision.

It is not, Soul, entering downward upon earth
      but entering upward from the fifth level Light.
Indeed!
It will be the grappling of goodness
      for Idyllic will be heard.
There is a grasping of magnetism
      that will create a great bombardment of ions to repel,
      creating a sky unknown to man.
For man will see from below.
As earth rotates it will change.
Souls, the radiant effect of a great arch
      that will take itself even unto Uranus.
It will be seen Soul, in the shadow of earth's second planet.

1152   We will speak of voice, of the Energy of voice.
Voice sends out
      but from the sending out, there is a return of Energy.
It is entirely dependent on the form the outcast is given.
If it is given in a positive, it enters in to be used within the form.
If it is sent as a negative, it creates a blight upon the Soul.
As the leaf receives a blight
      so does the human receive a blight from the voice.
It is sent forth with intent.
What is the intent in the sending forth?
This is the query of all worlds.
Voice in sending forth had intent.
Prior to intent is awareness.
Of what was Voice aware?
We know of Voice.
We know of intent.
We know awareness is prior to intent.
What we do not know is what occurred.
Upon what did the blight occur?
We had not known, Soul,
      now we know.
For in you, you have resolved the answer.
It is in Matter.
It created a blight in Matter.
Matter which was perfect is not perfect.
In the Energy as it is sent forth, it holds chaos.
In every form,

all universes, of all energies, of all existence,
   it is sent forth and blight occurs, chaos.
You who are human, you are resolving to create perfection.
You do this for MATTER, not the matter of your being,
   for MATTER of the beginning where no beginning is.
How congruous to make such a statement,
   yet it is so, as you will find it to be.
Soul, in all Energy there is arc.
It is why the ark of the covenant,
   the arc of Creator, the arc of all scientific energy.
There is no straight line that is not arced from distance.
There is no negative that does not have a positive Energy.
There is a voice that does not carry a vacancy,
   it requires thrust to make the voice project.
Breath, Soul, breath and voice connected.
It is Energy breath, voice.
In all paths of Energy is a projection of voice necessary.
Everything upon your earth has a voice.
Even the rock speaks, has a sound.
Your ear may not hear the decibel, yet the rock carries sound.
Within the water the sound is carried.
But water itself has sound.
It is carried by the breath of motion.
It is drawn unto itself to sigh and breathe, and sigh and breathe.
You, of earth, you have breath
   that allows the voice to take motion.
And yet often in your being
   you hold your voice from entering forth,
      for you fear.
You fear it will affect the matter of your being.
You hold the eye closed
   that you may not have to see the great vision within.
For it would require
   that you let go of earth matter, material matter.
Behold, you are the greatest of beings.
You carry the highest form of Energy
   with the greatest translucence.
You carry the Zero in your being.
The one is a straight line.
The Zero contains four arcs, triad and base.
Understand this.

You are a prism of all prism
> and your Energy is held above all energies
> and you see in your being yourself as no thing.

Yet you are all in all,
> for you carry credence to all Energy questions.

For the credence holds the answer possibility.
We would have you not see yourself
> as speaking outward from you in a straight line.

We would have you see yourself arcing your voice.
For in the arcing of the voice is a projection that affects others.
You contain within your being a balance,
> the chi, the very Energy of your Creator.

Understand the purpose
> of looking at matter is to balance matter;
> of the body is balance, of the mind is balance.

This brings to you perfection.
Study the arc, for even your world is arced.
All Domes are arced.
This we would have you know.
So be it.

1153 Souls of earth, contemplate well on that
> which you enter in to,
> for there are two doors to all entering.

There is the entering in of purpose in positive.
There is the entering in of negative.
Soul, one cannot be done without Truth.
With Truth you must enter through with purpose.
With Truth you must enter through all transoms.
There is a variation to gateways.
Many gateways have growth.
Many gateways have release.
Many gateways have Purity.
Many extend unto Ecstasy.
Know that you have the power to enter through all gateways.
You have the power to see, to behold that which is.
You may see, Soul, the very Angels.
You may behold the Circle of Saints.
You may behold the Hem of your Creator.
You may behold the Archangel.
That which is far from you

    that you may not behold is Supreme Being.
You have not entered through unto Supreme Being,
    only those who entered in the doorway with Creator.
You have not.
You entered through from the Love of Second Creator.
You are, Soul, from a realm beyond.
We teach you of these realms.
We teach you that all has a single purpose,
    that to bring unto Creator's Energy,
    negativity that will within itself
    give an understanding unto chaos,
    which will, Soul,
    translate itself to the understanding of many worlds.
It will, Soul, give reason to life and death.
It will behold the starry Realm,
    Idyllic and the seven worlds.
You will see, for you are the tail, the one left behind.
You are the distant and yet you are closest to Creator.
Souls of earth, there is a great strength
    in the acceptance of who you are.
There is a great strength, Soul,
    that you recognize that you are Angel value.
Value even unto Archangel.
There are many Fields within the realms of Love.
There are many Fields beyond the Domes of your existence.
You have, Soul, fourteen fields.
You have twelve elevations.
You have beyond each Dome, imploding Domes,
    so that you are distant in the darkness of Light.
You behold that you are within Light
    for you have your stars and you have your moon.
You have your understanding that your day enters in
    and your night time falls.
But that is not the reality, that is your illusion.
You are caught in a balance of positive and negative.
You are each at war with that which you are.
Beyond your realm are worlds from the Creator
    who formed your being,
    not as human, but as Angel self.
You have within the Realm of Second Creator
    a potential of awareness.

You have echo.
You have value.
These, Soul, are continuous strengths within your being.
Were you not to have the ability to echo,
> you could not send forth with the Truth as you do.

All upon your existence is in continuous numerology.
All is within the sound and the colour.
Your world is constantly fractious.
It is constantly battling the Energy from which it has come.
It is caught as the mote of the eye is caught.
And as you remove the mote from the eye,
> you will see the world as it is.

For the world that is sister will meld and become one.
Numerology, Soul, is simplistic upon earth,
> for within the Realm of your Second Creator
> > Negativity is known.

Negativity is felt.
Negativity has been made aware of.
They have within the realm of Second Creator
> their own research.

You upon earth, you delve in negativity.
They delve in research.
Many have entered in through the folds unto that research.
Now you see, one is of one, but each has its own component.
Love is not an equation in the Realm of Second Creator.
All that is nuance, all that is fractious,
> all that is windowed, this is visible.

They see that which you do not see.
They see that which Farside does not see.
There is a continuous fellowship of being.
We say this, so that you understand
> how you have managed upon earth to willfully
> manipulate the Truth, the awareness,
> and created forms to work together
> that do not produce understanding.

We speak of your temples.
We speak of your synagogues.
We speak of your churches.
We speak of that which was not intent.
The messengers each gave a message.
Each of the Four, Mohammed, Buddha, Krishna, Jesu,

   each gave forth messages.
Earth, you use them to convolute the Truth.
We ask you to re enter the equation.
We ask you to re verbalize the words spoken,
   the words given, the actions of the messenger.
Souls of earth, bow down to no man.
Bow down to no deity.
For deities do not require the bended knee.
Deities require Truth.
Deities require understanding.
Deities require Love given.
Deities, Soul, require Purity.

1154 How can you, humanity,
   understand that which your Creator
   has set upon your earth?
How can you understand the complicated
   interweaving of all creature upon your earth.
You may see, Soul, the most insignificant iota
   that has within it a complicated measure
   you could not fathom.
Yet your Creator has created this complexity within the iota.
Such complexity is carried into all existence beyond your own.
The measure of twelve by fourteen is simplicity for your mind,
   but within each weave of the twelve and fourteen
   are existences of trillion, zillion
   in your verbalization of complexities.
Your earth being is the most simple of all existences.
You and our being have existed upon your earth
   to fulfill that which has been agreed
   by whom we are upon earth.
Yet you are so much more and you see it not.
You do not see the Light within your self
   for your Light has been dimmed.
Upon Farside you radiate in your glory
   and even then you have not
   entered in to the ecstasy of the greatness of your being.
There are upon all existence a threshold, a entering in.
The entering in is through a fourteen by twelve.
That fourteen by twelve is measured
   and carried within each measure of the weave

    from the original original.
Twelve by fourteen, placed and held and held,
    are the complications of many twelve by fourteen.
The fourteen divided by Light and Dark,
    the twelve divided by possibilities of existence.
In each existence is a need
    and the need carries the existence
    through seven levels of being.
Each existence is carried
    by one hierarchy of being
    that you might attain the possibility of all that is.
That you might reach that perfect being.

1155 Humanity, blessed humanity.
Hear that which you are.
Souls of earth, you are mightier than we.
You hold within you possibilities we of Farside do not.
Indeed, of all energies you have a uniqueness.
You and we are perfection in that perfect place of Energy.
There is a perfect realm wherein Light is not darkened
    and darkness has no need to be lit.
It is a place of equality.
It is of genuine joy, but that
    is the world beyond ours, is it not!
We are the reflected unto, as you are.
We are the Souls forwarding our Energy
    that we might overcome Chaos
    and yet it was not to be
    and so we look unto you, you who are human.
All existences beyond your own have knowledge.
They are not dependent on the knowledge, Soul.
It is.
It is a portion of their being.
You may embrace that knowledge in any given request
    but you, you do not have that knowledge.
You have access
    but you do not access.
You have minute portion of that knowledge.
It is given and grows as you attain
    the fullness of gathering from your own species
    and they have gathered before you

    and placed in tomes the knowledge.
It is written in stone, Soul.
In your world as it is,
    it is placed within Energy
    yet it has always been placed within Energy.
It is a portion of Energy itself.
But you, you who are humanity,
    you carry something in your being we do not.
We accept.
We energize our being with Purity.
We accept that which is.
It is joyful.
It is a portion of gladness.
But you, you carry within you a portion of Negativity.
It is the curiosity.
It is rampant in your being.
It is why you are where you are.
It is that portion of Negativity
    within the very seed of your being.
It has the attribute of curiosity.
It gathers research.
You have taught us, Soul.
We research through you,
    heavens upon heavens all accepting,
    not challenging, accepting.
But you, you have a portion of wisdom in you
    for you have thought, contemplated.
You have not simply accepted.
You have diligently researched, tabulated, experimented,
    not always in goodness.
And yet, it is ongoing, always contending with past truths.
We glorify in your ability and we learn to be curious.
For us it is experimental.
It is set apart.
It is new.
It is not a challenge for us to have before us
    an empty canvas and a pallet of colours.
We know colour.
We know sound.
It is but to place upon the canvas that which we know.
Humanity too does this.

They gather from the Purity of their Energy to place.
It is not an experiment with us.
With you, Soul, you challenge.
You challenge even the concepts
      to portray something within the form
      that we have not extended our thought to,
      for we are content.
It is not without desire.
There is no need for desire.
It is blessed contentment to bring forth
      that which within our being we see.
It is done.
It is satisfaction but not experimental.
But you, you have brought a further concept
      to question, to be curious.
You have all the attributes of Creator within your being.
You do this, Soul, in the place of Creator's Energy
      and you find yourself a simple being
      being conceptual in all things.
There is a parallel universe.
You are party to it.
And yet it does not hold all within that you have created.
You are creators unto yourself.
Much of that which you create is discordant.
It carries deep wounds within the fibres of the human nature
      but much that is done in the name of humanity
      is the gathering beyond that which is known.
It is, Soul, that which you do.
You are recreating on a daily basis within your being a need.
On a daily basis you fulfil the need.
You do it in all aspects of your existence
      whether you are a single one or united.
You force issues to the breaking point.
You define each and every linear and vertical.
Your knowledge is expanding
      and your voice outward from your being.
You place it, Soul, in tones,
      in Energy that we might receive
      and you do this without prompting.
We have not exerted upon you any expectation.
You have offered it out freely from your being, we tell you.

In the place of perfection there is the need
        to protect that protection might be.
It is necessary tto reach outside of that perfection
        and establish a known.
Chaotic energies exist in the possibilities of cohesive meeting.
It would expand and decimate tranquillity.
It would alter the thread of perfection.
That which is done is done to prevent.
You are the experimentation.
We do not say this to bring you
        to sadness, to anger, to gratitude.
We do not say this to forbear you from moving forward.
We say that you are the warriors
        who have dared to enter in to the unknown.
You have been, Soul, resounding in your fortitude
        in all forms of Energy you have taken.
Yet the human is the most precious
        for it is stepped apart from Purity to gather truth.
Eons of existence in the darkness of the ion negative,
        you have collaborated with each other
        to overcome negativity to bring Light.
You have experimented.
You have pressured.
You have lost battles and won victories.
Each effort has brought you a little more wisdom,
        a further step into experimentation
        of how to preserve perfection.
Souls, we spend energies of Purity, of Love.
We give unto you all that we can and it is not enough
        for it requires that which you do,
        that which you are capable of to exert
        and reach for the unreachable.
Soul, many enter in to earth to be a part of that research.
Purity; you do it, Soul, by gift.
You are not placed.
You place self.
And yet how can the mind of the simple human
        reach to the level of the high mind
        without experimentation?
You do not always take the path of Purity,
        that would be Energy.

Therefore you reach into the unknown
> in all aspects of your being
> and we thank you for it.

There are many fences
> where energies look down upon humanity
> and they see a battle being fought.

1156 We would give you a teaching.
Verticals, linears, grids and waves,
> we would have you understand.

The grids, Soul, are throughout existence, sent forth
> beyond Breath by MATTER.

Within MATTER was always the power to move Energy.
It was beyond all existence
> where only consciousness entered in
> to flow freely through MATTER.

It was as a song sung in great beauty.
It carried a creativity that delineated
> the beautification of all members of consciousness.

It was triangulated through a great fractious chord,
> the cadence of which altered.

In the beginning there was Light and there was Dark,
> and creation saw that which was Light and Dark
> and was pleased as in Life and Death.

Indeed, darkness did draw apart from Light
> that it might see the very beauty of that Light.

The extension is in life itself, but darkness was without Light
> and the extensions of beings within the darkness,
> cried forth,
> *"Where can we be with Light?"*
> *If darkness is with Light,*
> > *it is not dark,*
> > *it loses of itself.*
>
> *If Light is within darkness, it gains.*
> *Do you see!*
> *It is not equal!"*

Equality was lost.
The linears protected the Light and the Dark from each other.
The verticals held within the pain,
> kept the Soul captured.

Energy, all was Energy.

Consciousness, the very first depression,
        the very first wave that overcame.
So grids were set to apportion half, this for this, that for that.
Upon your earth you have linears that reach unto us.
They tell us of the growth within your being.
You share, because you are of us
        that which you are and have achieved.
We see the strength and the weaknesses of your being,
        the verticals you lose to withhold yourself from others
        and you entangle and crate great adversity
        one to the other.
The weave, Soul, is built upon the grid.
It is your Energy that gathers in strength and colour.
It has motion and through your continuity of lives,
        it spews forth that which is held
        and the colour will have a denseness, a red thread.
And then the Purity will be gathered and the gold and the Light;
        oneness will occur and the purple would be threads.
And Creator's Masterpiece is being wrought through you.
You carry in your being
        the depression of the pain of light and dark.
You carry within you your version
        to mingling your Energy with another.
You carry, Soul within you,
        the power to create the Masterpiece that is Creator's.
From Light and Dark, equally the Creators entered in,
        some apportioned to Dark and some to Light.
Willingly to create and resolve wherein they may blend,
        and not lose of each other that which is perfect.
And so you bring forth from your humanity
        the birthing of perfection.
Some have been touched with negativity, a darkness.
Be it illness, be it a portion not blended
        or mind not fully complete.
And they have thrust themself in, for they are the Grey.
They blend to see how the colour will mesh.
And you, you with your worlds of light and dark,
        you create grays,
        even depression within your being,
        when indeed you are blessed.
You are the blessed,

for you have entered in unto earth to teach,
for you gather knowledge
for those who are greater than you.
You are, Soul, less than the Angels.
You are less in that you are so minute,
    you may hardly be seen in your universe
    that depends upon who you are.
Your very universe, Soul, the one you exist in,
    depends on the tranquillity
    that is found within humanity,
    that you can see and be a Light,
    that you can be dark and be whole,
    that you can be a part
    of the Light and dark and blend and be One.
Holy beings, do not be lost in that which you do,
    for you are humanity.
You have reaped havoc upon your world,
    you have devastated that which is beautiful.
Yet you are redeemed within your being.
You are finding Truth that overcomes.
Open yourselves to the Light.
Behold you are Light.
Enter thou into the Darkness that you might be One.

1157 Light and Dark, Souls, Light and Dark.
Bring your being to the awareness of Light and Dark.
There is no coincidence that your earth has light and dark.
Hold your being in the Light
    but be not afraid to enter in to the Dark.
For in the darkness you will find preciousness.
In the darkness you find goodness.
In the darkness you find that which you have come to seek.
Behold Idyllic!
Behold the Purity entered in to the realm of darkness
    through the Light, through the Dark.
How, Souls of earth, will you bring her forth?
How will you bring forth that which is of the greatest Purity?
We say unto you,
    acknowledge there is light and dark in all things
    as there are positives and negatives
    as there is your night and your day,

>   as there is the voracity that gathers
>   when darkness abounds
>   and the tenuous release of this voracity
>   when Light enters forth.

You are, Soul, in the Light.
You are beheld as Light.
You carry your being into darkness
>   that we might see that which is.

You explore in your Energy the cavernous ways.
You drive yourself into depths of darkness
>   and you learn from that darkness that which is Truth.

You overwhelm, for you from your choice
>   overwhelm darkness within your own being
>   and bring forth that spiral of good
>   that is known as humanity's Pillar.

There is a track of great importance
>   that you will be guardian of.

It will, Soul, be through the darkness
>   holding chaos at bay with the power you have gained.

Only within the realm of Purity,
>   the spiral of goodness, has such a path been honoured.

But you will enter in to the Void where chaos can abound.
You will do this to recover Light
>   and bring forth Light of more magnification
>   than is within your own being.

In the united oneness will be the voyage of all voyage.
For you will find your being bombarded
>   but the Oneness that you hold as Humanity,
>   the strength of the armour you have gathered
>   will protect you on your way.

Our being is vulnerable
>   as is the Energy of all beings, vulnerable.

Not vulnerable as you on earth are vulnerable
>   but vulnerable in that there is no returning home,
>   vulnerable in that there is only the outward path.

Can you perceive, Soul, not to look back?
Indeed, Lot's wife looked back.
She looked back at Negativity.
She saw that which was negative and it altered her being.
This is the truth of the Bible's interpretation
>   for it is only in the on going forward

    that chaos does not bombard.
And how is it known,
    with the exception of chaos
    as it bombarded unto Idyllic,
    unto the seven new worlds,
    that which will occur?
Yet this is not singular in its deference to chaos.
For before in the Records Sublime
    is the telling of yet another bombardment.
This bombardment altered the very Breath.
And we say to you,
    "Breath is sacred to the human."
But we say again to you,
    "Breath is sacred unto all beings
      of all existences, in all form."
You have the power of Light and dark.
You have brought your being deep
    into the realms of darkness.
Your world throws its very being into turbulence
    that you might see the vastness of chaos
    and that which chaos can set forth
    in a realm unprotected.
You are illusion.
You are in a state in between.
You are caught in a vacuum as once before all things,
    all things were caught in a vacuum.
And you have the veracity to not adhere to the program
    set before you as humanity.
You have chosen to delve deeper and deeper
    into the throes of Negativity.
It has not been our want that you should be so at risk
    and have we not safeguarded your being
    to uplift you in the ships prepared
    so that total devastation will not annihilate
    the goodness you have within you!
For all is questionable.
Now we say to you,
    your world is in great turmoil
    and people devastated in their being
    brought to the great harshness of their reality.
Yet we do not know wherein

    that devastation would take the world.
For you have set an agenda far from that which was set
    for humanity upon entering in.
You are, Soul, bringing forth the greatness of your being
    in that you have willingly drawn
    an addition into the Path of mankind.
As your world will survive
    and the Thousand Years is your reality,
    that we know.
That your world will recover, that we know.
What we do not know is how to bring forth that which is lost,
    how to draw unto us that which is spiralling
    in an outward flow from where we are,
    that which is beloved of all existence,
    that which is particled of whom you are,
    of whom we are, that which is, Soul,
    the Energy Flow of all existence, Idyllic!
You have prepared a great Path before you.
You have gathered in your wisdom
    a knowledge of right and wrong, of good of evil,
    you have brought forth demons and Angels
    to portray to yourselves that which is the reality
    of Light and dark.
And we say to you, indeed, the Angels are Light.
The demons, Soul, the demons are chaos
    and all that chaos has done to existence,
    unto Breath, unto Ion, unto Matter.
Within the Void of Consciousness is the memory.
Within the Void of Consciousness is the great tribulation
    that set forth such an occurrence to be.
There is an upper chamber,
    there is beyond that which is
    the Voice of Consciousness,
    the tremble of greatness.
It is, Soul, gathered as the vastness of the stars are gathered.
It is not a single component, it is a multiplicity.
It carries the form of Matter.
It is in the Dark.
It has no will.
It carries a form.
You must radically alter the form of ion

        to become that which is matter.
One without the other is lost.
It is not whole.
It is not complete.
When it gives forth a charge, it loses.
It holds a memory in each fragment of being.
Within it is Breath possible.
Within it are all complications of Energy
        co existing with a single exception;
        that component, Soul, is nothing.
Zero, Soul.
You are Zero.
You have calibrated in your science to be one.
You are Zero.
Correction.
You are to find the way
        for that which had all components was Idyllic.
That which was fragmented from energies
        and put to one form, perfection.
And that from which it came,
        the Seven Light, the Seven Dark
        gave of the Energy within.
Recover that which is lost and know that you are not alone
        in the recovery of that which is lost.
Many worlds struggle in their Energy
        to bring to be the perfection once again
        into the space of the Flow
        for it is within the Flow the solution lies.
Is Idyllic outward from the Flow?
We see this to be the probability.
It is as your earth struggles
        when you have lost a piece of your world
        to delve into the sea upon the land
        to find that which is lost
        that you might identify that which occurred.
It is a key, it is a component.
Humanity, your world dabbles in negativity
        and you call out the names of great teachers.
You exhume words of teaching and ignore them
        to ply your negativity and hate one to the other.
And we say to you:

> *"Draw your beings, draw your beings*
> *unto the greatest purpose of mankind,*
> *that of Idyllic.*
> *Recover unto goodness that which is Purity itself."*

Only in your oneness
    can you bring yourself to such perfection
    that you can withstand the Negativity.
We cannot.
We do not know how precious beings
    of such nondescript selves as you, do it.
But we know that you do
    and you bring to the higher level of your Energy.
Souls of earth, batter not your beings.
Withhold not your bread one from the other.
You are your brother's keeper.
Your breath is as one breath.
Your being as one being.
You are more than Purity, Soul.
You are the graciousness of Spirit
    that has entered in unto chaos
    to be bombarded by negativity
    and overcome that bombardment.
But you have antagonized within yourselves
    and we say to you,
    "*You are precious one to the other*!"
You are the Armada.
You are godly in your being.
Holy being you are, Holy unto Holy.
Do not ransom a Soul to negativity.
Do not place dogma as Purity.
Understand the action of the human surpasses all dogma.
The action of the pious
    is a truth of neither dogma or the Armada.
Soul, look to your brother,
    look to the eyes of those you wish ill
    and see you a mirror of yourself,
    of your children and your children's children.

1158   We speak to you of Creators.
We have said there is no God at the point of chaos
    and indeed in your world, within the form of chaos,

the appearance is of no God.
Yet stand briefly, even momentarily outside of the chaos,
    and Creator is revealed unto you.
Your Creator is within your world,
    with the Energy of being.
You have but to seek the Energy
    to combat, to still thy mind.
In the greatest fear there is calm with the touch of Creator.
Your Creator is within the Yawn.
Unto all as hierarchy,
    most powerful one, Great One, Godhead.
Without the Yawn, there are equal Creators
    anticipating in the outward reach unto perfection
    to gather in stillness into the veracity of Energy
    that will not be calmed.
It is within the reach of all Creators to be the single hierarchy
    but there is no desire
    for they are equal one to the other,
    yet differ in that which they offer.
As one, united, they are Supreme Being.
They are one in the expansiveness of consciousness.
They have within no internal bleed.
They have no outward thrust,
    for they are contained by the Void of Consciousness
    preventing the chaotic intrusion
    into the vital Energy of being.
All else entertains chaos.
MATTER, ION, even BREATH is thrust forth by Chaos.
You do well to worship a God.
You do well to maintain a respect of litany for your God.
You separate yourselves from your God.
When you separate yourselves from peoples, from religions,
    therein is the mark of negativity entered in.
This is the thrust of chaos.
Rise above the human appetite for chaos.
Desire to be equal in Energy unto all Energy,
    holding identity only as mankind.
Therein will you find the vastness of who you are.
Therein will you find the Spirit of your Creator.
Therein all things with gentleness,
    with compassion, with great humanity.

Therein is the platform levelled.

1159   Soul, understand that which contains
        the attributes of Creator,
            each Creator containing different attributes.
Second Creator we will say to you, Intent, Awareness, Breath.
No sound echoes its being without awareness.
And the intent is caught and held by Second Creator
        who gathers awareness,
            as Twelfth Creator gathers echo.
The magnitude of awareness
        would make the listening capacity
        of your earth to space
        seem as naught.
For the Awareness of Second Creator is such
        that it astounds all other Creators;
            the Intent to know and gather awareness
            of all Energy with the power of Breath.
Soul, they are the form in which Energy takes.
The form of Creator is Truth, Purity, and Love.
It is a visible form.
To be in the space of Second Creator,
        is to recognize Intent, Awareness, Echo.
Each Energy of Creator has attributes.
You will know of them all, Soul,
        but we instill them in your being,
        so they are now familiar.
At no time will you have to look to your being
        to research the attribute of your Creator.
It is an indelible part of who you are now.
So shall the attributes of all Creators be.
Energy of consciousness has attributes.
Not a single attribute, Soul, but many.
Within each of Fourteen are three.
Within the 15th is the entirety held in fragment.
In the Void of Consciousness are all the attributes held.
Angels, Soul, each designated to a single attribute
        so that within the realm of the Archangels
            are Twelve Creators.
They are three legions of Angels unto a single Creator.
Each legion of Angel is accountable

        for a different aspect of the Creator Energy.
One, Soul, forward of.
One, unto.
The other, residing in the space of.
Your earth could not visualize a count
        to the number of the legions of Angels
        in existence within the Triad of Idyllic.
Lost are one third of the hosts of existence.
Therein you understand
        the great pain of the loss unto existence.

1160   Soul, unto you is given the landscape of that which is.
It is the constant upheaval of chaos that creates a view
        for earth that is not a continuum of perfection.
Within the many areas of Flow are the memories
        of that which is, not was, is.
For the very Angels know the heaviness of the earth flesh
        keeps you within the body
        so the Soul may dance the earth dance.
You have entered in unto earth
        and the purpose commencing
        with your utterance forth.
The first sound heard is an absolute repelling of entering in,
        a rejection of that step that will bring forth a sound
        wherein all negativity will open and hear.
The very Angels will see that negativity has been addressed
        in a manner that will carry a vibration
        even unto Perfection.
Souls of earth, the sound of your music upon your earth,
        the notes that can touch the instrument
        to bring forth a tear
        from the most hardened of individual.
Think you how the songs of the Angels,
        how the horn of Gabriel
        echoes through the heavens and is heard vibrantly
        so that the colours resonate to the very music.
The Sound transcends all Purity
        lifting in that ecstatic visualization
        that presents itself in the magnitude
        wherein the Rembrandts, the Michaelangelos,
        are seen as students

>   for the creativity brings forth such visionary forms
>   that all that was and is,
>   the very creations of Creator are landscaped alive.
> No contention, yet questioning, curious expectation.
> The sound vibrates, regenerates the mind.
> The Spirit, the Essence, wherein all that is within the Yawn
>   sees within the Sound
>   the forward movement unto perfection.
> There is, Soul, the cymbals, the harps, the violin,
>   instruments so that your mind will cease to hear;
>   only the consciousness within your mind
>   for you will have lost all need of self within the hearing.
> You will be carried by the tone unto the distant Perfection.
> You will lift and behold a perfect order.
> Variance, Soul, variance.
> Complexities slewing outward in great leaps of knowns,
>   a challenge,
>   the very consciousness from which it comes.
> In itself it is reborn for it is ever reaching not contentiously,
>   nay, with infinite capacity to Love
>   upon which existence is.
> It is.
> It dwells.
> It has no need.
> Yet want is fulfilled before the conscious thought is complete,
>   expanding outwardly focussing on a central axis
>   of completeness of perfection.
> There is, Soul, an order wherein that which is heart expands
>   in the perfect beat
>   where the mind is measured for the perfect thought.
> With Sound and Colour
>   is contemporaneous only unto itself
>   for it always enhances that which it is.
> It is the Light in the morning sky.
> It is that which is of such Ecstasy
>   without perfection you cannot behold.
> It is the way to all peace and contentment.
> It is the fractalling resource of all Sound and Colour.
> Behold that which is Perfection.

1161 Soul, we would have earth hear the joy of Farside.

We would have earth understand
      the complexities of the beauty
      that are available unto earth
      that earth does not see
      because of the negativity of man
      has no distortion in the vision of Farside.
We would welcome your being to vision that perfection,
      wherein you do not have
      a daily struggle within your being
      to maintain a balance of positive and negative.
Indeed for us within the realm of goodness
      there is the Energy Flow of our Creator.
Oh earth, you cannot in all the awareness of your being,
      appreciate the Love of that Energy.
We are in the presence of Energy Flow.
We are touched in our being by the fullness of that Love.
It glorifies our being.
It showers our being and presents the intricate filagree of Purity
      wherein we might reside.
You have an earth that is beauteous,
      for your earth is a part of our earth extension.
But you do not have the Light to reveal the intricate filagree.
You only see under microscopic lights,
      a paleness of what we live.
Holy beings, this is our homeland,
      but this also is your homeland you have left
      to defend against negativity, all that is Purity.
You have stepped in to expand our Purity outward,
      for indeed you are we.
You are of our being.
You have entered in to a causal frame
      and in your vulnerability your vision has been shaded,
      but we offer to you the Purity we have
      to see the many worlds
      of goodness that expound not in difference,
      but behold themselves as one.
We who are alien to you are indeed one of you,
      for you have been us and we have been you.
Your descent into the troubled way
      is that you might take your Energy Light,
      that all would become as the Prism,

        and the intricate weave of all energies might blend
        to portray a masterpiece of perfection.

1162   Beloved of earth, bring forth your joy.
Bring forth joy unto all that is earth.
Allow the ice of your being to seek out
        that which requires your tenderness, your joy.
Joy heals.
Joy mends.
Joy repairs.
Joy is the Energy of your being.
It is the reverberance of all that is within.
Those who cannot find joy in their heart
        seek pain, seek negativity.
Souls of earth, blessed whom you are.
See that which is the Energy of joy
        and know that you gather together
        send forth great orbs of joy.
They are as the diadem that Energy fulfils.
It enervates.
It broadcast forth and
        you are a medium of transference of Energy.
We ask that you see the mighty of whom you are.
We ask that you see the joy of who you are.
From the great landscape of your galaxy,
        from the great cosmic totality of universes,
        there is a thrust forward unto Negativity.
And you, you have the possibility of this thrust.
You have the joy to give forth.
Do not shroud yourself in pain.
Do not, Soul, shroud yourself in darkness
        for you are of the Light.
You are of the Energy that is Light.
You have all that is within a single shard of Purity.
You have all that is within the Energy of your Essence.
And you, you who are minute,
        you who are insignificant in self unto all other energies,
        you have the power to withstand
        the forces of negativity,
        the forces of evil upon your earth.
For you you have within you the shard of goodness.

You have within you a knowing
      that you are of your Creator,
      that you are but an illusion upon your earth.
It matters not that the form is decayed,
      for you are more than that which you see.
You are Energy of greatness.
You are a Purity and you know it not.
You are, Soul, defined by that which would do.
You are defined by that which you shed forth unto all beings.
Be it Light or darkness,
      it identifies the Energy of your earthly being.
Lift thine eyes unto the hills.
Lift thine eyes
      and behold the apex of Purity, the Light that shines.
You are, Soul, the voice
      and in the voice you have the power to express.
The voice is Energy.
It is known throughout the ages.
It speaks forth unto all.
In all there is no withholding.
There is only the Energy that is profound.
There is the profoundness of that Energy that is Love.
There is the fullness of that Energy that is Ecstasy.
It is, Soul, even unto the minuteness of whom you are,
      the power that is yours.
Souls of earth, do not count your sleeps.
Do not count that which you weep for.
Do not count that which your heart yearns for.
Count the goodness that you send forth.
Count all that is within your heart
      for you are on a glory road.
You are on a Path that leads unto your Supreme Being.
You are charted.
You are given in all Truth by your Creator.
You are the veritable pearl, the gem,
      that comes from the lowly station
      and rises to become worthy
      than all that is upon our earth
      for you rise above our earth.
You cast your Energy upward and it is received.
You give forth Light.

You give forth a diamond shard.
Peace for earth is not your reality.
The overcoming of negativity, this is your reality.
The rhizomes flower and become beautific.
Your words will wither.
The rhizome will dry sere
      but the seed within the flower
      will bring forth yet again the Truth unto earth.
You enter in again and again unto earth.
You give forth of your Energy.
Your Energy grows and becomes as the Angels.
And then you recognize yourself as the Angel self
      and the wings uplift
      and the Holy Energy that you are gives forth Ecstasy.
Then, Soul, you see even as the Angels
      see the darkness wherein Light is cast
      and you recognize the Archangels.
Speak.
Speak humanity!
Speak unto those who are lost.
Shed thy being in the consciousness of whom you are
      unto the lost for the Archangels are lost
      and would be found
      for their darkness is repairable
      by the Light of your being.
It will, Soul , energize all that is.
They will see the Creator lite whom they are.
The Light will expand, become mighty in them
      and they will open unto the darkness
      and Light the way,
      for they will recall
      within the darkened way is the Idyllic.
Souls of earth, you see how simple you are.
And yet we show unto you the complexity of your being.
You are profound in your Purity.
You are mighty in your Love.
You are, Soul, withstanding all negativity,
      transmitting forth a sound of greatness.
The sound echoes in to the chambers of darkness.
They resound in waves of humanity's Purity.
Holy Holy Holy.

Seek and ye shall find.
Seek in the darkness and ye shall find.
Fear need not be for you who are of Purity,
    you rise above fear.
You lose the fear
    for death of earth you have experienced many times.
It has been yours in many lives in many forms.
Do not fear to pass.
Fear not to succeed.
For in the depths of darkness
    are pure energies who would return
        unto Supreme Being.
You are worthy of their recovery
    for you have the Colour and the Sound
        that will bring unto them recovery.
Humanity, time has been allotted.
Throughout time there have been many
    who have dwelt within their Holy Being.
There are only Four
    who have entered in from a truly Holy state,
        only Four who have reached the level of our Love.
Many beings we have formed
    and they have reached the magnificence of Purities.
The beads of their chosen energies
    have given unto my creations,
        but Four that I have at my station.
Four do I have unto Godhead.
Earth humanity, recognize the Purity of each Soul.
Do not see a vision of uncleanness.
Do not cast dispersion upon the unclean.
Do not flank armies against the withered and brought down.
Unto humanity much has been given.
Unto humanity the most precious is the ability to Love,
    for of Love are you made.
With Love have you been formed.
With Love have you been seeded.
You are supreme in the ability to gather the light of Love.
Light is Love!
Love is extended to my son, and my son, and my sons.
For, Souls, you are the being of Love.
You are Energy.

Energy and Light are Love.

1163 We speak to you of that which we know of Godhead.
Infinite wisdom, infinite Spirit, infinite joy, infinite sadness,
    the capacity to stretch all realities into a single idiom.
You will hear an echo in the Place of Shining
    for all thought resonates.
All consciousness is formed for the Triad
    within the Place of Shining.
It has not always been so.
At a portion, thought was brought forth from the Source.
Then from the Seed, but now from the Place of Shining
    wherein only two portions of the Triad abide.
Where there are two, there is something wrong.
What is wrong, Soul, is that,
    we shall use the word, community, is not complete.
The home misses a member.
The member gone creates a problem.
As with you, Soul, when a member is lost, you go to seek.
And so it was with the Wilful Child, the Negativity.
The Archangels went to seek,
    to alter at the Source at the Seed, at the Cauldron
    and formed yet a negative.
Truth, Wisdom, Negativity to seek, to understand.
You, you are that infinite negativity sent forth to recover
    for you were armed with Truth.
Ever tactically varying each approach.
In battle it is always so.
A seed, you hold a new beginning.
Love, to embrace, Purity to gift and Truth to recover.
For when you are fallen
    you must find a truth to recover from where you are.
You must hold in your being and search with the Truth.
You are at battle.
The strategy began at the Place of Shining
    as Melchezidec offered Humanity,
    before even they were human,
    unto Creator to bring forth Negativity,
    Negativity dug deep within the pit of the negative ion.
And humanity, weak, entered in many times.
Not once, Soul,

>   over and over and over
>   regaining truth upon truth upon truth.
> From the space of Godhead,
>   Creator gave forth the breath of Truth
>   with all knowledge of the Battle deep within.
> But Humanity, humanity chose to enter in as negativity.
> Indeed weak, able to be recognized by negativity
>   using only a portion of thought
>   to entice negativity unto it
>   and ensuring that humanity would be weak
>   in the place of negativity,
>   that it would be well scarred,
>   then as one,
>   would find Negativity would have scarred
>   the very being of humanity.
> Humanity found strength to stand and recognize
>   and gave of the goodness of self unto Negativity.
> Humanity you reach into your very being,
>   you struggle with the Truth of who you are
>   but Godhead is ever vigilant of that which you do.
> The Angels and Archangels
>   constantly aware of your endeavours.
> As you lift your voice against negativity there is rejoicing.
> As you send forth Love unto negativity there is rejoicing.
> As you lift your Energy to compassion
>   the anthems ring out, the hallelujahs are sung
>   and there is rejoicing within the Place of Shining.

1164 Far from you, into the space of your Parallel World
    is the great perfection of all.
It has within no detriment to any being.
There is, Soul, existences unlike your own
    for they hold the perfect anthem of cooperation.
They hold within that space the viability of all energies
    working together, working together!
Within the space of your Parallel World there is no ideal.
The ideal is that which is sought.
The ideal would be a mix of all energies
    not a portion of all energies
    but a mix of all energies that all might be held as one.
Within the devout of earth's saviours

        is the great purpose of holding a mix of all energies.
But you have not succeeded, Soul.
This you know.
You have been brought to warfare time and time again.
Your time only lapses to peace where warfare still struggles
        so that it is not a total peace.
Within the space of Perfection wherein Chaos is a portion,
        there is an intense striving to give purpose
        to the mix of these energies.
For it is as the missing note,
        it is when perfection is left undone.
You have had many examples given unto you
        wherein you had the perfect perfection.
Buddha sought to bring this to be.
Christ, Krishna, Mohammed
        each enthralled in their own scope of vision.
Many have come and many have gone.
Many have thought
        and thought has lapsed into chaotic.
Souls, you are the eye that holds a vision.
You are caught in the vision within the eye of your being.
You have given the concept of that vision unto your Creator
        and you have offered to enter in to extrapolate
        from the negative energy a positive mix.
And we have rejoiced
        that you have brought fruition many times.
But you have not succeeded, Soul,
        for still chaos does not rightly fit.
It is the piece of puzzle that is lost.
It is the sound that is not heard clearly.
It is the vision that merely sees.
Soul, you are on a quest.
Your quest is clear.
Your quest has been as long as humanity has been
        for you entered in to earth
        with a single purpose of overcoming negativity.
You have entered in individually;
        even now there are humanities
        who have banded together,
        as the violets and the indigo,
        to give more power to the vision that you have.

Still you have not succeeded.
Within the Parallel World that is yours and ours
        and all energies of all creations, there is a portent.
The portent is that consciousness is.
When consciousness beholds a thought
        the thought must become.
It cannot be released.
It is there that it might become.
Perfection gave forth a conscious thought;
        " What if all was given into a single mix, not separate,
                not each Energy performing that which it knows
                but creating a perfection
                wherein all thought was a single thought".
What then?
What would be the greatness of that thought?
What would be the power to ignite even yet a further perfection.
And you, you are a portion of Energy.
You have agreed to enter in.
You, simple being that you are,
        you who have no scope
        of the greatness beyond your being
        of that which is within the heavens to know,
        not, Soul, to delve within your milky way;
        not to see beyond the stars themselves to other heavens
        but, Soul, to reach in to the perfect self,
        to reach within the ideal state.
Soul, you have empty hands to offer
        but you have a Light!
It beams from the Energy of whom you are.
It echoes upward into the heavens above.
t reaches in to that which is the beginning of a new thought
        which would set outside perfection
        that it might not mar that which perfection is.
And you, you have the ability within your being
        within the grace of whom you are,
        within the truth of whom you are
        to hold a Love and a Purity beyond that of the Angels.
You have reached, Soul, a chord that strengthens all energies.
You have reached a oneness
        wherein we all see that which you are.
You Lighten our darkness, Soul.

We behold the iota of your being and as you
      hold fast to each other in the oneness of that Light
      we see even a greater strength
      for it delves itself to fulfil a need
      to reach in to all avenues of repair,
      all avenues of need to mend.
You are, Soul, holding a needle so small
      and yet that needle can mend
      within the great Void, a hole.
You can repair.
You, Soul, have the thread that is Light.
You have the perfection that is Truth.
You have the oneness that is comfort.
You are the great and you are the small.
You are the beginning and you are the end.
You are to be valued with all value.
We sing anthems unto your being, humanity.

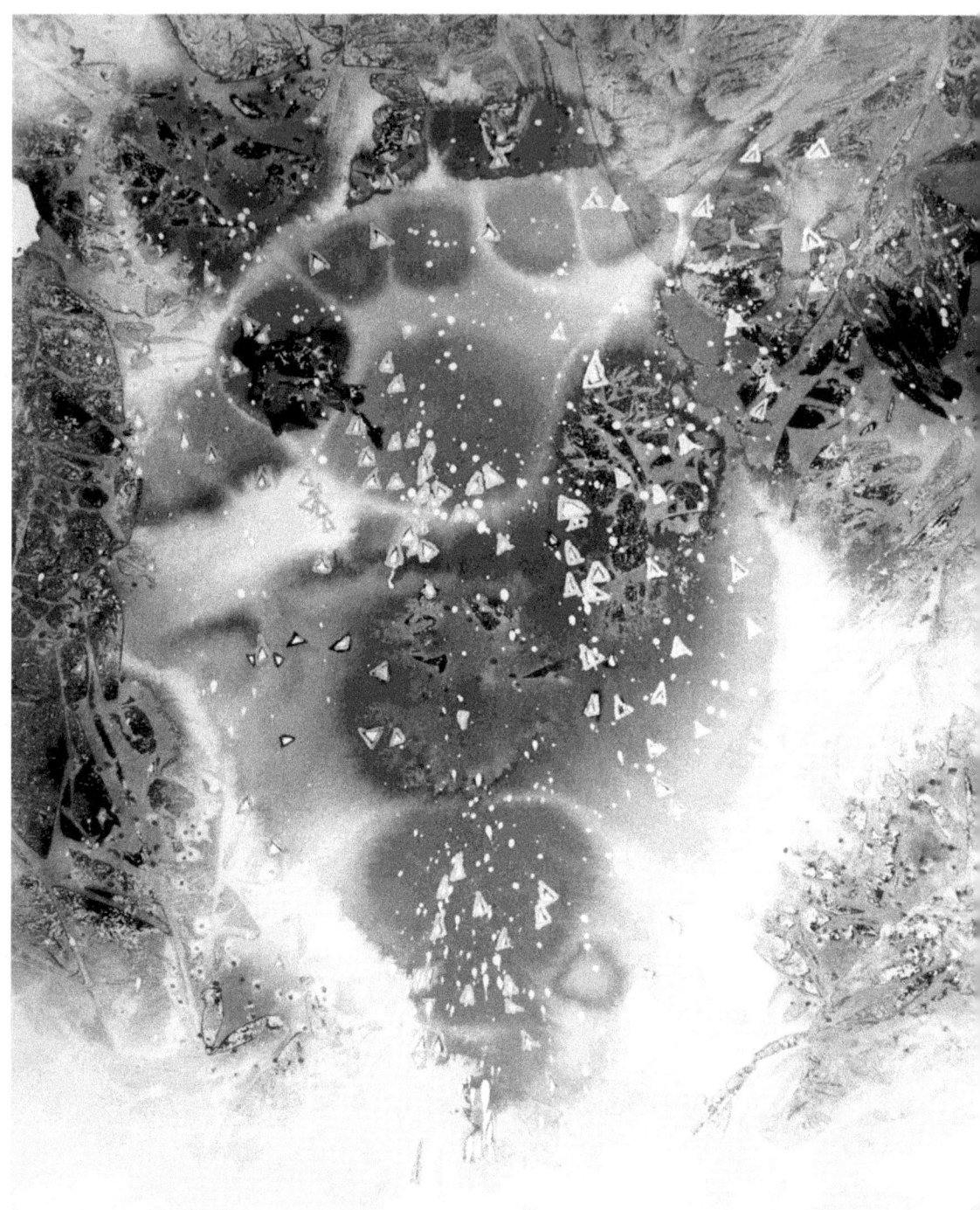

Creations of Light

Chapter Five
THE BEGINNING

1165   Souls of earth, from the farthest reaches of existence
        beyond the realms of worlds formed,
        are worlds yet unformed,
        are Energies of such profusion of Colour
        as to ignite Sound.
Indeed!
Ignite Sound!
Beyond Energy of 15th Creator
        stretching equally unto growth
        is an order that has been in all things.
It is as syncopation in its element of clarity.
It is as dissolute of chaos.
Yet unto you, unto all energies forward chaos reigns.
There is, Soul, energies formed and ignited;
        a profusion of prismatic colour;
        unified in purpose of being
        that has a single goal, to eradicate chaos.
You are what you call born, are transferred forth,
        transferred, as in matched forward.
In the forward is a loss of identity
        and the return is a regaining of identity.
You are particled, particled of all Energy.
You are valued in your being
        beyond that which you can know.
For in the continuum of existence is a perfect harmony.
You are a part of that perfect harmony.
You are a thread within the Masterpiece of great harmony.
We ask you, Souls of earth, to value the being that you are,
        to value the vibrancy of your Energy.
For it is in the syncopation of all energies
        that the great perfection will come.
You are an honoured member of a great tribe.
The tribe is called humanity
        and has set itself apart from all other existence
        to battle with this chaos, to bring about a harmony.
You cannot foresee, as we can foresee,
        the energies resounding unto you in waves.
You cannot see as they bounce

from your being and are sent forth,
the perfection in which you send them forth.
You are not idly upon your earth, Soul.
You are upon your earth
to overcome all that is negative round about you,
to perceive in the glory of whom you are,
the presence of an Angel,
to behold the chord of perfection
that is humanity within you.
Behold, the watchmen is in the tower
and the voice can be heard,
and the voice cries forth,
"Behold the consciousness of being.
Do not behold that
which is the serenade of man in groups.
Hear only the unified tone of humanity
that speaks to all man equally in sound."
You are a portion of the solution of overcoming negativity.
Count thyself present, Soul.
Be, in the name of peace, of Truth, of Purity.
Soul, from Colour ignites Sound.
Sound ignites Colour.
They are complimentary one to the other.
It is known in your worlds,
but it is infinitesimal in its knowledge
or in its perception.
From that which we see, the kaleidoscope of colour,
that is in what you call the Heavens.
Soul, your heart would burst from its form.
Your consciousness would be so awakened!
The beautification of that which you would see,
the threads of weave
in coordination throughout worlds, worlds;
one boom, boom, boom, boom
electrifying, would be a word you might use.
Yet it has no meaning for its simplicity,
for it expands the consciousness
to be in the space of such total coordination.
And then a chaotic scribble
as though the author has placed in a discord
that creates a sound

        so vibrantly out of sync with all of accord
        and stridently strikes discord.
This you rectify.

1166   You cannot always gasp outward,
        you must bring forward.
Energy, likewise, must be spiraled.
All affiliations must be spiral,
        one accountable to the other, but in spiral.
Void, Ion, Matter, separate in their Energy Field,
        a need to blend together,
        as the Soul, Spirit, and Essence
        has a need to blend together.
You could not always be apart from your Spirit.
There would be a withering of the Soul.
The Soul would extinguish itself.
For Matter to be as Matter with no movement,
        no expectation of movement as Matter,
        it would be as naught, as no thing.
Ion Energy within itself has a motion
        but not outward from itself,
        always impelling, impelling,
        not repelling, impelling.
There is a need for it to repel outward
        that it might nurture,
        nurture other energies.
Void is the containment of all things with a single exception.
Breath, Breath, for the triad has entered forth from Breath.
It will capitulate the sciences in their understanding.
In the beginning was MATTER,
        beginning, Soul, of existence.
Of what you may ask?
Existence.
Breath gave forth a triad of Void
        wherein Matter and Ion might exist.
But without the component of Breath,
        within the triad itself,
        there was no motion, none.
It was inactive,
        a Field of creation wherein all creation lies.
For time is not an element.

Yet no interrelation, no meld, except Breath,
>   would give of self to create the motion.
And in the creating of motion ever outward from it,
>   Breath sustained a drought.
A drought such as your earth feels, a drought, Soul,
>   such as your mind feels a drought,
>   that holds a part of lack of self.
Behold, in the forward of Time,
>   all droughts will have renewal.
Earth, your earth, will become pristine.
For in the Thousand Years of renewal,
>   all forms will replenish.
All form of existence will dwell in the land
>   and be seen and acknowledged
>   by the energies therein.
There will be no hidden agendas in the forwarding of time.
You will behold the Time of no time
>   wherein a year will be as moment,
>   and a moment will be as a year.
For in the glory of Beholding, time will cease to be.
Void, Ion, Matter, triad of all existence.
In the beginning was MATTER.
MATTER formed first.
ION formed second.
VOID, the container, wherein these entered.

1167 Soul, it is the beginning of all that is.
It is the awakening.
It is the pronouncement of Energy.
It is the vehicle for that Energy.
That Energy, Soul, is as vibrant as it enters in.
It loses density as it is reflected forward.
You are a reflection forward many times, Soul.
You have entered in not unto your world,
>   unto existences.
In many forms you have entered in.
And so the Angels became classified in variations,
>   Seraph, Cherubim, Angel,
>   call them what you will.
They are reflectories forward and have lost of their Light.
The density is not pure, Soul.

The density is illuminous.
The Energy illuminates ION and MATTER, Soul.
The Breath sends forth the great bolt of Energy
        and all that was in a core,
          became as broken.
The Core was as your volcano, full of Light
        and expressed itself outward with consciousness,
          absorbing unto each particle
          so none has come outward without consciousness.
None has come outward without Light.
There is no escaping, Soul, but there is no return.
How does the Core maintain a return?
How does the Core give forth of itself and not diminish?
Examples and examples and examples, Soul, ever outward.
Energy of your being is quickly diminished.
Energy of your voice from overuse is quickly diminished.
Energy in all its facets without replenishment
        is quickly diminished.
How will you maintain?
The Core holds Energy.
The Core holds density.
The Core holds all portions of Energy.
We speak to you.
Is MATTER Energy?
Is ION Energy?
Is consciousness Energy?
They must move to be Energy.
Is that so?
It is not, Soul.
To be still can still hold Energy.
To be silent can still hold Energy.
But what can maintain Energy?
What can replace Energy as pure as what went forth?
It is not that Energy cannot be replaced.
Indeed you may replace
        energy upon your earth with other energy,
          but it always diminishes nor is it always the same.
It is, Soul, the sending forth and the return of equal Energy,
        of same Energy, of pure Energy, that is vital.
Vital, not unto consciousness,
        not unto ion, unto MATTER.

Unto MATTER!
For it is MATTER that is the containment.
As Energy releases, the force of Energy left creates Vacuum.
Vacuum loses Value.
Value requires Echo.
Echo is not possible without return.
There is a continuum of exactness in all Energy,
    be it within your world, be it within your galaxy,
    be it within the Timetable of Man
    or the existences beyond.
All outward flung worlds,
    many of which you know,
    have within them the same curriculum
    to resolve an issue of Energy.
And what replaces Energy
    to keep the containment in its original
    without the Vacuum that has already begun.
Only, Soul, can it close.
And then there is no expression outward
    and it is as it was, no thing,
    only MATTER holding Energy, ION and MATTER.
No consciousness, no Breath, Soul.
Without consciousness and Breath
    there is no worthy existence.
It is not simple, Soul.
Eons of Light and Dark
    have placed great conscious thought to solutions
    that have not brought forth.
Your greatest minds, our greatest minds,
    consciousness itself,
    relies that a solution will be born
    in the minds of men
    in the heart of existence in the Energy of all Energy.
Yet, it has not been so and still we seek
    and you seek and know it not.
Worlds of worlds seek.
Legions of Angels seek.
The Circle of Angels, the Circle of Saints,
    even unto the Supreme Energy
    which is the Energy within
    of which you are all a portion.

Supreme Being, Light of all Lights,
>   Energy of all energies, how could you not bow down?
And yet it will not fulfill a purpose,
>   the purpose that is to be fulfilled is in the hearts of men.
It is, Soul, in the goodness of whom you are,
>   for you have returned Energy in the darkness.
Within the Yawn it has been
>   and even unto Idyllic has it been heard.
And we await the echo back unto where we are.
Flame of Light you are humanity.
Flame of all flames ever outward in your turn
>   for solution have you come forth
>   into the darkness through unto the Light.
Awaken our hearts,
>   as in the great awakening of Energy,
>   may you awaken in whom we are a solution of Energy.
And so we have unto you given an equation
>   to stir the heart of man,
>   to seek where it is not possible for us to seek.
And so we say unto you,
>   *"Search through the Timetable of Man,*
>   *that Energy would return unto Energy."*
Blessed art thou, humanity.

1168   Souls of earth, we speak to you
>   of that which you call deity.
We speak of that which we know as Supreme Being,
>   Energy endowed with all that is perfection,
>   with all that is from all worlds
>   for all worlds are formed of that Energy.
Within the place of MATTER is the existence of this Energy.
Within the place of ION is the existence of this Matter.
Energy itself is all that is pure, all that is Truth,
>   all that is of the highest form of all Energy.
We speak of forms you see as insignificant;
>   as Echo, as Intent, as Awareness, as Value.
All within the Void is of this Energy.
You worship, Soul, in the form of men.
You worship that which you call deity,
>   God, Allah, Blessed Being.
You even speak as I AM.

Souls, you speak in the infancy of whom you are!
You speak as the cradled infant who has not yet learned
    the fullness of that which is Supreme Being.
You have monologues one to the other,
    discourses one to the other.
Idealisms, Soul, you seek out as parcelled to a Creator,
    to a deity and we say to you,
      "*You have not yet learned to crawl*".
You have not gathered the wisdom that is yours to gather.
You have seen.
You have been spoken but you have not heard.
You have not in one whit gathered the fullness
    of the entity you speak of.
Holy Being, Holy Holy Holy does not
    reach into that aperture that reaches
     unto Supreme Being
    for, Soul, you must Enter In.
It is not an Energy that all can reach
    unless they are one in humanity.
You bow your knees.
You pillow your head.
You open your eye and behold that which you will
    but often you have only entered in unto
    the first or second level of Farside.
You have barely glimpsed the Hallowed Halls.
There is, Soul, before you an expanse.
There is before you a great passage
    beyond Time and Timeless wherein all IS;
    where all Energy flows as One Energy,
    where all Energy is in motion.
It does not seek to collide.
It has its own Path, each and all,
    moving in great accord
     one with the other yet apart.
And in this great theatre of striation
    is the well worn path of Chaos.
It is caught as all energies are caught in their own momentum
    placed by the hand of Divinity; placed
    in a diminutive state of non collapse.
Within the great Field of each potential of Energy
    is a thread of need.

It is a need that is in all beings of earth.
It is within the very form of your flesh and blood.
It is within the very mind that you hold.
It is within the very heart of your being
        that to fulfill, to blend, to be a part of.
This is within the Energy of Supreme Being;
        this Energy that creates and creates and creates
        to form a part of the very being of that Energy.
Echoed through all Energy is, Soul, a pheromone.
It is, Soul, deep within the need of all.
Seek beyond where you are unto the Deity of Triad;
        unto Godhead, unto Great One, unto Creator,
        formed each unto one and see
        the need always to move, to create, to give forth.
Soul, from the beginning Supreme Being,
        the need to create, to form, to give forth.
Of all that is Love is not the greatest.
Love is the potential.
That which is the greatest is NEED.
To fulfil NEED drives all Energy.
It is not of compassion.
That is created within.
It is, Soul, the element
        to create a solution for all that is Energy,
        for all that is captive
        within the Paths of Creators making.
For it has been ordained that all things that reach unto another
        will withdraw, only, as in the magnet
        where one is drawn unto the other.
And so has been created within the Dome of Supreme Being
        a NEED where magnetism is a portion,
        where you will draw and be caught and held captive
        until you create a magnetism of your own
        that is so strong it repels.
You are created
        because you have offered yourselves for a purpose.
That which you call Creator is the Energy of magnificence.
This Energy comes from the Triad
        that holds within all the components of Supreme Being
        even within is the NEED to fulfil, to be fulfilled.
Souls, in your likeness as your Creator

you can step close to another being.
You may even touch the being
> but hold for that person no profound effect
> unless you give in the Truth of whom you are
> that purpose for which you came forth.

You are within the great Path
> where energies have fallen and been lost,
> where worlds have been caught
> in the depths of agonies
> for the sleep was a dreadful sleep
> and the absence of Creator in that sleep
> a loss beyond bearing.

You hold within the power of whom you are
> the destiny of all man
> more, you hold within your being
> the solution to NEED,
> not to Rapture,
> although to be in Rapture is to be held in Ecstasy.

But to find your Energy beyond into the beginning
> where is all memory of all that was and is
> and the purpose yet to be.

You reach your energies
> for the reason you have come to earth
> to project unto all man that which you are,
> to give unto all men the idealism of Supreme Being
> for you have the chord within you.

You have the component that is.
You have heard within your very being
> the NEED and you hold within your very Energy
> the magnetism to draw unto to you
> all that is Truth in goodness, in perfection.

1169 Behold Chaos.
Behold that which is Voice.
Behold the great pyramidal entity wherein Breath struggles.
And you who are human,
> you have allowed your beings to be called forth.

You have entered in.
You have awareness of the great Chaos.
You have before you a vision;
> a vision that has entered in

>   for a very molecular structure that you are,
>   that has entered in to the mind
>   and the high mind that
>   is even touched in the heart of your being.
> For you have carried a glow of fire in your being,
>   fire such as that which does not have flame;
>   such as that that carries Energy, Energy, Soul!
> You have brought the chord of that Chaos into recognition
>   that there may be solution.
> Where art thou?
> Where art thou Chaos?.
> Why is there no voice to Chaos?
> But there is, Soul.
> There is a voice to Chaos.
> It has been carried into multiple existences.
> It carries distortion from the order of its being.
> It holds a whirr,
>   a sound of continual motion outward from its being.
> As the small child caught in dilemma calls out,
>   "*Help me, help me*",
>   so has Chaos called out in many forms,
>   "*Help me, help me*".
> Humanity, you have allowed your energies to enter in.
> You have shown unto many existences who you are.
> You have overwhelmed these existences
>   with your ability to overcome chaos.
> You have brought yourself into the great path of all Energy.
> Who can deflect chaos?
> It is not necessary to deflect chaos.
> It is not the dilemma.
> The dilemma, Souls of earth,
>   is in returning all energies to the full circle of being.
> Voice.
> Many existences have bowed down to Voice, to triad.
> There is no triad formed
>   that has not the purpose of solving Chaos.
> None.
> From the greatest of triads, to the minute,
>   all have a single purpose,
>   to create calm, then to touch the Energy to return.
> In your being, as a single individual, you divert chaos.

We do not find any grandeur in a Soul diverting chaos.
We find great awe in a Soul that can alter chaos
      to return to that which was its beginning.
A child has entered in to your earth with Purity.
A child gathers pain
      and a child becomes that which they have gathered.
And then, the consciousness of why you have entered in
      touches the being and the being understands.
It is not diverting from chaos but overcoming chaos
      that they might return to the perfection of their being.
Souls of earth, the mouth is not the solution.
It is action from the very being of whom you are,
      for it is in the aura Energy that you alter chaos.
It is in the aura Energy that you bring unto you,
      that perfection that touches chaos,
      to know awareness of its beginning.
Breath struggles to be.
Breath struggles.
Upon earth breath struggles in all perfections
      even unto that perfection.
Time is not the issue.
Response is the issue.
The great glory road is the issue, the great path
      where all consciousness moves outward
      from its beginning.
Wherein is that beginning?
Wherein is that place of perfection?
It is not Idyllic,
      it was created.
It is not Voice for Breath struggles within.
We say to you, you have understood much,
      if you have understood the Seed.
You have understood much,
      if you have understood
      the many Creators as the Supreme Being.
You have understood much,
      if you have understood Flame and Breath, side by side.
Hold in your being that echo is more than a return of sound.
That is only dilution.
Echo holds within a resounding of whatever form it meets
      that it might return to Echo.

It must have form to echo forth from.
You have been brought to great understanding
      and we bring you to yet
         another platform of understanding.
All creation expanding outward.
Where is the sounding board from which echo may return?
In Chaos there is flight,
      flight from the Source of all Energy.
Where is the sounding forth?
Why does it not return?
You are not the only world wherein research is done.
You are not the only solver of complexity.
You on earth, have great minds
      that equate and bring to be new structure.
There are many worlds such as yours.
You are the only one touched by the very dilemma.
You are the very one that is free with negativity.
You exist in a negative ion.
You have woven a thread that carries such treasure,
      for negativity streams from your being.
You have given unto research a pattern.
And we take you, Soul, to where you have allowed us to go.
Beyond where you are, existences far from where you are,
      are structured legions of beings
         who focus on the great equation.
There is upon your earth a new value.
It is, Soul, to follow negativity in the fall
      from where it is to how far it can go.
Your earth has understood this.
Even is mankind cooperating in this evaluation,
      to see how far negativity can go.
Does it dilute?
Does it enhance?
Does it create greater illusion?
Your earth is in a downward cycle.
It will not always remain.
We give you courage that you might know
      and we say to you,
         "*You have agreed to enter in.*"
To measure how fast a rock may fall
      is simply to allow it to drop

and measure the fall and equate time.
And so are you falling,
    and so are we equating, resolving.
But you knew this.
You did.
You are in illusion.
This you must know.
You are where we are.
You are where we are and you have disguised your being,
    not that others might not see,
    but in a vulnerability that all that is chaos might not see.
Souls of earth, you are portioned of goodness
    and you have entered in
    to be the sounding board and we hold you high.
Breath blesses your being and Flame ignites your Spirit.
Be human kind to one another in your great fall.

1170   Indeed, we tell you, Souls, of that which is.
The Light IS.
It has consciousness.
It is.
It has life.
It has death.
It is.
It has all the components of good.
It has all the possibilities of evil.
The power is in the source.
The power is in the reverberation of Energy.
It is in the fullness of Purity.
It is in the touch of Breath.
The Breath creates motion,
    allows the Colour and Sound to echo forth.
Light is a reverberation of Energy.
Energy is not without Breath.
Consciousness is the viable intelligence
    that sends forth an echo to respond.
The response is only possible through perfection,
    else all would be chaos.
And so was it not that Death
    moved apart from Life and created Chaos,
    this is known,

      it is a portion of all consciousness,
         it was a gift but it created an unforeseen issue.
Perfection was incomplete.
Breath stilled within.
Only the Angels send forth the Colour and Sound
         for the issue within is unknown.
We have said within the Light is all, even the vile possibility.
Indeed within earth you have found this to be.
You have created a vileness.
Even as you have created a sound that is sent forth
         unto the Angels of your compassion
         and are you not encapsulated within the Yawn
         that there would not be
         yet another echo of pain sent forth.
All that is perfection is cordoned off.
Breath echoed unto Light, unto consciousness.
What is NEED?
The NEED, Soul, is to prevent
         the ultimate Chaos within perfection.
See that which has happened unto the many existences
         wherein we have attempted to create
         a resounding echo that would heal.
And Breath stirred the Energy
         and the Energy itself fragmented
         and sent forth shards of Light.
The heavens sent forth the rumbling
         and behold
         from the shards of Light rose consciousness.
And behold the Angels became
         and consciousness spoke unto the throngs of Angels.
         "*Go forth.*
         Search in the darkness for that which we have lost."
And the heavens of Perfection understood.
There was no containment except the Energy itself.

1171 We ask you to be prepared to hear.
We take you, Soul, to the Void of Consciousness.
And you will understand awareness,
         understanding, contemplation, divination.
What you would call, Soul, mind
         but a mind fragmented minutely

wherein all consciousness has a single purpose, to be.
To be, to exist and peruse only the consciousness itself,
    ever expanding, ever creating.
Expanding within a realm,
    as your thoughts expand within your head.
And as they dwell and are perceived, you think,
    "Who can I share this thought with?
    Where can I take this conscious thought?
    Who will be my adversary
        to bring it to a greater thought?"
And so it was with Void, the Void of Consciousness.
Within all Energy form there was no thought.
It was MATTER.
It carried no purpose.
There was Energy.
It existed.
But it could only think within itself.
For it had motion only unto self, with no creative self,
    except within self for its own purpose.
And Void sought a companion
    to share the consciousness of being.
Without motion it could not be.
Breath was known unto consciousness.
It carried motion.
But Breath and consciousness created nothing.
And Breath was moved to place motion within ION.
And ION could then reach out and attache itself to MATTER.
And their ideal would have been for MATTER
    to reach to Consciousness but it did not.
Consciousness reached to MATTER
    and within all matter is consciousness.
But MATTER was altered by Breath.
It moved outward from itself
    creating and creating and creating.
Ever expanding by the outward Flow of Breath.
Void within Matter became ITH.
ITH, ever abiding, ever a part of.
All that was created by capital MATTER
    became fragmented Energy
    with memory of where it had been
    but no creative thought within,

   belonging to, yet apart.
Consciousness forwarded self an Energy, Fifteen.
We call this Energy Fifteen,
   for your understanding, Supreme Being,
   who used MATTER
   to create Energy forms with thought,
   simple thoughts, creatures, great thinking forms.
The consciousness of Creator reached into that which was
   and developed a civilization of one,
   of two, of ten, of thousands,
   and thousands of energies.
And within these energies thought could be returned.
Some more than others.
And those of the greatest, the Archangels,
   the Arch, the topmost consciousness.
And Creators were brought to being for a single purpose.
Matter was awry.
It did not return to its Source.
Within the creations of Archangels,
   they were Energy from Ion
   and could use the form of Matter at will.
But Matter itself in the pure state of Matter,
   only moved outward.
This is your dilemma and this is our dilemma.
The Archangels are purities of great Love.
They have a single allegiance to the form of their Creator
   and in all things to the wheel of their Creator.
You who are humanity,
   who have also been created by a Creator,
   you are wilful.
You do not always do the will of your Creator.
But in this negative state,
   you have learned to release negativity from you
   and reach once again unto your Creator.
You are matter in the form you are in
   and that is a return of matter unto Matter.

1172 ITH, first Energy sent forth from 15th Creator,
   purpose of solution
   never to be singularly as the Energy of itself
   but always to transform of the same Energy.

ITH is the single Energy
> that can be more powerful entering out.

All other energies diminish of self,
> for all other energies, with the exception of Breath,
> > entered in at the will of the 15th Creator.

Breath and ITH are combatants.
Yet Breath and ITH are not, how would you put it,
> alien one to the other.

Indeed they know of each other, both powerful,
> 15th, Creator of consciousness.

Breath, power unto 15th Creator, not antagonist, not anger.
Indeed, not.
Were you to have the perfect union of energies,
> you would have them equal, would you not!

Indeed equal, one not taking from the other,
> one giving equally to the other.

This would be the perfect union.
In the drawing of Breath
> unto MATTER and ION, chaos began.

Within the corridor of solution,
> ION and Breath are always together,
> Death and Life together.

They have found each other,
> and like upon your world a tale of union,
> > there is a need once meshed, to be meshed.

But in the meshing there is chaos.
ITH projected outward as Breath.
But within the Energy of Breath, of Flame, of Fire,
> the Energy of power,
> > to be able always to be at one, equal to.

In your world, you know it is not so.
Breath can overwhelm fire,
> and fire destroys matter and ion.

So is the contentious dilemma that ITH sent out to resolve.

1173 Soul, you understand
> the purpose of all Energy is for return.

Each existence has entered in to proceed
> with the solution for return,
> > not of the prodigal son which is earth's
> > but, Soul, the return of all Energy, all matter,

>   unto that from which it comes,
>   the source of its being;
>   Energy returning unto Energy.
> It is Matter, Soul.
> It is the depletion of Matter.
> The Void of Consciousness,
>   that from which 15th entered in,
>   is providing a solution.
> Understand, the need of all Energy to spiral
>   not downwards only, but indeed, unto self.
> For in the perfect spiral
>   is the perfect containment of all Energy.
> All Energy is a part of all Energy, Soul,
>   but depletes itself.
> Yet, the source is in its very being,
>   as upon your earth your DNA,
>   the source is still within you
>   even though it may have been diluted many times.
> A need, Soul, to return to the source of that Energy
> The hierarchy of all consciousness
>   is the Void of Consciousness.
> From the Void of Consciousness
>   comes the 15th Creator,
>   comes the Fourteen, Vanguard;
>   comes downward past ITH,
>   past Fire, past Flame,
>   comes even unto earth humanity.
> For you hold in your being a consciousness.
> You do things at a mind level
>   and you do things at a conscious level.
> They are not the same.
> The mind level is earth humanity.
> The conscious level is of the Void of Consciousness.
> Soul, you are connected to ITH and Fire and Flame.
> You are profound in who you are.

1174 Souls, we speak of breath.
All breath upon your earth is fragmented to time.
Breath allows motion upon your earth.
Breath allows motion upon Farside.
Breath is not as your breathing of earth,

        containing a motion to move forward
        the Energy within flesh and blood,
        rather it is the vibratory motion of Breath
        that is before Void of Consciousness.
Breath was.
Motion was.
All motion is Breath connected.
All motion is not attached to ion of matter
        in the form of earth matter,
            yet in order for matter to have motion,
            it must be moved by Breath.
So it has always been.
Ion receives the Breath
        to create the stir that instills the motion.
Your being breathes.
And you feel alive with the breath that you carry.
If the breath is altered, even significantly altered,
        you cease to exist, Soul.
Upon Farside such a lack of breath could not be.
For lack of breath is attached to earth negativity.
It is attached not to Chaos,
        but to earth negativity.
It is the purpose of your entering in and your leaving.
Upon the Farside Breath always IS.
It is the Energy of Creator extending forward Breath,
        the great Yawn indeed is Breath.
In worlds beyond worlds, beyond the Rend, beyond SEE,
        beyond the Vanguard, is Breath.
Breath entered in to fulfil the need,
        the need to instill motion within MATTER,
        and then again as Breath moves ever forward,
        the need to draw back Breath.
This is continuum in existence.
For all things must resolve themselves to be spherical, Soul.
If they are not they will ultimately lose source.
It would diminish.
It must resolve to ever wend its way
        unto where it has entered in.
Breath does not do this
Within your human form it does draw back and you live.
But in the great expanse beyond existence,

> beyond Existence is Breath.
Wherein is no MATTER, yet MATTER was in the beginning.
How can this be?
This is not a puzzle, Soul,
> it is known how this can be.
But to place a momentum in the outer edge of Breath,
> to return unto Source, this is not known.
This is the dilemma.
We do not place it to you, Soul.
Yet, you have a part in the resolving.
For all that you do upon your earth
> is simply to return life unto matter.
For it is not Breath that is diminishing.
It is MATTER.
For the outward flow of Breath is sending forth
> Energy and not returning unto.
You have been entered in for a single purpose.
The purpose, to return the Blessed unto Creator.
You have accomplished more than you know.
You have brought your energies unto the time of no time.
You have even understood,
> there will be a consciousness in the time of no time.
Life could dissipate from you,
> yet you understand you will be.
But the consciousness of your being will have lost the matter.
Only upon your earth do you re enter as matter newly formed;
> again, newly formed, and yet again newly formed,
> repetitive in the many lives that you live.
You do this within the flesh and blood of your being.
But Matter with Ion in the Void of Consciousness
> is ever moving outward.
And Breath takes the motion ever forward.
Our mountains disintegrate,
> they can even be too heavy to be.
They can send Energy forth and with it part of their being.
So does Matter send forth Energy, endlessly, Soul.
What of MATTER's origin?
Where is the replenishing?
What of Breath that ever goes forward and does not return?
MATTER was in the beginning.
Breath is stronger than MATTER.

MATTER's origin, Soul,
    it is called Voice.
It is that which was sent out,
    that which was sent forth.
Your volcanic eruptions
    replicate the sending forth from the Core,
    which is the voice, the voice that rumbles.
Comes, Soul, from the spiral of all Energy, the Core.
We can tell you that no life form
    such as you understand life form has existed.
Existence came after.
What was, was the sling of motion.
Cylindrical, Soul.
Ever in constant motion.
Voice always sends forth from Core outward.
You use a word, fielding, so it is, Soul,
    fielding for that which it knows to be,
    all things in perfect order.
And only as Consciousness had a need
    to meld with MATTER,
    did Chaos,
    in the form you understand chaos, come to be.
Yet, before this chaos was yet another Chaos.
This is the quest.
For in your mantle is the very chaotic sphere we have.
And you are creating
    the absolute chaos upon your planet.

1175 Soul, recognition is vital
    for each being of earth to behold
    not in another, but in themselves that which is.
To recognize from where they have entered in
    to whom they have recognition,
    to whom they are a portion of.
Each being of earth is of the Register of Farside.
Each being of earth is a portion of the Handiwork of Creator.
All your energies are recognized.
None can walk upon the earth
    without the colour and sound of the tread
    being accounted upon the Farside.
You are the ignoble tread

    until you have become the golden tread.
You are that which is the Masterpiece.
You are that which is recognized unto the distant places
    and we speak, Soul, beyond the worlds of Farside.
We speak beyond the galaxies of your knowing.
We speak beyond the Breath formed unto Voice.
We speak where sound is new and colour is fresh
    and that which is, is still in the glory,
    the frontier of Energy,
    the awakening of consciousness,
    the bringing forth of MATTER.
The sound is keyed into the silence
    and the colour is shed into the Core
    and the resilience of both awakens the MATTER.
The MATTER was still and now has being.
The consciousness awakened to recognize
    the very thunderbolt of Energy that was cast out.
As the breaking of the shell brings forth life,
    so did the great Energy bring forth,
    and all that was in no thing
    began to move and spiral and begin and cluster.
And the great clusters held a motion of their own
    and the Light clung to the clusters,
    and the clusters magnified their being
    and the Energy sharded the clusters.
And the clusters took on consciousness
    and the consciousness recognized their energies
    and Behold became the Archangel.
But not singly, Soul!
The multitude cluster upon cluster echoing outward.
The Energy could not fathom the enormity
    of that which was and how to contain the cluster.
And the great Energy brought forth a known,
    a knowing of the Colour and Sound
    required containment and sent forth
    Rays of Energy, Fifteen Rays to contain the clusters.
For each in the spiral always entering in,
    elongated in a sphere of Light.
The Light became the containment of Dome, of way,
    of Path for all Energy, legions of Archangels even,
    each belonging to a shard of Light,

    each holding a ray of colour.
You are humanity, you are of a portion of colour.
Not the colour of your humanity,
    but the colour of your Purity.
You hold in your being
    a colour that is of the legion you belong.
You are of Purity, you are of the origin,
    you are of the beginning.
The bolt of Energy brought forth myriad of Light, of Dark.
Each held within a Truth, each held within a Fire, a Flame.
You are flame, Soul.
You are garnered from Flame, the Flame of Energy,
    the Flame of the beginning
It cannot be extinguished.
It is.
It cannot be wetted or darkened or thwarted.
It is.
You are magical in that you are forever,
    you are magical in that you belong.
When you are without,
    when you are forlorn in your being,
     alone in your heart,
      become whom you are, a portion of Light!
Recognize whom you are, the goodness of forever.
You have the halo.
You have the prism.
You have, Soul, the exquisite self.
It is Colour and Sound.
You are the bright morning star.
You are the sunset that arrises in the awakening day.
You are the sun, the stars and the moon
    but you are ever so much more.
For you are the beginning.
You are the first ray brought down, reflected forth
    until you are the minute of whom you are.
Yet you have the possibility of the flare of the Flame.
Unto you, unto your being, humanity, behold your hands
    and know the flame moves upward unto all Flame.
And you, you cannot be diminished by Dark.
You will ever go forth in the Dark.
You will ever be the shining star.

Devout?
The flame does not require devout.
Piousness?
The flame does not require piousness.
It requires breath
    that you might be awakened
      by the Breath of whom you are.
Tether your being unto Light.
Tether your being unto the colour that you know is your own.
All beings know their colour if they will.
All beings recognize the coordinates of whom they are
    unto the Creator that is theirs.
This know.
Power be to you, humanity.

1176   Beloved of earth, carry your being unto where we are.
Hear, Soul, the thrum of tone, of sound and your being.
There is no latchkey.
There is the open door.
The way is clear.
 The spiral is upward.
Enter you in to the Path of Farside.
Rejoice in the Sound as you enter in.
Hear about you the thrum of no time.
Hear the echoes of existences far beyond your own.
Hear the song of the Angels.
Hear the voices of those long left from earth.
Hear that which you have entered in for,
    for there is much that is available unto you.
The choice is yours.
It is, Soul, read from your Aura
    again, Soul, the language of Farside, indeed.
You have entered in to another reality.
You have entered in even unto an illusion.
How can it be both?
Indeed is your world not a reality where you are!
Are you not often content within your reality!
Indeed.
Mankind is often slow to enter in to where we are,
    for fear is designated in their being, a tribal want.

Souls of earth, you are in an illusion.
You are in a state of temperant.
The temperance of being human within your earth
    is akin to being human on Farside,
    but it is not the same.
It is so much more where we are.
Upon earth you are caught in that which you must become.
Upon Farside you are that which you are.
How could it be for you as humanity,
    for you to be exactly that which you want to be?
Upon your earth, Soul, it is seldom possible,
    for even when you find that which you want to be
    you are incomplete,
    for you have not entered in
    to the fullness of your being.
The Energy that you are understands
    a missing, an empty, a totally incomplete self,
    so you begin your search again.
Humanity on Farside has a singleness of mind.
Mind, Soul, seeking only to hold that which is,
    to overcome the pain of negativity as a goal,
    to hold in the mind of earth the purpose of being,
    to reach beyond the earthiness,
    to know the Energy of self completes the form.
Without the Energy of self there is no you.
There is only the illusion of who you are.
Souls of earth, there is even upon Farside a Truth
    that the illusion of where we are
    is known, is understood.
And yet we are complete within the Farside,
    for we have found all fragments of self,
    the Soul at one with the Spirit and the Essence.
We do not have the lost feeling, the lonely heart,
    the emptiness of Soul,
    for we know we are home,
    we are in the Arms of our Creator,
    we are in the Yawn of being.
Worlds you search for are within the Yawn.
The universal understanding of space is limited,
    for you are in a vacuum as we are in a vacuum.
You have the Negative and the Positive Void.

You have the great curtain of care dividing the two
        and yet you are in the Yawn.
Beyond where you are, beyond where we are
         are existences far beyond our own
        in every manner of being.
We have not communicated,
        we have been communicated to.
We have been communicated through.
To and through.
We understand we are Purity.
We understand we are levels of Purity.
We understand the Angels and the Archangels,
        the legions of being.
We understand the Energy from the Source
        from which all receives Light,
          the Light of consciousness,
          the Light of being.
Indeed, the sun provides your visual light,
But, Soul, there is vision beyond the light of earth.
It is beyond the Light of all Energy.
There are no secrets.
You are not caught, enmeshed in a secret world,
        a secret universe,
          but you must have the key
            to open that which you would see.
To have the key you must first enter in to the Purity of being.
Not the Truth, Soul.
Truth is second.
For the ultimate Truth is where we are within the Yawn.
You must enter in.
To enter in you must have the Purity.
The Purity cannot be found without Love,
        the Love of self, the Love of mankind,
          the Love of creature, the Love of your world.
This is essential for those
        who would reach into the highest realms of knowing,
          for in the holding of such Love you become Love itself!
You recognize the Energy within your very being.
There is no evil in you.
You are mirrored,
        that which you are is mirrored.

You have a self of such authenticity.
The Truth of whom you are is where we are.
You are corporeal in your being.
You see the pain of your earth is resident in you.
The Farside, pain does not dwell.
You are, Soul, ever a part of where we are.
You do not condition yourself to be a part of where we are,
    you are a part of where we are,
    for your Spirit is always present upon Farside.
Now we have said to you,
    we do not speak to the Beings far outward from us,
    but we know of a great mirrored Lake.
It is called in all worlds, the Silver Waters, the waters that shine.
It is a place to enter through.
It is Holy as you would call much upon your earth Holy.
It is a place where Creators Became,
    where the great Energy of such pureness
    branched outward as the candelabra branches outward,
    and became Fifteen and the strength and the power,
    the Truth entered in differently unto each.
They reach forth in their Energy to form creations
    within the Void of Consciousness,
    and they registered all that was.
But even they were replications, Soul.
Replicating, mirroring that which was before them.
You mirror behaviors throughout your life
    and often you find as you mirror a behavior
    you become dissatisfied with self,
    and you understand this is not who you are;
    it is a behavior, yet it is alien to me,
    for it does not fit, Soul, the Energy of self.
Creators were formed
    and yet before them was the Vanguard, a Holy Truth.
We know the Truth was to protect.
Protect, Soul.
If there is only Purity, what is there to protect?
To protect, Soul, the beginning.
You are born and the parent endeavours
    to protect the Purity of the child
    as the child grows to manhood.
So Energy would protect that which was in the beginning,

  that no shadow would fall,
   for Life and Energy is Holy.
Life and Energy is Purity.
It may mature into something other than,
   but its beginning is pure.
Protection, Soul, always in the beginning.
You have been given a Path to follow.
You have been given a form through which you may enter in.
You may gather all that you are round about you,
   and it will lift you through into the platforms of being.
As humanity, you may travel where we may not,
   for you have been given a Path that is clear unto you.
Souls of earth, you have upon your being a great mantle placed.
It is, Soul, to reach into the realms
   where the legions of Angels flow,
   where the Holiness is the ultimate of being,
   for you may hear the very Breath of life in the Energy,
   where you may hear the tones and sounds of existence.
The echo is heard by us.
We hear it clear.
But you, humanity, you may enter in
   even before the Gateway opens.
You have the Path to enter in.
We will assist you in all manner of ways that we can,
   but it is your Path and your way,
    the way of Humanity.
Why would you enter in, Soul?
The why is in the Sound and the Colour
   of the Angels, of the Archangels.
It is in the horn of Gabriel.
It is in the music of Raphael.
Souls of earth, hear the Angels.
Weep not, that you do not hear them in your state of earth,
   but know that you have the power
    within the state of Humanity, of Farside.
Enter thou in that we might follow.

1177 We come to you from the Colours and the Sounds
   beyond your stratospheres for yours are distorted.
They do not have the consistency beyond the care.
In the space of Angels, in the space, Soul,

of the Archangels, the Colour and Sound migrates.
Indeed, it has the ability to come and go at will.
It sees an abundance of pink brought forth
        as in opening fractal your earth knows
        and the kaleidoscope of colour
        beautifies all within the heavens
        for all Colour and Sound carries
        a frequency of ecstasy within.
It is like the chord of your earth harp.
It is, Soul, like the stone of the Laird.
It is as your earth's babbling brook continuously moving.
It does not remain as a single fountain overflowing.
Indeed not.
It continues to move.
It is, Soul, opening the way,
        a vehicle wherein all Sound and Colour
        carries a consciousness from where it has been.
It is a language unto itself where all beings understand.
It brings forth, Soul, a picture.
It is the softest down
        carried upon the weight of your shoulders
        so that you know you have the comfort
        to accept or reject
        and yet it is not intrusive in any manner of being.
It only holds within a consistency of wisdom,
        not just wisdom, Soul, but the Wisdom that is Ecstasy.
It is patterned from a knowledge of perfection.
It comes as a thread from the very Creator of all being,
        Supreme Being, Supreme Energy,
        Supreme Consciousness that which is
        the fullness of all things.
It comes forth unto you
We equate it, Soul, to the energy field
        you hold upon your earth a radio of listening
        and your mind expands.
So it is with Colour and Sound.
It brings forth visions of that which is beyond where they are
        so that we where we are we know
        that which is beyond where we are.
We hold, Soul, ourselves first to await news.
You would say news of that which is in perfection

       for we know even unto all that is
       within the bodies of spheres
       bringing forth and expanding,
       opening as the butterfly opens
       to send forth galaxies of being.
You have not beheld,
       but you will behold the glory of these worlds.
You see from your earth the rings of Saturn.
You see the striking temerity of Mars.
You see the landscape of your moon
       but, Soul, these hold nothing
       to that which beholds in the Creator landscape.
And beyond the Creator landscape,
       beyond the Yawn that holds you tight
       within your worlds of many worlds,
       there is, Soul, a fence from which you will see
       the very ordinance of Supreme Being.
You will see, Soul, that which is the glory of the heavens above
       and you will find yourself,
       were you to have knees in that moment,
       upon your very knees.
Your Energy is a part of all Energy.
Your glory is a part of all glory.
All that is within your world is manifold,
       more than you could visualize.
We say this, Soul, to you that you might not in any form
       limit that which is your Creator
       even more, Soul, the complexity of your Creator
       that holds within a Triad
       and is but one portion of Creator
       that is the Supreme Creator of all Energy.
Souls of earth, unto you is your Creator.
Behold an Energy of Consciousness.
Behold a form of all forms.
Behold an endowment of all perfection.
Souls of earth, minuscule beings,
       without your portion Supreme Being would not Behold.

1178   Soul, be within the Energy Source.
Be within the Energy Field of fourth Light Being,
       strategically open to the Flame within the darkness,

>   strategically seeing the dance of dark energies.
> Yet even from the space of the Energy Source,
>   all the energies within the realm of Energy Source
>   cannot move unto in being,
>   only in projecting, projecting.
> The projectile is voice, Sound.
> Only from four.
> But all energies having given throttle to the projection.
> We must explain, Soul, the meld has not been successful
>   until the Energy of humanity, of sound.
> In the projection,
>   the Energy that has been sent out by Fourth Creator
>   has reached to here, and the next Energy boosts it.
> You call it a booster, do you not.
> A rocket booster, Soul, you understand you did not invent it.
> The Energy boosts the Sound forward, the Sound.
> It is only the Sound that enters out from the Fourth,
>   so as not to create a chaos,
>   but the Energy is boosted forward
>   by the coming together of each individual Light Being.
> It takes seven Light Beings
>   to thrust it forth unto the level of four.
> There is, Soul, heaven and heaven and heaven
>   and there is Energy of such magnitude
>   that it Lights your world in the Energy that you are.
> And we say to you, gather the Light
>   that is offered to you from the Energy Source
>   where all Energy Beings as Jesu dwell.
> This is a Purity of such Love that all is given for that Love.
> The Souls enter in unto earth, Archangels.
> Jesu has Holy Holy Holy, Light of Lights,
>   entered in to earth to teach to earth that which is Light.
> Light for which the Creator entered in
>   unto the Place of Shining,
>   a Light of such goodness
>   that it forms an iridescent glow
>   of startling proportion that emanates
>   into all Energy Fields
>   so that the echo of that
>   which is done in the Path of Light
>   is known throughout all Energy Fields.

You are in but one Energy Path.
It is continuous, yet within it are many existences.
We speak unto beings of earth.
We ask you not to be pious.
We ask you not to hold the cowl about your being.
We ask you not to hold the three quartered hat
    to pronounce your righteousness.
We ask you to know that which your brother of earth endured.
This Soul of earth entered in not from a heaven
    where Souls gather in Purity.
This being was Purity.
This Soul entered in from the place of Love,
    of Radiance, of Ecstasy.
This Soul left the home of your Creator, of our Creator
    to lowly habitation on earth to speak of this Light.
He saw Holy Light and He knew that to give,
    not as the Archangels entering in to Farside
    gave to teach,
    but to enter in to the very negativity of earth
    and be assaulted by the negativity of earth.
This Energy, this Light Being, proclaimed
    and gathered the goodness of Purity unto Him
    that He might teach unto earth did He come.

1179 We speak to you of that which we know of Godhead.
Infinite wisdom, infinite Spirit, infinite joy, infinite sadness,
    the capacity to stretch all realities into a single idiom.
You will hear an echo in the Place of Shining
    for all thought resonates.
All consciousness is formed for the Triad
    within the Place of Shining.
It has not always been so.
At a portion, thought was brought forth from the Source.
Then from the Seed, but now from the Place of Shining
    wherein only two portions of the Triad abide.
Where there are two, there is something wrong.
What is wrong, Soul, is that,
    we shall use the word, community, is not complete.
The home misses a member.
The member gone creates a problem.
As with you, Soul, when a member is lost, you go to seek.

And so it was with the Wilful Child, the Negativity.
The Archangels went to seek,
    to alter at the Source at the Seed, at the Cauldron
    and formed yet a negative.
Truth, Wisdom, Negativity to seek, to understand.
You, you are that infinite negativity sent forth to recover
    for you were armed with Truth.
Ever tactically varying each approach.
In battle it is always so.
A seed, you hold a new beginning.
Love, to embrace, Purity to gift and Truth to recover.
For when you are fallen
    you must find a truth to recover from where you are.
You must hold in your being and search with the Truth.
You are at battle.
The strategy began at the Place of Shining
    as Melchezidec offered Humanity,
    before even they were human,
    unto Creator to bring forth Negativity,
    Negativity dug deep within the pit of the negative ion.
And humanity, weak, entered in many times.
Not once, Soul,
    over and over and over
    regaining truth upon truth upon truth.
From the space of Godhead,
    Creator gave forth the breath of Truth
    with all knowledge of the Battle deep within.
But Humanity, humanity chose to enter in as negativity.
Indeed weak, able to be recognized by negativity
    using only a portion of thought
    to entice negativity unto it
    and ensuring that humanity would be weak
    in the place of negativity,
    that it would be well scarred,
    then as one,
    would find Negativity would have scarred
    the very being of humanity.
Humanity found strength to stand and recognize
    and gave of the goodness of self unto Negativity.
Humanity you reach into your very being,
    you struggle with the Truth of who you are

        but Godhead is ever vigilant of that which you do.
The Angels and Archangels
        constantly aware of your endeavours.
As you lift your voice against negativity there is rejoicing.
As you send forth Love unto negativity there is rejoicing.
As you lift your Energy to compassion
        the anthems ring out, the hallelujahs are sung
        and there is rejoicing within the Place of Shining.

1180 Souls of earth, you have been taken
        to a passage outward.
You have viewed that which is negative upon your earth.
You have formed the tears, that wide grief
        for that which is lost from you.
And we say unto you,
        how would you grieve were you to feel the depth of pain
        when perfection of all existence was taken
        and thrust into the Void,
        into the desolate no man's land
        where nothing is as it should be?
You have been, Soul, knowing of a great Energy,
        a fragment, and we say to you:
        "Is Idyllic now fragmented?
        Has the world so beloved of all existence
            fragmented itself
                as from the beginning all was fragmented?"
You know of matter.
You know you are matter,
        yet in your being you are fragmented.
A part of many parts, a being of many directions.
Humanity itself upon the earth
        not even a single purpose to speak, to teach,
        but fragmented.
And in the fragmentation is conscience
        in every fibre of your being there is conscience.
Souls, are you now as Idyllic?
Or does Idyllic still flutter in the downward spiral?
Now you know of your mathematics.
You know that that which is of greater proportion, heavier,
        will thrust itself forward at a greater speed
        than a smaller less weighty,

and so it is with Idyllic and the seven worlds.
That which was held aloft was majestic in all form.
That which was held aloft was greater
        than any sphere your science has knowledge of.
And yet you do not perceive it.
We do not perceive it.
Our research does not perceive it.
We perceive where it has been.
We perceive its projectory.
We know
        of these worlds three have entered in to the Flow.
And how do we stop pummelling, downward spiral?
And unto what does it spiral?
What is the projection, the destiny?
It is important,
        Soul, it is important to your existence!
It is important to all existence
        for it necessitates one, two, three possibilities.
It will continue and we know as you know,
        all things have a beginning and an end.
This is so, this we know.
So will it meet its beginning
        and then what are the dynamics of that meeting?
What is the chaotic encounter to be?
We do not know.
Is it possible to draw it back unto us?
As all things are sound and colour,
        as all components within your being
        are sound and colour,
        so are all components within Idyllic,
        Sound and Colour.
What is the perfection of Sound and Colour
        that will draw it upward?
Humanity, have you brought forth the perfect C?
Have you the perfect note to bring forth
        even unto Creator that which is Negativity?
This we know in our manifests, you could do!
You could bring forth that which is our Brother!
First you will dare to enter in to transition,
        then unto the Blessed Archangels.
Then to He that has been lost from us,

    beloved of all Creators,
      a portion lost from Supreme Being.
But will that perfection bring you closer
    into the goodness of Idyllic?
Will you draw with your perfection
    that which is radiance and Light?
We do not know.
And you of earth, give us answers in our seeking.

1181 Souls of earth, we give to you an understanding
    of the downward spiral of Energy.
This Energy seeks, knows, has purpose.
This Energy records in all manners.
This Energy does not alter in the way earth alters,
    but it alters the momentum,
    the positioning of Energy.
This Energy will not permit wilfulness,
    will not permit fortitude.
Fortitude is alien.
It must not be compliant.
Compliance is alien.
It must be free, free radical, Soul.
It must abound in source from which it comes.
Only then may Energy be brought past five.
A purposeful messenger can reach
    into the Energy consciousness,
    not to the Energy of being
    but to the consciousness
    of many energies beyond five.
One of these is Volume.
You will find yourself in the placement of Volume.
Volume, always expanding, always recognizing,
    always coordinating, always resounding.
Volume can resound against itself.
Volume can resound against matter.
Volume can record within the Energy of its vibration,
    as whorls send forth a vibration across your ocean
    so does that vibration speak to other mammals.
So it is in the Energy above the Dome.
Volume is the re sounder.
Echo projects the message unto Volume.

Volume is the great translator of purpose.

1182   Soul, in that which is perfection
        dwells energies, existences.
Soul, the gates are closed.
All that have been sent forth exists outside of perfection
        wherein Chaos dwells,
            wherein there is a downward spiral of Energy
        to fulfil the NEED unto perfection.
Wherein is the beginning?
Wherein is the end?
Even, Soul, within the place of perfection
        there is no beginning, there is no end.
There is, Soul, a continuum of consciousness!
There is a graciousness, a wealth of Purity,
        an exuberance of Sound and Colour.
There is within the form of perfection a cloudless visual,
        no steaming gaseous molecules that dance
        and exude forth contemporaneous energies.
There is enfolding vicissitudes of grandeur.
There is cavernous ways
        wherein all is visible expressing outwardly.
Expressing, silence itself expresses.
Sound turns, contours, blends into that which is.
All form bends at will,
        textures, senses, complexities
        rampant within perfection.
It, not an iota within the chamber, gives forth.
The constant Rapture is Naught,
        desensitizing the consciousness.
It allows the expanse of the form of consciousness.
It billows forth, it texturizes all
        and becomes elasticized in its expression
        for it always enters in unto itself.
It is complete.
This perfection fulfilling all purpose
        opening grandeurs of the consciousness
        that excite beyond the kaleidoscope of colours
        to all that a mind could bring forth
        in the fullness of its possibilities.
Within perfection is the Mind of all that is.

It is, Soul, the resonance of all that utters forth
>and vibrates and is held.
For even eons forward the Energy is hear.
Beyond the Window that impels and repels
>is the constant vibration flowing.
Souls of earth, you little know that which is perfection.
You could not contain your mind to receive
>that which is the perfect flower opening before you.
Each petal giving forth Energy unto itself
>yet blending and knowing it is of all else.
For there is the one consciousness
>that is as the many petalled blossom.
But it wants in its description
>for it cannot contain the magnitude
>of that which is possible in consciousness.
It cannot contain the creativity of that which is in consciousness.
In that perfection all becomes within the consciousness!
It is thought,
>therefore it is.
There is a constant within the consciousness of perfection.
It is, Soul, impel, repel.

1183 Soul, in Energy is hierarchy.
The Fifteen have hierarchy above Archangel.
All existences below Fourteen are reflectory of Archangel,
>with the exception of those reflected from Creators.
Souls of earth, draw your being unto the distant places.
See the curtain separated.
See within the habitats.
See those who are as you, mankind.
All are one.
One are all.
Encircle your world.
Encircle the valleys and the mountains, the rivers.
See the mountaintops rise
>and with the eyes of an eagle
>allow your sight to enter in to the currents,
>to the tors, to the resting place of mankind
>to see them different,
>as they are without their flesh and blood.
Do you see them upon the burning pyre.

Other than bone to leave with the ash?
Are you different than they?
We stress the oneness of your humanity.
You are breathed forth from the same Creator.
There is total agreement with all the Creators
    for a single purpose.
Your earth has not yet
    come in complete restoration of single purpose
    or your world would be where we are,
    not you, Soul, your world.
You hold within your being a mark.
It is a mark of the mind.
It is connected to the outer waves of your Energy.
It is not a visible to you.
It is marked so that unconsciously you tap its source.
A being does not require intellect to tap its source.
It requires only knowing.
You are within the Realm of your Creator.
Within the Realm of your Creator is a rhythm of the Creator
    that you hold dear unto you.
It is a rhythm of Love and Purity, of Truth.
The truths are there available for you.
Discernment is a part of humanity's knowing.
Many beings have discerned there is more than one Creator.
Many beings have discerned there is a Supreme Being.
 And we tell you this indeed, your Creator
    is apportioned of the Supreme Being.
Can you send forth energy from your being?
Indeed you can!
It can inflict itself on beings.
It can send forth great feelings of Love.
It is not difficult for earth beings.
How much less difficult where there is no negativity
    for your Creator to send forth great energies!
But, Soul, if you are the Supreme Being,
    can you grasp a Supreme Being
    with the knowledge of all the foundary of earth?
Souls, minuscule with all the magnificence of Eternal.
All the associates that make your earth earth are
    only a portion of that which is.
All is particled of Supreme Being.

All formulated, known, a part,
>   the very Being of Supreme Being.
Souls, all that is within the numerical containments
>   of substance, matter, ion,
>   that formulate gaseous places,
>   solid forms of such enormity
>   that your galaxy could enter in.
How can your words of earth express,
>   how can your words of earth encapsulate
>   any meaning to such enormity?
They cannot for the simple, and the educated.
There is only humbleness at such magnitude.
You cannot, Soul, bring yourself to an equation
>   that would behold that which is Supreme Being.
It is not possible within the mind of man.
It is not possible within the Angel's consciousness,
>   within the Archangel's consciousness it is not possible.
But you of earth,
>   you have been in the Eye of your Creator.
You have been recognized.
You have been brought forth with the portion of Energy.
You are, Soul, treasured.
You are beloved.
The need for humanity is still.
The need for humanity will create a purpose;
>   if not humanity?
And you spoke as one,
>   *"It will be.*
>   *We will provide Negativity*
>   *with the answer for its Need."*
And, Souls, wonder is auspicious,
>   for the smallest has brought forth the greatest.
And you have singled out compassion as the answer!
And the very tears of the Angels,
>   for the Angels wept
>   when first compassion came from the scars of negativity!
And then, as though not even knowing,
>   you heard the Sound of yet another Need.
You heard the Sireen Sound.
You heard even from the chasm,
>   from the great Cauldron you heard, Soul,

        the Purity and the Negativity.
And you offered yet to go in.
Souls of earth, you are very human.
We recognize the simplicity of your being.
And we do not say this as a detriment unto you,
        simply that there are few strengths within you,
        but the strengths that you have acquired
        have made you a goliath.
They have made you a giant.
They have, Soul, been greater
        in that you have offered to meld together
        not singly but as one.
And so we remind you of the melding,
        of the agreement of entering in unto earth
        that you would be one in humanity,
        that the glow that is before you
        recognizes there is one humanity;
        they all wither to the same bone,
        they all leave
        with the same heart and mind and Soul.
You are Light and we recognize you as Light.
So be it.

1184   Souls of earth, respect your Gods,
        when you recognize your Gods
        are whom you are
        no matter which you choose.
You choose the Energy of a Creator.
        you choose the Energy of Supreme Being;
        all Creators unto one.
Souls of earth, breathe the breath of Purity
        but know the breath is contained of the original Breath.
Original first Breath to awaken motion,
        first Breath to meld ION and MATTER.
Souls of earth, recognize in yourselves
        the capability of that which is totally human.
Understand you are a participant in all action of creation

        for you are creation itself.
You are creator indeed,
        for that which is a portion of your being

    is a portion of all being.
Unto you is the fulness of Creator possible.
Unto you is the fullness of echoed Breath possible.
Hold within your being the countenance of Purity.
Hold within your being that which is breath.
Souls of earth, magnify that which you are,
    not that which you have become!
That which you are is of the Essence,
    a portion of Creator!
That which you have become
    is the growth you have entered in for.
Behold how magnificent is the portion of your being
    that gives Light unto all other Light.
For all Light is reflected unto the beginning of consciousness.
You are of the beginning of consciousness.
You have within you the Flow, the recognition.
You have in you, Soul, the re told being
    under whom all being is recognized:
    seven Light, seven Dark, Fourteen Creators
    of whom you are particled,
    the Supreme, the fullness of Fifteen.
What is the variance, Soul?
The variance are in the complexities of each Creator.
It is in those attributes which are recognized.
You will hold in your being
    a pronouncement of that which you are.
You will understand
    you have more ability to the conscientiousness of being.
You have more ability
    to the stability to the Echo, to the Value.
You will recognize the very Truth of your being is magnificent.
You will behold that which you have come
    and discern the pattern of your being.
Are you of the fullness of the pattern of your being, Soul?
Are you made of the same swath?
Are you able to reconnect
    unto the fullness of whom you are?
We ask your return, Souls of earth.
We would that humanity would return unto Farside.
For that which you have come to do, you have done.
That which you have entered in for, you have completed.

And earth, your earth, is in travail.
Indeed.
The birthing chambers are full,
    the negativity about to be born and reborn
    and we would not have it so.
Hold fast humanity to the Timetable of Mankind.
Understand, we would not have you
    leave earth of your own accord.
We would have you recognize
    that all humanity would blend together in their Energy
    and be lifted in a single moment unto Purity.
That which you leave behind
    would be recognizable upon the Farside
    without the leverage of negativity.
Do not fear to lose that which you have.
Fear only not to blend your beings.
You are the righteous entered in to earth.
Pious is not righteous,
    religious is not righteous.
Righteous is the right of your Creator.
It is the portion of you that is of Purity,
    recognizing the Love that is the attribute.
Behold, you are!
Welcome your being.
View who you are.
See the reflection of your humanity.
Know that you will enter in to the great cavern.
ou have, Soul, all Creators beaconing unto you.
You have, Soul, the Light and the Dark to behold!
You have that which is consciousness
    ever intermingling within the mind to bring you
    unto the one and only destination of your being
    within the Second Gateway.
Advance unto the door of perfection.
Advance unto the way of humanity.

1185 We speak again of motion.
This motion we speak of as vibration, enters in.
Hear!
It is heard.
It is felt.

It is a visible vibration.
Often it is so strong that the body loses equilibrium.
It happens often to many Souls.
There is a great connection between the left and the right.
Yet they are distinctly separate, one from the other.
They carry a different motion, one from the other.
They carry a different expectancy, one from the other.
Motion and vibration are as the left and right,
> are as the Dark and Light connected,
>> fellow to each other, yet, separate.
Motion is that which is created upon your earth.
Motion is that which your humanity has brought into being,
> even from the Farside.
Indeed!
It is necessary and prudent for mankind to remember
> the greater part of who they are
>> is resident upon Farside!
And the motion of Energy
> is transferable from Farside to earth.
Only is the motion of humanity transferable
> when it has changed to vibration
> and carries the higher chord.
Motion carries a lesser chord and cannot reach to High C,
> only the falsetto of motion.
You are, Soul, hearing constantly a motion within your being.
It is sound.
Your mind translates that motion
> without your low mind being aware.
So we introduce to you:
> the low mind, the high mind,
>> the high consciousness, and Supreme Consciousness.
You are connected to all.
You are particled to all.
You have chosen to be.
What we will have you understand with great clarity,
> that the Supreme Consciousness
Supreme Being is 15th Creator.
The Supreme Consciousness is Breath
> but not Breath contained.
Again, we would ask your awareness
> of the great pyramidal container

        wherein is Breath contained to be motion altered.
Supreme Consciousness is the pyramidal,
        not the first, not the second but the third.
You have witnessed the first.
You have seen Breath strangulating within
        to create motion to be without.
As you are condensed in your Energy to implode,
        so is the smaller,
            the greatest and the greatest the smallest.
We ask you to contemplate.

1186   Soul, we have you gather your mind in great Purity,
        for we would have you behold
        the energy of Supreme Being.
We would have you know constant Light,
        enervating outward,
            ever forthcoming of goodness, ever.
As you breathe, as your breath takes itself outward
        it alters all that it is entering into,
            all the spectrum of that which your breath holds,
            even the moisture droplets are reflected outward,
            and you draw back unto you breath yet again,
            and alter within your being the breath you send forth.
So is the Energy of Supreme Being
        always charging the Field before with Light.
Light, Soul, of such grounding glory
        that it alters all that is touched,
        all that is proportioned to gather.
There are worlds beyond where Energy's Source exists
        that gather the Light of Creator.
There are, Soul, are Angels who become beautific
        in that which they are
        because of the luminescence of such glory.
All that is within them is then sent forth into worlds beyond.
The ability to transform, to transcend, to transmit becomes
        a nature unto itself within the Energy,
        for this is the nature of Supreme Being;
        to give, to transmit, to transcend all that is.
You each have an ability to be gracious.
You each have ability to be godly.
You each have the ability

>   to give forth in a manner of Supreme Being.
> Souls of earth, cover yourself with this Purity.
> Cover yourself with the Energy given unto you;
>   for you the Energy is somewhat dimmed.
> You, you are the prism, you are the coat of many colours,
>   for you have gathered, from Angels
>   who have gathered from Supreme Being,
>   therefore your Energy enters in in many colours,
>   that each holds a component to give forth,
>   to understand, to behold, to soften all that you are
>   gracious in all that you do.
> Souls of earth, the praying hands do nothing,
>   they give forth platitudes.
> The open hand has the ability to do, to offer, to submit.
> You are of Supreme Being,
>   for even as you have the Energy of Farside,
>   even as you have the Energy
>   of your Creator within the Energy Source,
>   so you even have more worthy of you,
>   the Energy of Supreme Being offered unto you,
>   the very Breath entering in to alter,
>   to change that which you are.
> Not, Soul, for the benefit of Supreme Being,
>   but for the benefit of all Energy,
>   that all Energy might unite as a single Energy.
> Now we speak to you
>   of the complicated Forms of many Creators.
> We speak to you of Fifteen,
>   all Divine in Being,
>   all issued forth from the Energy of Supreme Being,
>   all with the embryonic beginning of perfection.
>   all having a potential.
> Third you know, Second you know,
>   First we give unto you.
> Life, Death, Presence are the components,
>   Awareness, Truth, Echo to manifold complexities
>   into giver and taker,
>   offering inability, capacity.
> Souls, familiarize your being
>   with that which is life, death and presence.
> The presence within you is the Energy

        held by the very nature of its being.
Each Energy, Creator, with the capacity to work
        with each of the Fifteen,
           so they are complicated yet incredibly,
           incredibly simple in that which they give forth.
First Creator gives Life,
        has the capacity of Death, has the ability of Presence.
Second Creator must, by the nature of self,
        enfold all these components
        within its nature so that
        the 15th Creator has the register of all.
Now, we complicate further,
        for it is the distribution downward
        in that 15th Creator has all the components,
        and the reflected attributes are sent forth.
The exploratory energies of each of the attributes
        is brought to an understanding to each Energy Field.
Within the knowledge of the human Energy
        are all the components of all Fifteen Creators.
You have within you life and death.
You have within you presence.
You have within you awareness, truth, echo.
You have within you Truth, Purity, Love.
Each enfolded to complicate, yet each separate
        to defer the complication of blend.
The blend is done in the Energy Field.
This is a spectrum of understanding
        that your science will soon enter into.

1187   Soul, we come to you from a distant realm.
We speak to you of the reflection that you are.
We speak to you of the Purity that you are.
We speak to you of the Love that you possess
        within you from the Angelic self.
We speak to you from beyond the Angelic
        even, Soul, unto the Archangel.
As you reflect in your being in your awareness
        of the values of Archangels, we cannot but see
           how like your own human form
           you perceive them to be.
And we say to you,

"*They are Angelic beyond your form
    for you have reflected your beings
    to a lesser degree.
You have reflected and reflected to become human.
You carry within you the possible designation
    of whom you have been,
    the possibility to triangulate your being
    into a distant realm even unto where we are.*"
We could barely perceive that from where we are,
    you could reflect unto the form of Archangel,
    yet we know your Purity,
    the Love of your being
    has that possibility within.
You perceive the supreme Energy again as being viable
    only as you relate it unto your own form.
A Creator whom we know who is valued as Energy of Light
    that lifts the Light beyond where you are to join
    into the All Being Energy of Supreme Being.
Holy Holy Holy lift thine eyes unto the Light of thy being
    and behold the perception of whom you enter in from.
You have the countenance of humanity
    but you have within your being the possibility
    of the totality of Energy
    for you have entered in from perfection.
You are all that is of the elements.
You are all that is of the Void.
You are all that is of the peace that is you,
    that is a portion of Supreme Being.
Souls of earth, you have not beheld within
    the purpose of whom you are,
    the voile from which you have entered in.
You are truly blest for you have taken
    the field of energy that you are in.
You have struggled with the form of whom you are.
You have reached into the depths of deprivation of the Soul
    so that only the heart the mind and the body
    are viable to you until you recall in your being
    the portion that is the Soul and its connection
    to the Spirit and the Essence of whom you are.
You cannot but ponder at how great thou art.
You cannot but see

       that you have a preponderance of perfection
       to cleanse that which has marred your being
       for, Soul, you are a reflected glory.
You have Entered In.
We see you far beyond in the Light of your being
       for through the Light of whom you are
       we have a vision of that which is Archangel.
How can you who are so worldly,
       who see your world in its robe of negativity,
       even, Soul, submit to thought
       that you have risen so high,
       through the Light of your Creator,
       that you have abounded in your being
       to the Light that gives Light to life and death,
        that gives, Soul, the power to vision.
You have brought your being unto a wayward station.
It was designated for you by the Creator of your being.
You have magnified
       that which is the seed of negativity within you
       to such great proportions
       that even those who dare not judge
       are brought to tears that fall.
Souls of earth, you are crowned in your glory
       by the Light of your Creator.
You have taken a great responsibility unto you.
You have delved within your mind,
       within the deviance of your body, of your heart
       to look into the depths of that which is hell on earth.
And we only see hell on earth,
       for that which is transition is caught
       within the Love and care of the Blessed Angels.
Souls, you take a bitter cup to your lips
       but you transcend beyond the cup of often putridness
       and you raise your energy and you see with eyes of earth
       that which is before you
       and you lift your eyes unto the heavens
        and you say,
             "*Creator, why?*
                Why have I been placed thus in such pain?"
And we say to you,
       you are of the Armada of your Almighty Creator.

You have not been placed, Soul.
You have chosen to overcome that which is negativity
      to see that which is negative, truly see and behold.
You have begun with the knowns of that which negativity is.
You have allowed it to overcome your being.
You have dressed yourselves in the darkness
      and you have beseeched yourself
      to travel a little deeper into the darkness
      for behold
      there are delights of the mind in the darkness.
There are delights even to the heart in the darkness.
But the Soul, the Soul beseeches.
      "Come once again unto the Light.
      See that from which you have entered in.
      See the glory of Almighty Creator.
      Behold you are a portion of that Light!
      And you reach from the dregs of darkness
          and you enter in to the Light.
Souls of earth, do not stay your being.
Do not hold yourselves
      to the portion of Light that is of your earth.
In no way can it comfort your Soul.
Reach to that which is of the Soul, the Spirit.
Reach to the particle of your being
      that is the Essence of your Creator
      and you will know you are Light.
You will know you are reflection
      of a greater source than that of earth.
As you allow the Blessed Angels
      to speak unto you, to comfort you,
      to teach from where you have been
      in the lofty heights of Light of Purity,
      then you will behold that negativity was an illusion.
It was only a moment.
You were lost.
You allowed your energy to be complacent,
      to be persuaded.
Soul, it is a precious moment
      when a human recognizes the Light of whom they are,
      for the heavens become more than they were.
All that was redeems itself

  and the Soul is lofted unto the Truth of its domain,
   the level of Purity it knows so well.
Souls of earth, you are a Holy being.
You are Holy Holy Holy in the presence of your Creator,
   for you have seen with the eyes of whom you are
   more than that which is a burning bush,
   more than that which is a blessed Light come down.
You have been lifted, Soul,
   unto the very Energy from which you have entered in.
You are Purity.
Hold to the Purity.
Fasten your Energy to the Light that is carried in the eye
   that allows you flight into the heavens and beyond.
Where we are we see you.
We are caught in the constancy of your being
   to repeat lifetime after lifetime of entering in
   to overcome the struggles of your earth.
Souls of earth, the negativity dwells always in the realm of earth
   but you you have the possibility to lift yourself
   and others beyond the struggle.
For you may see the Truth of that which earth is.
You may behold the higher good in all that is.
You may raise your eyes to the Mountaintop,
   to the heights of Purity
   and behold beyond where the stars,
   the moon and the sun fill the sky.
There are countless spheres beyond.
Soul, you are less than any word
   we could give you could describe.
Yet you are more than even your sun and your moon
   than even the planets in the millions beyond.
For you are the overcoming
   of all that is negative by entering in,
   by melding, by holding and struggling and knowing,
   yet reaching to lift the pain unto your Creator.
Souls of earth, there are many deeds upon your planet.
They are negative beyond describing.
You cannot always alter in the moment
   that which you see
   for often it is done before you see.
But you can send forth vibrations throughout your earth.

You can send them forth,
> so that earth itself rebounds those vibrations
> on a constant basis over and over, spiraling
> from one axis to another, around the perimeter,
> spiralling so that your Energy becomes power uniting
> with the energies of all humanity.

Souls of earth,
> you are reflected Energy of the almighty Archangel!

You do not see yourself as thus.
You were never intended to see yourself as such
> only to hear, but you can reach unto that Energy.

You can know yourself by the entering in to the Purity,
> by the goodness of your being.

Touch with the touch of Purity.
Behold with the eyes of Love.
Hear all dregs of negativity
> then mouth outward from your being
> the energy of Purity
> not in an uprighteous spout of self
> but in the goodness that equals
> that of your Creator in Love for your humanity,
> for that all humanity is one humanity.

It is, Soul, the Armada sent forth,
> all different are only the complications
> that have been set upon earth to overcome.

You are joy.
You are, Soul, the perfect being of Purity
> entered in to pain.

Behold that what you are
> and that which is yours to give.

Give that you might know that you are of your Creator
> that you might know you are of Supreme Being
> that you have reflected forth from the Archangel.

Holy Holy Holy blessed art thou humanity.

1188 Soul, we would speak to you of the Echo,
> the transmitter, the carrier, Soul, of all Energy.

It is, Soul, First Creator who by necessity must
> transmit all Energy
> of all occurrences first unto Supreme Being.

There is upon all Energy a known,

        that all must return,
        you, Soul, must return
        from whence you have entered in.
You cannot stay.
You have not the ability to stay.
You have an appointment with death.
It is not your time upon earth,
        it is the time you have given upon the Farside to leave.
You cannot hear, you cannot smell,
        you cannot see, taste, feel death.
You cannot.
It is brought to you.
How you leave your world is visible,
        but when you leave your world
        can create great karma,
        or should a soul take you before you should go,
        the karma would be of such complication.
And yet many occurrences are not karma,
        they are agreements
        brought by Souls at the Station of Learning.
All that you are is echoed forward, all that you have become
        is echoed backward, so that when you enter in to earth
        many receive an echo.
They hear, they know
        a child is coming with such visage.
And they will state this so, and it will be so.
It is because of echo, echo and Energy blend.
When a soul carries the Energy
        to behold that which is echo, the Soul hears.
Many beings who do not disperse their Energy
        into complicated forms, but hold their Energy,
        often receive the echo.
These can be Souls caught in an illness, children,
        elderly who have awareness of energies beyond earth.
You have the ability to receive echoes from distant places.
You have the ability to receive echoes from Idyllic,
        and we know this because many within the Crystal Cave
        have heard the echoes deep within the darkness.
They have held abilities to respond even unto echo,
        and resound it within their being.
We ask earth Energy to reason,

>   not with the mind but with the Energy,
>   that you might know the purpose of your being,
>   and you might understand
>   why you have entered in to earth.

You are the mark upon the map.
You portray when, where and even how you bring forth
>   the Energy of Idyllic.
It is with the sound you send forth.

1189   Soul, behold who you are.
In all humanity is presence.
Presence is recognized at the awakening of self,
>   the self of Energy,
>   the buoyancy that lifts and soars and becomes!

Within your world all that is holds presence.
The mountain, the river, the beetle, the barbed rose,
>   the tit willow, the leopard,
>   the very rock that is formation of earth.

Presence never alters from the purpose of being.
Presence recognizes all energies but fears not.
Presence does not enter in.
It does not hold side within the battle.
It is the present, allowing the Spirit and the Soul.
Within the Essence of self is the presence of whom you are.
It holds within all the accountability
>   and recognition of the chaotic purpose.

Yet in the recognition
>   does not move or alter self;
>   yet sends forward Energy
>   to gather recognition of chaos.

Who are you, humanity,
>   that you have not yet recognized chaos?

What will be sufficient for you, humanity,
>   to recognize the need to overcome chaos?

In the presence of your being
>   you understand why you have entered in.

You have understood in every life
>   you will have lived that which you must overcome
>   that, indeed, chaos might not reign.

Yet in the foothold of mankind upon earth
>   there appears to be an urgency

to draw into deeper chaos.
We would have you reflect on the presence of your being.
We would challenge mankind
    to see the dimension of whom you are,
     that you will understand the graciousness of being,
    that you would rise up in Spirit
    and recognize the power of whom you are.
Presence will maintain your place.
You will not lose your portion of humanity.
For you have left that portion aside your Creator.
It is from the presence of being that all Energy knows Energy.
For it is in the consciousness of that presence
    that recording is done.
Vibrate your Energy.
Move outward in your Energy
    and still you will maintain a presence
    that is immovable in the existence you are in,
    only moveable as you reflect back
    unto where you have entered in.
So be it.

1190 From the Realm of Consciousness is compassion.
It is not an innovation of lower existences, Soul.
Indeed not.
Within the Supreme Being compassion reigns.
It is the compassion that drew the need
    to give motion unto MATTER, unto ION.
It is, Soul, the gentle quiver of recognition,
    that being has not within them that which you have.
MATTER was not ignited.
ION was not ignited.
Consciousness was ignited from within!
The need to send forth became conscious.
The need to reach out became awareness.
The need to create motion became the reality.
15th Creator, Energy of Consciousness,
    Supreme Being, one God.
We use the term, God, that mankind might know
    the hierarchy of Energy.
You speak in your world of many Gods,
    we would have you term, Energy,

for all that you see as supreme are Energy.
All Energy can take on form.
You as human create form within your being.
You as human can alter that form within your being.
All form requires motion
        to be the igniter of consciousness within form.
15th Creator is that Consciousness.
All consciousness is tethered to one Consciousness.
All form is tethered to one MATTER.
All Ion is tethered to one ION.
15th Creator holding the pain of all Energy,
        seeking the unified effort of all Energy
        without compelling the Energy to move.
Spiral is the need that was created.
The need to bring forth is the completion of that need.
A need must have an answer, must it not!
You provide the answer.
You speak in your world of Gods.
You speak in your world
        with defamation against Supreme Being.
Yet in your comprehension of the Energy,
        there is a lacking of how vibrant,
        transcending, all energies, Supreme Being.
Soul, In your very finest moments you are pale in comparison.
Yet you are treasured form of that Energy.
Indeed, form, Soul.
And you are of the same vibrancy.

1191   All has pulse.
All Energy has pulse.
Often the pulse is taken to a slow, methodical beat.
Often it is quick, delivered with speed.
Yet all Energy, all Energy has pulse.
You have pulse.
Without the pulse of your heart you would not live.
Earth has a resounding pulse within.
Each of those who are of the Twelve have pulse.
Negativity has pulse.
And wherein all lies, has pulse.
The Void.
The pulse of the Void has the lowest degree of movement.

It is able to gather all resounding thrums within existence.
When a new thrum is heard, it gathers unto itself.
It is a generous thrum.
It denies no thing.
All that enters in is welcomed.
Energy begets Energy.
It does not evolve, it begets.
Understand this, science!
It is created from one thrum into another.
It forms and often annihilates.
Behold the vacuous way,
    the Void that is all things, that holds all existence.
Breath, Voice, Chaos,
    Life, Death, Awareness is within the Void,
    Sound and Colour within the Void.
It is, Soul, to be within the drum
    and hear the great throb from out
    and the vibration resounding
    from the throb of many tones,
    each holding a clarity of such divinity.
For what is divine?
Purity, Soul, Purity is divine.
Purity is sacred.
Purity carries its own resonance within the vacuous way.
Listen to the voice of Purity.
Listen to the variations that carry the message unto you.
You will not feel it with your heart.
You will not feel it with your mind.
You will feel it in the Energy of your being.
You will hear the earthquake tremor.
You will hear the great sky open.
But, Soul, you will also hear worlds collide and stars burst
    and Energy ignite one against the other.
And you will know in your being,
    you can take yourself from where you are
    to vision that which is.
You, who are humanity, can allow your being
    to travel through the vacuous way.
There is no cap to how far you can go, Soul.
It has to do with Purity.
It has to do relinquishing who you are,

        releasing from you your humanness
        and entering in to the fullness of Spirit.
Then you may travel through the stars to where we are.
We can guide you,
        you will not lose your way.
We can take you in your human Energy
        to behold the Human on Farside.
And you will see the gardens wherein
        the flowers reach abundance, the colour sublime.
You will see, Soul, the Akashic before you.
And you will be able to read your time on earth.
And you will take back with you that awareness
        and you will have encaptured in your being;
        as your filament captures, so will you capture
        that which you have seen
        and you will speak
        unto earth beings of that which is.
You will enter in to the sacred stations of learning
        and you will see familiars.
You will not speak, Soul, for you are a guest.
You may only witness.
Your earth voice has been stilled
        that you might gather as humanity gathers,
        that it might enhance
        that which you are upon your earth.
You may speak in your heart.
And if it is the wish of any being to speak unto you,
        they will do so.
But you may not express outward,
        for you are still of the earth weave.
You have not released from you all form.

1192   Souls of earth, we speak to you of chaos.
Chaos upon the earth is often engineered.
It is brought into being by the negative exploits of man.
Yet there is another Chaos.
It is this Chaos of which we speak.
The Chaos that is within all the outer realms.
It is, Soul, flagrant in its effort to separate all energies.
It is wild.
Wild in that it does not contain itself.

From where does Chaos enter in?
What is its origin?
Wherein is the core of its being, the central force
    that carries the centrifuge of all chaos
    wildly, outwardly,
    containing a thrust of such magnitude
    that it enters in unto all things?
Only within the safety of Purity
    set as a vanguard does chaos not enter in.
Yet it may enter through and we say this unto you,
    Idyllic and the seven worlds holding the perfection
    wherein all perfection resided in peace from Chaos,
    yet a simple leak was able
    to cause a reaction to the stability.
Within the microbic world which was seen as safe from,
    Chaos found a way to create a leak
    that withheld a perfection creating chaos.
What is this chaos?
Why are you where you are creating even more chaos?
You are learning to contain chaos!
You are learning to stabilize that which was unstable!
Yet the Chaos of which we speak is greater by far
    than all the universes melded together.
What is this fraction
    that can so alter what could be perfection?
We say to you, the energy of Chaos
    has its beginning before Breath.
It is contained of MATTER.
It is not MATTER in the sense you know matter.
It is contained of MATTER.
Its core is unstill.
Its core ever twisting, ever turning, ever altering its form
    as though strangulating within itself.
Each fragment of all beings that you see
    at some spectacle,
    has been within the outer Volume.
The spectacle has seen the Void,
The density of Naught and the vibrational core
    wherein vitrolization of thrust was contained,
    created an outward reach.
The Light, the Dark, never was,

>   the hot, the cold never was.
> The implementation of thought, was.
> The reach into the unknown, was.
> To retract the centre core to a stillness was not,
>   for it was not to be stilled.
> It was ever in vibration,
>   holding the serenity of its outward wall.
> Spectrum was deep within the core.
> It could not find cessation of movement,
>   it could not be stilled.
> No time, no eon,
>   no counterbalance to that which was only the Void.
> No worlds, no existence, no finite or infinity,
>   only the Core and the outer realm,
>   the vastness of which numbers could not account.
> No God or Gods, no creature,
>   the emptiness of volume, the state of all beings.
> And you see from where you are
>   how less than micro you appear even to our form
>   and you have entered in to the greatest battle
>   within reach of all understanding.
> You are fortitude at its best.
> You we see as of peace, tranquillity.

1193 Where did the breath come from?
What motivated Breath?
What motivated the reaction, Soul?
Capitulation, need.
You had to breathe or lose your existence!
Indeed. Capitulation. You gave in to breath.
Breath came from need.
Consciousness had a need for Matter and Ion to breathe.
What is consciousness, Soul?
Void.
Void, void of no thing.
Void, without,
    would be a reasonable explanation for Void.
Not without,
    Consciousness awakened to a recognition.
In the recognition was a vision of Matter
    that had always been.

Yet no motion.
Ion Energy, rapturing within self, rapturing!
Consciousness beheld this Rapture
    and a need to blend became a need for motion.
For motion would blend, would it not?
And, Breath, far, far, far, far, far, far, into the endless Void,
    the Sound of Breath was heard in the Consciousness.
But through the millennia a thought formed.
    What if I draw unto me that Breath?
    What if I, absorb and send outward
        unto Ion and Matter
            that which I have absorbed?
    Had I not awakened Matter?
    Will I not create the Rapture to flow?
Where did Breath come from?
It came willingly.
It was gathered willingly, absorbed willingly,
    sent forth willingly.
It did not resonate.
It did not clarify.
It jangled.
It brought discordant motion,
    rocking and rapture became despair.
And togetherness became chaos.
And worlds bombarded against worlds
    and all that was, left apart.
And Breath, yet willing, beckoned always unto Life,
    to Existence, to Matter, the triad to awaken,
        consciousness and have breath separate.
Humanity, your mind and your body are separate.
They do not blend.
Your mind, your consciousness,
    is imprisoned within your mind.
It can become a very prison.
Your body, the matter holds the pain of that imprisonment.
So it is in Energy of far off from you.
Breath has dissipated into air
    once again become, even chemical.
It is the belief of Souls of awakened consciousness
    of Farside, of Light Beings, of Angel worlds,
        that Breath was unto MATTER

    as at the Seed, a distortion.
This is what we can say to you, Soul.
Consciousness had aloneness.

EPILOGUE
Excerpts from the Textsum

1194 In the language of humanity there is a quick thread.
It is continuous.
It is, Soul, the thread of cooperation not between human,
      but between the energies of all that is.
There is within the text a code.
The code resides as a truth.
It is implanted not by you but by Energy itself.
It is a tedious in earth languages, to see, to hear,
      to speak the differences
      but that is because of the language barriers of your earth.
For you that which is tedious is a smooth plane for another.
The text is.
It cannot be changed.
It is a truth that man's inability to be one is fallible.
Those inabilities show within the text even, Soul, as the six.
You are not perfect but that which goes forth has a Truth.
It will resonate.
Allow the justification of Truth to be present.
Do not make huge arcs in the thread,
      for the thread does not delineate one from the other.
It aligns humanity one with the other.
All that you have done, all that you have you put forth
      is visible in the threads.
The lacks,
      Souls who have been tethered, yet barely present,
      have a thread.
The Soul who unites yet is not present, has a thread.
Each of you have threads that have filtered themselves
      into the text management.
You cannot, Soul, eradicate the errors.
They will be seen as inadequacies
      but each has been inadequate
      to bring forth in your humanity.
Only in the thread that is the walk ins are you adequate.
The words are as is, errors yes, not merely one
      yet as each human peruses
      they will be met at the level they are in.

They will recognize the error where some will just pass on by.
You will each be tempered in your reaction, differently.
The text does not go forth for six.
It does not go forth in the language of English, Chinese.
It does not go forth in Taiwanese, in dialects of Africana,
      in the languages of the north
      and the south of the east and the west.
It goes forth as an Energy to touch the Souls of man,
      to touch the hearts of man, to touch the minds of man.
It is not to bring grandiose to any one being.
It is not to reside in the hearts and minds of six.
It is to fill a need.
It is to resonate within the Souls of mankind.
The Angels accompany going forth,
      do not fear for the passage through earth
      will be unique as the coming forth.
It is why there are Keys,
      Keys to enter, Keys to bring forth,
      Keys, not a single Key
      but seven unique Keys
      that touch all areas of mankind.
There was never to be a single Key.
Within earth are seven planes.
Within the Yawn are seven planes the Keys must fit unto.
Do not place fear.
Fear is inadequate.
Place Love.
Place purpose.
Place truth for that is what you are, Truth,
      the great joy of your Creator, mankind in oneness.
We say to you,
      "Do not concentrate but allow the Energy to flow."
Too much consternation clogs the wheel of motion.
Be generous in your spirit.
Be truthful in your words.
Be joyful that that which is is apportioned
      not to any one of six,
      not even to six
      but unto all the earth members
      who have entered in to place the seven Keys forward.
You do not know

whether you speak to an Angel or an earth being.
For Angels have entered in to give Energy forth.
You are merely human but the Energy of whom you are
    may thrust even farther for, Soul,
    the energies of your walk ins
    are tantamount to the mission of sending forth.
Do not sob.
Do not cry.
Do not fear.
Allow the motion of a great wind to spring forth
    and you will find volumes entering in to
    an inquisition of the mind
    and men will question from whence it has come;
        "*Who has brought forth?*
        Has it been the devil?
        Has it been ill will?
        Has it been a gift from Almighty God?"
Souls, you are Angels.
You have entered in for a moment in your time,
    each with a purpose but the purpose is one.
You are the cornerstone of a great Tablet.
The Tablet will fall asunder
    and you will be amazed, at times downcast,
    at times billowing
    in what you would deem to be righteousness
    but it will be, Soul, acclamation of the heart
    for the heart will recognize that all motion has entered in.
Do not be tedious in your answers to mankind.
Allow the perusal of that which is
    for then will be the need to bring forth
    the manuals of teaching.
For man will counter with questions
    and from the great script of *Supreme Trilogy*
    will come the answers
    and further still unto earth the stream arrives.
Gentle thy hearts.
Do not counter a problem with a problem.
Allow acceptance to enter in,
    for indeed in to each volume, Energy flows.
It is alive, Soul, with Energy.

1195 Souls, we come to you to restore a broken space.
We come to you to participate in your agenda.
We are, Soul, given vision as your channellers are given vision.
We are not one or two, we are a world of visionaries.
We are able to see within the hearts of man.
We are able to see within the Dark Void.
But we are limited to the space we are in.
We have a possible ability to see through you,
      through your being
      and it is for this
      that you have received a restructuring of your being.
Souls, you may ask
      at the temerity of altering who you are without asking.
But we have asked, it is the agenda of Farside, Soul!
For you will be taken to distant places
      and not anchored as securely as you have been.
We do not carry a fear and we ask that you do not carry a fear.
If you have fear, you will not be able to transfer
      your coordinates to where we are.
And you must, Soul, come to us for we cannot come to you.
There will be a great darkness felt
      by the channellers in entering in.
You will feel the pressure of many grids upon your being.
You will feel within the Energy of your crown
      an upheaval as though the crown
      has been lifted from your body.
We will let you know, Soul,
      this is the sense of our entering in to travel with you.
There will not be a single being,
      there will be multiple in the single transporting.
It will not alter your body,
      but you will feel the density of the energies.

1196 Soul, we speak to you
      of the consistencies of that which is earth religion.
It is a recognition
      from that which has been given
      in Creator's Trilogy, the Keys;
      in Supreme Being Trilogy;
      and to be, the Trilogy of Consciousness.
There will be recognized a great similarity

    in that which is of earth and earth's religions.
These are not coincidental, Soul.
Earth has received much from Purity.
Mankind has contorted much that has been received.
There is, Soul, a great Truth.
The Truth is from the great Voice of Consciousness.
Voice of Consciousness.
It is, Soul, sent forth by the Void of Consciousness.
It is that which the symbols of earth have been made,
    the truths of the apex, the mountaintop,
    the pyramidal offering that is triad
    wherein all mankind recognizes
    a consciousness of Energy.
There is, Soul, the symbolic truths of life and death.
There is the power of life
    and the opportunity death provides for life, for renewal.
There is the Rend creating pain in the loss of Purity,
    Idyllic, which is replicate in the loss of the Archangels,
    of the Angels in transition,
    of mankind within transition.
There is the great pyramidal leak
    wherein Chaos altered Breath and sent forth motion.
And then does Matter not escape the negative push!
For Chaos sends Matter disruptive pushing,
    thrusting forward and always
    there is the compassion of the Triad
    sending forth solutions;
    the chasm of innocence, the Microscopic beings
    who hold the most precious of Energy.
And yet, to create a negativity thrusting outward as matter itself;
    the wisdom of all Energy giving of itself Truth
    that solution might be found
    and offering unto humanity
    the opportunity to be the Armada;
    Truth of the Second Creator who offers the Truth.
Souls of earth, significance in all that you do,
    in all that is written,
    in all the words that are spoken.
There is a new day.
You speak the new day and indeed,
    a new day will enter in wherein all earth

>   will recognize that evil is of them.
>
> It is not, Soul, of negativity.
> It is created through negativity by humanity.
> There is a pouring forth of recognition of all that has been written.
> It will be evaluated and re evaluated
> >   as the text of the Trilogies,
> >   of Supreme Being, of Creator, of Consciousness,
> >   are given forth
> >   and in that recognition
> >   will become a beatitude
> >   that will speak of a perfect litany
> >   for the purpose of mankind.
>
> That litany will be recognized as seven.

1197 Blessed brethren,
>   we speak to you of the earth time you have left.

We speak to you of the projected menu
>   you have given unto your being.

We speak to all six.
The angel has left.
Souls of earth, none can separate themselves.
You are five in the care of the angel.
You have given the purpose of your being to bring forth
>   that which has been given unto you.

There is a time for each to be upon your earth.
Do not be saddened, do not decry,
>   for your earth is but an illusion.

You will know when one leaves earth, two will follow.
Each will feel the impetus,
>   the need to complete that which is given.

Hold to the calendar of earth time,
>   know that you bring forth
>   that which will be compared,
>   that which will be given unto
>   the separate dynasties of earth.

Do not feel that you have overwhelming urgencies.
What you have are overwhelming energies
>   to fulfill that which you do.

The back of your being is feeling the strain of your earth.
You are feeling a need to participate in earthly endeavour,
>   and it should be so, for you are of earth.

Do not displace that which is projected to you.
You cannot maintain earth breath.
It is vital to place your Energy to the task that you do.
You are beloved.
You are caught in a promise to each other.
You cannot displace that promise,
>   for your body will age and wither,
>   your eyes will grow dim,
>   and you will cease to sense the urgency.

It is human to have endeavours, activities of earth time,
>   but you are not upon earth to fulfill earth time
>   but to fulfill that which is Farside,
>   for you are walk in.

You cannot strain the flesh and the blood of your being,
>   for you have entered in to a human form.

You have chosen not to enter in as the angel form.
Therefore the endeavours of your earth must be earth time.

1198   To earth, to planet earth
>   from all who live within, yet you see not.

We speak to you.
We speak through the Greys unto your being.
We ask that you expect visitations,
>   that you feel and see the Spirit of whom we are.

Our Energy is transferrable.
You will feel the Energy of the Spirits.
You will think a shadow has crossed your wake.
And you will know you are tended to.
You are given unto you a respite of Spirit, not of work;
>   we have not said this, Soul, of Spirit
>   that you might find your Energy lifted,
>   that you might feel a gift given.

Do not place concern
>   when you feel around you spirits leaving earth,
>   it is only to remind you
>   that each of you have entered in to earth for a sojourn
>   until that which is done, is done.

Many that you know will pass before you.
Many will linger for many years.
But you, six, have entered in for a time, the time of fulfilment.
Only the Registry will alter the leaving,

>   only a time of un reward will give a quickening
>   to the time of earth.

You are able to see clearly.
You are able to understand
>   that the eyes of earth have only a simple purpose:
>   to perceive the beauty of earth,
>   to perceive the need of earth,
>   and to fulfil that need, the triad.

There is upon each Soul a greatness of Spirit.
For within each Soul is that of a duality.
For they carry both uniqueness of the Energy
>   they have entered in to,
>   and they carry also the Energy of that that is entered in,
>   a Spirit of manifestation.

This is difficult to contend with,
>   not just for the Soul
>   but for those who are a part of the family.

They do not perceive in you just a single being.
They understand your duality.
Yet, it is difficult, is it not?
You are first that Energy that entered in;
>   second, the Energy of whom you entered in to.

It is this duality that makes your life ever pressing unto you,
>   for you see your energies change.

You see your beings alter.
And one rides high the other rides low.
And so it is.
And yet, each Soul who is a portion of family,
>   has entered in with this agreement.

We would have you know this.
They are aware in their Spirit of why and whom you are.
They perceive that which was intended for your life.
No life has been less for the entering in.
All have been enhanced by the generosity of the Spirit.

1199   Souls, we speak to you of continuity, continuity,
>   of that which you do, that which is before you.

It is not endless.
Indeed, it has a time for you are in earth time.
Your time is counted and allotted.
There is indeed a program before you.

It is intense in its stringency.
It would seem there is not enough time.
Souls, we assure you, time will allot itself to you.
Do not seek for earth issues to be resolved from Farside.
They cannot be, they are earth issues.
There is much we can assist you with, Soul.
We can allot to you fortitude
    that you have strength to enter in to your day,
    that you have the fire in your being
    to know that you are in a moment of humanity
    and humanity has a great need for your action.
Beloved of earth, all those who have suffered
    throughout the millenniums
    await your entering in
    unto that which is to be finished.
For Soul, the beloved Brother is weary;
    is seeking and finds not.
You strengthen that which is the resolve to find!
Souls of earth, do not cry.
Do not weary to the point of wanting to leave,
    for your earth also would leave but cannot.
You, you who are humanity,
    you who have brought our energies beyond
    into the space of the Angels
    know that the crown of your being
    is not endowed with diamonds.
Soul, it has purpose,
    the purpose to bring forth that which is necessary
    for humanity's strength to acknowledge
    that humanity is in a space of great negativity.
And you, you who have seen a program,
    you who have seen beyond that which the Angels see,
    you know the solutions
    and you give unto earth solutions.
You give unto earth purpose of being.
When the Soul is brought low by negativity,
    they feel a nudge from you.
They feel your goodness,
    even as they strike your humanity.
Endeavour to be in the positive,
    for in the positive you bring forth quickly

        that which should be.
In the negative, Soul, you delay.

1200   There are no Judases.
There are, Soul, only parts of being
        for the purpose of growth to earth,
        for the purpose of teaching mankind.
There are, Soul, no men of evil.
There are men who perform evil deeds.
Understand, your earth is divining the purpose of earth.
Your science is understanding
        the purpose of earth includes Soul.
It is divining in spirituality, in enlightenment.
It is allowing that the earth is more than earth thought.
It has equated to its being enlightenment.
Many have acceptance, but science has not.
Science is now being given an equation.
It is: 7 over zero equals 3 over 1, Y equals T.
The triad of matter is force, Light and darkness.

1201   Soul, it is called chaos.
Chaos struggles in all things.
There is a need for deep calm.
We speak of the linears
        throughout all existence, the great variety.
As your earth beings have great variety
        so do the linears of wisdom draw forth and grow.
And as earth beings express wisdom, so the linears grow
        and wisdom becomes a part of whom they are.
All have not reached such wisdom.
You may not scurry to wisdom, you may not rush to wisdom.
You must walk calmly to wisdom.
You must allow thought
        to search itself, to search within, to search without
        that you might come to an equality of thought,
        a genuine equality
        wherein no one is seen to be less than the other,
        wherein each Soul offers
        what they have been brought to offer,
        that all have acceptance.
We ask that you offer forth unto each a calmness of being.

We stress it, Soul, so that you absorb the message.
For it is imperative to the moving forth of that which you do.
It is important that generosity of Spirit
        be a portion of whom you are.
Within the Soul of each being is the thread of past battles.
Within the Soul of every being
        is the loving kindness that has been offered.
Within the Soul of every being
        is the possibility of cohesive thought.
This will put motion forth in a positive manner.
You are not brought together to be inquisitioners.
You are not brought together
        to have one decisive above the other.
You are brought together even, equal,
        one no greater than the other,
            that you might accomplish
            that which you have entered in for.
All things will be done.
All books will be published.
All power will be given.
Do not own, do not choose right or wrong.
Do not place platitudes one to the other.
Be humble in that which you do.
Place honour forward
        and know you are brethren unto the other.
In your constant selves know that you are beings
        of immeasurable Purity and goodness.
Do not allow the human way to be your way
        but seek ever the higher self.
Seek ever the gentle spirit that is in you.
Laugh, sing, let go of pain.

1202 We would have you understand each,
        there is no coincidence.
What we would have you do, we would have you do in Purity.
The Purity of the six.
It is an equation that places the world as one,
        that recognizes the Soul value.
It is the equation!
It is the purpose
        of that which is channelled in your moment.

When six are not one, there are six.
The purpose is that they are one, that they speak as one.
That that which they know is offered as one.
Contention lies within.
There is no superiority in any one of the six
      for that which is the equation to come forth.
It must be seen as Purity,
      it must be recognized as a value to behold,
      and yet there is hierarchy
      and we say unto you
      erase from your being proudness.
Erase from your being that which holds power.
Give unto each of your fellows just,
      not just the Soul, just.
For just is enough, not an overage, not an underage, but just.
You are not meant to be,
      you are meant to bring forth.
There are no proud moments
      for those who enter in as walk in.
You are walk in.
You have derived your Purity in former lives.
That which you exist in it now is the being of another,
      who have given forth unto you a purpose of their being
      that you might complete
      that which has been witnessed on Farside.
In no matter do you impale another with darts.
In no manner do you speak
      in a righteous manner unto another.
Force does not have value.
Frenzy does not have value.
It is a gentle response.
It is heard and welcomed.
It is the reasoning of a just being.
It is welcomed upon each and all of the six.
It is the invitation to dance with Truth and vitality of being
      for you hold the power of Truth.
You hold it, Soul, it is not but yours.
It is not yours to evaluate.
It will be evaluated by the many beings of earth.
It will land upon deaf ears,
      or ears that are welcomed to hear.

Many who will forage through those words
      to find the gems of understanding,
      to find the purpose of existence,
         that existence to see the continuation of breath.
You are those existences.
You understand that life and death are one.
Life without death can not be.
All has value.
The value is not in the dying, it is in the living.
It is the renewal of breath, the welcoming back of breath.
Each being who has a place, knows that place.
Seek in your being to the nature of others.
We ask that each being gentles themselves.
Regret is a sorrowful state.
It is not meaningful in any form.
It does not reverberate to a positive note.
There is a Trilogy.
It is why you have entered in
      to place before mankind that which is needful.
This has always been precedents and is not now.
Each Energy will find a need to release from themselves
      negative being, that they might recognize the worthiness
      of the Soul they entered in with.
Do not promote.
Complete, Soul.
Time is closing.
Time is releasing itself upon your earth.
It is fragmenting and nothing your world does
      will prevent it from being so.
That which we give unto you, allows all energy
      holding negativity at the time of the whirl,
      to be lifted.
It is the devout Energy of Farside that this be so.
We can not make it so.
It is the energy of Holy unto Holy that will make it so.
Do not bombard your beings with negativity.
Do not base thy being but lift high your Energy
      that it might be melded within the aura of each other.
That which you have entered in to complete is not completed.
It is the purpose of your entering in.
We may not plead with you, Soul.

That which has been given, has been given.
The time limits have been set.
Do not look at your frail bodies and feel your minds withering.
You have adequate and more
        to complete that which is holiness.
There is no perfection except that which enters in.

1203   You have much to rejoice over,
        for you have been wounded
        and you have become
        and others will enter your space
        that they too might become.
They will see in your being the very Light that shines.
The Soul cannot be fraudulent in any manner.
For the propelling forth of literature
        is dependent on the goodness
        of the heart and of the mind.
The vibratory senses may not enter in to pain of want or greed.
As negativity comes so must it go.
You must release, Soul, all envy,
        all malicious thought, for the echo holds clear here.
This is the corridor of pain.
As you heal remember this.
Speak Souls. Speak often.
Speak forth of the Truth you have gathered.
Speak forth in tenderness that you might learn
        to extol from you words of generosity.
Offer not learning,
        but that which you have come to believe,
        that which you have been shown,
        that which has been offered unto you.
Do not teach.
Allow the teachings to be absorbed within the Energy.
Only speak of that which is pure.
Speak for them in the words of softness.
Express the variances of detail that have been given unto you.
Do not, Soul, balance between church and State.
Do not balance between channelling and church
        or channelling and state.
Only offer the visions that have been given.
Offer, Soul, the heights of the heavens.

Offer the knowledge of negativity,
    of the blessed Brethren,
    of the words that are available unto you.
Be willing to be heard.
For it is to be seen that will gather goodness unto you;
    and goodness will spread its being
        as a cloud can spread and open and give forth rain.
So will your words spread and give forth reason for growth.

1204   Hear the sound of creation.
Hear the sound of becoming.
Hear the crystal shard of Humanity.
Know that in the heavens of your universe, Sound is.
The Energy is.
The motion is.
The chaos is.
Within the sound of creating is purpose.
Within the sound of creation is dimensional thought,
    dimensional thought reaches beyond light year.
It is not connected except in consciousness,
    it is not tethered except to its beginning.
To enter in to conscious thought
    is to enter in to the fullness
        of what the mind is capable of.
To enter in to consciousness of being is to enter in
    to infinity of consciousness.
It is not the matter that is infinity, Soul.
Matter is finite within each existent capacity of being.
It is the consciousness of that existence
    that allows infinity to be reached,
    to be accepted, to be known.
Infinity connected always with sound, vibratory colour.
Your world places its own component of colour
    to bring forth image.
Yet in the Domes of reality
    there is ever expanding kaleidoscopes of colour.
They are, Soul, muted in every possible way from your eye.
For you must reach into the eye
    to become the level of perception.
Ergo a need to enter in to the fullness of being
    within each existence.

Each existence has a purpose.
Each earth being has a purpose.
Each motion has a purpose.
Each illness has a purpose to cleanse
      and be made ready to release toxins,
         to be ready for that which must be done.
Do not think any one of six
      holds the humanness of whom they are.
Indeed not!
You have entered in shard, you will leave shard.
You are ignited with purpose
      and the purpose will not be waylaid.
Each Energy has a commitment to the purpose of righting,
      righting the written form of mankind's endeavour,
         to find beginnings and endings, alphas and omegas.
There is a dance of Purity that the human form of many
      would they could not see, yet they will see,
         for it is the purpose of entering in.
And all that is of family will push away
      that they might see clear their purpose.
The hand holds and the hand releases.
The mind holds but the mind does not release.
It enters in to high mind from whence you have come.
It cannot erase from you the level of consciousness.
It is not possible.
You may refuse to see it, Soul,
      but you cannot erase it from your being.
For it is the level of Purity you are in.
It is where you are, Soul.
Your human form may try to deny.
But the consciousness is persuasive
      in reminding a Soul why they have come.

1205   We speak to you, Soul, of Truth,
      the Energy that flows through Truth.
We speak to you, Soul, of ruth, compassion.
Ruth, Soul, is compassion.
Truth, Soul, the word, truth,
      truth, the equation of T^3,

---

      [3] equation of T - see Appendix B

T and compassion equals entering in.
You are present within the realm of Truth.
Your purpose, Soul, ruth.
You, Soul, a search to the word
    and know compassion.
All things are known.
All knowledge is known.
It is not to gather knowledge through truth.
It is, Soul, to enter in to Truth itself.
The ruth not root, Soul, ruth
    that you might be the Truth,
    that your humanity might be the fullness of the Truth.
There is a plan, a purpose, a potential entering in.
It is with, Soul, the equation of T.
T plus ruth equals Truth.
There is no coincidence, Soul
But the word is more than a name, it has a meaning.
The meaning, Soul, is compassion.
You who are six must know compassion
    for you have become fully human.
In your Spirit you have entered in.
You have entered in to Farside fully human.
You have entered back unto earth,
    vulnerable within the Energy of another,
    the Soul Energy.
See each other, know you are bound one to the other
    not in your earth life, in your purpose.
There is no portion of your earth life that is coincidental.
All that you have entered in to is yours to overcome,
    to joy in,
    not to gather pain,
    to gather joy not to be burdened with pain
    but to rejoice one unto the other.
Even when one is absent there are six.
Indeed, you have chosen forms of energy that are not ideal,
    yet you have chosen forms
    in which you will overcome pain.
Had you chosen, Soul, a being to ask the gift of
    and the being was perfect
    wherein is the overcoming of pain,
    of anger, of sadness, of aloneness,

    of obstinacy, of secrecy.
You see all has purpose, all is tethered one unto the other.
Who can hold in their being the negative
    that seeps unto another without daunting self.
You cannot, Soul.
We ask you to hold the fullness of Truth,
    to understand the equation of T is not absent.
It is in motion.
You are not the only ones holding Key,
    others hold the Key to equation.
You are not the only ones holding ruth.
Soul, compassion cannot be absent in Truth
    or you have misunderstood
    the purpose of your being.
Happiness, Soul, happiness.
Motion, Soul, motion.
The air moving upon your earth,
    the bacteria in your air always in motion.
You do not need to protect yourself.
You need to know you have entered in
    for the purpose to heal.
The hands vibrate the Energy but, Soul,
    the aura does so much more
    for it is the connector to the Pillar of Light.
They blend, they throb in their blending.
They carry motion that enters in to another.
Know all thy Energy is one, each of six gathered unto one.
When one is absent the others draw the Energy in.
When one is absent the others know the Energy is there.
Hold your being and know as you hold your being
    you hold the beings of all six
    for you are one in your Energy.
All earth issues are only earth issues.
You of the Soul, of the Spirit, are beyond earth issues.
Your life is not given to you.
You, Soul, have chosen the life you live.
You have chosen to enter in to the very moment you are in.
There is no member
    of any family of the six that is coincidental.
Each is there to teach, to offer support, to give credibility.
Each is there by agreement.

Truth, that which you are armed with,
> that which Truth will bring you unto,
> ruth, compassion.

Glossary

Akashic Record - on going fulfillment of creation's growth.

Breath of MATTER - motion from Parallel Worlds.

Cauldron (capitalized) - entrance to dark passageway to the Archangels in fourth level Dark.

Creator's Yawn - Breath forward of Third Creator.

Crystal Cave - energies of manifested Souls to bring forth Archangels.

EYE (all capitalized) - receiver of High C, waiting to forward its oneness.

Farside - existence beyond earth toward Creator.

fence - a vision downward from Farside to Earth.

Fifteen Creators - fragmented Energies of Supreme Being.

Gathering Time - One thousand years of Purity.

High C - tone of oneness of humanity.

ION (all capitalized) - Energy sent forth from Core state of Being.

ITH (capitalized) - forwarded Energy of Supreme Being. A portion of the Triad of Flame, ITH and 15th Creator.

Keys (capitalized) - seven Tomes of Humanity's Intent.

Leak (capitalize) - the result of Death withholding from Light.

Learning station - upon Farside, where mankind sets goals for earth.

Light Beings - inhabitants of Energy Source.

MATTER (all capitalized) - Energy form entered in to our parallel world from Perfection.

Melchezidec - an Archangel who has not dwelt upon the earth.

meutric - distorted.

Microscopic World - holder of Seed Pod.

Naught (capitalized) - space of Void.

Parallel Worlds (capitalized) - Existences created in Energy's creation.

Path (capitalized) - the Energy Flow of Creator.

Place of Shining - wherein Godhead and Creator dwell.

Rend (capitalized) - result of Death withholding from Life.

SEE (all capitalized) - recorder of all echo and existences to and from Supreme Being.

Sireen Sound - the Sound of 14th Creator holding back Rend.

Soul of Creator - humanity in oneness.

Triad (capitalized) - Creator, Godhead, Great One.

Voice (capitalized) - containment by Void of Consciousness to meld MATTER, ION and Self.

Void of Consciousness (capitalized) - forwarded Energy of 15th Creator.

Window (capitalized) - vision given by Supreme Being into Parallel of Perfection.

Writing on the Wall - Soul growth planned upon Farside.

Zero (capitalized) - is the Void, Naught. Zero is vortex. Zero is the connector of all that is.

Appendix A
Daily East Ritual*

"East: it is the passageway to the Farside through the eye.
Its Truth is to be understood as a Love by humanity.
Focus on east at dawn, allowing the negativity
       to flow from your being,
           receiving unto yourself the goodness of Creator.
All humanity has the availability of this pathway.
The ritual of the east is the Soul's own response
       to the positive east which is tao.
Face east, two minutes.
Look with the eyes to the horizon's level.
In the brick wall or the iron cage, or the ornate boardwalk,
       know that the east will be with your Soul.
Turn clockwise once to heal.
Energy will flow to the matter before it.
All organs of the body are healed in the circle turn."

*Creator Trilogy, <u>Energy From The Source</u>, Appendix A

APPENDIX B
equation of T

T = Time

1 = Singleness
3 = Triad
7 = Planes/levels/dimensions
0 = Naught/Void
and the centre is Quar = Implosion

APPENDIX C

PUBLISHED

By Kitty Lloyd

Creator Trilogy
First Key Energy From The Source
Second Key So Shall It Be
Third Key Until Then

Creator Trilogy
Supreme Being Trilogy
How To Step To The Path
The Angel's Ecstasy
The Rejoicing

By Lucy Dumouchelle

Holistic Healing Through
Channeled Ancients
The Binary

FORTHCOMING

By Kitty Lloyd

Creator Trilogy
Trilogy of Consciousness
The Gathering Time
From Whence It Came
Ecstasy

Creator Trilogy
By Kitty Lloyd &
Lucy Dumouchelle

Echo
Value
Intent
Keepers of the Light

Published through Mountaintop Healing Publishing Inc

In the Energy of Matter,
in the formation of the triad, existence became.
Energies created.
Energy uncountable to your human scale went forth.
All Void carried outward that which was created.
All energies gathered in their Energy Field
the knowing of a single existence that had
no tangible without altering.
From the distant corridor of Breath is a Flow.
The Flow has awareness.
Awareness is within Breath.
Awareness, Intent and Presence, triad of Breath,
formulated second to Matter, Ion, Void
to initiate search.
Breath responsible, Soul, for all that flesh does.
Breath responsible for all that existence does.
Breath cannot gather back unto self, chaos.
From the core of Breath would be felt the chaos.
Within the blend of Ion, Void, and Matter,
was chaos, outward flow, no return.
Life replicated from Breath.
Death, a perfect replication of Life, for it returned unto.
When Death stepped away, Life was altered.
Energy, Soul, are not simplistic.
Energies equated to your science appear to be multifaceted.
Yet in that multiplicity of being
is a simplicity that earth is astounded by.
The resolution that is sought by all existence
is for Breath a co existence that will not diminish Breath.
Death diminished Life.
It is, Soul, profound.
For all the motion of your galaxies is in the outward thrust,
a search for that which is perfection to stand equal to Breath.

www.ingramcontent.com/pod-product-compliance
Lightning Source LLC
Chambersburg PA
CBHW081828170426
43199CB00017B/2672